UNDESIRABILITY AND HER SISTERS

MINORITARIAN AESTHETICS
General Editors: Uri McMillan, Sandra Ruiz, Shane Vogel

Minoritarian Aesthetics promotes scholarship that develops a minor position towards aesthetics and an aesthetic stance toward minoritarian experience. The aesthetic—the domain of sensation, beauty, value, taste, (dis)pleasure, and the sublime—instructs not only representations and judgments of the social, but the relational bonds that form between objects, subjects, and entities across spatial-temporal domains.

Deadpan: The Aesthetics of Black Inexpression
Tina Post

For Pleasure: Race, Experimentalism, and Aesthetics
Rachel Jane Carroll

Dissatisfactions: Queer Latinidad and the Politics of Style
Joshua Javier Guzmán

Undesirability and Her Sisters: Black Women's Visual Work and the Ethics of Representation
Tiffany E. Barber

Undesirability and Her Sisters

Black Women's Visual Work and the Ethics of Representation

Tiffany E. Barber

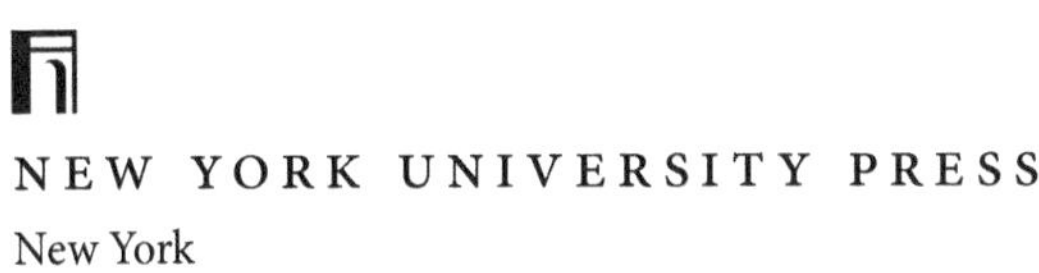

NEW YORK UNIVERSITY PRESS
New York

NEW YORK UNIVERSITY PRESS
New York
www.nyupress.org

Library of Congress Cataloging-in-Publication Data
Names: Barber, Tiffany E., author.
Title: Undesirability and her sisters : Black women's visual work and the ethics of representation / Tiffany E. Barber.
Description: New York : New York University Press, [2025] | Series: Minoritarian aesthetics | Includes bibliographical references and index.
Identifiers: LCCN 2024039857 (print) | LCCN 2024039858 (ebook) | ISBN 9781479829279 (hardback) | ISBN 9781479829286 (paperback) | ISBN 9781479829293 (ebook) | ISBN 9781479829309 (ebook other)
Subjects: LCSH: African American art–Themes, motives. | African American women in art. | Walker, Kara Elizabeth–Aesthetics. | Wangechi Mutu–Aesthetics. | Simmons, Xaviera, 1974—Aesthetics. | Narcissister, 1971—Aesthetics.
Classification: LCC N6538.B53 B37 2025 (print) | LCC N6538.B53 (ebook) | DDC 709.2/520973–dc23/eng/20250205
LC record available at https://lccn.loc.gov/2024039857
LC ebook record available at https://lccn.loc.gov/2024039858

New York University Press books are printed on acid-free paper, and their binding materials are chosen for strength and durability. We strive to use environmentally responsible suppliers and materials to the greatest extent possible in publishing our books.

The manufacturer's authorized representative in the EU for product safety is Mare Nostrum Group B.V., Mauritskade 21D, 1091 GC Amsterdam, The Netherlands. Email: gpsr@marenostrum.co.uk.

Manufactured in the United States of America

10 9 8 7 6 5 4 3 2 1

Also available as an ebook

CONTENTS

Introduction

The most disrespected person in America is the Black woman.
The most unprotected person in America is the Black woman.
The most neglected person in America is the Black woman.
—Malcolm X

Black women are not your mammy, America.
—Chanda Prescod-Weinstein

In the midst of Barack Obama's final year as president, the #BlackLivesMatter movement, and growing public awareness of the intricacies of intersectionality, Beyoncé released her sixth solo project and second visual album, *Lemonade.* In it, she brought new life to one of Malcolm X's most poignant social reflections that continues to energize academic and popular writing about the vulnerability of Black women and girls today.[1] Black women are the most undervalued people in America, the Black nationalist civil rights leader averred in a fiery 1962 speech about police brutality. When Beyoncé released *Lemonade* to critical acclaim in 2016, the album recalled this sentiment and the political moment that birthed it, joining the civil rights movement of the twentieth century with the new millennium's #BlackLivesMatter movement. Since its founding in 2012, the mission of the movement has been to counteract anti-Black violence with nonviolent protest, demands for defunding and abolishing the police, and community-based restorative justice in order to realize American democracy's full potential. Restorative justice contrasts punitive approaches to crime and retribution by encouraging victims and offenders to mediate a restitution that satisfies both parties. On this model, victims are active in the process while offenders take meaningful responsibility for their own actions to right their wrongs, which presumably leads to personal and collective redemption.[2] Seen as an expression of Black women's pain and triumph over everything from infidelity to familial strife to present-day police brutality, *Lemonade* was heralded as a revolutionary work of Black feminism and restorative justice.

The album is indeed visually sumptuous. In "Freedom," the camera pans around a home as women sit outside or prepare a meal. The video cuts between black-and-white and rich jewel tones—visual cues that differentiate the past from the present. "That night in a dream," Beyoncé recites in her introductory monologue, "the first girl emerges from a slit in my stomach. The scar heals into a smile." "A girl crawls headfirst up my throat," she goes on seconds later, "a flower blossoming out of the hole in my face"—a surrealist image conveyed through spoken text that merges motherhood with metamorphosis. One of the scenes in the video for this song about breaking one's chains features various cameos from other women—the mothers of Trayvon Martin and Michael Brown, actress Zendaya, and model Winnie Harlow, among them. This and every song on the album yield a single, but connected, narrative about strife and strength.

Viewers, listeners, and critics at the time labeled Beyoncé a cultural role model, a Black woman who had powerfully overcome the violence and weight of history by intertwining the personal and the political, a second-wave feminist adage. Samples of two field recordings from 1948 and 1959 that document the work songs of Southern Black prisoners and Jim Crow–era African American speeches and spirituals, respectively, buttress this analysis.[3] Incidentally, US vice president Kamala Harris secured permissions to use "Freedom" as her 2024 presidential campaign anthem at the same time that her opponent Donald Trump and other members of the Republican Party repeatedly issued racist and sexist attacks against her in live interviews, on social media, and in the political press. The song and album thus endure in the public imagination, as does Beyoncé's celebrity status, and much of the literature on the performer affirms her influence on US popular culture and politics.[4]

Lemonade, and the critical acclaim surrounding it, propose an ethos of repair and redemption that I interrogate in this book—the very notion that Black women's visual work must perform a recuperative function against historic and contemporary forms of violence. According to that logic, *Lemonade* and other similar examples in popular culture and fine art must elevate Black women's practices of care and self-love in response to the most insidious forces of oppression: patriarchy, white supremacy, misogynoir, and state-sanctioned violence. Case in point: Beyoncé's experiences with her celebrity husband's infidelity have melded the private devaluation of Black women by their partners with the national, sociopolitical devaluation of Black women in the United States.[5] As a result, the album prompted wide-ranging conversations about womanhood, feminism, musical genres, and who can claim Black identity and culture in a purportedly post-gender, post-genre, post-Black world.[6] For thinkers and writers who celebrated *Lemonade*'s utopian vision of healing and community in troubled times, #BlackLivesMatter was the catalyst for the album's intense engagement with Black culture and solidarity, especially among Black women. In so doing, the album also upheld a pervasive expectation concerning Black women's art—that other forms of cultural production, high and low, must have the same political and social ends.[7] This book invites readers to reconsider that expectation and to question the notion that only healing can lead to transformation.

This is not to deny the staying power of an album like *Lemonade*. Indeed, *Lemonade* has inspired countless think pieces, rave reviews, a new field of study named after the pop icon, and one crowd-sourced syllabus populated with more than two hundred Black feminist and womanist texts.[8] As writer, theologian, and lead organizer of the *Lemonade* syllabus Candice Marie Benbow puts it, Black women saw themselves as they watched chapter after chapter, lamenting the degradation they encountered in their intimate partner relationships and at the hands of a state "supposed to protect them."[9] *Lemonade* "left *sisters* exposed, yearning for a covering . . . for real healing and transformation."[10] The album's visual and sonic elements, in other words, were seen and felt as expressions of solidarity and sisterhood that coalesce into communal healing and wholeness. *Lemonade* also appeared to transcend taste barriers, solidifying the political, cultural, social, and aesthetic import—the value—of Black women's creative labors on a national and global scale. In this merger lay a call for freedom, as the eponymous song suggests, for the most disrespected, unprotected, and neglected.[11]

Undesirability and Her Sisters: Black Women's Visual Work and the Ethics of Representation collates an altogether different and disagreeable vision, what I term the "undesirable." The Black female bodies in recent works of public sculpture, collage, photography, and performance art by Kara Walker, Wangechi Mutu, Xaviera Simmons, and Narcissister discussed in the following chapters are neither coherent nor curative. Walker's practice—from the silhouettes for which she is most known to her large-scale, site-specific installations of late—refutes interpretive models moved by sentimentality not only for the past but also for wholeness derived from transparent meaning thought to yield communal belonging and healing. The acts of cutting, forms of blood spattering, and dismembering of bodies that constitute Mutu's collage practice more broadly and her cyborgs in particular engender ways of being not predicated on wholeness or harmonious racial integration. Simmons's disavowals of the self and the face within the staged portraits she creates willfully fail to reconcile the fissure between absence and presence that has energized theories of photography and Black representation for much of the twentieth and twenty-first centuries. Narcissister's multifaceted presentations of anticlimactic self-realization and sex trouble well-worn theories of Black feminist performance that, as performance studies scholar Uri McMillan describes, "often emphasize wholeness and positive self-representation as part of the recovery process to salvage the black female body from the historical violence of the visual sphere."[12] All four artists wrest staid modes of aesthetic theory and criticism away from a binary of rupture and repair by tarrying in negativity vis-à-vis toxicity, bottoming, opacity, and race play, clearing new ground for Black women's visual work that is equal to the political and sociocultural realities of the new millennium.

Unlike conventional readings of Beyoncé's *Lemonade*, and the greater ethos of self and communal empowerment, the artists in this book eschew wholeness and cohesion and instead embrace such sensibilities as rupture and repulsion. Their visions of the negative and nonnormative upset and upend, resulting in unexpected pathways for Black women's survival and self-understanding. Nausea, dismemberment, self-effacement, and self-objectification underlie their articulations of undesirability. Such minor aesthetic effects and enactments reconfigure the limits and possibilities of kinship and collectivity during an era defined by hope, change, and transcendence, on the one hand, and terror and anxiety on the other. In disavowing sociocultural mores and medium conventions, Walker, Mutu, Simmons, and Narcissister widen the analytical and thematic frames of art's engagement with everyday life, group identity politics, and what counts as progress and empowerment in the new millennium.

While the artists I examine are not themselves pop culture icons like Beyoncé, their work and the ways they navigate their own star status within the art world nonetheless raise important questions about marginality and representation. At the same time, the figures and makers in this book blur the boundaries between popular culture and fine art to perform Black womanhood and Black feminism in confounding ways. As *Lemonade* evinces, their work arrives at a time when more people than ever before are engaged with Black women and their creative output across media. From popular music, electoral politics, and social media to television and film to fine art, triumphant statements about Black achievement and intersectional feminism abound. Black visual culture more generally has garnered unprecedented art market visibility, corporate support, and viral social media attention in the past decade—what many thinkers and makers have called a New Black Renaissance.[13] That, in part, has to do with the salience of the #BlackLivesMatter uprisings, which prompted museums, magazines, small businesses, global brands, and media networks to issue dozens of declarations touting their commitments to racial justice and solidarity. Even as affirmative action rollbacks and other civil rights attacks at the local and national level supersede institutionalized diversity, equity, and inclusion measures, imbibing fine art, popular culture, and social media has become a public proxy for pursuing social justice and redressing anti-Black violence in the past and present.

Within this milieu, narrow ideas about cultural and political representation, racial and gender solidarity, and art's transformative "power" continue to constrain Black women's visual work in the popular imagination and, by extension, in fine art. Work here refers to the creative act as a form of reproductive labor that has aesthetic, political, sociocultural, and monetary value. It also underlines how Black women's visual and embodied alterity works on and in the US public imaginary. How does the increased visibility of Black women artists—at once historically marginalized yet hyper-visible in public and civic culture—impact how we theorize minoritarian aesthetic practice within art history and Black and feminist study? What are the limits and possibilities of kinship and sisterhood in the twenty-first century? In times of racial reckoning and upheaval, what do we expect Black women and their art to *do*?

Although Beyoncé's labor and image have both been the subject of scholarship that cuts across disciplinary tastes and boundaries, mainstream and academic reactions to her art, her stardom, and her wealth delineate a troubling cultural logic that the art world figures in this book contest. With the increasing commercialization of the art market in the digital age, museums and galleries prioritize blockbuster shows and crowds to drive revenue and social media attention. This increase coincides with, and often invigorates, an intensified focus on and consumption of work by artists of African descent in the new millennium even as they remain minor voices within the art historical canon and museum collections. In this milieu of art, culture, and social media (discussed further in chapter 1), the fans and influencers who celebrate Beyoncé's particular brand of feminism wield the same, if not more, power and social capital as the critics and curators who promote Black women's representation in exhibition spaces. These groups, in turn, influence cultural perceptions of Black women's marketability and desirability. *Undesirability and Her Sisters* locates and interrogates these interlocking phenomena within the context of present-day understandings of progress and struggle wherein racial representation has become a metonym for racial reparation.

Filtered through the prism of twenty-first-century political rhetoric concerning hope, reparations, and aspirations for racial and gender transcendence in response to anti-Black terror in the afterlife of slavery, my analyses in the following pages constitute a nonnormative Black feminist art history. My methodological approach is grounded in a conception of cultural production that exceeds conventional notions of resistance and reparation as primary models for identifying and comprehending minoritarian subjects' relationship to power in the wake of contemporary art's post-Black turn and the mainstreaming of intersectionality. A term borrowed from the art world that has become a popular framework for appraising contemporary Black culture, *post-Blackness* describes changing ideas about identity politics and multiracial promise. Intersectionality is the Black feminist concept that mutually reinforcing vectors of our identities (race, gender, and sexuality chief among them) constitute our subjectivities. Both discursive turns, coincident with Black art and visual culture's increased visibility in the art world and the wider world, have shaped twenty-first-century political and popular discourse about justice and representation, from Beyoncé to Barack Obama and beyond.

My mode of interpretation necessarily retools how scholars, museumgoers, students, critics, art enthusiasts, and lay audiences understand both the aesthetic and political value of Black women's artistic interventions as well as affective responses to their work. Despite the rise of Black women celebrity artists, from pop star Beyoncé to prototypical post-Black artist Kara Walker, and deeper public understanding of Black women's complex identities, books solely devoted to Black women artists are rare. *Undesirability and Her Sisters* transmutes both the dearth of humanities and museum scholarship on Black women artists and the constraints that Black women as subjects bear as a result of homogeneous interpretations of intersectionality, even and especially when done under the guise of celebrating Black feminism. The visual work herein also proffers a new metric for evaluating art and its histories with regard to individuals who, despite their growing visibility and popularity, remain relegated to the margins in terms of their social positions and the critical reception of their work.

Black Women's Visual Work

From womanist theology to public intellectual discourse, Black women's visual work in the United States has been synonymous with kinship, sisterhood, mothering, and reproduction. To heal the ruptures caused by slavery and its afterlife, metaphors of kinship have been used in Black aesthetic and womanist discourse as means for imagining bonds and obligations between individuals of African descent and their communities. Restoring fragments of identity and cultural history to some sense of wholeness also animates much of the literature on Black aesthetics while Black women have historically been constrained by protocols of behavior, reproductive value, and aesthetics in the public and private sphere. In the art world, these protocols materialize in expert and lay expectations that Black women artists address their work to slavery and its legacies in order to effect racial healing and empowerment, to thus testify to and ultimately redress the sociological, economic, environmental, spiritual, and physiological conditions of their own subjugation. To that point, art of the Black diaspora in the West has long been coded as a response to slavery. Consider, for instance, transhistorical studies of Black women's creative labors as caregiving, cultural production, and political participation that often consolidate sacrifice with self-care and salvation.[14] In this complex formulation, the slave past is the origin point for Black political realities in the present. Indeed, art, in this formulation, is meant to function as one form of restorative justice. This "ongoing and elusive process" of repair and liberation in the post–civil rights era, art historians Huey Copeland and Krista Thompson write, comes "into view through repeated attempts at its visualization."[15] These desires for repair in the present vis-à-vis repeated visualization emerge from a Pan-African, intersectional view of kindred experiences of oppression and dispossession in the afterlife of slavery. Kinship and sisterhood in this context typically refer to racial and gender affinity, common ancestry, or togetherness as sources of redemption and the bases of a shared politics.

For Black women, the act of making kin—familial and fictive—has also been tied to kind and kindness, especially when this reproductive work takes the form of caring for children—and nations—not their own. Black women's reproductive labor on this model of kinship and sisterhood engenders both revolutionary care practices and unique ways of being in the world—a triple otherness that I call undesirability, a visual and embodied alterity and queerness that materializes at the intersection of race, gender, and sexuality. #BlackLivesMatter, #MeToo, #CiteBlackWomen, #SayHerName, #ThankBlackWomen, and intersectionality are just a few of the slogans and ideas that have come to the fore in the twenty-first century, demonstrating the influence that Black women and Black feminist thought have on contemporary art and activism. Yet art history and feminism, despite the institutionalization of intersectional discourse, perennially fail to account for the racial, ethnic, class, geographic, and sexual differences that comprise the capaciousness of Black female being and becoming.

As Black feminist theorist Jennifer C. Nash outlines, "The wholesale abandonment of addressing how factors beyond race and gender shape black women's experiences of violence demonstrates the shortcomings of intersectionality to capture the sheer diversity of actual experiences of women of colour."[16] "Re-considering intersectionality," and the ways we theorize minoritarian identity expression in contemporary Black women's art, "enables activists," and artists and critics, "to ask under what conditions organizing as 'women' or 'blacks' or 'black women' makes sense, under what conditions temporary coalition-building makes sense, and how to organize across and beyond difference."[17] Just as categorical binaries are not enough to accurately depict intramural and extramural lived experience along racial and gender lines, aesthetic binaries of injury and repair, rupture and redemption constrict and homogenize Black women's art, its understanding and its possibilities. Walker, Mutu, Simmons, and Narcissister, however, re-form Black womanhood and sisterhood as contested, messy terrain that exceeds woundedness and victimhood, requiring theorists of racial and gender representation to abandon their commitment to recovery and repair as well as sameness and universalism.

Evoking olfactory, sonic, surface, and haptic responses—minor aesthetic strategies in and of themselves not often discussed in art historical scholarship—the dismembered, perverse, and repulsive figurations profiled in this book challenge normative modes of depicting Black women and their bodies as at once empowered and vulnerable. In so doing, they directly undermine expectations for Black women's work to be aesthetically pleasing and to redress racial and gender subjugation. In threading these ideas together, this book unravels the common theorization that representation, solidarity, and repair are mutually constitutive and unequivocally socially good. *Undesirability and Her Sisters* also contributes to recent and ongoing debates about the ethics of self-representation—the ability to act or speak for oneself, to mean and matter, and to ultimately refuse recognition—when calls for reparations and global justice proliferate.[18] The multifarious ways that Walker, Mutu, Simmons, and Narcissister reject notions of racial and gender fidelity and duty, bodily integrity, and multiracial kinship forsake social and aesthetic norms regarding what Black female figures can and should do in times of social and political upheaval. Their undesirable visions of race, gender, class, and sex—discordant, dark, and heterogeneous—coalesce into a politics without a program predicated on dissidence and bad behavior whereby negativity is productive but not generative. This shift, commensurate with present-day identity politics, charts new pathways for thinking about the ends of aesthetic criticism, Black women's art and world-making, and the value of representation.

Centering undesirable representation explodes the boundaries of Black female being and becoming as distinctly minoritarian formations. With an acute focus on non-normativity, *Undesirability and Her Sisters* investigates how Black women's aesthetic and sensory apprehensions of the world produce necessarily and equally minor stances toward beauty, value, taste, and pleasure on the one hand and the relational bonds that form between objects and subjects on the other. This is a decidedly queer position that stems from Black women's historical and ongoing subordination and the ways in which Black women have been regarded as reproductive objects themselves rather than social actors and agents. *Undesirability and Her Sisters* additionally underscores how steadfast the binary between fracture and unity has become within critical theories of feminism in the academy, in the art world, and in everyday life. Within theories of intersectionality in particular, Black female bodies "are ossified into homogenously marginalized beings who symbolize," Black feminist and visual culture scholar Amber Jamilla Musser explains, "a type of unchanging otherness from which more contemporary theory is drawn."[19] Just as rupture and repair continue to animate conversations about race and belonging in the new millennium, they also energize debates concerning feminist praxis and the everyday value of women's creative and reproductive labors.

Undesirability and Her Sisters challenges the positioning of intersectionality as the pinnacle of ethical feminism for both non-Black and Black practitioners as well as its hold on Black feminism's generative capacities. At its core, intersectionality disrupts claims to universal sisterhood within mainstream feminism. But as Amber Musser and scholar of Black feminism and queer theory Sharon P. Holland point out, intersectionality also excludes the Black queer female figure who "marks an undisciplined sector of the discipline: the representations of her have shifted from the dangerous and volatile to the abject and weak."[20] This is also true of mainstream objections to how Black queer femmes marshal political power and the threats they pose to the status quo. Members of the Republican Party and the alt-right press, for example, continue to vilify the Black queer femme founders of the #BlackLivesMatter movement by calling them terrorists. Further, Holland argues, Black queer women's "figuration at this point in our critical history looks profoundly like that of . . . a dead zone (think 'impasse')."[21] For Holland, the Black queer female figure is at once a reminder of historical wrongs and a social outlaw who remains outside of any political future. The works in this book revel in this dead zone, embracing the Black female figure as an outlaw that is always already queer.

As Musser, Holland, Hortense J. Spillers, David Marriott, Roderick A. Ferguson, Zakkiyah Iman Jackson, Tavia Nyong'o, and others have shown, queerness's paradigmatic racial coding—white and male—causes theorists to misrecognize, or forget altogether, the constitutive role that Blackness and Black womanhood have played in historical and philosophical ideas about queerness, abjection, negation, and subjecthood.[22] Scholars such as José Esteban Muñoz, J. Halberstam, and Gayatri Gopinath have also made important contributions to expanding the dimensions of queer theory to include considerations of race and racial difference. However, these analyses stop short of foregrounding how Blackness changes the terms of gender and sexuality to crystallize a fundamentally queer position. Black queer theorists remind us that Blackness's "existential negation" disfigures the coherence of gender and sexuality as normative categories.[23] Here, Blackness is a priori to queerness, the foundation of and for queerness as a way of being and seeing otherwise that arises from abjection and its embrace. This equation necessitates a reconsideration of both Blackness and queerness as modes of embodiment and valuation that exceed racial and gender performativity, identity, or even sexual practices.[24] Queerness in this book describes Black women's social location as gender and sexual minorities—the most disrespected and neglected—as well as the strange and perverse forms and figurations on display in the following pages. By queering both form and identity as the basis for recognition, recovery, and repair, the art of Walker, Mutu, Simmons, and Narcissister puts pressure on what constitutes "womanhood" and teases out the gender category's political density beyond relational bonds.

Cultural historian Saidiya Hartman's groundbreaking scholarship on the afterlife of slavery has become one of the most familiar and fruitful nodes for recent studies of sisterly relation, racial kinship, and Black intimate life within and beyond contemporary art. Hartman's work has recently moved outside of the academy into arts and culture institutions, influencing how scholars and arts professionals think and see the overlapping forms of oppression that circumscribe present-day Black women's visionary, world-making possibilities. Combining historiography with what she calls critical fabulation, Hartman illuminates how slavery spurred irreparable conditions of loss and dispossession that continue to constrain Black women's lives and creative labors in the present. As a practice of redress that is itself marked by conditions of impossibility, she recovers famous young Black women's wayward acts of resistance and stories of numerous, anonymous others who transgress the confines of the law to find belonging, intimacy, love, and freedom. For Hartman, Black women summarily operate outside of gender norms, whether they want to or not. Black visual and cultural studies scholars such as Tina M. Campt, Imani Perry, Amber Musser, and Therí Alyce Pickens have also recently written about the fugitive, vexy, counterintuitive, undisciplined, and mad practices of refusal that Black women have used to push against varying systems of violence, captivity, enclosure, and representation. Building on this growing body of Black feminist theorizing, *Undesirability and Her Sisters* enfolds queer negativity into histories of American and African American art to forge new insights into Black feminist praxis specifically and minoritarian, identity-based aesthetics more broadly.

Several scholars within related fields such as Black studies, queer studies, Latinx studies, and cultural studies have critiqued the coercive grammar of desire as it relates to positive representations of identity in performance art, literature, and film after multiculturalism.[25] Many have also sought to transvalue images and aesthetic practices that tie Blackness to abjection, ugliness, or other cultural stigma concerning disability and disease. Despite the pathbreaking work of the aforementioned visual and performance studies scholars as well as that of Kobena Mercer, Richard J. Powell, Darby English, Nicole R. Fleetwood, and Uri McMillan, this is not the dominant position within art history. Curiously and relatedly, Black diaspora studies remains knitted to authenticity, objectification, and visibility as the primary grounds for political organizing and resistance. From the confines of this intellectual and representational space emerges the dangerous assumption that other analytical lenses are theoretically insignificant or of little historical value.[26] The following pages alternately underscore nonnormative aesthetic effects and thematics often considered to be counterintuitive to art history's ocularcentrism or politically harmful to Black and feminist liberation struggles. This emphasis highlights how the architectures of capitalism, including the art market, rely on extraction, dispossession, occupation, and catastrophe. In refusing to act as expected, the Black women artists in this book repudiate the commodification logics of art as a marketplace—as an enterprise in itself—thereby unsettling how the very labor of resistance produces and manages them as racialized gendered subjects. Within this matrix, undesirability is a minor interposition that has major methodological implications.

The visual work of Walker, Mutu, Simmons, and Narcissister also widens the space between destruction and creation, reordering the assumed relationship between morality, womanhood, and the creative act. The same goes for sisterhood. My titular use of *sister* references a number of interlocking formations and identity categories that arise at the intersection of race and gender: a filial relation (a female sibling), a fellow woman committed to feminist issues, a nurse or caregiver, and an intraracial term of endearment for Black women as a marker of common origin or struggle. The queer forms and aesthetic strategies outlined in this book function as strange "sisters" to one another, not in strict relational terms but in terms of a *minor* ensemble of rupturing that corresponds with Black female being in its repulsion of habitual, commonsense narratives concerning comportment, collectivity, and progress. Each artist in the following chapters recalibrates different dimensions of the word *sister* as a gendered and racialized term. Pairing undesirability with the multivalent term *sister* delineates Black women and their visual work as complex forces of multiple meaning that exceed compulsory group politics organized around race and gender affinity. This framing opens up the boundaries of Blackness and womanhood as well as the ways sisterhood and solidarity have been thought within modern and contemporary theories of aesthetics, politics, and activism.

Undesirability and Her Sisters illustrates how Black women artists' relationship to America's (slave) past, to racial and gender otherness, and to aesthetic practice has changed. The repulsive, errant, counterintuitive, and kinky aesthetic strategies outlined in this book reject propriety. But such strategies are not reducible to mere rejection, thus shifting attention from a Beyoncé-era, post-Black way of categorizing Black women's art to one more concerned with non-normativity. This turn to negativity parallels an emergent strand of queer theory within Black feminist praxis, highlighting a mutual exhaustion with contemporary rhetoric surrounding racial and gender identity having particular and positive (in both senses of the term) meaning. Such strategies and their effects reach beyond post-identity discussions and toward negativity as a productive way to illuminate the complexities around Blackness, womanhood, power, and personhood.

In the art that populates *Undesirability and Her Sisters*, there is no aspiration for healing or wholeness. Walker, Mutu, Simmons, and Narcissister neglect to heal the wounds of racial and gender oppression, fail to insist on visibility and inclusion, and refuse to enact self-love. They thus undermine several presumptions: that slavery is the nexus of Black shared experience, that increased transparency creates a more just world, and that cross-racial intimacy is not only possible but desirable and necessary for social transformation. As stratagems of refusal, they move away from a unified notion of Black female being and sisterhood, while also jettisoning assimilation, metamorphosis, and repair as goals. In foregrounding the ties that bind Black feminist art praxis, negativity, and non-normativity in the twenty-first century, Walker, Mutu, Simmons, and Narcissister chart new ways of being, seeing, and thinking about Black womanhood not always accounted for under the banner of Black feminism and intersectionality.

Beyoncé's Feminist Brand

Beyoncé has come to embody a redemptive, millennial brand of feminism that the art and artists in this book defy. For self-identified Black feminists, Beyoncé exemplifies intersectionality, a term that legal studies scholar Kimberlé Crenshaw coined and popularized to describe how mutually reinforcing vectors of oppression constitute Black women's lived experiences. Black feminist scholars and fans have generally attached themselves to the elements of Beyoncé's creative output that encourage cohesion and recuperation, resulting in a monolithic, homogenous view of Black feminism and Black womanhood at the expense of other possibilities, namely, undesirability. According to Black classical music scholar Naomi André, Beyoncé exhibits a new Black feminist cool.[27]

Since departing Destiny's Child for a solo career in 2003, the singer has become a global icon. She and her husband, rapper and philanthropist

Jay Z, have occupied the Louvre, supported contemporary struggles for Black freedom, and amassed one of the most robust collections of art of the Black diaspora. Her paradoxical performances have inspired heated debates about contemporary Black feminism, racial belonging, intellectual property, capitalism, and aesthetics. With every surprise album drop, Beyoncé breaks the internet and sets new technological, discursive, and entrepreneurial trends—from music to motherhood. As literary scholar Stephanie Li writes on Beyoncé's pop culture influence, "Her pregnancy transforms her into a fertility goddess; her heartbreak in *Lemonade* becomes the pain of a black woman collective; her videos and lyrics produce memes and slogans that become personal [and political] anthems."[28] Additionally, her fans have claimed her albums, her work ethic, her dance moves, and her offspring—the fruits of her creative and procreative labors—as stimuli for social transformation. She is, in a word, phenomenal.

The pop star's cultural vitality also stems from the moral power she wields, individually and collectively. As an icon for millennial women's empowerment, Beyoncé expresses and remakes Black womanhood in a world where feminism is neither a dirty word nor passé. In front of giant screens emblazoned with the word *feminist*, she sings of being flawless and of overcoming obstacles and disappointment. She pens letters in support of equal pay, and she starts and steers trends that persuade her fans to adopt certain beliefs and actions. Her 2014 Video Music Awards appearance, where she performed singles from her self-titled visual album of 2013, caused *feminism* to trend at record-high volumes on Twitter (now called X) while also visually and sonically mapping a twenty-first-century genealogy of feminist thought for women of African descent. "Flawless," a feminist anthem of sorts, samples lines from Nigerian writer Chimamanda Adichie's oft-cited 2012 TEDx talk "We Should All Be Feminists;" at the 2014 VMAs, a gigantic black screen displayed Adichie's statements and the word *feminist* in white capital block letters. *Time*, *Huffington Post*, *Slate*, and other major outlets declared this performance not only a definition of feminism, but also an act of reclamation of the word and practice as activism. From this angle, Beyoncé achieved something seemingly unfathomable: she brought feminism to the masses. Talking about gender and gender equality essentially went pop. This popularity and desirability was also marketable and profitable.

In "Formation," the performer encouraged Black women everywhere to carry hot sauce in their bags while boosting Red Lobster's sales by 33 percent thanks to a lyric about eating at the chain restaurant after coitus.[29] Meanwhile, the video for the song was publicly hailed as a #BlackLives-Matter anthem. Since *Beyoncé* (2013) and *Lemonade* (2016), the singer has become the embodiment of millennial, intersectional feminism, an arbiter of Black feminist solidarity that competes with and arguably eclipses the whiteness and supremacy that contemporary phenoms like Taylor Swift embody.[30] In full view of millennials reluctant to claim the words *feminism* and *feminist*, Beyoncé runs the world while nurturing her career, her marriage, her sexuality, and her role as a mother.

Because of this influence, Beyoncé's work—her creative output and the cultural-political labor she performs—seems to be beyond critique. Aside from her unattributed citations of preexisting artworks, registering any disapproval of the singer's output or status could invite retribution from the Beyhive.[31] She, in other words, transcends critique as a millennial intersectional feminist whose Blackness and womanhood are seen not as injuries or afflictions but as beacons of promise that are often in fact unattainable. Alternately, Beyoncé's visual and sonic works are fraught with cross-racial desires for freedom and recognition as well as upward mobility for Black and non-Black fans alike. She is a solo artist who, as cultural critic Wesley Morris proclaims, thrives in sisterhood as a bandleader, a dancer, a conjurer of histories, and an untouchable symbol of racial and gender progress.[32] Despite these endorsements, Beyoncé's revivification of (Black) feminism leaves much to be desired. In songs seemingly about independence and empowerment, her lyrics still largely fixate on how men and their behaviors affect women. Meanwhile, her visual displays of accumulated wealth border on unethical decadence. Only recently have Black feminist scholars taken her to task for her promotion of capitalism and opulence in the face of genocide and ongoing struggles for racial freedom and sovereignty within and beyond the Black diaspora.

Within this representational space, *Lemonade* remains a watershed moment for fans and feminists. The album's eleven chapters—intuition, denial, anger, apathy, emptiness, accountability, reformation, forgiveness, resurrection, hope, and redemption—construct a narrative wherein metamorphosis repairs individual and collective hurt. During one vignette,

Beyoncé realizes how much she has sacrificed for her partner and dives into deep water. As the singer emerges, several other Black women link hands with each other to elevate and edify her: a resurrection. Through closeness and physical touch, these women form a helping, healing circle to guide Beyoncé toward acceptance and self-love. This motif of healing recurs in a scene where Lesley McSpadden, Sybrina Fulton, and Gwen Carr hold pictures of their slain sons: Michael Brown, Trayvon Martin, and Eric Garner, respectively. Surrounded by a cohort of familiar Black girls, women, and mothers, Beyoncé conjures a multigenerational picture of Black womanhood where relationship turmoil parallels Black women's intersectional experiences of oppression. This enactment of communal healing, according to essayist Morgan Jerkins, redresses generations of Black women's silence and hurt—from heartache to the loss of their children—adding a new dimension to the feminist platitude "the personal is political."[33]

As a twenty-first-century Black feminist text, *Lemonade* legitimated the public expression of Black women's rage, a direct counter to what historians Evelyn Brooks Higginbotham and Darlene Clark Hine respectively call the "politics of silence" and "the culture of dissemblance." Both Higginbotham's and Hine's concepts are foundational to understanding nineteenth- and twentieth-century Black life; they name the strategies of *not* openly expressing dissatisfaction or rage that Black women employed as a means of survival during the Jim Crow era. Black women reformers at this time, Higginbotham and Hine argue, believed that silence and the promotion of proper, respectable Victorian morality would end the lie that Black women were immoral by nature. Within this framework, Black women appeared to embrace the unsavory conditions of employment and domestic life available to them at the time. Doing so in the face of pervasive stereotypes and negative estimations about Black women's sexuality in the minds of their non-Black and Black male counterparts could protect the sanctity of their inner lives and garner greater equity for all African Americans. Only with secrecy and a self-imposed invisibility, Hine declares, could ordinary Black women accrue the psychic space and resources needed to hold their own.[34] Silence and dissemblance, in this context, function as practices of resistance and liberation.

With its many chapters and songs like "Formation," *Lemonade* visualizes a different kind of comportment and (Southern) Black femininity evocative of, yet unmoored from, Victorian sensibilities. For its proponents, especially those who identify as Black women and Black feminists, *Lemonade* articulated hope and a way forward, a light at the end of a dark tunnel of oppression. Consequently, the album appeared to infuse feminism and the value of Black women's work with new meaning in the new millennium. The album's arc from degradation to healing follows an old adage: *When life gives you lemons, make lemonade*. For Benbow and other *Lemonade* fans, Black women's artistic production personified the power to transform and transcend, to move beyond "pain and create worlds of hope for generations to come."[35] In this frame, the present and future promise of Black women's visual work—and the beauty it constitutes—is an antidote to their social status and the undervalued labor they perform in the cultural landscape of an unequal America.

Black feminist attachments to Beyoncé demonstrate the limits and possibilities of seeing Black women's visual work as a remedy for the historical and contemporary effects of racial and gender oppression. Her brand of feminism—fearless, flawless, and family oriented—and its larger-than-life capitalist branding are seamlessly virtuosic and triumphant. *Lemonade's* narrative arc also teleologically ties Black womanhood to heteronormativity, a tethering that the undesirable Black female bodies in this book undercut. On the whole, *Lemonade*'s sonic and visual narrative spotlights how the artist moves past pain and rage to elevate the benefits of heteronormative coupling and Black motherhood as pathways to individual and collective hope, redemption, and well-being. Although the songs and interludes on *Lemonade* cycle through a litany of negative feelings that could be characterized as expressions of undesirability, marriage, mothering, and reproduction personify the pinnacle achievements to which Black women can and should aspire. In this version of progress and social respectability politics, Black women's values must align with dominant norms concerning femininity and futurity rather than alternative forms of kinship that rhyme with the messy terrain of undesirability. Alternately, another implicit assumption arises from this disciplinary script and in the album's revelatory responses: reproduction is continuous with reparation; that is, Black women and the procreative capacities of their bodies and their art have the power to mediate as well as mollify traumatic experiences. Notably, Beyoncé's latest award-winning album, *Renaissance*, was celebrated for its centering of historically marginalized Black queer voices and music genres. From this angle, Black women's art and world-making functions as a mode of historical recuperation, an enduring idiom of Black cultural resistance expected to recover and redeem the past by bearing witness to and reconciling collective trauma in the present.

This treatment—a social and aesthetic burden that the Black women artists profiled in this book exorcize—has been lauded as a means of compensation, as reparations, for historical ills and oppression, with the trauma of slavery occupying the most notable of these instances. These suppositions are symptomatic of hermeneutic readings of art that argue for its epistemological authority. They resemble what queer theorist and aesthetic philosopher Leo Bersani calls redemptive criticism and what literary scholar Stephen Best calls melancholy historicism with regard to slavery studies—a kind of crime scene investigation in which the forensic imagination is directed toward the recovery of a "we" at the point of "our" violent origin.[36] Influenced by Sigmund Freud's psychoanalytic theory of sublimation, redemptive criticism and melancholy historicism begin with the suspicion that a text's truth lies in what it does not say; readers must, therefore, dig deep to decipher its hidden or repressed meaning.[37] Two anticipated results arise from this analytic approach. First, a text achieves wholeness from its newfound complete or transparent meaning vis-à-vis close reading and looking. Second, the status of readers and viewers as superior cognitive beings is reinforced. Within this paradigm, art not only produces knowledge about social relations and historical experience, it is also an act of self-mastery and collective healing. In the process, understanding is achieved through interpretation, and "life," chides Bersani, "can be redeemed through an act of cognition" or "self-comprehension."[38] The creative act following this model gains its transformative power by simultaneously reducing experience and producing an aesthetic object that gives life a heightened sense of value through its emphasis on wholeness and cohesion.

The nausea-inducing, dismembered, self-effacing, and self-objectifying Black female bodies that litter the pages of this book, along with their makers, depart from this paradigm. The repulsive, frenzied figures herein refuse humanistic attachments to the liberatory potential of art that rely on a productivist work ethic such that Black women are expected to advocate for themselves, diversify the institutions in which they live and labor, and denounce and remedy their own subjugation. Such art, in my view, emphasizes the messy terrain of struggle, its ethical imperatives, and its impact on quotidian life by modeling forms of refusal that dispense with Black women's compulsory engagement in electoral politics, representation, sociocultural critique, and debate, arenas that typically result in further discipline and punishment for minoritarian subjects. In so doing, Walker, Mutu, Simmons, and Narcissister bring new meaning to race, gender, class, and sexuality as intersectional contingencies in Black feminist art and criticism. Instead of transcendental beauty, wholeness, and individual and collective becoming, the artists construct alternative modes of embodiment that are neither seamless, nor healing, nor exoticizing, nor essentializing. The perverse figures in *Undesirability and Her Sisters* eschew sublimation and synthesis as appropriate, or even necessary, responses to racial and gender subjugation. In troubling normative notions of memory, materiality, and kinship, the artists in this book and the characters they create disturb the ways in which historical formations of Black women's creative labors energize and regulate protocols of imagination, representation, and desire in the present. As a result, they destabilize liberal ideas about collectivity and equality as measures of social progress and well-being, proffering instead heterogeneous, unwieldy strategies of survival and self-understanding indifferent to propriety and futurity.

"Post-Black" Women's Work

Contrary to normative inclusion in the national body or desires for intraracial and interracial kinship as a form of repair, Walker, Mutu, Simmons, and Narcissister depict Black female bodies and identities as unstable sites for indexing the performance of proper subjectivity along racial, gender, class, and sexual lines. Such "undesirable" representations break from broader political and cultural aspirations toward wholeness and togetherness as signs of wealth and health, conceptions of personhood—and, by extension, liberal humanism—informed by rational, post-Enlightenment subjectivity.[39] These modes of selfhood operate on the level of the individual body—the corporeal self—and on the level of the body politic—the nation. Wholeness, here, is interwoven with the creation and maintenance of whiteness and democracy and is concomitant with discourses about political enfranchisement. Within these discourses, "in-tact," beautifully composed, desirable Black bodies are imbued with the ability to counteract visually oppressive regimes born from structural violence. *In-tact* here refers both to *intact*, whole, unimpaired bodies and to bodies that personify ideas of respect and tactfulness inherent to the rhetoric of racial duty and uplift. This affinity and desire for wholeness—internally and externally—is the first point of departure for my use of the term *undesirability*.

The analyses in this book juxtapose post-Black aesthetic discourse with intersectionality's mainstream popularity and #BlackLivesMatter, phenomena and events that have opened up novel and sprawling conversations about representation and recognition in the new millennium. Post-Blackness, according to curator and museum director Thelma Golden, who coined the term with artist Glenn Ligon, defines cultural producers of African descent born after the civil rights era who are "adamant about not being labeled as 'black' artists, though their work [is] steeped, in fact deeply interested, in redefining complex notions of blackness."[40] The term went mainstream when contemporary African American celebrities such as Raven-Symone, Common, Pharrell Williams, and Touré Neblett proclaimed to be "rooted in, but not restricted by, blackness."[41] America's first Black president, Barack Obama, has also been associated with both post-Blackness and post-racialism as proof that African Americans and the nation could move beyond four hundred years of racial antagonisms.

Like Beyoncé, Obama's political and cultural rise has been a touchstone for debates concerning the right and wrong ways to picture and perform Blackness (publicly and privately) amid intraracial and interracial aspirations for collective uplift. For eight years during his presidency, an array of Black artists attended White House events; their work hung on the White House's walls while acts of anti-Black violence spiked. This tension between Black achievement and anti-Black violence underscored the cutting contradictions within Black America as well as the nation as a whole. Obama's two-term presidency was, in performance studies scholar Brandi Wilkins Catanese's summation, "a diagnostic [and reparative] symbol of America's ultimate triumph over racial prejudice"—a sign that the nation had solved the problem of the color line.[42] The election of Kamala Harris, the first female, first Black, and first Indian American US vice president, brought this ethos of triumph and repair to the surface of post-Black and intersectional discourse again in 2020. But some have found fault with post-Blackness, especially with regard to art-world politics. "Racism is real, and many artists who have endured its effects feel the museum is promoting a kind of art—trendy, postmodern, blandly international—that has turned the institution into a 'boutique' or 'country club,'" artist David Hammons quips.[43] Golden herself admits that post-Black is "both a hollow social construction and a reality with an indispensable history."[44] For all its controversy, post-Blackness represents a sea change in how artists and scholars conceive of aesthetic categories and values in racial and gender terms.[45] However, much of the literature on post-Black artistic production fails to activate new modes of criticism beyond the loss and recuperation binary that energizes narratives of progress. It also neglects to account for the art market's collusion with capitalism, imperialism, and desire alongside the persistent demands for Blackness's visualization at the same time that Black bodies endure unique and increased forms of scrutiny and surveillance.

Darby English, one of the most provocative thinkers and writers on African American art and its histories, reflects on the post-Black moment and Golden's exhibition, *Freestyle*, which ultimately solidified the term's cultural impact. "The show," he states, "registered the undeniable emergence of a thrilling range of tones and textures. You couldn't really like or dislike 'Freestyle' as a whole. That's how full of difference it was. It acknowledged and embraced fragmentation and multiplicity in the cultural field."[46] Within the exhibition itself, he continues, "you had to negotiate form to get to meaning, and meaning was so precarious. . . . A formal crisis rooted in [Black] diversity engendered a conceptual crisis. There had to be a conversation."[47] English highlights the important shifts that post-Blackness initiated a generation ago in terms of identity-based exhibition making, Black aesthetic criticism, and progressive sensibility more broadly. The complicated feelings and language of nuance that post-Blackness occasioned at the start of the new millennium have since devolved into one-note captions, and form has given way to content in an image-saturated world. *Undesirability and Her Sisters*, by contrast, investigates the speculative, errant, ambivalent, and irreconcilable ways of Black women's visual work as pathways to a new, negative ethics of representation and relation.

The second facet of my use of *undesirability* relates to the most salient aspect of post-Blackness: the fact that contemporary Black artists "live in a world where their particular cultural specificity is marketed to the planet and sold back to them."[48] Blackness in this configuration is manufactured, packaged, and circulated as a fetish object, thus detaching it from Black interiority and subjectivity. Black and non-Black artists, then, can choose to wield Blackness however they want but only insofar as it functions as a commodity. Put differently, Blackness is both present and absent in our contemporary consumer culture, contained yet excessive, in full view but at the same time obfuscated. The aesthetic strategies analyzed in this book illustrate how present-day Black women artists self-consciously engage with their identities and bodies as commodities, as both desire and lack, in an increasingly globalized art market informed by the "white gaze" and essentialist racial thinking. While Beyoncé's feminist brand promotes Black women's redemptive narratives without engaging with fetishism and class critique, Walker, Mutu, Simmons, and Narcissister disrupt the ways in which Black womanhood has been codified into representational space, culturally and politically. Their undesirable figures confront Black womanhood as a matrix of identifications and projections that are, to paraphrase English's thoughts on Blackness as art, equally real and unreal. In so doing, the figures episodically and self-consciously repel the totalizing forces of the art market as a system of control and containment.

The perverse figurations in this book likewise transgress the boundaries of intersectionality, which, as Jennifer Nash tells us, has become "shorthand for the single best and most ethical kind of feminist work possible."[49] Such dominant narratives of Blackness and feminism that enfold theory into praxis as the cutting edge of revolutionary activity have mobilized assertions of loss, return, and progress to forecast what each discursive field has or could achieve. In *Why Stories Matter: The Political Grammar of Feminist Theory* (2011), Clare Hemmings outlines how Western feminist theory's three presiding narratives—progress, loss, and return—have developed over the last four decades in response to political advances and feminism's global co-optation. For the first narrative genre, emphasizing progress shows how feminist theory in the West continuously expands to welcome new and diverse voices. Through "the subsequent efforts of black and lesbian feminist theorists, among others," Hemmings explains, "the field has diversified, and feminism itself has become the object of detailed critical and political scrutiny."[50] Here, "woman" and feminism are no longer seen as unified or universal categories—a good thing—and a strict focus on gender as a feminist object gives way to defending the merits of feminism itself. Narratives of loss—of feminism's demise at the turn of the new millennium—counter narratives of progress by proposing that the shift away from woman or gender as the object of feminist theory has led to a "depoliticization of feminist commitments."[51] Additionally along these lines, Hemmings argues, "Conservative institutionalization of feminist thought and the generational popularity of 'post-feminism' are empty parodies of a feminist social movement that has incontrovertibly passed."[52] Lastly, narratives of return attempt to rescue Western feminist theory. Proponents of return narratives yearn for a feminist past unburdened by post-structural critique, relativism, and political incapacity.[53] They also champion democracy and pragmatism to bridge the gap between loss and progress, emphasizing the materiality of embodiment and structural inequalities in order to move beyond "the opposition between fragmentation and unity."[54] Whether celebrating a move beyond unity and identity, lamenting the demise of a political agenda, or proposing a return to a vision from previous decades, all three narratives are claims about the past, present, and future value of feminist praxis.

Within these three narratives, Amber Musser explains, Black feminist thought is sidelined in order to produce an arc that positions progress, loss, and return as antecedents to a homogenous present. This move "also positions feminist thought as extractive. It draws insight from these positions but does not treat this knowledge as more than accumulative, which is to say that Black feminist thought is imagined not to reorient a standard narrative but merely to represent a previously underacknowledged subject position."[55] This ossification flattens Black feminist thought's potential and contributes to Black feminists' impulse to safeguard intersectionality as if it is property that has been lost or stolen. From Nash's point of view, Black feminists attempt to rescue intersectionality from its wholesale incorporation into the academy more broadly and into predominantly white Women's studies departments in particular. Not unlike the buttressing that *Lemonade* garnered from Black feminists, this defensive posture also forecloses Black feminism's potential.

Nash implores Black feminists to separate their care for Black feminism from ownership over intersectionality, to essentially let go of their desire to control what Black feminist thought inspires in and from others.

The mode of Black feminist theorizing that energizes the arguments in this book reaches beyond identity politics and the new culture and morality wars, resulting in what I term an "anti-redemptive ethics of Black representation." The minor, unruly, queer potential of Black female being and (un)becoming invigorates each chapter, illuminating the multiple ways that Black women's visual and embodied alterity reorders the terms by which art history and Black and feminist study must engage with race, gender, class, and sexuality under and against market forces. Spurred by restorative justice projects and ongoing struggles for freedom, the affirmative and largely heteronormative ethics at the heart of Black aesthetic discourse within these fields has heretofore constrained the possibilities of Blackness and its queer dimensions. The visual work highlighted in the following pages, by contrast, embraces the bottom (a term often associated with queer sexual dynamics) as a social location, as a bodily region, and as a nonnormative worldview. In so doing, the figures in this book engender a different kind of value: constructions of Black female embodiment that adamantly refuse to be fixed and disciplined. The aesthetic objects herein consequently extend recent studies of how abjection subtends the sociocultural, psychoanalytical, and aesthetic dimensions of race, gender, sexuality, desire, and disability.

In the 1960s and 1970s, performance and body art involving urine, semen, saliva, feces, blood, and other bodily fluids coincided with radical, leftist politics. With the 1982 English-language publication of Julia Kristeva's *Powers of Horror* alongside the rise of AIDS, new ideas about feminist politics and art practice, as well as the criminalization of homosexuality, further inspired deployments of the pained, diseased, "other" body to debunk cultural myths. The English translation of Kristeva's text also cemented the enduring richness and applicability of the concept of abjection in cultural thinking, in contemporary art practice, and in feminist and queer scholarship on both sides of the color line.[56]

Drawing on French psychoanalytic theories of the monstrous and Jacques Lacan's ideas concerning filth as the constitution of the subject, Kristeva describes abjection as the dissolution of the distinction between the self and the "other." Kristeva herself associates the aesthetic experience of the abject with poetic catharsis. In her formulation, artists repair the trauma of disease and oppression by immersing themselves in the impure process of abjection in order to protect themselves from it.[57] More than a transgression of cleanliness, however, abjection is "what disturbs identity, system, order. What does not respect border, positions, rules."[58] Black women's cast-off, neglected status in America's social hierarchy places their bodies outside the "proper" boundaries of sociability. Black women's visual work, by extension, constitutes a unique form of minoritarian aesthetic practice that issues from Black women artists' self-conscious engagements with subjection and abjection as twin phenomena.[59]

Contrary to a transcendent version of Blackness or a misapprehension of history and its material conditions, Walker, Mutu, Simmons, and Narcissister construct inassimilable Black female forms that radically refuse integration and reconciliation. Their aesthetic strategies foreground Black female bodily abjection and turn away from social and aesthetic norms concerning respectable sociability, mutual belonging, wholeness, self-becoming, and sexual pleasure as remedies to subjugation. In transgressing boundaries of decorum, comportment, and racial and gender harmony, their work disobeys representational mandates that demarcate the right and wrong ways to picture and perform Black womanhood and sisterhood in the twenty-first century. Consequently, they call forth a historiographical ethics of representation and relation that treats both the past and the present with their own particularity. To this end, undesirability as a way of being and seeing otherwise resists "the impulse to redeem the past and instead rest[s] content with the fact that our orientation toward it remains forever perverse, queer, askew," as Stephen Best puts it.[60] Examining the queer negativity of Black women's artistic production in the new millennium thus exceeds contemporary art discourse to highlight the impact of gendered labor on Blackness and its persistent visualization in America's current political, public, and aesthetic domains.

Undesirability beyond Beyoncé

Beyond Beyoncé, the ethos of making lemonade—turning a negative situation into something that positively benefits oneself and one's community—pervades public discourse about Black women's work, from cultural production to caregiving to political participation. While Black women, whether performers, artists, or politicians, are more visible than ever, narrow ideas about representation and its power continue to constrain their work and image, begging new questions about the role of Black women's influence on culture today. When Democrat Doug Jones defeated Republican Roy Moore in Alabama's highly contested special Senate election of 2017, for example, social media erupted with posts and tweets thanking Black women for "saving America." In a state where African Americans usually make up one-fourth of the electorate, Jones's win was seen as a step in the right direction for the South and for the nation, a momentous event in the wake of Donald Trump's upset victory of 2016.

The white supremacist agenda that Trump espoused in the executive orders he signed while in the White House during his first and second presidential terms and that he continues to propagate in the press and in the social media sphere counteract the postracial order Obama appeared to initiate. For these reasons, Black women's extraordinary political showing in a region and country still acutely riddled with the problem of the color line functioned as a sign of racial and gender progress at the time. Black women politicians and voters in Georgia and elsewhere received a similar wave of support and recognition during the 2020 US presidential election when Joe Biden defeated Donald Trump and with the 2021 Senate runoffs that shifted congressional power to Democrats. Belatedly recognizing Black women's centrality to the US nation-making project, Democratic National Committee (DNC) chairman Tom Perez called Black women "the backbone of the Democratic Party."[61] This statement was a response to an open letter penned by Black women activists and elected officials chiding the DNC's efforts to regroup by pursuing working-class white voters and taking Black women, the party's most loyal support base, for granted.[62] Perez also used it as a slogan to promote his "Seat at the Table" tour in 2018, the title for which is taken from singer (and Beyoncé's sister) Solange's 2016 award-winning album of the same name.[63] Perez's misguided statements were ultimately an attempt to appease Black women's dissatisfaction concerning the Democratic Party's predominantly white male leadership. Astrophysicist and public intellectual Chanda Prescod-Weinstein and others rejected this rhetoric.

Prescod-Weinstein's admonishing tweet in the above epigraph, "Black women are not your mammy, America," calls attention to how the nation cannibalizes Black women and their procreative labors for the sake of political unity. Invoking the mammy stereotype—the most well-known and enduring racial caricature of African American women, which Walker and Narcissister both appropriate and alchemize in darkly humorous ways—lambasts the assumption that it is Black women's essential duty to remedy America's toxic civic culture, an interpolation that equates saving the nation with nursing the nation back to health. From this angle, Black women's visual work in the new millennium is paradoxically and problematically integral to the nation's well-being. Black women, to put it plainly, are seen as nursemaids for a broken political system that has, since its inception, regarded Black women's bodies as expendable and gratuitously open to sexual exploitation and violence.

Prescod-Weinstein's language further animates one of this book's fundamental principles in that it rejects the idea that Black women are inherently resilient subjects who retain an innate creativity even in the midst of patriarchal white-dominated cultural opposition.[64] This ethos surfaced in additional social media retorts that proclaimed that Black women voters in Alabama in 2017, and again in the 2021 Georgia Senate runoffs, acted not to save the country but to protect themselves. Instead of patriotism, their actions in this vein embodied forms of recuperative care for themselves and their immediate and extended kin within and beyond state lines. As a result of the mainstreaming of intersectionality, the reparative labor that Black women are expected to perform in redressing their shared undesirability is twofold for conservatives and progressives alike; vis-à-vis political participation, Black women are warrior outlaws who reify the injustices of an existing social order *while they also* equate voting with "proper" subjectivity for maintaining a state that relegates them to the bottom of its hierarchy. The visual work in this book and the novel analyses it prompts emphatically reject notions of propriety and reparation in ways that mirror Prescod-Weinstein's public repudiation of the various constituencies that attempt to claim Black women's labor for their own benefit. It also considers for the first time how Black women's triple otherness—an alterity at the intersection of race, gender, and sexuality—spurs nonnormative aesthetic strategies of repulsion and negativity that refuse to be political in any conventional sense. That is, the figures in the work, their actions, and their makers remain outside of the field of political action properly conceived (within the means-ends logic that subtends the definition of politics in the West).

Repeated deployments of repulsion and negativity connect the artists and artworks in this book, as does their disregard for a bounded, unified understanding of Black female being. Here, repulsion operates on two levels, first as abhorrence and second, in terms of physics, when two objects turn away from each other upon contact because they share the same magnetic charge. In bringing these threads together within contemporary Black feminist art practice and criticism, *Undesirability and Her Sisters* identifies and advances a latent strand of queer negativity that energizes and expands the boundaries of intersectional theory. The female figures who populate the art of Walker, Mutu, Simmons, and Narcissister emphasize the ways that Black women, their undesirability, and their creative labors continue to be foundational to twenty-first-century conceptions of the nation, of racial progress, and of reproductive futurity. Yet the "sisters" in the following pages are marked by rupture, opacity, and frenzy, not repair, pleasure, or desirable metamorphosis. As a result, the art and artists in this book stretch persistently archetypal ideas of Black womanhood and the parameters of kinship and sisterhood beyond flawless figures or strong Black women who overcome relationship and racial strife. Additionally, while I have grouped Walker, Mutu, Simmons, and Narcissister together, the perverse, disparate figures they produce do not cohere into a picture of togetherness. They instead rebuff representational norms that conscript Black women's creative labors into caregiving endeavors believed to beget self-determination and social transformation. In so doing, they expand the aesthetic and ethical terrain of what it means to be Black and woman in the twenty-first century, revealing the omnipresence of historical injury as well as unexpected, at times counterintuitive, strategies of survival in an era of new racial and gender meaning.

Each of this book's four chapters spotlights the work of a different artist, charting an important new genealogy of Black women's art equal to the challenges of our time. In addition to an individual artist, each chapter focuses on a specific aesthetic strategy and signature artistic medium, all of which bear a special relationship to the construction of race, gender, class, and sexuality in the United States. The first two chapters outline how Kara Walker's recent large-scale installations and Wangechi Mutu's collages modify art historical narratives about representation's transformative power in our current era of racial and gender reckoning. These chapters also advance provocative claims about the political value of Black women's visual work in the age of social media and #BlackLivesMatter. Renowned for her room-size tableaux of black cut-paper silhouettes, Walker's recent monumental public sculptures draw viewers into jarring versions of trans-Atlantic slavery and present-day race relations that are, in the artist's words, "totally demeaning and possibly very beautiful."[65] For Mutu, women disproportionately sustain representational burdens that paradoxically relegate them to a lower social status and position them as sites of structural and metaphorical support. To counter this cultural tendency, the artist places female figures at the center of her art as protagonists, "as a platform to reveal the resilience and physical/mythical power of the female body."[66] How the artist manipulates this power, however, confounds conventional understandings of women's capacity to band together or quickly recover from traumatic situations.

Simultaneously provocative, alluring, and unnerving, the art of Walker and Mutu stages an apt reckoning with historical experience by short-circuiting the white gaze, breaking with Enlightenment ideals concerning humanity, and undermining essentialist Black thinking with regard to the memory of slavery. Two of the most celebrated artists working today, Walker and Mutu create bodies of work that demonstrate their evolving engagement with their own identities as artists, as Black women, and as mothers. They are the best-known artists in this study, with the largest amount of scholarship on their work, yet critics routinely default to narratives of recuperation and repair when describing each artist's practice. My analysis, by contrast, focuses on the ways in which the two artists foreground images of undesirable Black female being and becoming despite their success and how critics tie themselves in knots describing them as redemptive and uplifting.

Walker's fashioning of the Black female bottom in *A Subtlety*, the first public art commission of her career, and in *Fons Americanus*, her first public art commission in the United Kingdom, provides the basis for the aesthetic strategies analyzed in this book. The two works coalesce the unique experiences of Black women who have historically and generally been relegated to society's margins, particularly in the context of slavery and ongoing legacies of racial and gender-based oppression. Walker's fashioning of the Black female bottom merges "bottoming" as a form of submissive sex with "being at the bottom," a position of devaluation, vulnerability, subordination, objectification, and powerlessness within a given hierarchy—racial, aesthetic, class, and otherwise. Within this matrix of identity, history, memory, and power, Black women are persistently figured as fungible objects as well as minor characters devoid of interiority or formal inventiveness.

Chapter 1 examines how Walker's work dispenses with the impulse to meet absence with presence, loss with recovery, and erasure with visibility as viable and desirable forms of empowerment and enfranchisement. Most importantly, her enactments of the Black female bottom exceed depictions of victimhood; her troubling imagery is a blunt repudiation of the redemptive power of art itself and its capacity to ennoble past experience as romantic or reparable. The artist's two site-specific installations demonstrate how architectures of capitalism and containment rely on dispossession, occupation, ruin, and catastrophe. This includes the art market. In her work, Black women's bodies are sites of creation and reproduction without futurity that invigorate the market's extractive logics. To this end, Walker's public art commissions and recent works by Mutu, Simmons, and Narcissister model aesthetic strategies that are neither derivative nor transcendent. Embracing subjection and abjection, the dismembered, self-objectified, inassimilable Black female figures at the center of these artists' practices function as preconditions to an alternative ethics of being and relation that magnifies the unfinished project of racial and gender empowerment in the twenty-first century. Such strategies consequently expand the boundaries of intersectionality by underlining how domination and submission co-constitute Black women's lived experience in an era defined by the persistent visualization of Blackness alongside the continued devaluation of Black female bodies.

Chapter 2, "Alien Kin," focuses on Mutu's visually arresting collages. Her visual work connects Walker's satirical re-imaginings of the American slave past with hybrid constructions that double as metaphors for racial and gender otherness. Trained as both a sculptor and an anthropologist, Mutu uses art historical strategies of accumulation to create unique depictions of human and nonhuman relations that animate the limits of bodily trauma and collective memory in an era of techno-optimism and post-identity desire. Notably, the majority of her art depicts the Black female body as the ground from which nonnormative conceptions of reproduction, futurity, and humanity spring. "I think there is a shift not in using the black body 'as a political gesture' per se, but a movement towards using the black body," she has said, "for a variety of gestures not just pertaining to race or gender in the most obvious manner."[67] Indeed, her cyborg bodies comprising human, animal, plant, and machine parts alert viewers and critics to the contemporary conditions of fragmented existence and the vicissitudes of humanness. Suspended within nebulous, unstable environments where ruptures on the surface and within the picture plane proliferate, her complex figures exist between disgust and regeneration.[68]

To the artist's critics, the cyborgs are empowering, compensatory amalgams of Black womanhood and mutual belonging—self-regenerating hybrids that affirm collective intersectional futures across time, species, and environments. In my reading, the recurrence of cutting, blood spatter, and dismemberment as the bases for construction in Mutu's work proffers alternate, at times violent and undesirable, forms of transformation that leave the body undone. Her dismembered figures, as a result, destabilize assumptions concerning bodily integrity and the continuous relationship between a shared slave past and contemporary Black political realities, as does her view of herself as a Black, East African woman working in the United States. Rather than symbiosis, the human, plant, animal, and mechanical parts in Mutu's collages animate anti-communal mutualisms that come into view via dismemberment between human and nonhuman species. This transgressive dismemberment, as I call it, disavows reparative resistance and upends the presumption that slavery is the nexus of shared Black experience and identity. Transgressive dismemberment joins recent critical studies of ugliness, negation, failure, unbecoming, and repulsion within feminist, queer, and Black cultural theory. I apply these theorizations to Mutu's collages alongside Black feminist writings by Farah Jasmine Griffin, Hortense J. Spillers, and Octavia Butler to further articulate the value of undesirable Black female embodiment.

The second half of the book turns to practices of self-display that mobilize themes of individual and collective becoming within landscape, portraiture, and performance. Chapter 3, "Against Revelation," outlines Xaviera Simmons's critical engagements with photography's semiotic properties, namely the index and its function, and the ethics of historical reenactment and performance. Since its inception, the practice of photography has spurred debates about its histories, its utility, and its effects. Early thinking on photography considered the medium to be transparent and truthful, that is, contiguous with the real. In the latter half of the twentieth century, conceptual and post-conceptual photographers began exploiting the contingent relation between presence and absence that was thought to inhere in the medium. In so doing, they effected an "unbridgeable distance from the original, from even the possibility of an original," art historian and cultural studies scholar Douglas Crimp explains, and by extension, a referent.[69] Simmons extends these photoconceptual interventions to issues of surface and depth that arise from photography's imbrication with the Black (maternal) body.

Questions concerning the self and the referential authority of photographic images, both analog and digital, persist in the present, and Simmons's output during the first quarter of the new millennium confronts these questions head on. Active since the early 2000s, she has garnered appreciation within the art world; however, she has yet to receive concentrated monographic attention. As such, her measured output and conceptual concerns elucidate another dimension of the minor explored in this book. Rather than crafting transparent photographic images of fixed identities that reconcile the fissure between absence and presence, the figures in Simmons's found and staged portraits are often grainy and obscured, with parts of the body—namely the face—totally hidden. This act of refusal, along with the techniques of masking and self-disavowal that the artist deploys across her practice, constitutes a language of opacity that embraces inscrutability in an era when emergent digital-imaging and surveillance modalities, calls for transparency, unprecedented forms of Black visibility, and so-called racial and gender progress proliferate. By presenting transient bodies, identities, and opacity as integral to depictions of the self and Black female being and becoming in contemporary art, Simmons's work challenges what constitutes identity and loss by exposing the limits of photography and historical reconstruction in the wake of trauma. More specifically, her expansive practice defies well-worn norms concerning Black image making as a means of (self)-representation within histories of photography, disrupting the relationship between indexicality and racial reckoning.

Narcissister's dance-based performances of kinky sex, which many critics describe as reclamatory acts of self-love and care, are the topic of chapter 4, "Masks, Mayhem, and Kink." Presented in the form of live stripteases, video works, and collaged self-portraits that approximate the do-it-yourself aesthetics of porn, sex tapes, YouTube parodies, and the pop music video all in one, her work turns away from social and aesthetic norms concerning fine art, appropriate sex, and Black dancing bodies. Behind eerie Barbie masks of various shades, some featuring just one orifice—an opening for her mouth—Narcissister, a self-identified "sister" with mixed-raced heritage, redirects our gaze to her body in abject sex acts that do not end in orgasmic climax. In *Every Woman*, her best-known work, she performs a reverse striptease to Chaka Khan's "I'm Every Woman," pulling clothing and accessories from between her legs, her mouth, and the Afro wig she wears, all the while refusing to reveal her identity. She cannot see or look back at us with her own eyes; alternately, we see only part of her. Her own gaze is obscured, as is her own apprehension of the world outside of her self-made artificiality and plastic mask, turning her focus inward. From this angle, Narcissister appears to be the sole object and subject of her sexual exploits. For these reasons, many critics see Narcissister's persona and performance practice as radical reclamations of the racially and sexually degraded self, observations not in accord with the repulsive nature of her performances.

Her practice of flipping in and out of costumes, multiracial masks, and abject sexual scenarios congeal into race play, in my view, a form of kinky sex that at once relishes yet exceeds erotic fetishism. Kink in this context encompasses the sexual quirks that the artist performs, the cultural signifiers—curly-haired wigs and merkins—that she wears, the erotic entanglements of race, gender, and sex that she animates across her practice, and her repulsion of aesthetic and social norms concerning the mixed-race female figure. Similar to Mutu's cyborgs, Narcissister caricatures the myriad ways in which American racial discourse promulgates images of hybrid figures as loci for multiracial desirability and promise. The artist's cleverly suggestive moniker and her kinky enactments of race play consequently transform narcissism from a kind of ego-loving self-absorption into undesirable self-objectification.

In short-circuiting drives toward wholeness, racial healing, and reproductive futurity, the artists in this book picture inassimilable, anti-communal ways of Black female being that are not reducible to group self-definition, past trauma, or multiracial transcendence. This non-relational current animates undesirability, as does a sense of enervation that stems from well-worn ideas concerning biological and artistic reproduction as the grounds for eliminating the sting of racial and gender subjugation in the present. By harnessing undesirability, Walker, Mutu, Simmons, and Narcissister delineate conditions of Black female being and becoming that crystallize at the border between disenchantment and disaffection, all while refusing coherent minoritarian subjectivity and unity as well as a discernible way forward. In so doing, these artists unsettle social and aesthetic norms regarding what Black female figures can and should do in times of social and political upheaval. Their visions of racial, gender, class, and sexual existence are predicated on dissidence, where bad behavior—the discordant, the dark, and the heterogeneous—is commensurate with the challenges of our time. Rejecting ideas about racial and gender fidelity and duty, of bodily coherence, of kinship, and of futurity, entreats viewers and readers across multiple fields and disciplines to think differently about the ends of art and collectivity. This paradigm shift breaks open the myth that civic welfare and progress can be achieved through harmony and an unwavering faith in social progress, and it matters now more than ever. Considering the current US political climate, ongoing racial and gender violence, and debates about the relationship between art and social protest, this work is urgently of its time.

1

The Black Female Bottom

Experience may be overwhelming, practically impossible to absorb, but it is assumed . . . that the work of art has the authority to master the presumed *raw material* of experience in a manner that uniquely gives value to, perhaps even redeems, that material.
—Leo Bersani

With every exhibition and new body of work, artist Kara Walker inspires debates about the right and wrong ways to picture and perform Black womanhood. Much of the controversy surrounding her stems from the publicity and attention her darkly humorous installations receive from the predominantly white art world, from her well-known silhouettes to her recent public sculptures, which amplify the qualities of materiality to the point of perversity. Throughout her oeuvre, undesirable figures recur—the topsy turvy, the mammy, and the negress, an alter ego that the artist adopted early on in her career—as do other stereotypes about Black women's bodies, their sexualities, and their reproductive capacities. In constellating bondage, hybridity, opacity, and self-objectification, her figurations of what I call the Black female bottom—a dynamic physiological, material, and conceptual space—lay the groundwork for a definition of undesirability that functions as an aesthetic enterprise, one that Mutu, Simmons, and Narcissister take up and extend in the following chapters of this book. Black female bottoming, here, exceeds the visual. It pivots on "a too-muchness," as Walker puts it, that inundates viewers with disgust, nausea, and repulsion.[1] These minor aesthetic strategies upend the value hierarchies of beauty and desirability against which Black women are measured and debased in the past and present.

The publicness and pornographic edges of both Walker's imagery and her status as a world-renowned Black woman artist have also provoked vitriolic responses from viewers, critics, and fellow artists. She is the

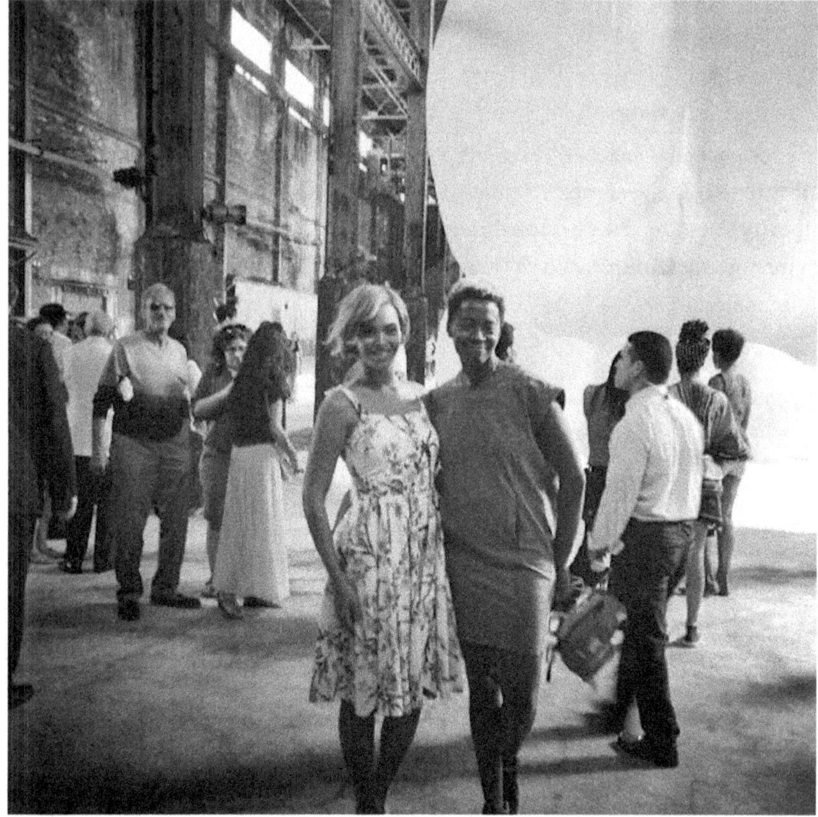

Figure 1.1. Photographer unknown, digital color photograph, BeyLite Instagram, 2014, Fair Use.

most known artist in this study with the largest archive of exhibitions and writing devoted to her work, and her fame and visibility have put her on the same stage as Beyoncé in the social media sphere and in scholarship. In 2014, the two stars posed together in front of Walker's first public art commission, *A Subtlety, or the Marvelous Sugar Baby, an Homage to the Unpaid and Overworked Artisans Who Have Refined Our Sweet Tastes from the Cane Fields to the Kitchens of the New World on the Occasion of the Demolition of the Domino Sugar Refining Plant*. For some scholars, this meeting inside of the factory-sized installation was evidence of a kind of kinship that transformed *A Subtlety* into a site of sisterhood and healing. But the sculpture itself—a large-scale sphinx with an oversized backside and the head of a mammy made entirely of refined white sugar that dripped in the searing heat of the summer—was the very embodiment of abjection.

According to literary and cultural studies scholar Sarah Brophy, Beyoncé's mere presence appeared to transform Walker's "grotesque" approach to the history of slavery into "an image of black feminist solidarity" that the public nature of the work reified.[2] Alternately, literary studies scholar Jarvis McInnis saw Walker and Beyoncé as kindred artists who could reclaim and "reterritorialize" sugar refineries and plantations to upend racial-sexual violence. For McInnis, Walker's *A Subtlety* represented a singular alternative "to the impossibility of justice and repair," and Beyoncé's *Lemonade* served as a treatise on "racial healing, feminist insurgency, and self-determination."[3]

This chapter, however, considers how Walker's material choices and self-conscious engagement with her own social status and hyper-visibility in the marketplace circumvent viewer expectations and the weight of slavery's transnational legacies. Instead of an affirming display of solidarity and racial repair, I argue that the artist's recent public artworks—namely *A Subtlety* of 2014 and *Fons Americanus* presented by the Tate Modern in London in 2019—represent undesirable figurations of the Black female bottom. Playing on social degradation and sexual submission, such figurations upend value hierarchies as well as transcendental ideas of race, gender, and class. The result is an expanded understanding of post-identity discourse and intersectionality in contemporary art.

In 1995, Walker crafted *The Means to an End . . . A Shadow Drama in Five Acts*, an unruly antebellum plantation scene at small scale that would come to unsettle not only viewers but also exhibition venues. Produced in an edition of twenty in collaboration with Landfall Press, the work unfolds over five panels from left to right and back again, addressing the viewer as both onlooker and reader. A child, solid and black, dangles from the breast of a barefoot woman. A young girl sits askew on the back of a strange four-legged animal. Her arm reaches out as the animal races toward another off-kilter female figure whose pantalooned leg steps in the opposite direction over a trail of amorphous lumps, made to resemble either feces or rocks. The trail culminates in a head and hand emerging from the ground. The head tilts up, fixated on the figure looming over it: a male atop a grassy ledge, outfitted in a top hat and coattails.

Extending his leg as if to enter the chaos sprawled before him, he holds an unclothed child by the neck.

The Detroit Institute of Arts (DIA) acquired *The Means to an End . . . A Shadow Drama in Five Acts* for its permanent collection a year later. But when it was exhibited only three years after the acquisition, the artwork was suddenly removed.[4] Several board members and representatives of the museum's Friends of African and African-American Art, a longstanding auxiliary group responsible for fundraising and acquiring works for DIA's African and African American art collections, complained that the piece had offensive racial overtones. "We are a big public museum, the only one in this town," DIA's chief curator, David Penney, told *Detroit Free Press* reporter David Lyman at the time.[5] "As a result, we have a tremendous responsibility to our community."[6] This sense of duty is directly tied to the racial makeup of Detroit in the late 1990s. Envisioned as a racial utopia, Detroit has often been referred to as a "chocolate city" because of its large Black populace. The number of African Americans living in Detroit exponentially increased between 1910 and 1980 due to the first and second Great Migrations.[7] Looking to find jobs and escape Jim Crow segregation in the southern United States, Detroit's Black residents instead found themselves excluded from white areas of the city through violence, laws, economic discrimination, and redlining. Because of this, Walker's print spurred generational debates regarding the roles and responsibilities of Black art, its makers, and its collectors in a market and city wrought with their own histories of systemic racism inflected by class and neighborhood tensions.

This early instance of censorship in Walker's career underscores how publicness and place have imbibed her practice with intramural desires for Black women's respectability in contemporary American art. It also highlights the dispossessive force—the undesirability—that issues from Black women's public displays of nonnormative identity performance and sexuality, representations that go against the grain of respectability and privacy. Walker's work borders on the pornographic, and for many viewers, this fact is at once titillating and disturbing. This precarious balance has generated a swarm of controversy about the artist, who first began exploring racial and sexual themes as a graduate student at the Rhode Island School of Design. In 1997, three years after her first solo show at the Drawing Center in New York in 1994, Walker was awarded the prestigious MacArthur "genius" award, an accolade that precipitated a maelstrom of criticism from older African American artists.[8] Betye Saar, Michael D. Harris, and Howardena Pindell were among the most vocal denouncers of Walker's use of so-called negative images, likening the artist to a race traitor.[9]

And yet her work reveled in the negative. Her kinky entanglements defined a post-slavery imaginary where "monstrous intimacies" between Blackness and whiteness proliferate, as Black literary and cultural studies scholar Christina Sharpe describes.[10] Phenotypical allusions underscore these intimacies in both book print form and in the room-sized installations for which the artist gained notoriety, and closer inspection reveals each figure's racial markings. The repeated outlines of exaggerated agape lips, unkempt hair, and barefoot, half-naked bodies in ragged clothing rehearse stereotypical figurations of Blackness made popular in nineteenth-century American sentimental novels, blackface performances, and physiognomy textbook illustrations. Conversely, the well-kept coattails, pigtails, and even the blank gallery and museum walls to which her black cutouts are adhered conjure a genteel whiteness that starkly contrasts the deviant acts on display in black. Walker's engagement with the blackness of the silhouette in the physiognomic sciences, however, takes on a very different valence that prefigures the perversity she explores in her more recent work. This sustained engagement, one that pivots on playing in the bottom registers of color and form as sites of undesirable racial and spatial intimacies, engenders paradigm-shifting analytics for the study of Black women's visual work in the new millennium.

For Walker, the silhouette is the ideal art form for upending normative ideas about Black women's reproductive capacities and the persistent entanglements of race, sex, gender, and class in the afterlife of slavery because of its status as an ostensibly simplistic art form. Typically sidelined as feminine parlor craft or collectible ephemera, the silhouette for Walker is an already demoted art form. Nineteenth-century cycloramas and genre paintings function similarly for the artist. She appropriates and transmogrifies these outmoded, "second-class" art forms, to use her terms, to upset value hierarchies of American art and life that define Black subjects as second-class citizens.[11]

Also known as profile portraits or shades, the silhouette is a pre-photographic method of figurative representation composed of solid outlines of a subject made from pieces of cut black paper mounted onto a white or light-tinted background. Silhouettes first gained popularity in the mid- to late 1700s. But because silhouettes generally dispensed with European conventions of portraiture such as stylized poses and mise-en-scènes, they were derided as derivative within the fine arts. Alternatively, within handiwork trades, silhouettes were seen as viable forms of portraiture. At the same time, Swiss physiognomist Johann Kaspar Lavater used the medium to analyze facial types and discern a subject's moral character. Rather than providing realistic renderings, Lavater used silhouettes to picture and exaggerate differences—those of race and class among them—through processes of abstraction and distillation. Silhouettes-as-portraiture were also used as etiquette manuals during the Victorian era in both Britain and America to teach young girls how to comport and dress themselves in order to be "good ladies."

Thus, within the bourgeois origins of portraiture, the blackness of the silhouette was not at first racially charged; its function was to reproduce the trace of a (white) bodily presence—conversely, to function as a sign of its absence. In this schema, the blackness of the silhouette—its opacity—operated as a signifier both of emptiness and of fullness: it indexed the body that casted the shadow that then served as the form's outline and content. "Within bourgeois portraiture," moving-image studies scholar Alessandra Raengo tells us in her writing on Walker, the index, and Black visual culture, "the silhouette was animated by the desire to transform a hole into the possibility of wholeness."[12] Through the affective investment of the viewer, the silhouette, in other words, becomes a mark of personhood.[13] And once the outline and its contents are imbued with sentimental memory and nostalgia, they become a projection of desire. The indexicality of Walker's silhouettes thus entails a spatial and affective theory of identity and difference, of self and other, and ultimately, of abjection and bottomhood.

The silhouette, Lavater wrote, is "the emptiest but simultaneously . . . the truest and most faithful image that one can give of a person . . . because it is an immediate imprint of nature."[14] For Lavater, the silhouette's "modesty" and its "weakness," its lack of texture and detail, made it the most suitable form of representation for physiognomic analysis.[15] "It provided," Raengo intimates, "an abstract map of the body onto which it was possible to seemingly read, but in reality project, an imagined relationship between its inside and its outside, its outward characteristics and its interior essence."[16] The blackness of the silhouette, here, is a meeting point between mimesis and contiguity, between trace and race. It becomes a racially *overdetermined* index "through mimicry of the chromatic attributes of certain bodies' skin," Raengo asserts, "and as a signifier of the Other."[17] Where the silhouette captured the essence of an individual—their virtues and their likeness—with very little detail for Lavater, Walker appropriates the silhouette to exaggerate the Blackness of picture-making traditions even more and the persistently entangled nature of racial and gender relations in the afterlife of slavery. From this angle, Walker's art urges viewers to see the very presence of the construction of race in the image, anticipating Xaviera Simmons's engagements with indexicality and theories of photography discussed in chapter 3.[18] The silhouette figures explode the boundaries that preserve the assumed contiguity between the inside and outside of racially marked bodies and the standards of etiquette, or good behavior, that the form was originally intended to enforce with regard to both race and gender; Walker's silhouettes, in short, behave badly.

The stereotypical features of her *black* Black figures rely on racist visual codes and figurations that were popularized in nineteenth- and twentieth-century American novels and films such as *Uncle Tom's Cabin* and *Gone with the Wind*. Topsy turvy in the former and the mammy character in the latter surface again and again in Walker's art, troubling the relation between Blackness and representation by altering how we generally *see* race, class, gender, and sexuality in unexpected ways. Furthermore, Walker's scenes of abject violence and satire set in the antebellum American South hijack narrative conventions and the silhouette to complicate "a pre-existing text of blackness," as art historian Kobena Mercer outlines in his writing on tropes of the grotesque in Black avant-garde art. This hijacking extends from the medium to the conservative expectations of racial solidarity, uplift, and respectability that come with it and Black art more broadly.[19] These expectations, art historian Gwendolyn DuBois Shaw argues in her path-breaking book on Walker's silhouettes, flatten the possibilities for Black women's experiences of pleasure and agency. Feces doubling as rocks, ballooned penises propelling their owners into the air, silhouettes of wet-nurses and pickaninnies suckling one another, and other kinky scenarios punctuate how race is necessarily a sadistic, libidinal fantasy that is both terrifying and titillating.

Walker's topsy-turvy, post-slavery world imbricates racial and sexual fictions to illustrate how Black sexual expression has long been marked as deviant in America's public imaginary. All her silhouette figures, most of which are black in color, are engaged in freaky business: women and children suckle each other's breasts; others, impaled and dismembered, are seen defecating on pristine white walls; more, still, are caught in acts of autofellatio and forms of sexual degradation. Beyond these monstrous intimacies, Walker's silhouettes are black holes that function as spatial terrains that prompt a wider view of Black female sexualities and their potential, especially in regard to queer theory and nonnormative creative expression. Such black holes, Black feminist and science studies scholar Evelynn Hammonds argues, appear empty but are in fact "dense and full."[20] Taking black holes in space as a point of departure, Hammonds questions the perceptual tools and economies of visuality used to categorize, and thus formulate, Black women's sexuality as deficient yet ever expanding, dense, and unknowable. "Rather than assuming that Black female sexualities are structured along an axis of normal and perverse paralleling that of white women," she argues for theories of Black female sexualities unmoored from heteronormative white female sexuality.[21] In so doing, "we might find that for Black women a different geometry operates."[22] By drawing black and white into such peculiar, gravitational relations vis-à-vis color, phenotype, and kink, Walker makes visible how Black sexualities muddy the boundaries of normalcy and knowability. That is, the *imagined deviance* of her black figures, regardless of their racial markings, effectively contaminates sexualities historically thought to be pure and pristine—a post-slavery landscape of excrement, waste, toxicity, and filth.[23]

Walker's silhouettes have come to define her career, and they have inspired an equally exhaustive amount of literature on the subject. Much has also been written about her text-based works on paper, films, and cycloramas. But the relationship between her silhouettes and her public artworks remains underexplored, as does Walker's articulation of the friction between Black womanhood and publicness in her life and career. Instead of rehashing the robust body of scholarship and criticism on her silhouettes, this chapter proffers a new perspective on the artist that conjoins her recent shift to public sculpture with Black female bottoming. Although this trope is present in her earlier work—it appears in her silhouettes as topsy turvy, the mammy figure, and her own embrace of the negress as an alter ego—the Black female bottom has grown in both scale and materiality in her public sculptures of late.

A Subtlety and *Fons Americanus*, two of Walker's major public artworks of the past decade, amplify how fantasies and fictions about the Black female bottom in American culture, as a body part and a spatial and environmental concept, refract and constrain Black women's creative and sexual expression. Scale and materiality in these works perform excess that in turn produce more excess at the level of ingestion, olfaction, and planned ruin. One a factory-sized installation and the other a sprawling fountain, *A Subtlety* and *Fons Americanus* transmute the displays of racial and sexual abjection in Walker's silhouettes to aesthetic experiences that materialize in conjunction with but ultimately breach the bounds of the visual and the commercial art market. The first inundated visitors with olfactory and gustatory effects that mirrored the decaying and degrading ruins of the space it occupied. The second also addressed space and ruin, that of the Black Atlantic and its relationship to British and American imperialism. It towered over its viewers, positioning them as lower figures overwhelmed by the fountain's height and figuration; its structure, on the other hand, placed the Black female slave, a recurring figure in Walker's works, at the top—a reversal that prioritizes the bottom. Both installations espouse negativity as a productive strategy for grappling with the complexities of Blackness, womanhood, and subjectivity in the art world and the wider world.

Walker's public artworks embrace bottoming's association with submission and abjection to fashion novel modes of being and relation that emerge from toxicity, decay, decomposition, and nonreproduction. Across intricately cut silhouettes and monumental installations that double as anti-monuments, the Black female bottom emerges as an aesthetic intervention, a site-specific character, a social and sexual position of submission and degradation, and a space of sensual excess.[24] This excess actively challenges the social and structural constraints of a marketplace that demands that Black women artists be both marginal and hypervisible, vulnerable yet also in active pursuit of their own healing and

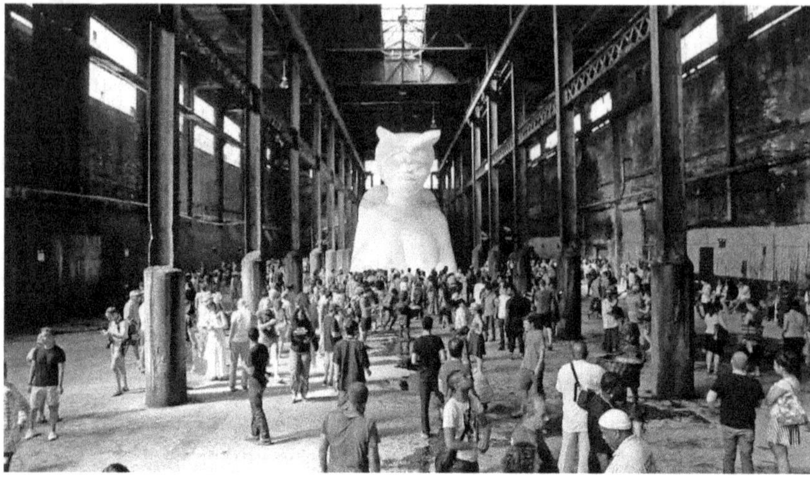

Figure 1.2. Kara Walker, *A Subtlety, or the Marvelous Sugar Baby, an Homage to the Unpaid and Overworked Artisans Who Have Refined Our Sweet Tastes from the Cane Fields to the Kitchens of the New World on the Occasion of the Demolition of the Domino Sugar Refining Plant.* Polystyrene foam, sugar. Approx. 35.5 × 26 × 75.5 feet (10.8 × 7.9 × 23 m). Installation view, Domino Sugar Refinery, 2014. A project of Creative Time, Brooklyn, NY. Photo: Jason Wyche Artwork. © Kara Walker. Courtesy of Sikkema Jenkins & Co. and Sprüth Magers.

empowerment against all odds. In untethering Blackness and its embodiment from the binary of trauma and redemption, Walker expands the terrain of art's engagement with Black women's social and sexual lives in the new millennium.

The Difference a Subtlety Makes

For nine consecutive weekends in 2014, a colossal sugarcoated sphinx could be seen in the now defunct Domino Sugar Refinery in Williamsburg, Brooklyn. Droves of people, myself included, stood in line for hours in New York's summer heat to ogle *A Subtlety* and to snap a picture of it. When I finally made it into the refinery, I was overwhelmed, not so much by the sight but by the smell. The molasses-caked walls emitted a scent so strong as to be nauseating, and the various elements of the installation, like the refinery itself, were rapidly disintegrating. The sphinx's fifteen "sugar babies," a cadre of candy-coated, resin-cast servant boys with stereotypical Black features positioned throughout the looming space, were completely coated in molasses, melting and crumbling to pieces like the refinery's walls. Five feet tall with cherubic faces all a similar shade of brown, some of the sugar babies stood amid melted pools of dark liquid that resembled the color of blood, a mix of humor and horror similar to the grotesquerie that subtends Walker's signature silhouettes. Over the course of the exhibition's run, the sugar babies' baskets, historically intended for the collection of fruit, sugar cane, and other crops, slowly accumulated the dismembered arms and heads of the other molasses boys that had collapsed and shattered from New York's intense summer heat.

The thirty-five-foot-tall, seventy-two-foot-long sphinx itself was monumental and nude, a stark-white female figure with the head of a mammy, a stereotype that originated in slavery. As in her silhouettes, Walker resuscitates undesirable images of the Black female form—minstrel, monstrous, stereotypical, and more—but does not redeem them. In American literature and visual culture, the mammy is typically depicted as overweight, desexualized, yet gratuitously open to the threat of sexual violence, a condition of the Black female slave experience. This figuration incited criticisms that the installation made light of ongoing racial harm and pain that stems from slavery and Black women's historical and contemporary subjugation.[25] Walker is no stranger to this type of critique. Across her oeuvre, her figures walk the line between stereotype and archetype, obscenity and irony. The difference with *A Subtlety* occurs at the level of materials, publicness, posture, Black female bottomhood, and space.

One of the most talked about temporary, US-based public artworks of the twenty-first century, *A Subtlety* realizes the artist's long-standing interests in aesthetic strategies of repulsion and refusal. The installation unseats Blackness as a sacred, untouchable signifier, extending and transmuting the force of her silhouettes to engagements with the Black female bottom. *Bottoming* is a term typically associated with gay male anal sex and BDSM (shorthand for a variety of erotic practices and roleplaying involving bondage, domination [or discipline], sadism [or submission], and masochism). Popularized in Leo Bersani's psychoanalytic writings about perversion and gay male pleasure, *bottoming* and *bottomhood* as keywords and theoretical concepts have undergone revision in recent years. Twenty-first-century scholars working at the intersection of psychoanalysis, race, gender, sexuality, and culture challenge queer theory's "masculinist bias"—its exclusion of women and how its framing feminizes those at the margins.[26] Nguyễn Tân Hoàng, Jennifer Nash, Darieck Scott, Amber Musser, Kathryn Bond Stockton, and others illustrate how bottoming and bottomhood undermine normative sexual, gender, and racial hierarchies. Hoàng's writing on Asian American masculinity and same-sex representation in film locates bottomhood as "a sexual position, a social alliance, an affective bond, and an aesthetic form," all of which have the potential to coalesce into a cross-racial, mutually pleasurable, oppositional politics that center on relationality.[27] Most importantly for my purposes, Hoàng, following Heather Love, proposes a politics of bottomhood that refuses to redeem bottomhood as resistance. Departing from Hoàng, my conception of the Black female bottom in Walker's work—a systematically forced and enforced position—is firmly rooted in Black women's triple otherness and undesirability. It builds on Jennifer Nash's notion of Black anality, Darieck Scott's idea of the Black power bottom, and Amber Musser's writing on sensation and sensuality as new analytics for appraising the limits and possibilities of Black female being.

Nash extends Evelynn Hammonds's analogizing of Black female sexuality with black holes to query how the Black female anus, rather than the Black female buttocks, acts as a significant and signifying space through which Black sexual difference—and Blackness more generally—is imagined and represented in popular culture and pornography.[28] Because of art historian Sander Gilman's groundbreaking scholarship on Saartjie Baartman, also known as the Hottentot Venus, "Black feminist theory," Nash writes, "has long argued that the buttocks are the location of imagined black sexual difference," as well as Black women's sexual excess.[29] In this schema, Baartman's body functions as a "master text" for theorizing the myriad ways in which the dominant visual field inflicts violence onto Black women's flesh, from freak shows of the past to popular media and pornography in the present.

Nash's Black anality troubles Black feminist preoccupations with spectacularity and excess as counters to historically reductive and demeaning frameworks of analysis that label the Black female body as grotesque, strange, unfeminine, lascivious, and obscene. She instead claims that Black pleasures can be imagined and oriented toward the anus, thereby elaborating on anal ideologies such as spatiality, waste, toxicity, and filth. More than exploring the production and circulation of anal ideologies and how they constrain and violate Black sexual freedom, she excavates moments of "race pleasure" where Black female bodies attach themselves to anal ideologies in ways that engender delight in Blackness itself.[30] According to Nash, Black women strategically deploy anal ideologies to expose the kinds of pleasures that Black subjects can take in Blackness—its hyperboles and its painful fictions. Here, her work dovetails with Darieck Scott's concept of extravagant Blackness and what he calls Black power bottoms, both of which revel in paradoxes that speak to "the very core of what blackness is in our culture and how we embody it," he argues.[31] Such paradoxes include "luxury that is necessity, freedom that is imprisonment, and perhaps surprisingly, their correspondent vice-versa formulations;" bottoming in particular "evokes the willed enactment of powerlessness that encodes a power of its own, in which pain or discomfort are put to multifarious uses."[32] Though Scott's work primarily interrogates the socially constructed linkages between Black maleness and abjection, his work is an important revision to the whiteness of anal ideologies within theories of race and psychoanalysis.

Significantly, Scott acknowledges, "women can be—*and by the normative or traditional definitions of gender*, often are or [are] supposed to be—'bottoms,' too."[33] Walker's practice of Black female bottoming saliently evidences this possibility, merging erotic fantasies of the Black female body with domination and submission. In so doing, her art opens up new pathways for understanding Black women's triple otherness, their queerness, and their creativity within the context of sexual and sensual excess. As a preeminent scholar writing on these topics, Amber Musser's theorizations of what Walker terms "too-muchness" elaborate on the interrelations between race and masochism in the US imaginary. Her groundbreaking scholarship on sensation, surface, queer form, and "the undisciplined" proffer new epistemologies of selfhood and pleasure that unsettle intersectionality's framing of Black and brown female bodies as homogenously sexualized, objectified, abject, and wounded. Walker's *The End of Uncle Tom and the Grand Allegorical Tableau of Eva in Heaven* (1995), according to Musser, transmogrifies "sexuality, agency, and subjectivity for black women."[34] In her analysis of the artist's masochistic tableaux, Musser argues that paper and vinyl function as skins, making material how Black female flesh has historically been seen as a flat surface absent of sexuality yet full of projected fantasies from without and within. Musser's more recent writing on *A Subtlety* furthers her analysis of what she terms Brown jouissance, a form of extreme pleasure that stems from extra-visual sensations and sensuality. Walker's exploitations of materials and bodies in her anti-monuments, Musser argues, underline how Black women meet structures of violence and domination with annunciations of aesthetic and material excess that nullify mastery, certainty, and pornotropic capture. By commingling excess and disgust through nausea, decay, toxicity, and physical recoil, *A Subtlety* upends assumptions about art's capacity "to master the presumed raw material of experience in a manner that uniquely gives value to, perhaps even redeems, that material," to use Leo Bersani's words.[35]

Disgust is a minor aesthetic category that receives little critical attention, literary scholar Sianne Ngai explains, while "theories, poetics, and ethics of 'desire' abound."[36] Beauty and pleasure have similarly occupied superior positions over disgust and repulsion in philosophies of art. In classical studies of aesthetics, Carolyn Korsmeyer, philosopher of aesthetics, feminism, and emotion theory, writes that disgust is "the one emotion that could not be incorporated into an experience of beauty."[37] This excessive quality is part and parcel to how Walker's recent public artworks break down normative hierarchies of aesthetic and political value. Disgust and other minor feelings have garnered more consideration in recent years, thanks to scholars returning to key studies such as "Disgust," Aurel Kolnai's long essay from 1929, and the rise of affect theory and queer theory. Disgust, Korsmeyer advocates, should be counted in the hierarchy of senses as one capable of positive use in artistic representation; "It is a pancultural, hardwired reaction designed for protection against contamination."[38] Disgust is slippery and paradoxical, though; it invites allure *and* aversion, thus possessing positive and negative valences. On this score, literary scholar Glenda Carpio believes disgust and its relative dark humor to be cathartic in the context of contemporary representations of slavery, modes of survival that heal the past in the present.

Performance studies scholar Tavia Nyong'o echoes Carpio's sentiments in his writing on the proliferation of stereotypes in popular culture and everyday encounters with racist memorabilia. "Through disgust," he writes, "we reassert our *dignity* and attain distance from the pleasure that the stereotype urges upon us. This oppositional distance places the racist object in a new frame, one in which the object is re-signified."[39] For Nyong'o, disgust is a form of communal resistance, a coping device that protects people of African descent from the harm that racist imagery seemingly imparts. Disgust in this schema becomes "a totem of *our racial survival*" because it "reasserts the boundaries of the body when it comes in potential contact with literal or metaphorical excrement. The *pleasure of disgust comes when we recover bodily integrity*," Nyong'o continues, "in the face of the dis-equilibrium presented by somebody else's shit. In the particular case of racist kitsch, disgust apprehends the object as a kind of body that we are not, or, at least, one that we are no longer."[40] The disgust and repulsion that inheres in Walker's art, however, refutes recovery, easy consumption, and integration, even as it begs such responses; it is inassimilable, undesirable. From this angle, *A Subtlety* and its rendering of the Black female bottom prompts a reconsideration of art that re-signifies racialized gendered stereotypes. Formally, conceptually, and environmentally, the Black female bottom in *A Subtlety* exceeds the sculpture's oversized backside. The installation strategically saturates visitors with filth, toxicity, and decay in dynamic ways that disorder individual and collective desires for mastery, coherence, unity, and resolution, producing instead unexpected, counterintuitive, disarming, and *necessary* encounters with the promise of destruction and dispossession.[41] *A Subtlety*'s "power" thus emerges from lingering in spaces of negativity and nonreproduction.

Similar to the generational outcry over Walker's silhouettes and tableaux, *A Subtlety*'s 'publicness' inspired controversy about racial fetishism and the artwork's perceived lack of respectability. Critics and viewers seemed to prefer the artist to engage the trauma of history with reparative means rather than fully acknowledge the approach she did take. To this point, the material of the sphinx—refined sugar—proved to be more affective than the black vinyl of her silhouette cutouts. Many of the spectators and critics, amateur and professional, who encountered Walker's installation feared that *A Subtlety* was "recreating the very racism [the] art is *supposed* to critique," as writer Nicholas Powers puts it.[42] Numerous blog posts and even a staged protest by Black artists—an effort to flood the refinery with people of color under the banner, "We Are

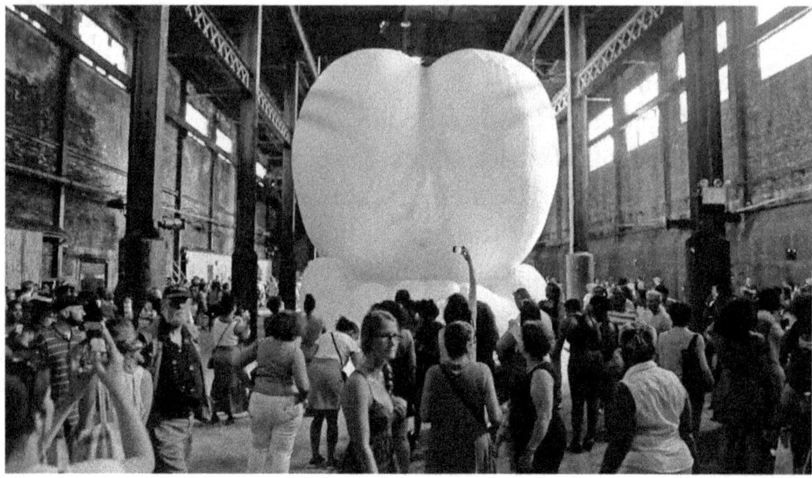

Figure 1.3. Kara Walker, film still from *An Audience*, 2014. Digital video with sound, dimensions variable. Artwork © Kara Walker. Courtesy of Sikkema Jenkins & Co. and Sprüth Magers.

Here"—reproached Walker's sphinx and its babies. Such responses assume a direct connection between the work of art and its viewers where the work of art has the power not only to master but also to repair and redeem the historical trauma of slavery to which Walker's work attends. But instead of creating a respectable space for racial mourning and healing, *A Subtlety* confronted viewers with a shadowy form from a collective past, a haunting articulated by an uneasy relation between race and capital in a putatively "post-racial" twenty-first century. Against the backdrop of social and political antagonisms where colorblindness and anti-Black violence uneasily coexist, *A Subtlety* conceptually and materially brought together Blackness, slave labor, and sugar production as constitutive elements of the United States and the African diaspora on the shores of New York.[43] Rather than redeem the experience of slavery and its effects, however, Walker's sugar sphinx caused revulsion.

In addition to penned criticisms and organized protests, viewers took selfies of themselves making lewd gestures in front of and behind the sphinx and posted them on social media. In a surprise reversal, Walker secretly recorded viewers' ludicrous, spectatorial engagements with the sculpture's private parts, "spying," as she calls it in a public talk with filmmaker Ava DuVernay.[44] Walker composed the footage into a twenty-seven-minute, eighteen-second video with sound, *An Audience*, which she premiered as part of *Afterword*, her November 2014 solo show at Sikkema Jenkins in New York. A time-lapsed clip from the video went viral, raising a host of questions about race and representation, the artist's role in society, and the relation between public and private when historically subjugated bodies were the center of global debate.[45] Save for the figure's left hand and sugar offspring, the sculpture and building were both destroyed.

Kristin Iversen, writer and managing editor for *Brooklyn Magazine* at the time, notes that the power of Walker's work "lies in its bold reappropriation of images of black women and its insistence that viewers acknowledge the power and the pain behind what they are consuming for what can best be described as pleasure."[46] Such comments fortify the assumed authority of the work of art, amounting to a narrow focus on cultural content with little attention to form. This position assumes that art can redeem life, enlighten viewers, and right historical wrongs such as slavery in Walker's case. In so doing, it trivializes art *and* experience, reducing their radical potential. Iversen is right to highlight Walker's inventive risk-taking, but what is missing is recognition of the repulsion that the artist's sugarcoated, larger-than-life, mammy-faced sculpture incites and the idiomatic play on words and images that inheres in it. Typically, in a sentence, there is an understood literal, or empirical, connection between the words and the objects, actions, or characteristics expressed. This creates and conveys the meaning of the sentence. But idioms alter the typical sentence structure by disordering the rules of composition, and the whole of a phrase changes when placed within a specific context. Walker's *A Subtlety* operates in the latter way. Walker has said that "[the mammy sphinx] had to have the 'too much' and it also had to be easy to see . . . sweet on the eyes–or something."[47] Here, Walker relies on an idiomatic expression to connote the meaning of the work, and other idioms concerning sugar and sweetness apply to *A Subtlety*. To sugarcoat is to make something difficult or distasteful appear more pleasant or acceptable; to sweet talk someone is to coax or cajole them with flattery.

Language and narrative have always been fodder for the artist's enactments of dark humor, and *A Subtlety* is no exception. The installation

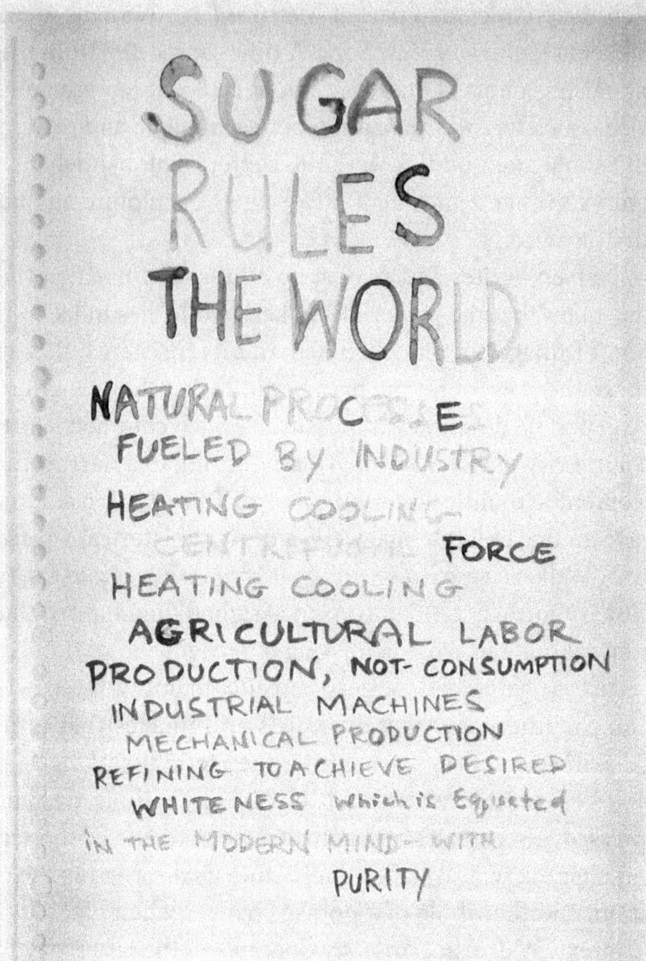

Figure 1.4. Kara Walker, detail from *Sugar Makes This World*, 2013–14. Ink, watercolor, and graphite on paper, suite of nineteen, 11.75 × 8.25 inches (29.8 × 21 cm). Artwork © Kara Walker. Courtesy of Sikkema Jenkins & Co. and Sprüth Magers.

envisages several definitions of the term subtle: the use of clever methods to achieve something; a distinction so fine and precise that it is difficult to integrate and comprehend; highly skillful and keen insight; and the ability to operate insidiously while in plain sight. The size and smell of Walker's sugar sculptures—the sphinx and its servant offspring—caused revulsion, overwhelming viewers to the point of sickening them. In other words, Walker's *A Subtlety* was hard to imbibe and digest.

By centering repulsion and queer strategies of reversal and inversion, *A Subtlety* consequently rezoned sugar's historical context from that of ancient traditions of opulence and consumption to that of the unsavory, toxic terrain of chattel slavery and its afterlife in the New World. Citing Sidney Mintz's *Sweetness and Power: The Place of Sugar in Modern History* (1985) as a source of inspiration, Walker highlights the history of sugar and subtleties as commodities and culinary treats that originated in the royal courts of North Africa and the Middle East. "Sugar was rare," she remarks in an interview with Kara Rooney of *Brooklyn Rail*, "even considered medicinal. It was like gold, extremely precious. At a certain point coming from the East in the 11th century, there began an enormous effort, at the bequest of the sultans, to make these strange, grandiose marzipan structures. Once they were fashioned, they would present and give them to the poor on feast days."[48] In Walker's reference, a subtlety was originally intended for mass consumption and considered a medicinal agent that inebriated the masses, distracting them from their plight. These sugar sculptures provide a point of departure for the idiomatic wordplay that Walker serves up in her installation.

Although the artwork's inspiration stems from a distant source, *A Subtlety* figuratively coats racist imagery with the historical experience of colonial-era sugar production in the present, connecting sugar to the production and trading of other commodities—goods, food matter, physical labor, and bodies—the economic core of the transatlantic slave trade. Simultaneously, the monumental mammy, its sugar babies, and the factory in which they were temporarily housed became trademarks for a historical mode of racialized identity formation and nation-making unique to the United States. *A Subtlety*'s iconographic reference to the mammy stereotype imitates Aunt Jemima, whose abstracted personality and caricatured body became the trademark of other processed sweet foodstuffs: pancakes and syrup. In "National Brands/National Body:

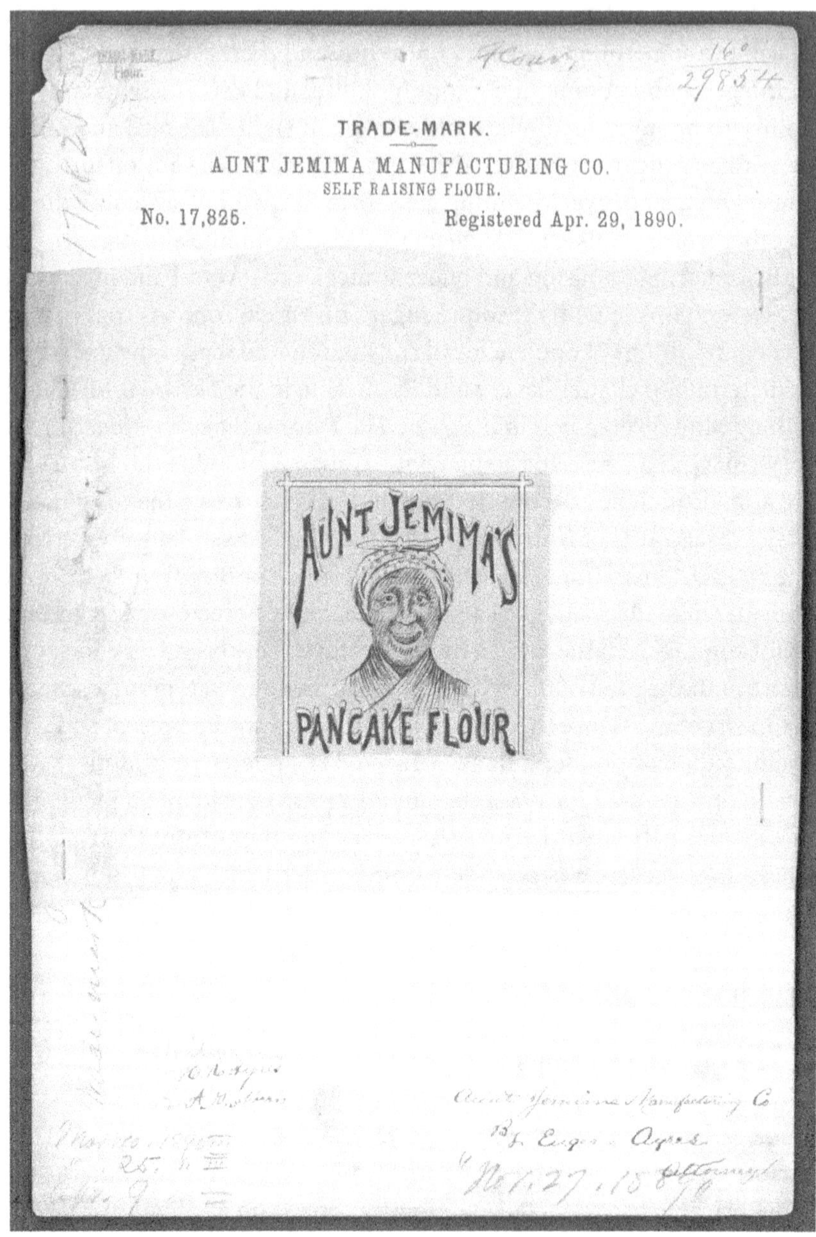

Figure 1.5. Trademark registration by Aunt Jemima Manufacturing Co. for Aunt Jemima's Pancake Flour brand self-rising Flour, April 29, 1890. One item; sheet 26 × 29 cm. Library of Congress Prints and Photographs Division, Washington, DC, open access reproduction number LC-DIG-trmk-1t17825 (digital file from original, front) LC-DIG-trmk-2t17825 (digital file from original, underneath overlay on front).

Imitation of Life," critical theorist Lauren Berlant links Aunt Jemima's emergence in American advertising with a growing consciousness about national identity in the United States. Aunt Jemima's introduction onto the national stage at the Columbian Exposition of 1893 coincides with "the origin of American progressive modernism, the alliance between industry and the state to produce new 'frontiers' of production and invention, and the induction of advertising itself as an arm of American sovereignty."[49] The mammy figure's "logocentric style," as Berlant terms it, "encouraged consumers to link products with personalities."[50] Thus, the "promise" of Aunt Jemima resides in the displacement of "racial nostalgia, national memory, and progressive history" onto her abstracted body as a mechanism for post–Civil War national consolidation.[51] The origins of the Domino Sugar Refinery, its structure and its products, also contributed to this consolidation.

Originally built in 1856 by the Havemeyer family, Domino was the first of dozens of sugar refineries that contributed to Williamsburg's emergence as the industrial center of the Port of New York in the nineteenth century. Built from blocks of polystyrene foam and coated in sugar bleached to a blinding, monochromatic white, *A Subtlety's* site-specificity played a key role in the installation's conception, creation, and display. By the end of the Civil War in 1865, the refinery had become the largest in the world, employing over four thousand workers and processing more than half of the sugar consumed in the entire United States in a single day's output. Within this context of post–Civil War nation-making, a post-Enlightenment dialectic between embodiment and abstraction emerges that is key to *A Subtlety*'s enactment of the Black female bottom as an intervention in the factory. On one side of the dialectic, Berlant asserts, is whiteness and maleness. "The white, male body is the relay to legitimation, but even more than that, the power to suppress that body, to cover its tracks and traces, is the sign of real authority, according to constitutional fashion."[52] On the other side of the dialectic reside women and African Americans who, because of their gendered and racialized positions, are denied subjectivity because they lack the power and privilege to suppress their bodies.[53] As such, gendered and racialized subjects within the US public imaginary are endowed with "an always-already-violated body," a surplus corporeality that translates to hyper-embodiment, "an obstacle and not a vehicle to public pleasure

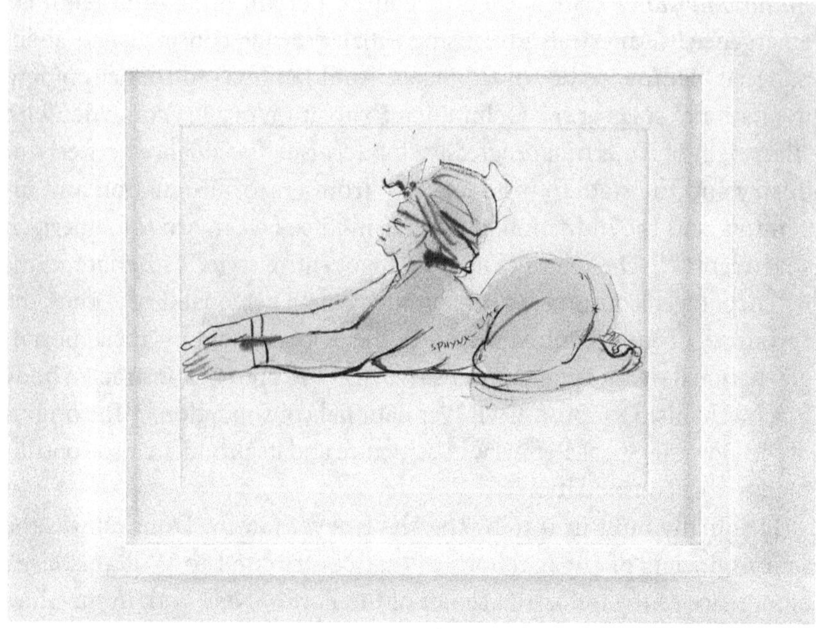

Figure 1.6. Kara Walker, detail from *Untitled, 2014*. Ink and watercolor on paper, suite of eight, approximately 9.625 × 12.5 in (24.4 × 31.8 cm) each. Courtesy of Sikkema Jenkins & Co. and Sprüth Magers. © Kara Walker.

and power."[54] A structure so large yet so "subtle" as to be too much to take in all at once, Walker's monumental mammy figure magnifies Black women's subjection relative to issues of hyper-embodiment and public pleasure.

In this reading, the encounter between embodiment and abstraction is precisely where pleasure and repulsion meet.[55] *A Subtlety*'s rotund, implausible body with its stark white coating amidst the intoxicating sweetness of the refinery's air repulses the senses. Rather than the safety and security that commodities typically generate according to Berlant, Walker's mammy evoked *dis*comfort. The mammy's racist history looms large here. In the preparatory sketches for *A Subtlety*, Walker draws and redraws the figure, a Black female slave who performs the role of nurse and caretaker of white slave owners and their children. But contrary to the amiable, nonthreatening, obedient, and asexual servant, *A Subtlety*'s mammy caricature confounds aesthetic and social norms in two ways.

First, the over-embodied, offending figure surpasses the referential classical form, an idealized female body in the shape of a nude sphinx, which many viewers further objectified through lewd gestures and selfies shared on social media. Documentation of these fetishistic antics in front of and behind the sphinx confirm that Walker's monumental mammy was in fact a register for contemporary brands of race and gender that refer to the particular and peculiar American institution from which it springs.[56] In this context, the sphinx's nude body doubles as icon and trademark, monument and meme. Second, the mammy head coupled with enlarged breasts, oversized buttocks, and exposed vulva quixotically transmogrified the glaringly white sphinx. That is, the stereotype's deviant Blackness sullied the classical form's purity, imbuing it with a toxicity that caused both revulsion and contemporary racial anxieties to surface in a putatively post-racial present. In this vein of disgust, the monumental mammy was so spectacular, so objectionable, that viewers were compelled to capture and consume it, thus animating a compulsory desire to possess and discipline the racialized reproductive body. But instead of a procreative vessel with an afterlife sustained by permanent presence or an enfranchised lineage, the slave qua sphinx is a site where reproduction without futurity proliferates. The eventual demolition of the sphinx and factory heightened this effect. Like the parasite-host relations that populate Mutu's collages and the kinky onanism at the core of Narcissister's practice, the slave-sphinx and her disintegrating offspring deviate from social and aesthetic norms concerning morality, motherhood, kinship, wholeness, and reparation. As embodiments of pure dysfunction, they behave badly and act *negatively*.

This is where the sugar sphinx finds its sweet spot, its "too-muchness." Depending on the time of day, sunlight would flood the refinery, bouncing off the stark-white mammy sculpture to produce an overexposed photograph where the sphinx's features were bleached, or indistinguishable—the sphinx's breasts and areolas, for instance—and colors were unnaturally bright, or completely white. Thus, the mammy sphinx was a site of overexposure twofold, through material conditions that repulsed viewers' senses of smell and comprehension, as well as by disordering the technologies of seeing used to capture it—a double nullification. In its sugary form and imitation of Aunt Jemima, *A Subtlety* produced an excessive Blackness that was literally too much to behold and stomach.

Furthermore, the sugar sphinx embodied repulsion in its size, its inscrutable expression, and its left hand. The thumb clenched between the sphinx's left index and third finger recalls the Afro-Brazilian *figa* symbol, a talisman of good luck that has traditionally been a symbol of fertility, of protection against harm, and a flippant gesture meaning "fuck you." From bodies to racial categories to cultural expectations, Walker disrupts it all, and any cohesive ingestion of *A Subtlety* is muddled by overexposure and repulsion. The installation's formal components and its effects—coated color relations, nausea, physical recoil, and a big fuck you—dynamically refuse synthesis both as an art object and as a vehicle for public discourse.[57]

When Creative Time commissioned *A Subtlety*, sugar production at Domino had already ceased, and much of the complex was slated for demolition, with the land scheduled for new mixed-use development. The building was destroyed in October 2014 and repurposed into high-end condominiums by Two Trees, the underwriter for the installation, just months after *A Subtlety* was dismantled. For these reasons, the artwork has been read as an act of collusion that leveraged the artist's own creative capital to drive gentrification in the area. In one response to this triangulation of artistic labor, economic capital, and gentrification, anonymous women of color created a counter-archive under the banner "I died for sugar back then . . . and sugar is killing me NOW!" Along with #WeAreHere, this counter-archive mediates the thousands of images of the sphinx's oversized features that circulated under #karawalkerdomino, thus adding to the installation's enduring significance of "complicity and resistance," as Tavia Nyong'o puts it.[58] These interventions underscore the limits of both institutional critique and public art in the new millennium. Although valid, focusing on Black women's creative labors solely as sites of capitalist reproduction reduces their work to real estate endorsements rather than interrogating the marketplace of flesh, as Hortense J. Spillers terms it, to which Black women's bodies have been consigned. Walker's Black female bottom within this schema systematically fails to redress accelerated capitalism precisely because of the paradoxes of nonbeing and nonreproduction that the bottom engenders. Her art refuses to instantiate or correct historical experience in the present, repeatedly violating intramural calls for beauty and racial responsibility that frame Black art and Black female embodiment as modes of cultural

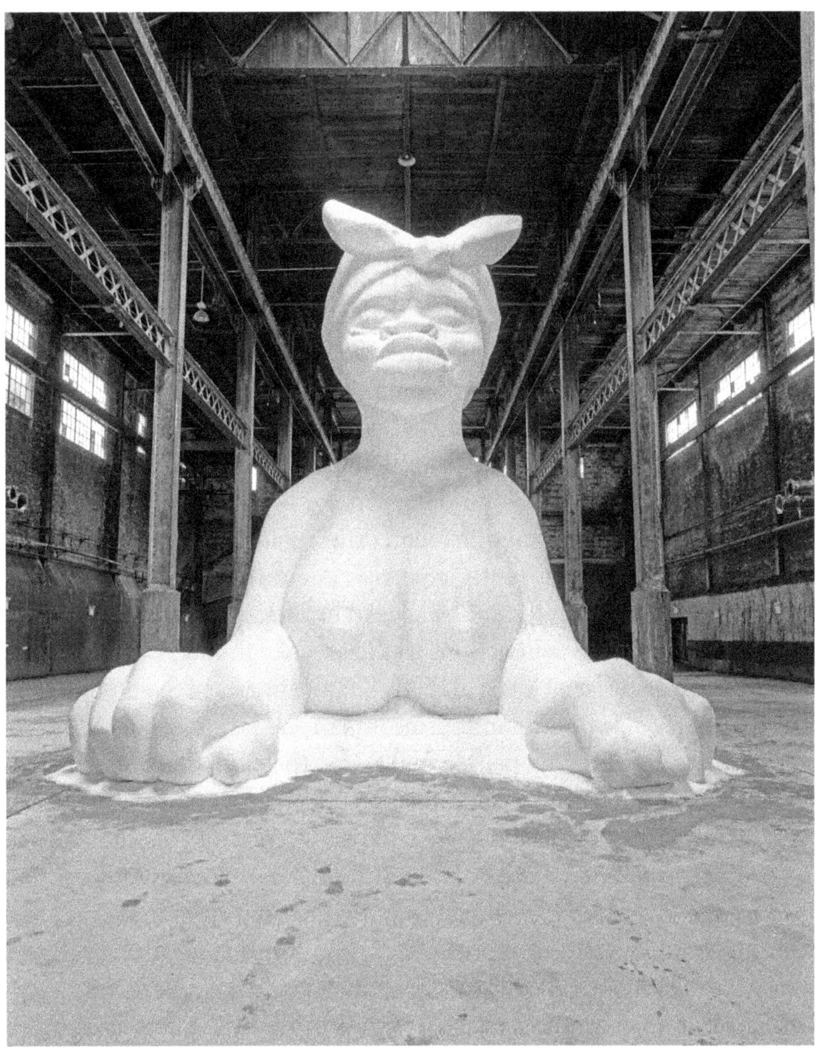

Figure 1.7. Kara Walker, *A Subtlety, or the Marvelous Sugar Baby, an Homage to the Unpaid and Overworked Artisans Who Have Refined Our Sweet Tastes from the Cane Fields to the Kitchens of the New World on the Occasion of the Demolition of the Domino Sugar Refining Plant*. Installation view, Domino Sugar Refinery, 2014. Polystyrene foam, sugar, approx. 35.5 × 26 × 75.5 feet (10.8 × 7.9 × 23 m). A project of Creative Time, Brooklyn, NY. Photo: Jason Wyche Artwork. © Kara Walker. Courtesy of Sikkema Jenkins & Co. and Sprüth Magers.

resistance.[59] *A Subtlety*, in my view, instead responds to and amplifies the toxicity of the factory and its location, both the waterfront and the neighborhood. Bridging site specificity and materiality with the sphinx's nonreproductive capacities and pose, the Black female bottom engenders a dispossessive force that exposes the multivalent contours of violence and toxicity at the core of the West's hollow yet insidious constructions of hegemony and the human.

The factory's molasses-caked walls and location in "the most toxic place to live in America," according to the late Williamsburg community leader and activist Luis Garden Acosta, are key to *A Subtlety*'s undesirability and its figuration of the Black female bottom.[60] Since World War II, Williamsburg has been a working-class immigrant neighborhood primarily populated by Hasidic Jews, Italians, Dominicans, and Puerto Ricans. The heavy decline of industry in the 1960s onward precipitated a marked increase in unemployment, crime, gang activity, and unsanctioned drug use. Concurrently, concerns about the long-term environmental effects of oil spills and leakages, the lack of clean water and air, trash piles, and their connections to the area's high rates of asthma and cancer have also risen. Alternately, Williamsburg has seen an uptick in the construction of new condominiums in the last three decades. Yet "developers aren't telling people that this is the city's most toxic neighborhood."[61] Once home to multiple gas, oil, energy, and food refineries and warehouses, the neighborhood sits on top of a bed of crude oil and other dangerous chemicals. *A Subtlety*'s nausea-inducing intervention exposes and unravels the linkages between environmental crisis and empire. The convergence of prostration, allusions to sex work, oversized body parts at hyperbolic dimensions, the toxicity of sugar's byproducts, and the factory's surrounding environment fortify the Black female bottom in *A Subtlety*. Not merely an alibi for capitalist-driven gentrification, *A Subtlety* made the Domino Sugar Refinery further unfit for habitation.

Thematically, conceptually, and materially, *A Subtlety* connects slavery's sugar history with present-day issues concerning labor exploitation and gentrification as structures of violence and domination that require the Black female body to be both present yet debased. Commissioned as a temporary public art project, *A Subtlety* was not staged in a museum. Thus, anyone willing and able to queue for long periods of time could experience the installation for free. This public accessibility paired with

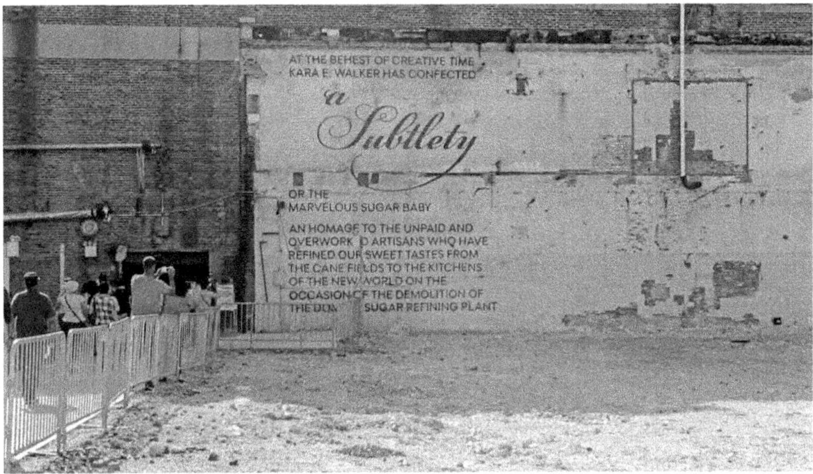

Figure 1.8. Kara Walker, film still from *An Audience*, 2014. Digital video with sound, dimensions variable. Courtesy of Sikkema Jenkins & Co. and Sprüth Magers. © Kara Walker.

the sphinx's public nudity, contoured by her shapely oversized breasts, buttocks, and exposed vulva, created a unique aesthetic experience that pivoted on lewdness, repulsion, toxicity, and planned ruin. The "whole project," Walker stated at the time, "is predicated on the space being demolished at the end of the run of the show," and as funerary monuments, sphinxes in the ancient art contexts of Egypt, Greece, and Italy were commonly installed to ward off evil and guard the dead.[62] Beyond the decay of the refinery, Walker's choice of materials also mattered. "It was very important to me," the artist confesses, "to have the figures made out of a substance that is so temporal, and so subject to change."[63] This attention to planned ruin vis-à-vis temporality and the promise of decay and death engender, like her silhouettes, a counterintuitive approach to redressing the trauma of slavery.

As homage to unpaid and overworked artisans, the marvelous sugar baby also merges social and sexual bottoms with Black labor histories, histories that emerge at the nexus between sickness, sweetness, and sex. In popular parlance, a sugar baby is a young adult woman who dates older men that are financially stable in exchange for companionship, gifts, and sex, and from the nineteenth century onward, Black female sexuality has been linked to prostitution and disease. Walker's adoption of the negress as an art persona highlights this history and the ways in which the art world exploits Black women's bodies and labors. Art work, in other words, is sex work.[64] Furthermore, Bersani writes in his canonical essay on homosex, female prostitutes were imagined to "spread their legs with an unquenchable appetite for destruction."[65] In linking the plantation with the outmoded workhouse, the decaying factory, the art market, and sex work as a conduit for destruction, *A Subtlety* extended the spatial logics of the Black female bottom into new territory. It also solidified Walker's status as a new kind of public figure, as writer Doreen St. Félix observes.[66]

Along with materiality and site specificity, the sphinx's pose and form are crucial to Walker's deployment of the Black female bottom. Prostrated with oversized buttocks and breasts perched in the air, the sphinx's pose is one of submission. Part stereotype, part mythological creature, Walker's hybrid figure is paradoxical in its melding of the mammy figuration with a feline body. Although typically regarded as sacred and enigmatic, the Blackness of the mammy and the exposure of the cat (another word for vagina) in terms of the sphinx's body and its female genitalia (rarely present in extant sphinxes of antiquity) merges the Black female bottom with hyper-visibility and perversion at the level of social degradation and sexual subjection. The publicness—indeed the outsideness—of the sphinx's alterity and its reproductive parts (the vulva is the outside part of the female reproductive system, whereas the vagina is the passageway) rhymes with the sculpture's construction; it is hollow on the inside. The marvelous sugar baby is therefore all surface; there is no interiority.

Furthermore, the melding of the mammy and the over-endowed, prostrated sphinx in a decomposing enclosure raises important questions about the mattering of race and gender in the new millennium as well as what it means to be desirable as a woman and mother. The massive steel beams of the Domino Sugar plant appeared to encage the creature while visitors ogled her, poked at her, and photographed her. In this way, *A Subtlety* recalls the Hottentot Venus's display as a freak show and ethnographic museum attraction in early-nineteenth-century Europe. "Crudely exhibited and objectified by European audiences and scientific experts because of what they regarded as unusual aspects of her physiognomy—her genitalia and buttocks," as Evelynn Hammonds

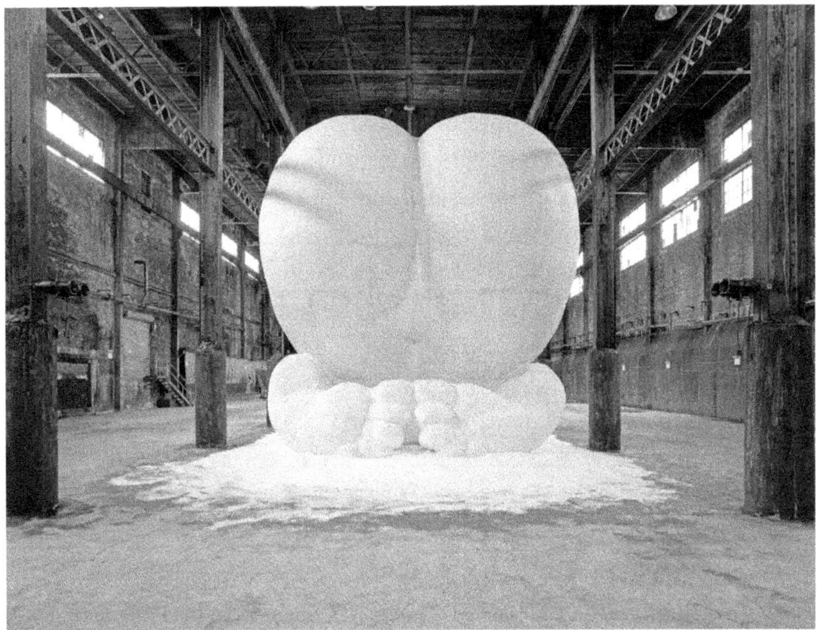

Figure 1.9. Kara Walker, *A Subtlety, or the Marvelous Sugar Baby, an Homage to the Unpaid and Overworked Artisans Who Have Refined Our Sweet Tastes from the Cane Fields to the Kitchens of the New World on the Occasion of the Demolition of the Domino Sugar Refining Plant.* Installation view, Domino Sugar Refinery, 2014. Polystyrene foam, sugar, approx. 35.5 × 26 × 75.5 feet (10.8 × 7.9 × 23 m). A project of Creative Time, Brooklyn, NY. Photo: Jason Wyche Artwork. © Kara Walker. Courtesy of Sikkema Jenkins & Co. and Sprüth Magers.

outlines, the Hottentot Venus's "primitive" genitalia became a sign of her primitive sexual appetite.[67] "Thus, the black female became the antithesis of European sexual mores and beauty and was relegated to the lowest position on the scale of human development."[68] For these reasons, Black feminist theorist Janell Hobson argues, a "big booty" signifies sexual excess and is "often associated with and [serves] as a stand-in for black women's sexualities."[69] *A Subtlety*, Hobson writes, also recreates the ubiquitous pop culture image of scantily clad Black models on all fours. In so doing, "Walker connects contemporary black women's bodies to a history of animalizing the bodies of women and Africans, as well as to a history of empire and New World slavery."[70] Combined with the rotting factory and its beams of containment, marshaling the Hottentot

Venus as a specter and an analogue buttresses the notion that Walker's sphinx is an animal in a zoo. Her use of sugar as an attraction is also at play here. Both phenomena center the Black female body and bottom as tropes of disorder, underlining the impact that slavery and colonialism have had on definitions of race, gender, and human life.

A Subtlety's staging of Blackness and animality, Amber Musser tells us, displaces the liberal subject; Black women, that is, fall outside of the purview of normative understandings of agency that are subtended by whiteness and fantasies of consent.[71] The figure's hybridity as queer-woman-animal instead gestures "toward a consideration of sexuality that revolves around the body and its pleasures. In this schema, the relationships between agency and subjectivity, perversion and normality, lose meaning."[72] The fulcrum of Musser's argument is corporeality and its fragility, and her interests in alternative and otherwise relational formations recall Hortense Spillers' theorization of Black women as interstitial and iconographic—"the paradox of non-being."[73] Writing about Black female sexuality and its absence within feminist art and thought, Spillers, like Walker, excavates the abuses and uses of history, hierarchies of power, and the negative aspects of meaning making. Rather than an embodiment of carnality born from the conditions of slavery and its afterlives, Spillers argues, Black American women became the principal point of passage between the human and nonhuman world—the distinguishing factor between humanity and "other."[74] At this level of radical discontinuity, Black is vestibular to culture, a point further explored in the next chapter. Through this stage of the bestial, the Black female remains exotic, "her history transformed into a pathology turned back on the subject in *tenacious blindness*."[75] This system of signs cultivates and engenders domination and subordination. *A Subtlety*'s copulation of blinding whiteness and Black abjection elaborates this dance of power, meeting it with toxicity and reproduction, all without futurity.

Walker's use of sugar and molasses as flesh becomes even more potent here. This centering of matter combined with the hollowness of the sculpture and the fraudulent animal-human hybridity it recruits for its form puts pressure on the newness of environmental humanities and contemporary theories of materialism within nonhuman and posthuman discourse. On the whole, these debates neglect the "recursive anti-black, sexuated economies of exchange and assignations of meaning, value and significance," to use Zakiyyah Iman Jackson's phrasing, that subtend feminist new materialist theory.[76] More than cataloguing how American empire was produced against and with minoritized subjects, *A Subtlety* articulates Black female abjection as a precondition for the human, as Jackson argues, that in turn facilitates and maintains hierarchical order. In its blinding opacity, *A Subtlety* is both sublime and abject, a disorderly figure that upends normative notions of beauty, agency, humanity, and power in both art and everyday life. The pleasure that such unruliness engenders has no aim or agency other than the episodic experience of the feeling itself. Furthermore, the sphinx is not based in reality; nor is it an amalgam that appears in the natural world. It is a mythological creature; it is iconographic, a passageway that yields toxicity and repulsion, not redress, enlightenment, or total integration.

A Subtlety thus fosters vulnerability, overexposure, nonreproduction, perversity, submission, and subjection without redeeming any of these acts or non-acts, a queerness that exceeds sexual identity and practice as well as victimhood and woundedness. Indeed, as Musser notes, *A Subtlety* is not a "triumphant reclamation of black female agency."[77] This self-conscious fashioning of negativity and powerlessness consecrates an act of surrender that is not based on lack but rather a refusal to resist and repair. Although controversial and seemingly counterintuitive, the Black female bottom's against-the-grain operations neither evacuate nor deny political effects; they instead reinvest in racialized gender subjugation to articulate unruly conceptions of being that arise from a strategically queer position—being at the bottom—wherein presence and self-objectification are coeval.

Not Your Mammy

Just as *A Subtlety* stages a radical reckoning with American imperialism's toxicity and contemporary reach, Walker's 2019–21 Hyundai-funded public art commission at the Tate Modern's Turbine Hall mobilizes the Black female bottom to upend the normative orders of industrial architecture, monumentality, empire, power, capital, and the environment. And like her silhouettes and *A Subtlety*, *Fons Americanus* appropriates forms of art and archetypes from bygone eras, namely the classical and Romantic periods. *Venus*, *The Ship*, *A Maroon Rebel*, *The Pietà of Emmett Till*, *The*

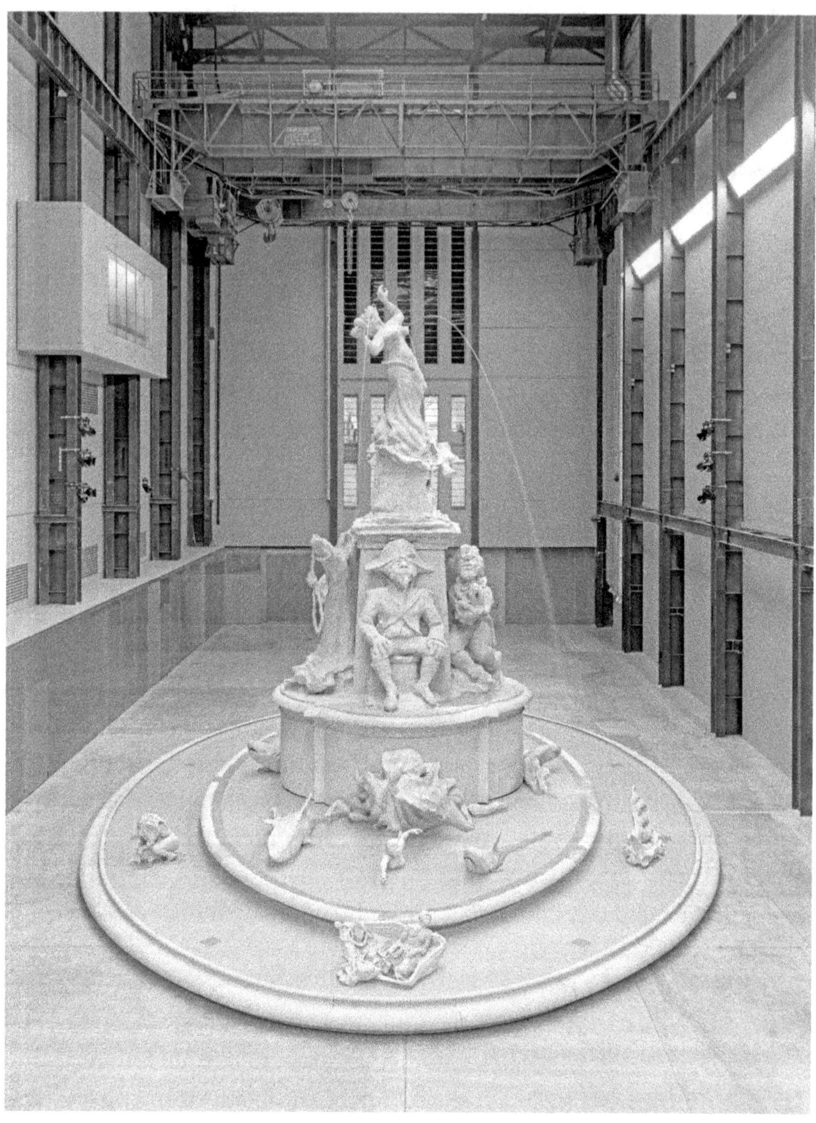

Figure 1.10. Kara Walker, *Fons Americanus*. Non-toxic acrylic and cement composite, recyclable cork, wood, and metal, main: 73.5 × 50 × 43 ft (22.4 × 15.2 × 13.2 m). Installation view, 2019. Hyundai Commission: Kara Walker—Fons Americanus, Tate Modern, London, UK, 2019. Photo credit: Tate (Matt Greenwood).

Physical Impossibility of Blackness in the Mind of Someone White, *The Captain*, *the Kneeling Man*, *The Angel*, and *Retrieving the Body* all comprise a range of figures, shapes, and forms in *Fons Americanus*.

Composed of figures in various states of decomposition and deliquescence, *Fons Americanus* represents the classical and the colonial not as sites of romantic longing for a lost or beloved past but as the horizon of dysfunction and impending decay and disappearance. The forty-two-and-a-half-foot-tall working fountain and its four tiers were loosely based on the Victoria Memorial in front of Buckingham Palace that dates to 1910. "Drawing from and inverting the meaning and titles of famous (and not so famous) artworks and poetry from the colonial era to the present, my Fountain yokes together racist representation and violent expressions of power, issues which tend to become romanticized and often depicted in pastoral settings," Walker states.[78] Here, late Victorian Neoclassical and Beaux Arts monuments, Eurocentric ideas about primitivism, and romantic icons such as the Trevi Fountain and the Fountain of the Four Rivers in Rome, Italy inspire its form, and like *A Subtlety*, the concept of the bottom figures prominently in the work.

Bottoming in *Fons Americanus* coalesces in the arrangements and appearances of bodies. *The Pietà of Emmett Till* in the lowest pool at the rear of the fountain is completely fused into the surrounding structure, so much so that it is hard to tell the two forms apart—a state of becoming that derives from the figure's gradual dissolution, much like the sphinx's sugar babies. The crowning Venus figure at the fountain's apex spouts water from her orifices and throat, which has been cut—another undoing—while the bottom half of her body blends into the plinth on which she stands. Four figures populate the tier below her. A minstrel caricature of Queen Victoria titled *Queen Vicky* holds her large breast out of her dress, towering over the crouching figure beneath her. Neither water nor milk, however, emerges from her chest.

Nearby is *The Kneeling Man*, a second caricature that Walker identifies as West Indies governor Sir William Young begging for mercy in the face of rebellion. "He is an amalgam of *European Colonial Interests*," Walker writes, "full of Capital and Promises and Religion (and quite possibly) Lies, deceit, and corruption."[79] A seated Toussaint Louverture and a noosed hangman's tree join *Queen Vicky* and *The Kneeling Man* on the second tier. The tree lifts two of its mangled branches towards Venus in

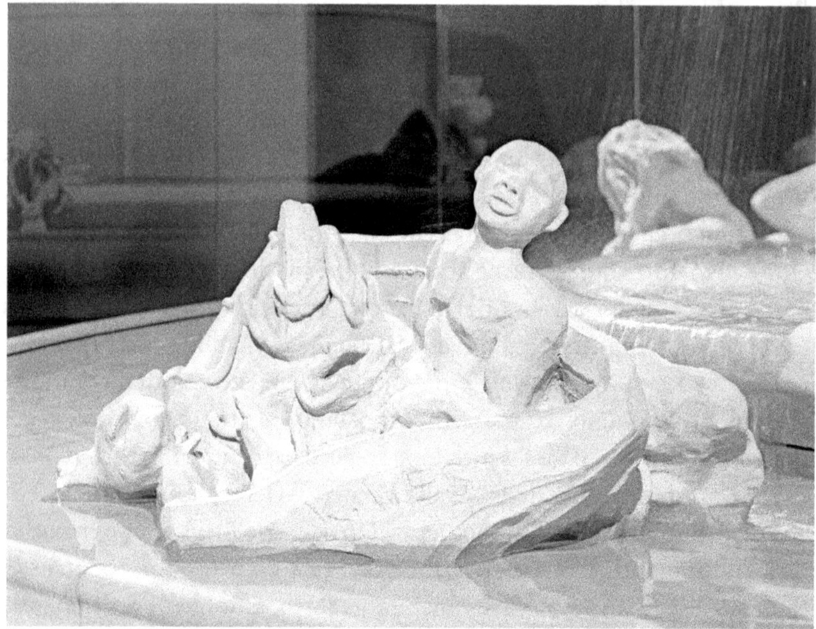

Figure 1.11. Kara Walker, detail from *Fons Americanus*. Non-toxic acrylic and cement composite, recyclable cork, wood, and metal. Main: 73.5 × 50 × 43 feet (22.4 × 15.2 × 13.2 meters). Installation view, 2019. Hyundai Commission: Kara Walker—Fons Americanus, Tate Modern, London, UK, 2019. Photo: Tate (Matt Greenwood).

a similar pose to her raised hands. Even with all the water pouring from her body, the tree's growth is stunted. It is all trunk, with few branches, no leaves, no flower, and no fruit. On the two watery tiers at the base of the fountain, sharks, ships, and more disfigured bodies abound. These tiers integrate references from John Singleton Copley's *Watson and the Shark* (1778), J. M. W. Turner's *Slave Ship* (1840), Eugène Delacroix's *The Barque of Dante* (1822), Winslow Homer's *The Gulf Stream* (1899), and Damien Hirst's *The Physical Impossibility of Death in the Mind of Someone Living* (1991). Combining these significant works from the Western art historical canon traverses and collapses disparate styles, time periods, mediums, and geopolitical regions.

Yet Walker's amalgamations refuse smooth or seamless integration, wading further into the limits and possibilities of negativity as a productive and creative source of disorderly pleasure and power.[80] The scattered figures in the fountain's tiers collect the water from Venus like the sugar babies in *A Subtlety* collect molasses and body parts. While the molasses children crumble and disintegrate from the heat, the Black figures in the waters of *Fons Americanus* swim, drown, and come undone by way of a different elemental force: the Black female figure above them. Separate from but adjacent to and in conversation with *Fons Americanus* is the stand-alone sculpture *Shell Grotto*. It is more intimate than *Fons Americanus* because of its less monumental scale, yet it is every bit as discomforting. A white scalloped shell opens to reveal a pockmarked ground. A white base undulates with serpentine lines, shadowed holes, and curvaceous edges. At the center, a bust of a young Black figure with an unidentified gender and sex emerges from a dark hole. A single tear streams down their face. The figure looks upward, out of the hole, their eyes open wide in terror. It is difficult to tell whether they are emerging or descending from the crevice, a hole that takes the shape of a stretched anus.

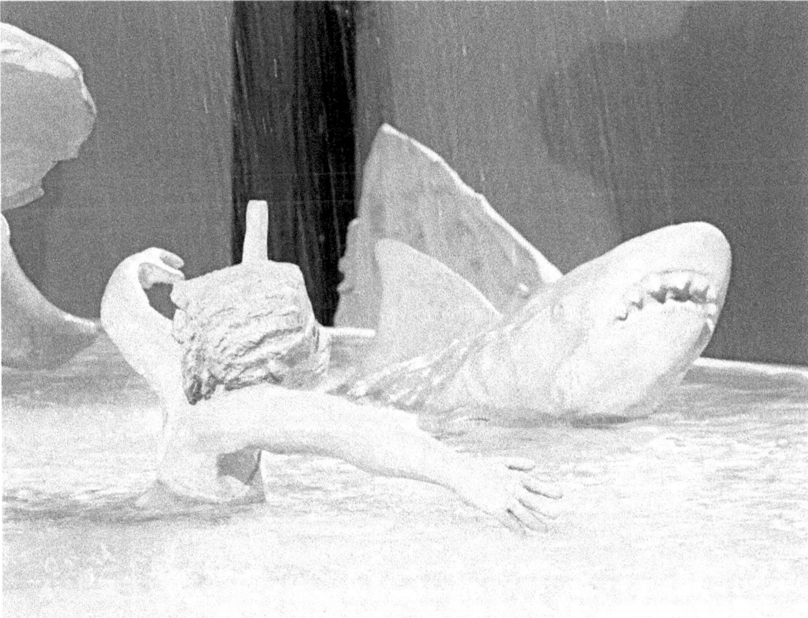

Figure 1.12. Kara Walker, detail from *Fons Americanus*. Non-toxic acrylic and cement composite, recyclable cork, wood, and metal, Main: 73.5 × 50 × 43 feet (22.4 × 15.2 × 13.2 meters). Installation view, 2019. Hyundai Commission: Kara Walker—Fons Americanus, Tate Modern, London, UK, 2019. Photo: Tate (Matt Greenwood).

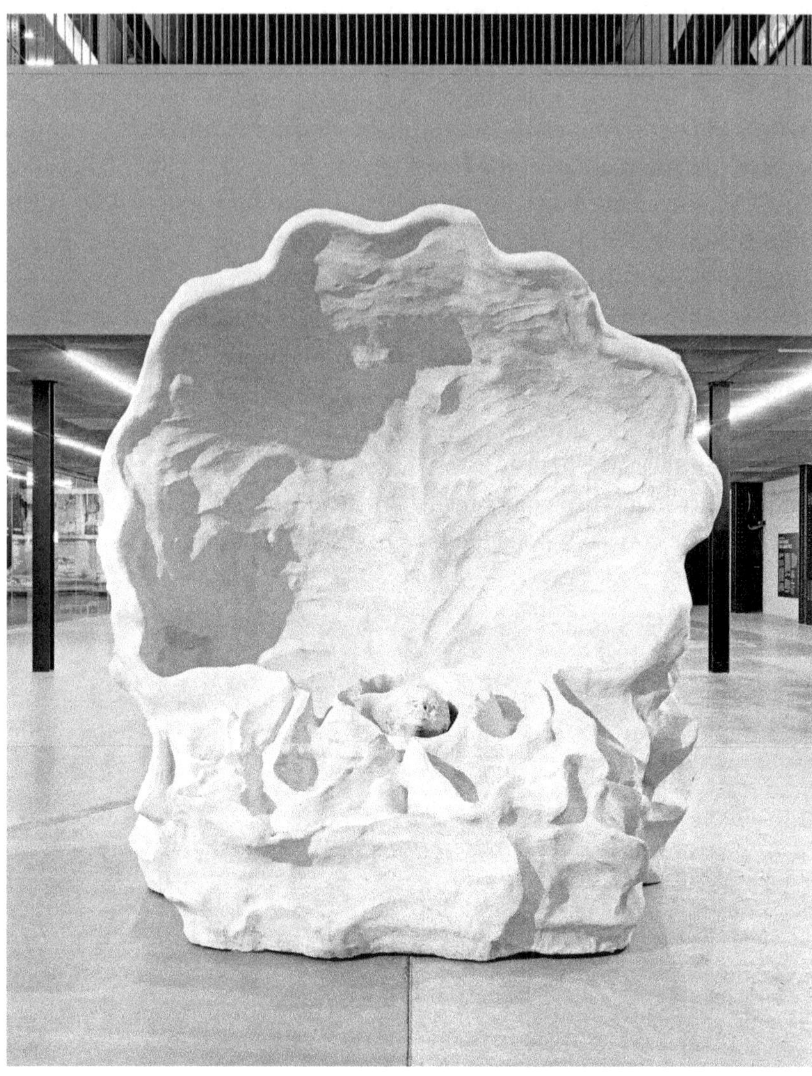

Figure 1.13. Kara Walker, detail from *Fons Americanus*. Non-toxic acrylic and cement composite, recyclable cork, wood, and metal. Main: 73.5 × 50 × 43 feet (22.4 × 15.2 × 13.2 meters). Installation view, 2019. Hyundai Commission: Kara Walker—Fons Americanus, Tate Modern, London, UK, 2019. Photo: Tate (Matt Greenwood).

For Walker, *Shell Grotto* references a specific place where Indigenous Africans who refused to board slave ships were tortured and drowned on Sierra Leone's Bunce Island, a British slave trading fortress at the western edge of the Black Atlantic. The stretched hole in the base of the shell on the ground of Turbine Hall is at once a killing ground, a metonym for those at the bottom of the Black Atlantic, and an instantiation of the non-procreative anal opening that conflates desirability and degradation.[81] "The last resting place of the rebellious unbreakable African, a dry-well into which uncooperative non-slaves were thrown away to die," the artist writes, was designed to be the first image to greet visitors.[82] By design, Walker situates the hole and the anal opening as a grave and the primary entrée into the tiers of bottoming that constitute *Fons Americanus*. Her openings and invitations are racialized terrain, sites of racial-sexual meaning making, that function beyond mere penetration. Bottoming here is also about social subordination and quotidian acts of racial and sexual violence that stand at the edge of spectacularity.

The spouting, disabled Venus atop the fountain is the pinnacle of Walker's machinations of the Black female bottom in *Fons Americanus*. Made of whitened cork, the artist's Venus emerges from a shell, like Sandro Botticelli's *The Birth of Venus* (1486) and Thomas Stothard's *The Voyage of the Sable Venus from Angola to the West Indies* (1801). Her arm is reminiscent of the *Winged Victory* at the apex of Buckingham Palace's Victoria Memorial. But unlike the smooth and gilded *Winged Victory*, Walker's Venus, like the rest of *Fons Americanus*, is roughly sculpted. Modeled after the artist's small clay sketches that were then reproduced at large scale with the help of a robotic arm, marks of tools and fingers linger on her face, arms, breasts, and belly. A fleshy figure that has simultaneously been underworked and overworked, her disfigured flesh bears the gashes and labor of her creation. With shark-infested waters of the Black Atlantic below her, her head tilts back toward the ceiling. Her neck is slashed, placing her in an impossible position. Suspended between life and death, the Venus spurts water from her neck and her nipples into the pools beneath her as she lifts her arms and curls her fingers. This expression of ecstasy combined with the figure's status and physical undoing—her unbecoming—unsettles the venerative function of commemorative sculpture. By placing her at the summit, Walker also inverts the fountain's hierarchical flow. The debased, dying figure is now

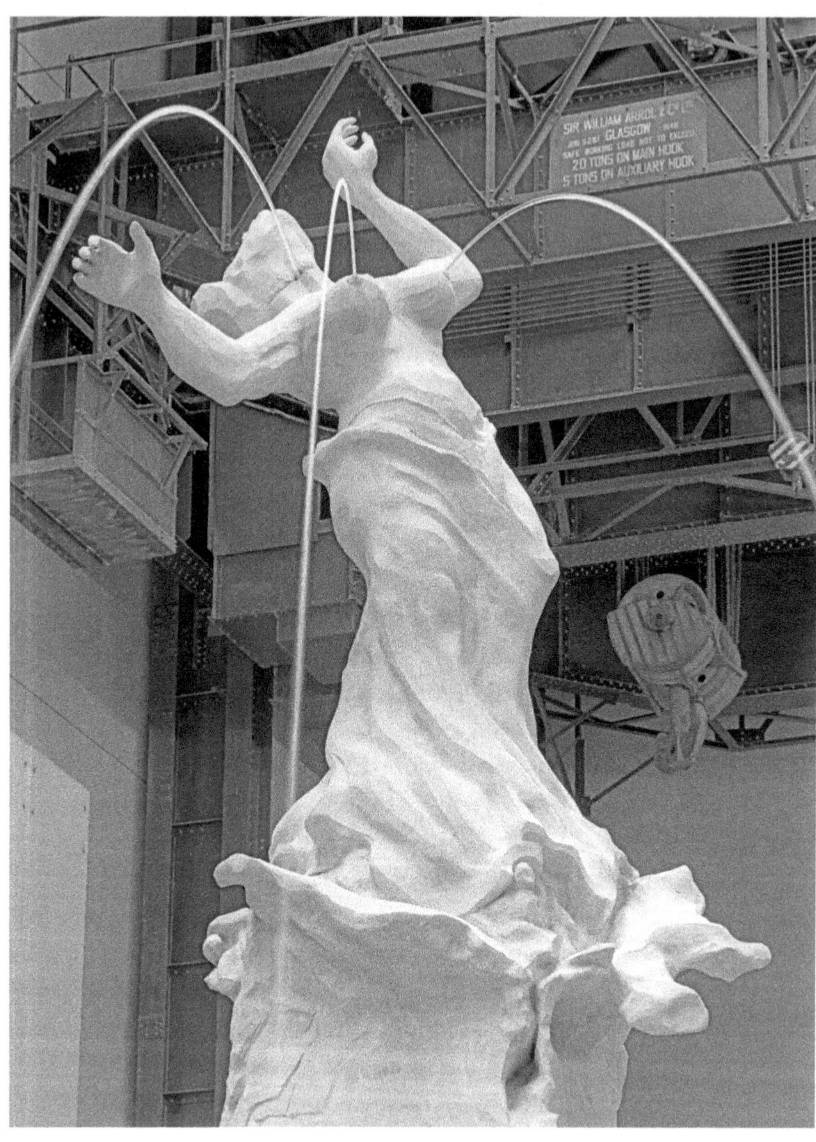

Figure 1.14. Kara Walker, detail from *Fons Americanus*. Non-toxic acrylic and cement composite, recyclable cork, wood, and metal. Main: 73.5 × 50 × 43 feet (22.4 × 15.2 × 13.2 meters). Installation view, 2019. Hyundai Commission: Kara Walker—Fons Americanus, Tate Modern, London, UK, 2019, Photo: Tate (Matt Greenwood).

a kind of power bottom that harnesses pleasure and pain in alternative, counterintuitive ways.

A dysfunctional, undesirable, inverted version of *Winged Victory*, Walker's Venus fails as a heroine. The force of her transgressive presence stems from a composed negativity; because of her position—socially, aesthetically, and physiologically (suspended between life and death)—she is incapacitated. Strategically disabled from nourishing and saving others, she compositionally refuses the concomitant roles expected of the mammy as nursemaid and Black women as caregivers and social change agents. The Black female bottom atop *Fons Americanus* consequently embodies a shadow feminism that, as queer theorist Jack Halberstam describes, "finds purpose in its own failure."[83] Walker's Venus exemplifies reproduction without futurity.

The Venus at the apex of the fountain thus initiates a discourse about "ill-gotten cultural inheritance[s]" across the Black Atlantic.[84] For Walker, the work is an allegory for "all global waters which disastrously connect Africa to America, Europe, and the hope (or threat) of economic prosperity."[85] The fountain is also site-specific in two ways; it is located in the Tate Modern's Turbine Hall, which once housed electrical generators for the now-defunct Bankside Power Station; and it also gestures toward the Black Atlantic while upending how the concept endures as a post-slavery geography and imaginary. Famed art historian Robert Farris Thompson first introduced the concept in 1983, and Black British cultural studies scholar Paul Gilroy elaborated the framework in his oft-cited book of the same name from 1993 to describe the enduring linkages between the transatlantic slave trade and the origins of Western modernity.[86] Gilroy's Black Atlantic also underscores the fluid and dynamic qualities of Black identity formation that exceed essentialism and national borders as well as culturally hybrid forms of music, art, literature, and religion that have and continue to serve as sites of Black resistance across the diaspora.

In *Fons Americanus*, Walker binds extra sensuous instantiations of materiality and monumental ruin together with the transnational memory of slavery in Great Britain, thus connecting two prominent locales within the Black Atlantic world—the United States and the United Kingdom. Like *A Subtlety*, *Fons Americanus* was never meant to have a physical afterlife. Eschewing permanence, the fountain's materials were dismantled and recycled at the close of the exhibition. With a focus on sustainability and planned ruin in addition to site specificity and structures of containment, the fountain juxtaposes decomposition and disorder with imperial and environmental control across the Atlantic world.[87] Comprised of softwood and baked cork as well as a nontoxic acrylic and cement composite used for casting and sculpting, the fountain features Walker's signature topsy-turvy aesthetics in its materials and depiction of the mammy stereotype as a kind of Venus. Her choice of materials and their disposal links recyclability with imperialism's desire to collect and catalogue everything in the natural world—the kind of cabinet-of-curiosity logic also at play in the freak shows and world's fairs that became popular in the West at the turn of the twentieth century. Such events were conduits for wider, symbolic displays of the West's technical superiority and power over nature and colonized lands and peoples. Walker's work, and Mutu's work in the next chapter, places the racialized gendered body, and the Black female bottom in particular, at the center of this matrix of power and representation. In so doing, her public sculpture at the Tate exposes art's entanglements with legacies of imperial violence and upends normative notions of agency, force, domination, and submission. Within all of this lies an embrace of perversity and negativity.

Similar to Xaviera Simmons's blackface rendering of Venus discussed later, Walker's Venus inverts the aesthetic value of both the nude female form in classical art and the logics of commemorative sculpture. An amalgam of several sources that include the aforementioned as well as the mammy and the negress, Walker's crowning figure also recalls the anonymous Venuses that spur Saidiya Hartman's notion of critical fabulation. Critical fabulation corrects normative, romantic explications of slavery and the Middle Passage by acknowledging the impossible task of recuperating lost stories, while also giving voice to those absented from the archive.[88] Rather than the classical image of white Western beauty, Walker's Venus embodies the effects of loss and rupture that issue from being systematically banished from home, family, and country. The artist envisions her Venus figure as a "*Mother, wetnurse, whore, saint, Host, lover—she is the daughter of the waters*," a passageway that yields more of the same. Reproduction without futurity is on display once again, here, in liquid that circulates without resolve.[89] "*The amniotic fluid at the beginning of this journey is now transformed into mother's milk and lifeblood*," as Walker describes, yet the Venus's sacrifice and labor nourishes no one.[90] The water that flows from her body feeds the tiers below her. But it does not initiate change or progress, nor does it comfort the figures that suffer beneath her, wedged in place, fixed in pain. In being productive but not generative, she forces a distinction between Black women's work as artists and caregivers and art's capacity to mitigate historical trauma.

Walker's paradigmatic turn to public monumental sculpture as an ideal medium for grappling with the material and sociopolitical remnants of slavery's legacies in the West coincide with Black women's hypervisibility along with the acceleration of white supremacist activity in the US public sphere. This shift in the artist's practice also corresponds with the increase in her own publicness—her celebrity status and her hypervisible exposure as a Black woman artist with international appeal who is "still wrestling with [her] relationship to what [her] art might do in the public space."[91] Of the influences for *Fons Americanus*, Walker recalls, "I wondered how to return the gift of having came to be—through the mechanics of finance, exploitation, murder, rape, death, ecological destruction, co-optation, coercion, love, seafaring feats, bravery, slavery, loss, injustice, excess, cruelty, tenacity, submission and progress—conceived here in the United States, to live in this time and place, with this opportunity, this ability."[92] Walker's reflections link her creative practice with her body's reproductive capacities and offer further insights into her self-conscious engagements with structures of marginalization and containment vis-à-vis the Black female bottom. "My work," she tells us, "has always been a time machine catapulting me backwards across decades and centuries to arrive at some understanding of my 'place' in the contemporary moment."[93] This position, for Walker, is a fraught one that demands self-objectification and minor strategies of refusal.

On the occasion of her September 2017 exhibition of new paintings at her New York gallery two years before *Fons Americanus* debuted, Walker issued two corresponding public statements that rejected the social and market protocols that constrain Black women artists working in the United States. Once again explicitly bridging Black women's visual work with sex work, the first statement was a tongue-in-cheek press release written in the darkly humorous vernacular that has become one of the artist's signature modes of communication. "Collectors of fine art will flock to see the latest Kara Walker offerings, and what is she offering but the finest selection of *artworks* by an African-American living woman artist this side of the Mississippi," the first line of the statement reads.[94] The statement goes on to narrate how scholars, art historians, and students of color "will study and debate the *historical value* and *intellectual merits* of Walker's diversionary tactics," "wonder whether the work represents a *departure* or a *continuum*," and "exercise their free right to culturally annihilate her on social media."[95] The final half of the press release lists the future reactions of parents and their censorship, former lovers and their recoil, as well as the withdrawal of support, the bemused silence, the winces, the disturbing delight, and other anticipated actions from critics, academic societies, gallery directors, as well as, finally, the president. The statement ends with a prediction: "Empires will fall, although which ones, only time will tell." Walker's press release and the accompanying artist statement satirize the linkages between the art market and imperial expansion. Her declarations also undermine the burdens of representation that demand both her presence and subjugation in the art world and the wider world.

Against the backdrop of ongoing anti-Black violence and the 2016 Unite the Right rally in Charlottesville, Virginia, Walker's 2017 statements generated a string of commentaries in the news and on social media. The perspectives ranged from valorizing the artist for her bravery in confronting systems of oppression while remaining committed to artistic freedom, to dissatisfaction and dissent directed at the artist's refusal to stand up and be counted as a Black woman artist amid present-day social and political upheaval. "It's too much," she declared in the artist statement that accompanied the press release for the show, "knowing full well that my right, my capacity to live in this Godforsaken country as a (proudly) raced and (urgently) gendered person is under threat by random groups of white (male) supremacist goons who flaunt a kind of patched together notion of race purity with flags and torches and impressive displays of perpetrator-as-victim sociopathy." Walker's interjection crystallizes the triple otherness that stems from Black women's historical and contemporary position at the bottom of the social order. It also underlines Black artists' frustration with a new millennium enamored with aspirational and affirmative engagements with race, gender, sexuality, and class that ultimately fail to yield social progress much less physical or legal protection.

Like *A Subtlety*, the social media attention that her statement garnered brought a measure of visibility to the conditions under and against which minoritarian figures, and their aesthetic strategies, exist and work. Despite the fact that Walker is well known for pointing up the limits of art's potential to repair historical trauma, critics and fellow artists still desired for her to salve the long history of racial strife in the United States. She refuses however, then and now, to embrace the top as a position of power and privilege despite her increased publicness and celebrity, eschewing debilitating social and aesthetic expectations regarding what Black women and their art should do. "I know what you all expect from me and I have complied up to a point," she states. "But frankly," she continues, "I am tired, tired of standing up, being counted, tired of 'having a voice' or worse 'being a role model.'" Psychologists and social scientists often identify role models as motivators for individuals, and for historically stigmatized and disenfranchised subjects especially, to set and accomplish ambitious goals in high-stakes achievement settings.[96] Walker rejects the disciplinary function of role models, underlining political theorist Joy James's provocations about the impasse between revolution and love, between theory and praxis, wherein no consensus currently exists on how to respond to the predatory formations and permutations of racial capitalism.[97] In so doing, the artist and her unruly "progeny" approximate what James calls "the captive maternal" that is better understood as an epistemic function rather than an identity marker. Walker's genuflections and prostrations in turn resist the conflation of respectability politics with achievement and freedom. The baseline work that the captive maternal figure, the Black female bottom, performs—the burden of praxis—stabilizes the very social and state structures that prey on her. The labor it takes to be on top—to be a top—is exhausting, Walker thus declares, from the mammy to the Venus to the contemporary Black woman artist herself. She instead rolls her eyes, folds her arms, and waits.

Walker's embrace of the lower registers of art and identity, her marshaling of demoted art forms, her mocking of ennobled art genres, and her sustained engagement with debasement vis-à-vis dark humor, defecation, the grotesque, disgust, toxicity, planned ruin, and repulsion all constitute the Black female bottom. These instantiations lay the groundwork for the aesthetic strategies and analyses that unfold in the following chapters of this book, culminating in Narcissister's topsy-turvy performances of kink and race play in chapter 4. Such self-conscious enactments, in my view, respond to the art world's consumption of Black women's work and image, hence Walker's portrayals of the negress as a subject and a maker persona. Her depictions of the perverse entanglements between body and environment, form and affect—molasses boys carrying the dismembered limbs of their kin, for instance, as they, too, slowly disintegrate—highlight the ways in which Black women's bodies and labor have been figured as sites of reproduction without futurity. This phenomenon, different compositions of which permeate the rest of this book, can also be seen in Walker's choices of materials and their relationship to the passage of time. Her large-scale public artworks break down and intentionally erode. Their ruin is deliberate, calculated, premeditated; both *A Subtlety* and *Fons Americans*, respectively, were designed to decay and disappear. Additionally, in perpetuity, both sculptures can only ever present a fragment of themselves—as photographic documentation, as ephemera, and as actual fragment vis-à-vis the molasses boys and the sphinx's left hand, in the case of *A Subtlety*. Thus, Walker's staging of reproduction without futurity becomes an opportunity for the artist to episodically disrupt the commercial market that constrains her creative potential by demanding that the Black female subject persistently visualize and relive her own subjugation for capital gain.

Furthermore, the freaky, sadomasochistic behaviors that Walker's figures exhibit turn the power dynamics of Black-white race relations in the United States on their heads, from the plantation past to the putatively progressive present, because the concept of agency and who wields it cannot be easily distinguished. Interwoven in a morbid dance of power, her figures appear beautifully crafted and harmless at first glance, but then become more complex and grotesque the longer and harder we look. It is not immediately clear which figures are white, which are black, which are dominant (the masters), and which are submissive (the slaves). There is no cohesion or racial harmony in Walker's work. *A Subtlety*, in particular, forcefully denies the possibility for shared kinship, or affirmative relationality between color and racial categories, by refusing synthesis, whether in terms of formal conventions, racial comity, cultural discourse, or aesthetic experience. In this way, she and the other artists in this book enact a form of Black feminist self-regard akin to literary studies scholar Kaiama Glover's conception of counterintuitive practices of freedom that privilege the self in ways unmediated and unrestricted by group affiliation.[98] This is an ethics of representation and relation that stems from embracing the disorderly and unruly contours of Black female being. Moreover, instead of establishing continuity between the past and the present, Walker's art holds open the gap between the imagined antebellum era that her figures conjure and the afterlife of slavery on which they are brought to bear, refusing to sublimate both the trauma and distance that continues to temporally accrue between the two sites.

Amid debates about the promise and pitfalls of progressive politics, the #BlackLivesMatter movement, the ubiquity of social media, and a growing public awareness of intersectionality, Walker's Black female bottom draws together racial and sexual abjection as conditions of being that stand outside of sociability's "proper" boundaries. But instead of meeting these conditions with reverence, repair, and restoration, Walker refuses to obey, to comply. Such errantry cannot be digested nor disciplined. Taken together, the artist's myriad interjections and inversions represent a fever pitch. As one of the most visible and viral Black women artists working today, her repeated rejection of behavioral protocols in the face of multiple levels of scrutiny contests the ways that civil society simultaneously demands Black women's exposure and their subjection. By refusing the commonsense logics of long-established systems of representation within the art world and everyday life, Walker's Black female bottom troubles the idea that social transformation is both possible and desirable. Her self-conscious engagements with subjection and abjection illustrate how the increased visibility of Black women's cultural and political labors impact how we theorize art of the Black diaspora.

The next chapter further explores how prominent Black women artists, as subjects, negotiate and refuse the traps of racialized and gendered protocols of representation, interpretation, and self-making that coalesce under the guise of celebrating Black feminism. Like Walker, Kenyan-born artist Wangechi Mutu's engagements with racialization and Black womanhood place the Black female body at the center of debates about new materialisms, environment and empire, hybridity, and the limits and possibilities of reproductive futurity in the new millennium. They also upend the idea that the past is continuous with the present, that Black women have a duty to maintain an ethical relationship to that past, and that Black women should produce positive images of themselves and their sisters as a means of compensation for historical ills and oppression. Mutu specifically draws a distinction between American Blackness and African

Blackness, distancing herself from the slave narrative as a defining feature of the former. This is an important distinction, for she is the only African-born artist in this study. Yet her work engages the legacies of slavery in the United States and the Black Atlantic world by interrogating the conditions of dismemberment and racial kinship separation that subtend Black diasporic experience.

In her fifty-nine-minute video *Amazing Grace* (2005), Mutu appears in a flowing white dress as she walks slowly along the sandy shores of the Atlantic Ocean singing "Amazing Grace" in Kikuyu, her native language. Titled after the famous late-nineteenth-century African American spiritual and filmed in Miami, Florida, the video's source text and location inform Mutu's articulation of Blackness across continents. At the end of the video, the artist disappears into the sea, edges away from the US shore. Her back is to the camera. As the ocean water envelops her, she looks out across the Atlantic where slave ships traveled the Middle Passage to the "New World," a journey into and out of slavery to which the song "Amazing Grace" alludes. A hymn about the assurance of salvation and divine love still sung at Black cultural gatherings today, "Amazing Grace" celebrates deliverance from the miseries of oppression. In using "Amazing Grace" as both the work's title and sonic framing device, Mutu situates Blackness historically, visually, sonically, and transnationally at the edge of a body of water so often associated with a shared Black past—the Atlantic Ocean. But rather than staging a present that is both recovered and whole, Mutu stages a history constituted by loss, alienation, dismemberment, and rupture over and over again in her practice. These features recur throughout her most-known works, her collages.

As multiply marginal figures, Mutu's cyborgs (in type and effect in collage) contest how claims to slavery as the nexus of shared Black experience have come to define African Americanness. They also destabilize Blackness and womanhood as definable entities that align with one another. As sisters in kind, spirit, chosen community, and political posture, Black women have been treated as prototypically intersectional subjects that make visible the shortcomings of conventional feminist and antiracist work in the new millennium.[99] The artist's repeated centering of dismembered racialized and gendered bodies within posthuman discourse and the adopted country where she lived and work for the first twenty-five years of her career unravels one of intersectionality's central threads: that race and gender are transhistorical constants that mark *all* Black women as indivisible beings in relationship to identity and oppression.[100] Her representations in turn reflect an aspect of lived experience in the American context that cannot be articulated in any other way but in the visual field because of American culture's fixation on Blackness as both invisible and hyper-visible.[101] Mutu's art, like Walker's, compels us to see that simply being Black and woman *does not* necessarily equate to group membership or solidarity. Her figurations not only appraise the dividing line between the desirable and the undesirable in terms of race and gender; her constructions also redraw how these attributes mutually constitute Black diasporic particularity.

2

Alien Kin

An apt reckoning with historical experience ought to require a failure or a short-circuiting of the redemptive function.
—Stephen Best

Such reckonings ought to compel us to consider whether there can be a black feminist ethics of nonrelationality.
—Rizvana Bradley

The art of undesirability, the premise of this book, unsettles common beliefs about the ability of Black women's creativity and biology to alleviate the toxic reverberations of racial and gender oppression. The artists and minor aesthetic strategies discussed upend normative ideas about agency and reparation vis-à-vis extra-visual form and affect. For Kara Walker and Wangechi Mutu, the two most known artists in this study, these strategies untether Black women's art from a curative, redemptive impulse to expose the unfinished project of racial and gender empowerment in the twenty-first century. Mutu is best known for her grotesque, yet dazzling representations of hybrid figures in otherworldly environments. In these spaces comprised of photo-fragments, paint, and other materials, Black and racially ambiguous cyborg women hover, suspended in motion. Formless backgrounds and impossible landscapes constitute these fantastic worlds, where images of uteri, birth scenes, cyborgs, and mother figures such as Eve and the Madonna proliferate.[1] The artist depicts wounds as signs of immediate and ongoing trauma—whether on the female bodies that populate her works on paper, in the backgrounds of her collages, or on the gallery walls of her installations. Blood spatter punctuates each composition, as remnants of human and nonhuman encounters where violence is both disabling and a strange form of birth.

Mutu's complex images do not proffer linear narratives that interlink the bygone with the present. Nor do they seek to answer the conundrums at their core: How or why can cyborgs also be mothers? Her interspecies figures and environments, riven with dysfunction, instead bring questions of mutualism and relationality to the surface, challenging the capacity of the art establishment and the humanities to reconcile historical and bodily trauma with the desire for new and progressive forms of togetherness. Composed of organic and biomechatronic parts, her cyborgs differ from other bionic characters that circulate widely in popular film and television. Such technologically enhanced figures are both a product of and a foil to the rapid and unregulated acceleration of technology, war, capital, and other sources of global conflict. In contrast to biorobots and androids, cyborgs are living organisms whose enhanced abilities derive from the integration of some artificial component that relies on feedback to function properly and optimally. Part human and part machine, cyborgs in the popular imagination are generally heralded for overcoming adversity, saving the world from itself, and restoring humanity to some sense of wholeness, even as their hybridity relegates them to the status of the "Other." The human and nonhuman intimacies and entanglements on display in Mutu's collages are, by contrast, the product of *undesirable* intercourse that does not yield high-functioning integration, all of which has profound implications for how scholars in every field of the humanities and social sciences analyze the relationship between Blackness and Anthropocentric consciousness.

The Anthropocene, and the apocalyptic discourse it has inspired within recent scholarship, defines the current geological period during which human activity has drastically changed the earth's climate and the biodiversity of its environments, potentially irreversibly so. The acknowledgement of such human impact, according to philosopher Axelle Karera, often neglects the *racial* realities of our current ecological crisis and the ways in which the Anthropocene reifies and relies on racial hierarchies to operate.[2] Mutu's work places Black women, "protagonists" as she calls them, at the center of this discourse.[3] She enfolds gender into critical conversations about race and the environment, visualizing how rising tides, oil drilling, and other forms of extraction disproportionately impact minoritarian subjects—both human and nonhuman—and their surroundings. The cyborg here functions as a signifier for both racial and gender otherness as well as for the types of bodies that might emerge and thrive in an increasingly uncertain world riddled with post-apocalyptic rhetoric and conditions. The parasitic dysfunction between disparate species and locales in Mutu's art significantly and repeatedly refuses oneness, a compelling blueprint for considering what tools and strategies are necessary for navigating such moments of crisis and rupture. The birth scenes, alien mothers, and cyborgs that recur in her collages, videos, sculptures, and works on paper animate the limits of bodily trauma and collective memory during a new era of techno-optimism and post-identity desire that denies and displaces the racially gendered antagonisms that continue to shape and determine everyday environmental conditions around the globe. In refusing to cohere into a picture of seamless, or even radical, togetherness, the alien kin that populate the artist's oeuvre, posed as they are in inhospitable, nebulous landscapes and at once physiologically and racially unrecognizable, model a Black feminist ethics of non-relationality.

Though critics often read Mutu's cyborg figures as mixtures between species, races, plants, and cultures that overcome fragmentation, sociopolitical upheaval, and the frenetic intersubjectivity of postmodern life, transgression, disability, and dismemberment are foundational to her praxis. Alternately, scholars and curators have problematically marshaled the artist's biography as a Black African immigrant woman to interpret her figures as signs of strength and resilience, at the level of the self and the nation. In the following pages, I advance a different reading. The parasite-host dysfunction that animates the mutant ruptured forms in her collages, in my view, insistently and incessantly stage non-relationality, breaking open the ties that bind historical and bodily trauma with hybridity as the horizon for coalition and community in the new millennium. Enacting alien kinship in this way challenges the trappings and slick aesthetic categories that proliferate in critical theories of art's potential, namely the elevation of beauty and wholeness, the idea that art can redeem suffering, and the assumption that interdependence holds emancipatory promise. The dismemberment and blood spatter in Mutu's work contrasts the "new ontological appreciation of interrelations of humans, environments, and societies" that feminist philosopher Nancy Tuana finds symptomatic in writing on the Anthropocene.[4] The artist's versions of alienness and non-relationality not only diagnose how race and gender complicate the terms of posthuman, postcolonial consciousness. They also offer a new analytic for evaluating Black feminist art praxis, one that undermines the psychological and material underpinnings of racist and sexist thought in aesthetic and political discourse writ large.

An established art market darling, Mutu rose to fame after renowned art historian and curator Kellie Jones included her installation Cleaning Earth in *Life's Little Necessities*, an auxiliary group exhibition for the Johannesburg Biennale in 1997 that created a groundswell of press and attention for the artist.[5] Much has since been written about her practice and what art historians and critics understand to be the conceptual scaffolding of her work. Trained as a sculptor and anthropologist, she uses a collage aesthetic to explore the transnational contours of Black female being, historical and contemporary experiences of trauma, interspecies relations as metaphors for multiracial mutualisms, and practices of resistance. Overwhelmingly, her growing circle of fans and critics praise her hybrid, human-nonhuman figures as rejoinders to fragmentation, crisis, and the intersubjective frenzy of postmodern, technologically networked life. Drawing from interviews with Mutu, curator Isolde Brielmeier, for instance, insists that the artist seeks "ideas, missing pieces, something that is whole."[6] Similarly, curator Josée Bélisle states, "She invests her 'girls' with a power of resilience and formidable doses of heroism."[7] Yet such readings limit the world-making aims of Mutu and her contemporaries to displays of adaptability, repair, strength, resilience, and transcendence. The artist's biography is often enlisted to exemplify this posture.

Born in Nairobi, Kenya, Mutu moved to New York in the 1990s to study fine arts and anthropology, eventually earning a BFA from Cooper Union and an MFA in sculpture from Yale University. As a transnational Black feminist artist, her immigrant status at the time was positioned as the compass around which the artist oriented her work. As a result, art critics have long detected a search for home and belonging in her collages, sentiments motivated by the repeated presence of trees and roots in her art. "Unencumbered by didacticism and informed by theory without adhering to dogmas," art historian and curator Kristine Stiles declares, "Mutu works with the cool reason of a world citizen and an intellectual whose art embodies the cosmopolitan ideal."[8] For Stiles, this translates to a multiplicity of truths and forms of intersubjectivity that stimulate human and nonhuman healing and well-being in the wake of trauma.

Alternately, art historian and museum director Courtney J. Martin argues that Mutu's collages and the fragmented bodies that populate them represent a postcolonial body politic; collage is analogous to "the composite nature of the nation" that is continually made and remade.[9]

Such readings of collage position the artist's preoccupations with bodily mutation as forward-looking, redemptive visions that engender radical becoming at the level of the self and the nation. They also naturalize mutual relationality and dependency, thereby fetishizing unity without attending to the racialized and gendered antagonisms that persist and fortify unequal power dynamics in the present. The mutant figures, species entanglements, and visual markers of uncertainty and indeterminacy that recur in Mutu's art, on the other hand, highlight the value of queerness and anti-sociality within Black aesthetic practice and, for others, the ways that fracture is assumed to warrant repair. Her alien mothers and cyborg figures emerge from alternate, undesirable forms of transformation, and neither wholeness nor repair results from this unconventional approach. Similar to Walker's repulsive silhouettes and anti-monuments, Mutu's art merges longing and loss with refusal and failure, each marking a point of crisis in progressive discourse about racial belonging and intersectional feminism in the Anthropocentric twenty-first century. The artist's approach to Blackness's origin story is key to this reorientation, especially in how she distinguishes between perceptions of Blackness in East African countries and in the United States. From this angle, Mutu's amalgamations interrogate the space that accumulates temporally and geographically between original sites of trauma and how those traumas come to bear on the present across space and time.

Rather than hybrid, reassembled bodies that achieve self-determination and multiracial, mutual belonging—broken vessels that seamlessly come back together—I see Mutu's cyborgs and collage aesthetic as instantiations of transgressive dismemberment and expressions of undesirability.[10] For the purposes of this chapter, I define dismemberment as the acts of cutting and breaking apart of bodies *and* medium conventions that pervade the artist's practice as well as the undoing of racial and gender categories that her work invites. Transgression, relatedly, connotes offensive acts, or violations of accepted or imposed boundaries. Together, dismemberment and transgression foreground the acts of cutting and constructed violence that constitute Mutu's practice on the whole, acts that in turn produce ruptured bodies that break with the basic tenets of figuration and what we expect Black women's visual work to recover and repair. Creating image worlds where violence proliferates ardently short-circuits recuperative narratives of wholeness, resilience, and triumph—what Kara Walker calls the "we-shall-overcomeness" of Black representational space—to reckon with the depth and range of Black women's lived experiences.[11] In repeatedly rupturing figures that transgress race and gender and placing them in amorphous landscapes, Mutu disaggregates skin, the body, and geography as stable sites of subjectivity and as reservoirs for re-memory. Her figures do not experience or enact cathartic emancipations from racialized gender oppression nor do they remain subject to it. Alternately, her own ideas about Blackness and womanhood urge viewers and critics to reconceive how representation in the visual field circumscribes the present and future terms of being and belonging for women of African descent in a world that alternately vaunts and denigrates them.

This chapter traces Mutu's strategic deployments of alien kinship and transgressive dismemberment by examining her contributions to the Venice Biennale (2015), her *Yo·n·I* series (2007), and her *Family Tree* commission (2012). Each body of work marks a turning point in the artist's career when she experimented with new forms and materials: mud sculptures in Venice, ruptured cyborg figures in her first solo show in London, and site-specific drawings and installations for the first survey exhibition devoted to her art, respectively. Most importantly in these series, the female figures display the effects of deracination and alienation. The worlds her "protagonists" inhabit are at once marked by disorder, change, and excess, from amorphous globs of junk and putrefying matter that grow and devour their surroundings, to the accumulation of dense layers of images in her large-scale collages. Mutu's excessive forms that play with skin color as a site of racialization are examples of Amber Musser's theorization of Brown jouissance. Excess, for Musser, "circumnavigates questions of sovereign subjectivity and desire to show us epistemologies rooted in opacity and sensuality."[12] Such representations of decomposition and disorder, like Walker's work in the previous chapter, demonstrate how Black female embodiment acts as an interstice, a passageway that is foundational to human and nonhuman relations in an era of new racial and gender meaning.

To develop this theme, I read the figure at the center of *Non je ne regrette rien* (2007) from the artist's *Yo·n·I* series alongside Dana, the dismembered protagonist of Octavia Butler's *Kindred* (1979). In my analysis, Dana's experiences anachronistically prefigure and parallel the forms and formations of disorderly and *disabling* kinship that proliferate in Mutu's oeuvre. The collage and novel share cyborg thematics that mobilize science fiction and fantasy tropes that have become popular prisms through which to imagine alternative Black pasts, presents, and futures in the academy and in the art world. They also stage racial kinship separation in ways that provoke new understandings of Black Atlantic life with regard to slavery and its legacies. *Non je ne regrette rien*'s inclusion in *30 Americans*, an exhibition that has traveled to multiple venues since its premiere in 2008, further emphasizes the import of Blackness to the American imaginary and to the mainstream art world.[13] Yet both texts (despite the novel's name—*Kindred*) break with the "overcomeness" convention to which Beyoncé and Walker draw attention—that "making lemonade" and sublimation resolve suffering and trauma—within Black aesthetic theory. Juxtaposing Mutu's collage and Butler's novel engenders a minor stance toward aesthetic possibility borne from Black women's contemporary experiences with both historical trauma and present-day oppressive forces. It also claims theoretical space for Black women's visual work, which is often sidelined in favor of literature, music, and other forms of Black cultural expression. This non-relational, minor stance—in theory and in practice—unsettles the cyborg and interracial coupling as progenitors for progressively just futures within the liberal, posthuman imagination.

Comparing these two Black-woman authored texts—one visual, one literary—exposes the limits of making the past continuous with the present, of redemptive criticism, and of mutual belonging as antidotes to historical trauma. It also brings intersectional discourse into contact with disability studies. *Kindred* is Butler's 1979 speculative novel about slavery and time travel, and her science and speculative fiction writing has become increasingly popular because of its forecasting of the apocalyptic and racially unjust end times that mark twenty-first-century existence. In the wake of Black Lives Matter uprisings, the COVID-19 pandemic, legislative assaults on women's reproductive rights, and ecological disasters spurred by climate change, scholars, public intellectuals,

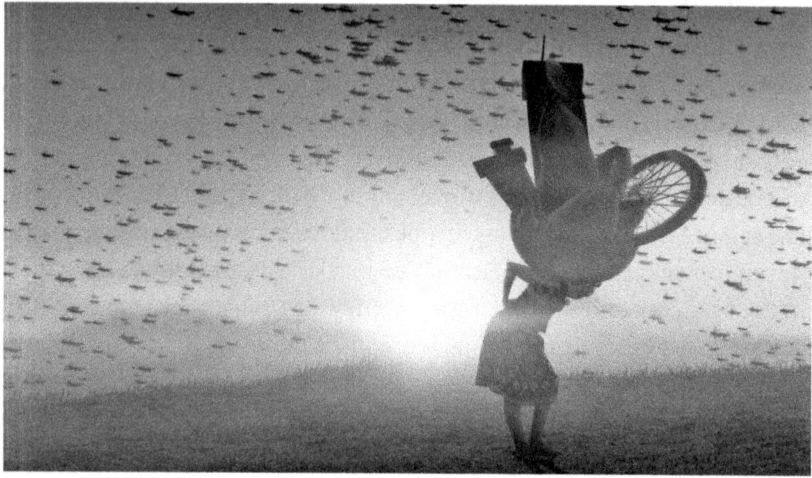

Figure 2.1. Wangechi Mutu, *The End of Carrying All*, 2015. Three-channel animated video (color, sound), edition three of three, two AP, dimensions variable. Courtesy of Gladstone Gallery, New York, Victoria Miro, London, and Vielmetter Los Angeles.

educators, and critics have turned to Butler's fiction to make sense of the sociopolitical present and to imagine new futures. Relating Dana's self-imposed dismemberment to Mutu's splintered cyborg protagonist underscores the minor, undesirable ways that Black women artists navigate social and political upheaval as well as issues of agency and disability in the afterlife of slavery. Analyzing these texts together highlights the interwoven ways in which racialization in the United States and public desires for wholeness and multiracial progress regulate aesthetic protocols for Black women at the level of imagination, representation, and cultural production.

The False Promise of Collage

Mutu's contributions to *All the World's Futures*, the title and theme for the 2015 Venice Biennale, exemplify her conceptual concerns with fragmented existence, ongoing legacies of racial and gender violence in our collective present and future, and the affective tension between disgust and regeneration. They also establish an important vantage point for reevaluating the political value of Black women's creative labors in the new millennium. For *All the World's Futures*, Mutu presented three original works featuring disorderly and dismembered female figures. Each artwork depicted a scene of creation, an origin myth drawn either from the artist's imagination or well-known cultural texts such as the Bible. All three pieces featured transmuted female figures that were frightening, mysterious, and productive, albeit negatively, even undesirably, so. The "Black" women—either animated or made of dark-colored pulp and photo fragments—appeared as vessels, passing through landscapes and cone-shaped cages in search of the earth's edge, new worlds, and knowledge. What they generated, however, was junk and curious waste. Notably, the majority of Mutu's art depicts the Black female body as the ground from which nonnormative enactments of reproduction, futurity, and humanness spring.

In *The End of Carrying All*, a ten-minute animated video, a barefoot Black woman wearing a head wrap and a cotton print dress trudges across a dismal landscape of grasses as she balances a basket on her head, the sun in the background casting both the lone female figure and the landscape in soft silhouette. Flocks of birds migrate low across the sky. As the basket on her head grows bigger, she stumbles under its weight. Objects including a bicycle wheel, a small house, and a satellite dish overflow, multiply, and pile on top of each other fantastically and of their own accord. The woman's back bends, her body bowing under her burden's increasing mass as she slowly approaches the edge of the world.

At the end of the ten-minute video, the earth rises up and swallows the protagonist. This final act of consumption sends a ripple through the bleak landscape, as if to suggest the possibility of transformation while at the same time stopping short of *animating* that transformation; the video fades to black once the earth settles before looping back to its beginning. The faint sound of birds is the last thing viewers hear. Here, the form and the loop suggest renewal in their return to the beginning. But the content of the video portrays a strange death; neither the character nor the landscape is seen to regenerate after this scene. This video plays on conventional Eurocentric representations of racialized and gendered labor in spaces designated as "Third World" while also providing a strong critique of the exploitative logics of uneven capitalist accumulation and economic development. *The End of Carrying All* pairs art historical strategies of accumulation with material consumption and excess to uniquely depict human and nonhuman relations. The video also contests Western conceptions of otherness, whether race, gender, nationality, geography, or sexual identity. The heavy load the female figure in the landscape carries is both the burden of representation and the weight of superfluous material consumption and waste. What gets animated is not positive transformation and renewal, but violent upheaval at the edge—and *end*—of the world. What gets accumulated in *The End of Carrying All* is not wealth, but junk.

This strategy of material accumulation comes to bear in a very literal way on *She's Got the Whole World in Her*, the artist's sculptural installation for the biennale. Half woman, half mermaid, a black, mud-colored figure covered in pulp made from junk mail perches on her stomach and peers into an earthen globe suspended before her. An expansive geometric structure resembling a crinoline cage surrounds her hind parts. Plumes of black and burgundy feathers flourish at her heels and in the crease between her buttocks and legs. A collection of curios—miniature gnomes and fauna—trails behind her. The subject of the collage *Forbidden Fruit Picker* is also a female figure perched atop a barren mound between a pair of serpents with a taste for blood and a decaying, foreboding tree, the base of which features a brown fetus turned upside down among a nest of disembodied hands. The sacred and profane come together in the sculpture and collage, one title referencing a Christian song ("He's Got the Whole World in His Hands") while the other's iconography re-presents Eve in the Garden of Eden.

Front and center filling a third of the frame, the figure in *Forbidden Fruit Picker* is foregrounded in such a way that her scale dwarfs the looming tree and landscape behind her. Her form is stable and immediately in view, yet she is vulnerable and suspended in motion. Her collaged body is composed of photographic fragments of human, animal, and motorcycle parts cut from magazines—a cyborg. Compositionally, Mutu's *Forbidden Fruit Picker* bears a striking resemblance to Giovanni Bellini's *Madonna of the Meadow* (ca. 1500), from the pyramidal structure of the female figure to the expanse of the landscape that frames her. The conflicting images and species in *Forbidden Fruit Picker*, however, refract Western art history's reverence for images of the Virgin Mary and Western society's disdain for unruly women such as Eve through the lens of Black women's queer negativity. Unlike Bellini's painting,

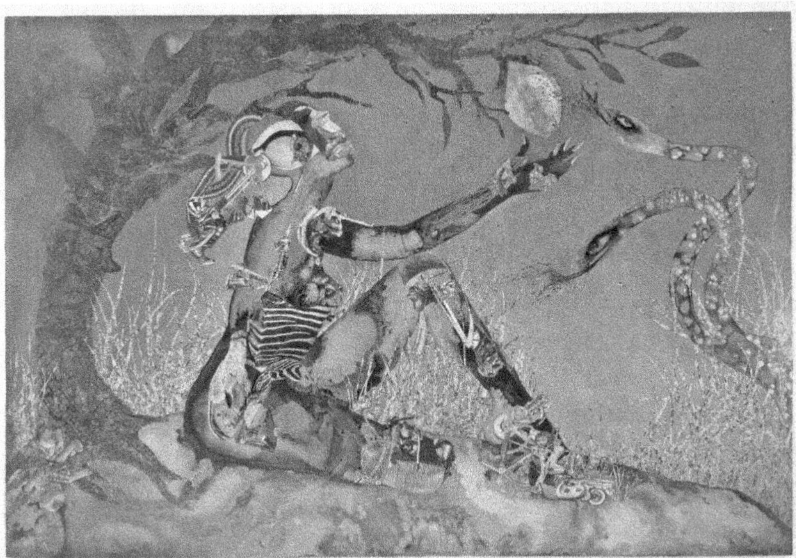

Figure 2.2. Wangechi Mutu, *Forbidden Fruit Picker*, 2015. Collage painting, 39 1/2 × 58 5/8 in (100.33 × 148.89 cm). Courtesy of Gladstone Gallery, New York, Victoria Miro, London and Vielmetter Los Angeles. Photo credit: Alessandra Chemollo.

there is no intimacy between the female figure and the child in Mutu's collage. Rather than vibrant, healthy trees that frame the protagonist and horizontal bands and diagonal lines that unify the composition's pictorial space, the artist's use of atmospheric and linear perspective and three-dimensional form disorders any relational logic between natural forms, human forms, and nonhuman forms.

Mutu's collages across her practice mix up where and how humanity begins and ends as well as what it means to create, live, and exist with other beings. Creation, for the artist, is not a process based on the seamless and successful interdependency and interconnectedness of all life on the planet despite the aspiration and desire for such futures. Her cyborgs embrace what curator Okwui Enwezor calls "the attributes of negation and repulsion" that emerge from "conflict among each . . . competing image species," a friction that also arises in the space between fragmentation and unity.[14] Conflict abounds in *Forbidden Fruit Picker*. The mechanical parts and new technology that retrofit the human form do not appear to work well together nor do they appear to aid the figure.

And rather than the shame typically associated with Eve's transgression, the collage fixes the figure in the act of disobedience, not the aftermath when Eve *and* Adam are exiled from the terrestrial paradise.[15]

This dark, ominous picture of "the first mother" at the beginning and end of the world recasts the future promise of women's biological and creative reproduction. "Females carry the marks, language and nuances of their culture more than the male. Anything that is desired or despised is always placed on the female body," Mutu asserts of the burdens women carry.[16] Self-assured, the forbidden fruit picker reaches for the lurid, ripe fruit hanging from the tree before her; but she does not touch it. Even as the composition gestures toward hope and renewal, there is something very pending in this image. This is not a picture of successful collaboration and coalition between human, technology, environment, and other species; the figure's suspended motion instead stages an ambivalent relationship between aspiration and attainment. Each element—plant, animal, human, and technological—remains on the surface, unassimilated. Each element, moreover, remains deviant in its own way—"other." This unruly Eve—a mix of entangled objects and textures—is, lastly, dismembered, her right leg missing its lower half.

The recurring motif of disorder and dismemberment in Mutu's 2015 Venice Biennale contributions reframe the political value of the artist's more-recognized artworks: her collages. Rather than producing figures that achieve synthesis across biological and cultural life, her composite images comingle the realities of being uprooted with the irreparable conditions of dispossession and alienation. To construct her collages, she uses several sources, what she has elsewhere called the fecund "shit" of consumerist society.[17] She cuts and pastes together photographic fragments from *National Geographic*, glossy fashion and beauty magazines, pornography magazines, ethnographic postcards, anatomy textbooks, coffee table books such as *Africa Adorned*, and automotive schematics. Her images, which also include hand-drawn and painted elements, are often mixed with decorative or abstract patterns and techno-enhanced bodies that yield provocative juxtapositions.

Because of her use of collage and the cyborg, her hybrid and multiple figures are often considered models of embodied resistance to racialized gender constructions and sexual subjection on the one hand, and feelings of fracture and displacement on the other. Scholars of postcolonial critique, feminist collage, and Afrofuturism—a flourishing cultural movement that combines science fiction, history, and fantasy to redefine Black diasporic experience—have celebrated the artist's incorporation of technological devices and science fiction elements as metaphors for racial and sexual otherness. Hybridity within these frameworks is seen to subvert the oppressive forces of colonialism and Western imperialism by turning the gaze of the subjugated back onto the colonizer while multiplicity suggests a pluralism in which an abundance of identity formations is not only possible, but also extant along various and potentially fluid axes of power. This liminal state of being at the border of two or more cultures thus functions as a strategic reversal of subjugation through subversion while multiplicity has signaled, for others, a utopian project of inclusion. These views postulate identity boundaries as malleable, the effects of which engender transformative instances of commonality and coalition, a way towards racial progress and mutual belonging.

From this angle, Mutu's cyborgs function not just in a posthuman sense; they are hybrid, multiracial creatures composed of disparate animate and inanimate parts that seemingly demonstrate the possibilities and benefits of mutual belonging in an uncertain world and future.[18] According to curator David Moos, "Her composite bodies become a merger of cultural signification, presenting a new hybrid of the female figure by blending distinctions between parts and whole, face and limb, outside and inside, into writhing emblems of excess and interpenetration."[19] Alternately, her cyborgs are seen as transgressive, self-generating, and self-affirming amalgamations of Black womanhood.[20] Black cultural studies scholar Michael E. Veal, for example, describes the artist's oeuvre as a "commentary on womanhood [that is] spiritual and alchemical;" her Black female figures are "potent agent[s] of regeneration," survivors who, in their "beauty," demand justice, realignment, and new ideologies of romantic love in a post-Black, post-gender world.[21] In these formulations, the cyborg finds its ideal expression in collage.

In choosing collage as her primary medium, Mutu joins a cadre of twentieth and twenty-first century artists that appropriate and juxtapose photographic fragments with hand-drawn and painted elements as a means for reckoning with sociopolitical upheaval. The act of bringing disparate parts 'into union' reconciles the fractured, oppressed subject, "collage as repair," as curator Trevor Schoonmaker puts it.[22] Art historical, feminist, and postcolonial studies of collage in modern and contemporary art have frequently associated the medium's so-called revolutionary edge with oppositional, utopian ideals. "Throughout the 20th century," surrealism scholar Gwen Raaberg writes, "a succession of revolutionary arts movements . . . laid claim to collage, assuming special rights to the form and avowing its special powers. In the contemporary arts," she continues, "collage is so prevalent that it is sometimes considered synonymous with postmodernism. Significantly during the last decades [of the twentieth century], feminist artists have particularly been attracted to this mode."[23] At the turn of the twentieth century, avant-garde artists in Europe adopted collage to expand the possibilities of painting—considered to be the epitome of high art—and to make sense of a rapidly changing world. Assembling and affixing found and readymade images to canvases permitted collage artists to abandon their reliance on paint and to mirror and respond to the drastic, unprecedented shifts in industry, urbanization, and war. Collecting or bringing "together" readymade and unrelated materials created something singular in both product and process, yielding an altogether unique work of art and a new political consciousness.

Often considered a paradigmatic minoritarian medium within art history and Black study, the prevalence of collage in the latter half of the twentieth century made it nearly synonymous with "postmodern cultural fragmentation."[24] Moreover, "artists who were culturally marginal," women and artists of color among them, appeared to gravitate toward collage in order to articulate their feelings of otherness.[25] African American artist Romare Bearden, one of American art history's most known collage artists working mid-century and one of Mutu's influences, described his own aesthetic practice as a political project.[26] Collage in Bearden's formative years, according to Kobena Mercer, allowed him to express the feeling of double consciousness—the sense of always looking at oneself through the eyes of others—that largely structured notions of Black experience at the time. For Bearden, the "distortion of scale and proportion, and abstract coloration" were "the very means through which [one tries] to achieve a more personal expression."[27] In 1964, Bearden began working exclusively in collage, a move that corresponded with debates about the social responsibility of African American artists during the civil rights era.[28] "The formal dynamics of collage" in Bearden's practice, Mercer tells us, were "especially relevant to the hyphenated character of diaspora identities historically shaped by the unequal interaction of African and European elements . . . articulating an anti-essentialist understanding of black identity."[29] Mutu's collages of dismembered bodies likewise contest the burdens of representing Blackness and its embodiment. But Mutu's present-day collages depart from Bearden's modernist depictions in important ways. Whereas Bearden conjured the improvisational qualities of collage to animate a joining together of the divided "African" and "American" subject, Mutu's practice exists at the nexus of dismemberment and violence, a rejoinder to utopian ideals of Black expression and mutual belonging.

Prevailing theorizations of early-twentieth-century collage by Dada artists in Berlin and surrealist artists in Paris as well as African American and feminist artists later in the twentieth century undergird the impulse to read Mutu's collages as pictures of a new and improved humanity during a time of political upheaval in the new millennium.[30] Centering unruly, dismembered, Black protagonists in inhospitable landscapes as Mutu does, however, splinters longstanding ideas about the merits of togetherness and the coalitional investments that drive narratives concerning contemporary art practice, intersectional feminism, and US race relations in the afterlife of slavery. The ruptured bodies in her work do not portray mutualism; they instead explode racial coexistence and unity as the basis for cooperative sociality along interracial and intraracial lines. For her, "Collages, assemblage, and mixing genres are merely tools to facilitate the rewriting of [her] memories and history" of colonialism, racialization, and gendered forms of violence and oppression.[31] Her collages consequently unsettle historical reconstruction and wholeness as desirable models of Black representation in the present. The artist's imagination of Blackness's origin story is central to this intervention.

Creation stories figure prominently within Mutu's oeuvre, a strategy that the artist uses to evince how her experience as a Black woman artist living and working in the United States differs from that of her home country. In an interview with Okwui Enwezor, she explains:

> When I say I'm an African artist, I mean it's part of my practice, part of who I am because I was born and raised there. But often when people say I'm an African artist, it's reductive—it's exotic, it comes from a world that's in the past. Even broaching the idea of race is very complicated

> because Africans have a different historical experience to those who were abducted and brought here to the USA. [There are] equal senses of alienation and exile but the myth that's loudest is the slave narrative, which doesn't apply to a huge amount of Africans, myself included. I always say that I was racialised in America, I understood my blackness before I got here but not because I was from a black-majority country. We don't break things down in terms of black and white, but we do have the colonial issue. My work relates to the forced creation story that the colonialists invented us [Africans, black people].[32]

Mutu's remarks challenge the idea that (a) African-born subjects have an essential, immediately legible relationship to Blackness that binds them to other members of the diaspora and (b) that African Americans bear a fundamental affinity to and for Africa as the basis for their Blackness. In both instances, slavery remains the ghost in the machine of kinship across race, gender, sex, and geography.[33]

In distinguishing African Blackness from American Blackness, Mutu emphasizes the difference between "African-American identity and what could be described as a *cultural politics of blackness*," as art historian Derek Conrad Murray outlines.[34] The artist's mention of the slave narrative also urges viewers and critics to reconsider where we locate and forge racial and gender kinship within and across geographic and cultural contexts. As discussed, kinship, "re-memory," loss, and melancholy have become defining features of visual and cultural studies scholarship of the Black Atlantic. The "continued proximity to the unspeakable terrors of the slave experience," Paul Gilroy posits, defines Black modern identity and Black diasporic belonging across time and space in the Atlantic world.[35] Furthermore, "most commentators who write on the role of memory for contemporary African-American subjects," according to literary scholar Ashraf Rushdy, "maintain that the act of remembering is curative and leads to a sense of wholeness."[36] For twentieth-century Black artists and intellectuals grappling with the trauma and memory of slavery in the United States, sociologist Ron Eyerman observes, representation became a means for achieving cohesion and racial belonging. Whether or not individuals themselves had been slaves or had any knowledge of or feeling for Africa, "It was the memory of slavery and its representation through speech and art works that grounded African American identity."[37] Against the backdrop of slavery's enduring legacies in the United States and globally, Mutu's dismembered protagonists disorder the figures and grounds on which racial and gender continuity and the politics of belonging cohere. Her cyborgs and the parasite-host relations that comprise them challenge the promise of collage, cultural identity, reproduction, and kinship as stable terrain on which to stake Black collectivity in the past, present, and future.

Cyborg Grammar and Black Women's Mattering

The distance Mutu draws between her Blackness and her experiences of racialization in the United States throws into question the idea that the slave past and cultural unity more broadly provide ready prisms for apprehending and embodying racial and gender kinship across the Black diaspora. Alternately, her depictions of human and nonhuman relations picture fraught and undesirable intimacies that, in their non-reproductive and dismembered state, *destabilize* assumptions about hybridity's transformative potential via the collage medium and the cyborg body. While she samples equally from African vernacular forms, historical avant-garde strategies made popular in Europe at the turn of the twentieth century, and American mass culture, her work also merges politics and aesthetics in ways that exceed persistent projections of hybridity and multiplicity as "transcendental panacea," in Tavia Nyong'o's words.[38] Her amalgamations instead visualize extraordinarily difficult relations and uneasy instantiations of racial and gender sociability by way of rupture and parasite-host configurations.[39]

Her 2007 *Yo·n·I* series dislodges the cyborg as an idealized figure of hybridity to portray new visions of racialized women as unruly material beings. Suspended in formless environments, the dismembered figures articulate the fungible space that Black women's reproductive labor occupies in the art world and in popular and academic discourse. The title of the show, her first solo exhibition in London, derives from *yoni*, the Sanskrit word for divine passage or sacred space rooted in the worship of female reproduction, creatively, sexually, and biologically. According to the show's press release, "The artist . . . placed careful emphasis on the spelling of the title to invite a reading of *Yo·n·I* as 'you and I,' a sense of unity and belonging rather than division and conflict."[40]

Yet the series' repeated use of dismembered form, the disjuncture inherent to collage, and the ruptured imagery that confronts viewers openly repels interspecies mutualism and optimism. The images in this series instead underscore the unequal relation between Blackness and humanness and the role this relation plays in the patterning and fashioning of collective futures in the new millennium and beyond. A different kind of relationality surfaces in the transgressive dismemberment on view in Mutu's *Yo·n·I* collages—a non-relationality that is essential to undesirability and the Black feminist ethics of representation analyzed in this book.

A nude female figure, with its head thrown back and its body extended under a serpent that appears to consume it, sprawls at the center of *A Dragon Kiss Always Ends in Ashes* from the series. *I Belong to You, You Belong to Me* is an entangled tower of phantasmagoric bodies, organs, and appendages. Paradoxically, what binds these bodies and organs "together" is the act of rupture. The motif of the soiled, burst torso present in this image appears later in Mutu's collages as does the nebulous background, splotchy skin, writhing roots, and blood spatter, all of which have become commonplace in her art. *La Petit Mort* (The little death) from the series speaks directly to the promise of ecstasy and transmutation. The cyborg figure's splayed legs mirror the protruding pink vulvar appendages that appear covered in dark-colored tendrils across the bottom left portion of the image; a patch of soil and pearl excretions replace the vagina. A detached head hovers near the top edge of the image, as does a ruptured squid entity to the right of the figure. Evocative of female transformation, the little death in this instance is not an orgasmic state of unconsciousness or transcendence but rather one of physical dismemberment—an undoing.

Non je ne regrette rien (No I have no regrets), one of the most striking and unsettling of the *Yo·n·I* collages, confronts viewers with a complex scene of dismemberment and dispossession.[41] A maimed figure—part human, part animal, part machine—is suspended in the middle of a grey and brown haze. Severed from its upper half and projected into a cumulous abyss, only its lower limbs remain. Separated like scissors, the bottom leg extends as the top leg bends at the knee, reaching upward in a shape that mimics a scorpion's tail. Instead of a knee joint, the top leg is equipped with a motorcycle wheel that connects to spinal tubing, and instead of a foot, the bottom leg is fitted with an amalgam of animal hoof,

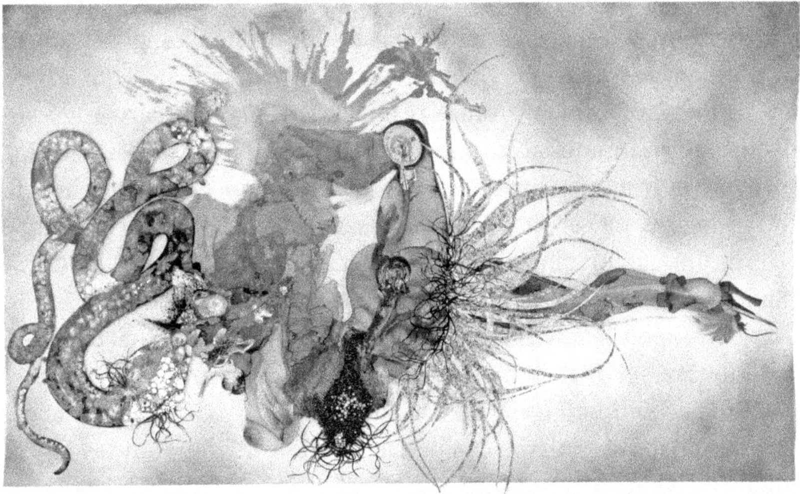

Figure 2.3. Wangechi Mutu, *Non je ne regrette rien*, 2007. Ink, paint, mixed media, plant material, and plastic pearls on Mylar, 54 × 87 1/8 in (137.16 × 221.31 cm). Courtesy of the artist and Vielmetter Los Angeles.

stiletto, and blooming flower. The stiletto and blooming flower are stereotypical signifiers of female sexuality, and the figure's splotchy, brown-painted skin suggests racial Blackness and ethnic brownness while also declining to confirm either. Green and grey-scaled tentacles cover its pelvic region.

A serpent on the left, its skin imbued with violet, red, and other earthen hues, coils around the exploding figure. Although the serpent flanks the ruptured female body, the creature does not appear to directly interact with it in such a way that distracts from or undermines the status of the protagonist. It appears *in relation* to the ruptured female body, a parasite-host configuration that frames the aberration at the center of the image. Mesh that resembles a network of cell fragments and black-colored soil spill out of the figure's burst torso. Dark, multicolored roots sprout from the figure's lower abdomen and overlap its sprawling tentacles while the roots invert plant and floral imagery that in art history is typically associated with white femininity and fertility.[42] Colliding color fields of ochre, green, and pink spatter the grey background, spewing from the figure's top leg from which its foot appears to have been violently amputated.

The composition is arranged in such a way that it is difficult to tell whether the coiling serpent is responsible for the figure's splintered state or the plant parts have breached the body internally. Consequently, the arrangement of human, animal, plant, and mechanical parts suggests a disturbing and impossible mutualism—a corrupted form of kinship—that derives from the disparate parts of a dismembered body, which fail to synthesize, rather than the parts' seamless fusion, new growth, or rebirth. Instead of affirming bodily agency and the political efficacy of mutual belonging, *Non je ne regrette rien* explodes the Black female body as a locus upon and within which racial, gender, and sexual codes and coalitions materialize in the past and present-as-future.

Mutu's *Yo·n·I* collages mark a number of turns within the artist's own practice that mirror discursive shifts in the humanities regarding Black women's reproductive capacities and how to picture futurity. First, the multiply split subjects depart from the artist's early composite figures, which tended toward bodily and representational wholeness.[43] The sparse, blank, and often ivory-colored backgrounds in *Pin-Up*, her first series of collaged female figures, differ from Mutu's *Yo·n·I* collages by drawing viewers' eyes directly to the figures and their proto-cyborg contours. The works in the *Pin-Up* series, many of which are untitled, feature poses and images culled from ethnographic postcards, health and beauty magazines, and pornography, each mixed with ink and watercolor on paper. In response to particular instances of disfigurement, political violence, and female mutilation on the African continent, Mutu's pin-up girls display physical deformations that might result from enduring a stampede, mass rape, or laboring in the Sierra Leone "blood diamond" trade.[44]

In one work, the composite female form, surrounded by floating balloons, poses in spiked, coral-colored heels just left of center. Lips agape, the figure suggestively looks over her right shoulder while the left side of her body is hidden from view. Her head and long, golden hair are adorned with a pink flower in full bloom. Her skin is a saturated dark brown tone. Her torso, fitted in a cream and pink polka-dotted one-piece that resembles a 1950s-bathing suit, is pitched slightly forward, accentuating her buttocks and breasts. In another untitled work from the series, the figure's mouth and legs are splayed open toward the viewer, a pose that reappears in Mutu's later works. The figure is bare chested, brown, and distinct from the previous work in both its explicit sexual posturing and its anatomical composition. She is also missing her left forearm.

Despite their composite form and missing limbs, Mutu's early figures are relatively proportionate, anatomically correct bodies. Between 2003 and 2004, however, this tendency toward figurative wholeness and visual coherence began to change. In 2003, Mutu expanded her scale, trading notebook-sized paper for enlarged pieces of Mylar and vellum. In *Alien Polka Ponder* and *I Have Peg Leg Nightmares*, both from 2003, the protagonists appear to be simultaneously composed and *de*composing. Their skins look like exoskeletons that break apart even as they define the figure's bodily edges. The segments of flesh, made of glitter, glossy magazine extracts, and duct tape, hover and gravitate toward one another, at once a *part of* and *apart from* the figure. In another untitled work from 2003, the artist trades floating circles of skin and surface for spattered paint, blood spewing from the barrel of an inverted pair of legs. A monkey hangs from the figure's back, a popular reference to an affliction and its palliative remedy as well as an oppressive load one can neither rid oneself of nor forget. These two works foreshadow the corrupted mutualisms that pervade the *Yo·n·I* collages where the Black female figure is a receptor for and carrier of a certain kind of burden: cultural baggage. The weight of the parasite-host relation, meanwhile, bends and lays waste to her body.

The *Yo·n·I* protagonists thwart wholeness, extending the artist's early strategies of dispersal and waste into a refusal of synthetic relations that form the core of Donna J. Haraway's subject-defining writings on the cyborg from 1985. Haraway's approach to feminist theory broke new ground within posthuman studies and continues to animate critical understandings of kinship as they play out in the Anthropocene. "A cyborg body is not innocent;" she writes, "it was not born in a garden; it does not seek unitary identity and generate antagonistic dualisms without end (or until the world ends); it takes irony for granted. . . . Intense pleasure in skill, machine skill, ceases to be a sin, but an aspect of embodiment."[45] For Haraway, the binaries that demarcate gender are visionless, whereas creating a new landscape of representation in which technology is incorporated into bodies—thus creating cyborgs—might create a world without gender. "We require regeneration, not rebirth," she explains, "and the possibilities for our reconstitution include the utopian dream of the hope for a monstrous world without gender. . . . Cyborg imagery can suggest a way out of the maze of dualisms in which we have explained our bodies and our tools to ourselves."[46] To some degree, Mutu's figures fulfill Haraway's cyborg dreams by dispelling an Enlightenment ideal of a whole, self-possessed body. It is clear, however, that Black womanhood—a collision of gender and race—continues to be a problem for Western aesthetic thought, as evidenced by Haraway's contradictory approach to what she calls "New World black womanhood."

Here, Haraway sees Black women's subjectivities as sites of figuration that "resist representation" and catalyze "new turns of historical possibility," even if paradoxically.[47] In "Ecce Homo, Ain't (Ar'n't) I a Woman, and Inappropriate/d Others: The Human in a Posthumanist Landscape" (1992), a postscript to her manifesto, Haraway borrows theorist Trinh T. Minh-ha's sign of an impossible figure, the inappropriate/d other, to describe "New World black womanhood."[48] To correct the racial shortcomings of her original manifesto and unsettle critical theory's attachments to master narratives, she begins the essay with a "focus on the discourses of suffering and dismemberment" in order to reclaim hope and humanity through "self-contradictory," "nongeneric," radically nominal, and "negative" ways.[49] But to do so, she imports the history of Black female slavery, and specifically, Sojourner Truth's iconic speech "Ain't I a Woman?." Haraway thus holds onto difference, in one formation or another, even as she aims to displace "the Enlightenment figures of coherent and masterful subjectivity" and restore human connectedness.[50] How can Black women simultaneously be sites of figuration yet also resist representation and restore connection? If a cyborg is post-gender and without the cultural baggage that stems from binary categories, is it also post-sex? Post-nation? Post-race?

Haraway's expanded view of the cyborg cannot possibly meet its goals precisely because of the role Black women's reproductive labors play in the liberal imagination as interstices and impasses. The ungrammatical aspects of Black womanhood that are structural rather than merely social constrain the possibility of a liberatory cyborg politics that transcends gender.[51] Race and its intersections with gender and sex, in other words, remains a problem—an impasse—in this new world. Referring to literary theorist Hazel V. Carby's description of Black womanhood under conditions of slavery, namely how the cult of true womanhood positioned Black women as abject counterparts to white women, Haraway asserts:

> In the New World, and specifically in the U.S., black women were not constituted as 'woman,' as white women were. Instead, black women were constituted simultaneously racially and sexually—as marked female (animal, sexualized, and without rights), but not as woman (human, potential wife, conduit for the name of the Father)—in a specific institution, slavery, that excluded them from 'culture' defined as the circulation of signs through the system of marriage.[52]

Black women (as slaves) bear and produce property, in this logic, but they do not own or possess it. As a result, naming and valuation as signs of legacy, inheritance, and origination bear no meaning for Black women because for them, names are merely empty signifiers granted through the dominant discourse of the Master.[53] They are uniquely "ungrammatical" in relation to language and the law, as Hortense Spillers provocatively claims in her late-twentieth-century writings on Black female subjectivity.

Following the novel semantic field that Spillers defines, the dismemberment that predominates Mutu's visual work likewise engenders an evocative epistemology for understanding contemporary racial belonging and Black female being in the West in the afterlife of slavery. Within this visual field, Blackness disfigures gender, and the modifier "Black" renders female bodies the stuff of un-matter. This designation places them outside a classical configuration of how bodies as matter come to mean, originate, generate, and regenerate. Matter, as critical gender theorist Judith Butler explains, is associated with reproduction, origination, and causality. "The classical configuration of matter as a site of *generation* or *origination*," she writes, "becomes especially significant when the account of what an object is and means requires recourse to its originating principle."[54] The recursive origins and principles of Mutu's collage practice trouble the mythic contours of "the human" by exposing how racialized female bodies, and their labor, energize modes of thought focused on creation, such as science and religion.[55]

Whereas Haraway's theorizations of the cyborg neglect an explicit examination of race, the intersectional alterity of Mutu's cyborgs foregrounds the racialized dimensions of reproductive futurity and posthuman discourse. In so doing, her work presents the refusal of synthesis as a survival strategy for Black women in an anti-Black world, an important addition to feminist theories concerning the limits of the human that followed Haraway's pathbreaking scholarship. Chela Sandoval, Janell Hobson, and Zakiyyah Jackson have constructively critiqued how Haraway's conceptions of the cyborg's liberatory possibilities overlook racialized gendered bodies.[56] For Sandoval, Black and brown life *is* cyborg life, from pre-automated labor to the ways that subaltern, outsider existence energizes oppositional consciousness and politics in the West. Hobson, in her writings on historical consciousness and the Black feminist imagination, claims that bodies still matter as sites of resistance in that they mobilize, destabilize, and decolonize the meanings of race and gender in an increasingly digitized and globalized world. Jackson complicates this claim by reordering the enduring relationship between Blackness, animality, and the human in the history of Western science and philosophy. In *Becoming Human*, Jackson unearths how constructions of racialized gender, Black maternity, and anti-Blackness are indispensable to future thought on matter, materiality, and posthumanism. At stake in all of these revisions is what constitutes resistance and power under and against the totalizing forces of racial capitalism. By enfolding race, gender, and sex in ways that reject wholeness and revel in boundary confusion, Mutu's collages likewise trouble the cyborg's liberatory potential.[57]

Despite the existence of lines that shape recognizable limbs, painted tones of flesh and blood, and visual gestures toward internal organs, Mutu's cyborg bodies do not project a unitary human form. Nor do they present Black womanhood as homogenous or universal. The multiple bodily registers in each collage—human, machine, plant, animal, alien, Black, female—resist coherence and mutual belonging, and their environments lack intelligible details and definition; they are formless, nebulous. Her compositions consequently collapse figure and ground to produce another form of rupture that coincides with the exploded, deformed bodies that inhabit them. In their ruptured state, Mutu's cyborgs act as impossible, undesirable figures that dismember how Black female bodies are seen and acquire meaning. In so doing, her art engenders a critique of the void—the specter—that Black women's visual and embodied alterity occupies within posthuman discourse and critical theory more broadly.

The Mylar surfaces in *Yo·n·I* materially reinforce the discursive and conceptual dismemberment present in the series. Mylar is a synthetic polyester film that causes paint to pool and appear to float on the surface of the material. Of her use of Mylar, Mutu says:

> Around 2002, I began making a lot of work on Mylar—collage works, always focused on these subjects that were female, somehow transforming into or from cyborgs or chimeras of animal, plant, and human mixtures. These sort of mythological creatures: in poses, in action, in dance, caught in motion in their worlds.[58]

These orchestrated acts of suspension and capture find their material complement in Mylar, further emphasizing the conditions of dislocation and dispossession—of bodies, of time and place, and of imported media—that constitute Mutu's work. The material also produces a glistening sheen that draws the focus to her piece's many surfaces, to the skin of the work and that of the figures therein. Here, the material support of the collages is both skin and background; put differently, figure and ground meld into one another, an added dimension that obscures the knowability of race and gender in these images as well as the relationship between surface and depth at the level of identity and form.

Mylar also allows the artist to play with splotchy, layered skin to trouble the ways in which racial signifiers attain meaning. In *Yo·n·I*, skin takes on new significance in its rupturing because of the way it mediates the interplay of race and gender (as social constructs) and biology (the anatomy that defines female and male). By correlating racialized female flesh with dislocation, the series underscores how categories such as "Black" and "woman" came to be the quintessence of what Spillers terms "a particular figuration of the split subject that psychoanalytic theory posits."[59] For Spillers, the split "nature" of Black female being occurs not only along the lines of racial and gender difference but also in regard to body and flesh. Black female flesh acts as a surface, an unprotected, disfigured, open site for violation and violence derived from the historical, physical, and psychological effects of slavery.[60] The unfavorable responses that Kara Walker's *A Subtlety* roused in both viewers and critics exemplify this. In their triple otherness, Black women are dispossessed and excessive; with their insides turned outside, they are displaced from symbolic orders of white Western subjectivity.[61] As Musser argues in *Sensual Excess*, aesthetic forms have the capacity to "rearrange knowledge by engaging differently with fleshiness and how we apprehend it."[62] Mutu's manipulation of surface at the level of technology, nature, and the materiality of the body, in other words, registers the complex relationship between race and gender at the level of surface and flesh. Much like Xaviera Simmons's images in the next chapter, the artist's collages highlight the role that skin color plays in processes of racialization *and* materialization as well as its status as a signifier for Black identity. Along these lines, the nebulous environments and messy parasite-host relations in *Yo·n·I* challenge posthumanist conceptions of matter as lively and exhibiting agency.

In the last four decades, scholars of feminism, visual culture, political philosophy, psychoanalysis, and Black life have interrogated the anti-Black blind spots of academic writing on posthumanism and new materialisms, especially those organized around reparative notions of forgiveness and futurity. In the United States, these discourses remain tethered to slavery. As Spillers reminds us, "The quintessential 'slave' is *not* a male, but a female."[63] Anti-Blackness becomes a structural necessity for relational ethics in this schema, and the parameters that position redress as the only outcome for slavery's resolution in the present hinge on humanizing Blackness. But as Alexander Weheliye, Kodwo Eshun, Axelle Karera, and Zakiyyah Jackson remind us, Blackness has always been at odds with Enlightenment ideals of what constitutes humanity.[64] Experiences of colonization, Middle Passage slavery, and racial subjugation necessarily exclude Black bodies from narratives of humanism; in the case of Blackness, as Eshun puts it, "the human is a pointless and treacherous category."[65] Relationality, for Karera, "is inherently not only a position that the black cannot afford or even claim. The structure of relationality is essentially the condition for the possibility of their enslavement."[66] Black women are thus systematically suspended, subjectless outlaws who exist outside of Western post-Enlightenment gender categories; they exist, moreover, outside of the category of the human. Yet their sublime capacity, as Jackson attests, saturates social orders of matter and hierarchical arrangements of gender and sex in the globalizing West.[67]

In addition to the physical and material ways in which Black female embodiment ruptures the space of liberal humanist ethics, Mutu's collages, like Simmons's photographs in the next chapter, add new dimensions to recent theorizations of the Black epidermal surface—skin—as liquid and relational. Exceeding the Anthropocentric reliance on nature-culture, human-nonhuman dualisms, and ocular-centric understandings of surface as finite and flat, her compositions throw foundational concepts like visibility and relationality into crisis. Whereas literary and Caribbean Studies scholar Michelle Ann Stephens sees skin as a "threshold, a point of contact, a site of intersubjective encounter . . . between the self and the other," Mutu's machinations of paint and cyborg imagery recast the generative limits and possibilities for subjects historically seen as quintessentially other, abject, and alien—the stuff of un-matter.[68] The Black female cyborgs hurtling through space, time, and barren landscapes gain more traction here, for it is the extra-human processes of generation and destruction that articulate the matters of race and reproduction in the afterlife of slavery, both physiologically and pictorially.

The Black female body in Mutu's art is a contested site of creation, origin, reproduction, and matter. Persistent dismemberment in *Yo·n·I*, along with suspension and dislocation, also redraws the parameters of representation and kinship as well as the usefulness of the cyborg as a technologically enhanced survivor ready to face the future. The recurrence of ruptured bodies thus exposes the limits of communal relations as loci for racial and gender belonging. Her cyborgs refuse to come together as racially coherent beings, forcing a distinction between reproduction—both procreative and creative—and racial reparation as ingredients for human progress and historical transformation. These visions of matter, of identity and image, and of the future, core to all of the artists in this book, become more complex when considering the Blackness of Mutu's forms. Her cyborgs, and the rupture in *Non je ne regrette rien* from *Yo·n·I* in particular, exaggerate the extra-material conditions of fracture and undoing that inhere in collage and racialized female embodiment. From pornographic photo fragments, kitschy glitter and pearls, representations of intestinal hemorrhaging, plant soil, and the use of mesh to signify scaly flesh that alternately appears ripped apart, the piece becomes more repulsive the closer we look. In so doing, it articulates a different horizon for sisters in crisis, one predicated on non-relationality, that urges viewers and critics to rethink what it means to be Black, woman, and human in the twenty-first century.

Dismembering Kin

Analyzing Mutu's work through the lenses of dismemberment, non-relationality, and disability shifts academic, art world, and popular media conversations about the liberatory promises of kinship, bodily coherence, and technological advancement in the Anthropocene and the afterlife of slavery. Rather than amalgamations that overcome adversity and oppression, her cyborgs and the speculative landscapes they inhabit engender disorder and disability, not wholeness and reparation. Because of this, her cyborgs are often compared to the Black female characters and aliens that populate Octavia Butler's post-apocalyptic speculative fiction. In the months and years following the most recent wave of Black Lives Matter uprisings and COVID-19, both Mutu and Butler have enjoyed renewed and enduring acclaim for the provocative blueprints their work offers for navigating uncertain futures. Each artist mobilizes Afrofuturist aesthetics to center Black women in critical visions of tomorrow, but only recently have their respective bodies of work been analyzed with respect to disability.

Claiming Mutu's and Butler's protagonists, and the impossible interracial unions that surround them, as sites of dismemberment and disability holds special relevance for the memory of slavery in the United States and the violence that stems from this rupture. Building on budding literary studies scholarship on Mutu, Butler, and disability studies, I read the figure at the center of *Non je ne regrette rien* alongside Dana, the dismembered protagonist of Butler's *Kindred*. Although *Kindred* anachronistically prefigures Mutu's collage, it parallels the forms and formations of disorderly kinship in the artist's oeuvre. Neither the cyborg nor Dana is unequivocally saved or restored by integrating technology and racial others. Instead, the worlds that Mutu and Butler construct resist the assumed inherent value of futures wherein technological advancements "liberate" humans from their reliance on the planet's resources and where cross-racial intimacy vanquishes anti-Blackness.

Kindred is a story about a contemporary Black woman who, due to unexpected instances of time travel, finds herself shuttled between her

1976 Southern California home and the pre–Civil War Maryland plantation of her ancestors. A struggling writer who works odd jobs at a temporary labor agency she likens to a slave market, Dana along with her white husband, Kevin, have just moved into a new house when the time travel begins. During the course of the novel, she interacts with her distant ancestors—slaves and slave owners—and must save and free her direct ancestor, Rufus (a white man), in order to secure her own existence in the future that is her present. In the most pivotal scene, she becomes lodged between the world of her time and the world of her ancestors. A fatal skirmish ensues, resulting in Dana losing her left arm when the portal between past and present, an actual wall, entraps her. Although Dana makes it through the wall, she must violently self-amputate her arm in the process, leaving her limb in the past. Dana's body consequently becomes a battlefield on which issues of racial kinship, possession, ownership, and agency are played out across the protagonist's past and present. For these reasons, *Kindred* is typically considered a paragon literary text that posits a continuous relationship between a shared slave past and a Black political present that hinges on building a portal whereby Dana physically reconciles her Black and non-Black kinship relations. Like Mutu's work, it has also been heralded as a canonical Afrofuturist text.

During her second trip to antebellum Maryland, Dana realizes she has been transported to the 1800s to intervene in her own history, to ensure that her direct ancestor Hagar is born. Essentially, she is made responsible for her own lived historical experience in the past as well as her own *becoming* in the present, a riff on and re-gendering of "the grandfather paradox." This well-known science fiction trope is where inconsistencies of time travel emerge through changing the past—a person travels to a time before their own grandfather has children and kills him, thereby making the time traveler's birth and existence in the future impossible. Through time travel and encounters with her ancestors, Dana must secure her future existence through an imposed, forcible dismembering that is uncertain, painful, and dangerous, vis-à-vis matrilineage and the captive maternal. The time travel is activated by one of two occurrences, either when Rufus is in danger or when Dana fears for her own life. Although *Kindred* appears to emphasize continuity and multiracial mutualism, it also breaks with that continuity. Dana saves Rufus so that he can father the bloodline of her future, but she eventually has to kill him after her foremother's suicide in order to prevent him from keeping her in the past. In this way, she and Rufus are connected across time but constituted through racial and gender distance.

Many critics have read Dana's experiences of dislocation across time and space as empowering rewards that stem from intersubjective relations, yielding an enlightened, awakened self. For Octavia Butler herself and her critics, Dana's physical loss imbues her with a new form of self-consciousness. Literary scholar Robert Crossley notes in an essay included in the twenty-fifth-anniversary edition of *Kindred* that Butler's fiction centers "on women who lack power and suffer abuse but are committed to claiming power over their own lives and to exercising that power harshly when necessary."[69] In an interview with author Randall Kenan, Butler elaborates on Crossley's observations by saying, "I couldn't really let her come all the way back. I couldn't let her return to what she was, I couldn't let her come back whole and [her dismemberment], I think, really symbolizes her not coming back whole. Antebellum slavery didn't leave people quite whole."[70] Butler thus frames Dana's self-amputation as a way to imagine the psychic and physical dismemberment that slavery and its afterlife spurs.

For Butler, apprehending slavery's brutality in the past and present requires alternative modes of knowledge because such a past makes it inherently impossible to return to any semblance of wholeness or preconceived notions of reality. In this frame, Dana's dismembered Black female body challenges Western concepts of subjecthood by forging not only a *felt* understanding of history but also an enriched self, borne from overcoming isolation, or alienation, as well as an unsavory familial past. Although dismembered, she is literally formed by the intersubjective relationships and shared experiences that she now carries with her. But negatively. As a result, many have argued, Dana's felt understanding of history privileges an embodied particularity that reflects the Black female slave experience in the United States, experience antithetical to a humanism vested in any pretenses to universal rationality.

In addition to unseating humanistic norms, several literary scholars have extended Dana's loss as a metaphor for the "lasting damage of slavery on the African American psyche," to use Grace McEntee's words.[71] Pamela Bedore likens the loss of Dana's arm to the loss of the character's innocence regarding the supposed progress of racial relations in the present.[72] For Ashraf Rushdy, who extols the "acute representations of familial and historical relations" in Butler's "novel . . . about [loss and] recovery," Dana's missing arm is payment, an indebtedness that results from the risks that stem from changing the course of history.[73] Her physical and psychic losses, he insists, "are sacrifices made in her successful attempt to alter the past."[74] In other words, her loss and memory-as-narrative are modes of recovery that remedy history. Ruth Salvaggio also sees Dana's dismemberment as a distinct "birthmark" that represents part of a "disfigured heritage."[75] These interpretations elaborate the melancholy historicism that underlies neo-slavery studies and Black arts criticism.

For literary scholar Farah Jasmine Griffin, contemporary novels about slavery written by Black women refashion dominant, demeaning discourses of Black female bodies as ugly, inferior, and inhuman into sites of "healing, pleasure, and resistance."[76] This transformation, what she calls textual healing, has been a flashpoint for narrative reparations of the Black female body and racial belonging within Black cultural studies since the early 1990s. While Griffin acknowledges that Black bodies can never return to a pre-scarred state, she insists on a notion of healing achieved through coherence and self-determination. Motivated by faith in Black women's writing, specifically, and literature, more broadly, to recuperate and redeem a traumatic past, textual healing claims the maimed (Black female) body in a *narrative* of love and care. In this framing, "loss gives rise to longing," to use Saidiya Hartman's words, in order for Black women to "get along" and guard against destruction from outside forces; neo-slave stories, in this framing, function as forms of compensation.[77]

Non je ne regrette rien and *Kindred* both depart from Griffin's notions of textual healing and the recuperative mandates of Black cultural production more broadly. Their imaginings of dismemberment, whether through an African American or African lens, prompt an understanding of contemporary representations of slavery and its afterlife that break from the impulse to redeem the past in the present. This perspectival shift is unmoored from a binary of rupture and reconciliation. The protagonists in each work of art trouble the ethics of historical reconstruction projects and posit dismemberment as an essential element of contemporary Black female being, particularly in terms of initial sites of trauma and the distance that accumulates between then and now.

Near the end of *Kindred*, just after she slits her wrists in order to precipitate a return to "the present," Dana is summoned back to the plantation for the last time because Rufus is distraught over the suicide of his slave. Alice, Dana's foremother whom she physically resembles, hangs herself after Rufus claims to have sold their two children, Joe and Hagar, as punishment for Alice's attempted escape. In this scene, Dana recognizes how much she resembles Alice: "Her head was bare and her hair loose and short like mine. . . . It was one of the things that had made us look even more alike—the only two consistently bareheaded women on the place."[78] Although Dana favors Alice, her relationship to slavery differs from her ancestor. In the pages after Alice's suicide, Dana contemplates accepting a brutal reality that, for Griffin, is a quintessential feature of slavery and a primary need for textual healing: rape. This is the turning point of the novel. Dana immediately dismisses her thoughts of conceding to Rufus's sexual violation, and in a flash of violent resistance, stabs and kills him for attempting to rape her (as Alice's surrogate). This ends the time travel and the conditions of Dana's bondage as she is abruptly transported back to 1976 Los Angeles. Meanwhile, Rufus's lifeless hand grips her left arm, which she forcibly rips from the wall in order to remove herself from the literal and figurative restraints of her past.

Dana's psychic and physical dismemberment from the imprisoning bonds of her ancestral past—her refusal of rape and her self-amputation—are significant in two regards. The first is the interracial rupture that necessitates Dana's self-amputation. By this point in the novel, she has become acclimated to living in the past. Each trip back demands more time spent than the last, and at times she is unable to distinguish between her Los Angeles home and the Weylin plantation. As a result, she and Rufus grow closer in both time and space. This closeness makes plain the resonant dialectic of their relationship—a mutual, multiracial dependence violently enabled by slavery—that comes into view through time travel, a bond from which Dana must eventually sever herself.

Secondly, and perhaps most evocatively, fear catalyzes Dana's time travel in such a way that she cannot be raped within the structure of the narrative. This impossibility suggests that rape is not the trauma, or the historical experience of slavery, to which she is tethered. Replacing Alice with Dana forces a substitution of one Black female trauma for another, from rape to dismemberment. This contrast between rape and dismemberment marks each one as a unique form of trauma that emerges from specific historical experiences and relations. This differentiation also punctuates the anti-redemptive stakes of *Kindred*'s end. That is, redemption, or textual healing, makes sense if the trauma is rape, but something else is required if rape is not the primal scene of Dana's becoming. As a contemporary Black woman, she has a different relationship to the past and slavery, one based on something altogether different: dispossession and dismemberment.

The fact that Dana is withheld from networks of kinship often considered anchors for Black female slaves in bondage further confirms this point.[79] Twice orphaned, as a child and by her aunt and uncle's disavowal of her interracial marriage, she exists within a paradigm of individualism and isolation, a conventionally male construct and privilege within narratives about slavery informed by American Enlightenment principles of self-reliance and independence.[80] Similarly, Mutu's cyborg figure is isolated from its surroundings, thus denying neat categorizations of kinship based on race, gender, species, or otherwise. Like Dana, the dismembered figure in *Non je ne regrette rien* is dislocated as it floats above an unstable, indefinable environment that obscures spatial orientation and refuses to anchor the viewer in a specific time or place.

The expressions of dismemberment in Butler's novel and Mutu's collage expose how efforts to redeem the past and the excised Black body are futile. Insofar as Black female figures are marked by violence, the text and the artwork reveal that aspirations toward wholeness are fundamentally untenable, a condition even more exaggerated by the distance in time and space that accrues from the original moment of historical trauma. For once the historical conjuncture has passed, anthropologist and curator David Scott avers, the cognitive and political understandings of wholeness and recovery unique to that moment no longer "have the same usefulness [or] salience."[81] Spanning the speculative landscape between neo-slave narrative and future text, the two aesthetic objects and the violently separated figures on which they center, refuse closure and consequently thwart a drive toward wholeness, mutual belonging, and historical recovery.[82] In their refusals of social and aesthetic norms, *Kindred* and *Non je ne regrette rien* short-circuit what sociologist Alondra Nelson calls a "dialectic between defining oneself in light of ties to one's history and experience and being defined from without (be it in virtual or physical space, by stereotypes or the state)" specific to representations of Black women.[83] The dismembered Black female body in *Non je ne regrette rien* in particular represents a hybrid figure whose very being materializes through alterations and transformations that ultimately refuse synthetic reconciliation.

Dana's alienation therefore comes to mean more within the context of her self-imposed dismemberment. Unlike her counterparts, she cannot experience rape within the form of the narrative. This fact and her estrangement from her family give rise to a constructed individualism—an otherness—whereby Dana elides accepted embodiments of Black womanhood as well as racial kinship. Her likeness, *not her experience*, connects her to her foremother, and rather than a multiracial mutualism that ensures hers and Rufus's well-being, she is returned to the post-integration present un-whole and disabled. Thus, for Dana, killing the "master" necessitates a certain loss defined by the inability to access historical trauma, the refusal of her ancestral past, and the removal of a piece of herself in the present. Finally, at *Kindred*'s end, Dana discovers that no historical records of Joe and Hagar exist. During a visit to Maryland in an effort to process what she and her husband Kevin experienced (he was also transported to the past during one of Dana's trips), Dana finds that Rufus's house is gone and there are no newspaper articles, legal records, or proofs of sale that confirm Joe and Hagar survived. Although she herself is alive, even this is inadequate evidence:

> 'You've looked,' [Kevin] said. 'And you've found no records. You'll probably never know.'
>
> [Dana] touched the scar Tom Weylin's boot had left on [her] face, touched [her] empty left sleeve. 'I know,' [she] repeated. 'Why did I even want to come here. You'd think I would have had enough of the past.'
>
> 'You probably needed to come for the same reason I did.' [Kevin] shrugged. 'To try to understand. To touch solid evidence that those people existed. To reassure yourself that you're sane.'[84]

At this moment of realization, the force of loss is palpable. Despite her longing to apprehend a violent, traumatic past that results in her dismemberment, this reveal refuses to turn the past into what literary theorist Walter Benn Michaels' terms "an object of cathexis . . . something that might be lost or found, defended or surrendered."[85] In its absence, the archive fails to bear witness to Dana's historical experience and intraracial lineage, underscoring the multiple levels of her loss, physical and psychic. This loss subtends the filial bond that exists, however tenuously, between Dana and her foremother, a bond meant to anchor Dana in the present and conceivable future. Her marriage ties are also rattled by this lack of evidence; the future of her romantic relationship as well as the possibility of mutual, even multiracial belonging are thrown into question, further solidifying Dana's alienation. In the case of her genealogical links and within a humanistic understanding of mutual dependence as necessary to social well-being, *the promise of kinship* that both an archival and affective reckoning is expected to effect is unmet. The project of historical reconstruction is thwarted here, anticipating David Scott's notion of a failed future "whose lack of specifiable or retrievable content" is without completion or closure, redress or redemption.[86]

Just as *Kindred* fails to corroborate the past and reconcile it in Dana's present, the multi-species, parasite-host relations in *Non je ne regrette rien* refuse synthesis and racial redemption by dispensing with the promise of interracial sex and intimacy. Rather than a desirable means of transformation, the dismembered figure represents a failure of its prosthetic devices to guard against the incursion that results in its mutilated state. The transgressive force of the ruptured racialized female body is therefore potently articulated in the imaginative failures and expressions of dismemberment, not reparative resistance. Mutu's cyborgs are the result not of healing but of the uneasy intersections of human and nonhuman difference. Undesirability, then, derives from non-mutual, indeed irresolvable, anti-communal connections between the human, plant, and machine parts that constitute her collaged figures. Most significantly, the exploded figure in *Non je ne regrette rien* exceeds the discursive boundaries of Dana's dismembered body. Dana's "future" is formed through her experiences with the past; her body literally bears the marks of her encounters, a detail that becomes even more crucial upon the discovery that official records of her family do not exist. Mutu's figure, on the other hand, is neither constructed by and through history nor is it secured and redressed through the violent mutualism that constitutes it. Transgressive space here is marked by violation and repulsion, and the formal qualities of collage envelop viewers in a process of deconstruction and disordering, in turn troubling how we apprehend both history and racial formation as linear and legible. Appendages spill over the edge of the work as the figure hurtles through the gray abyss, a space demarcated and confined by the frame of the image. The figure thus contests the spatial logic of the structure that contains it; the work exceeds the boundaries of its frame just as the body transgresses its own limits. Neither nature, nor machine, nor human anatomy solely constitute the exploded figure at the center of *Non je ne regrette rien*. All of these elements are present and yet none are mutually exclusive or constitutive.

Dismemberment, consequently, *is* the tie that binds Mutu's cyborgs and Black female bodies across the diaspora in the afterlife of slavery. Rather than overcoming alienation in order to experience synthesis, reconciliation, or transcendence, the transgressive dismemberment in *Non je ne regrette rien* denies "easy recourse to the body as the locus of an essentialized self," as curator Hamza Walker puts it in his essay on the problems and capaciousness of Blackness in post-Black art.[87] Therefore, the future text at which we arrive in *Non je ne regrette rien* is one where racial difference is not reconciled, and the racialized reproductive body is beyond repair. Hybridity and multiplicity fail to cohere into a project of racial and gender progress as the cyborg is pushed to its limits. The individual ruptured figure in *Non je ne regrette rien* gains more momentum, here, as it hurtles through space untethered, for it is in the figure's transgressive dismemberment and anti-communal isolation that it comes face to face with the repulsive force—the dispossessive force—of loss, excess, and negativity. Dismemberment in this frame engenders an apt reckoning with historical trauma by visualizing how alienation effects and conditions contemporary Black female being and kinship. Mutu's collage practice consequently results in something more urgent and more disturbing than repair. The dismembered figure confronts dispossession and dislocation with a defiant declaration, "No, I have no regrets."

Alien Kin

The parasite-host relationships that populate Mutu's collages allegorize natal alienation and its circumscription of Black Atlantic life, reconfiguring the degree to which the Black female body's relationship to reproduction (biological and symbolic) can be family and future oriented. Typically understood, reproduction refers to the biological and anatomical capacities for procreation, or the sexual or asexual capacities of organisms to regenerate. However, by the time The Federal Act of 1808 curtailed the international importation of any new African slaves into the United States, the reproductive capacities of Black women were not only economically beneficial, they were also indispensable to sustaining the institution of slavery and its afterlife. This is the genesis of what historian and sociologist Orlando Patterson calls "natal alienation," "the loss of ties of birth in both ascending and descending generations," a constitutive element of African-American identity and sociability.[88]

The acts of cutting in Mutu's cyborgs mirror the effects of kinship separation and alienation, the severing of ties—material, physical, filial—that stem from slavery's legacies. This schema of separation and incoherence makes Black filiation impossible in any normative sense, thus forestalling the apparent security proffered by nuclear bonds. In his reading of Hortense Spillers' "Mama's Baby, Papa's Maybe," critical theorist James Bliss asserts, "'the Black family' is refused entry into the symbolic order except negatively as a site of pure dysfunction."[89] This refusal engenders "reproduction without futurity," an element seen in the alien mothers and strained kin networks of Mutu's more recent bodies of work, as well as in Walker's figurations of the Black female bottom and the performance art of Narcissister discussed later in this book.[90]

Mutu's alien mothers and the focus on Black women's reproductive capacities across her practice—from photographic appropriation to ovular imagery and birthing scenes—refashion the uses of alienation, generation, and creation for the new millennium. This bears out in an untitled mixed media collage and painting on vellum from 2004 where the figure of the cyborg and the mother are one in the same, making dismemberment the horizon of reproductive futurity. Motorcycle wheels and fenders replace the shoulder and vaginal region of the figure along with pin-up legs and the spattering effect that appears in the artist's early bodies of work. But the blood spatter in this work issues from a butterfly violently emerging from the female figure's stomach, a parthenogenic and nonhuman birth more akin to the science fiction one at the heart of *Alien* (1979), a Hollywood film franchise centered on monstrous births in outer space. This kind of procreation not only transforms the host, but also gives way to strange offspring.

In a famous scene from the 1979 film, Kane, a male character played by John Hurt, is attacked and orally penetrated by a recently discovered alien creature. After an impossibly brief period of incubation, the alien spawn bursts forth from Kane's torso in a strange re-visioning of the primal scene.[91] Instead of offspring born from copulation, the alien 'baby' is produced through parthenogenesis, a form of asexual reproduction in which the growth and development of an embryo occurs without fertilization. Parthenogenesis typically involves offspring originating from a single organism and inheriting the genes of that parent only. But in the *Alien* scene, as in the scene in Mutu's untitled collage, the offspring does not take on the genetic traits of its temporary host; the baby's violent eruption fatally rips apart Kane's body, affirming that the male body (and the Black female body, in the case of Mutu) is incompatible with this futuristic reproductive process. Variations of this scene reappear in the next three films in the *Alien* franchise wherein the part-alien, part-human white female body of Ripley, the heroine played by Sigourney Weaver in each of the films, is solely responsible for the proliferation of humanity.[92]

Mutu's 2004 untitled collage on vellum, on the other hand, centers a Black maternal figure depicted as an alien cyborg body and the point of origin from which another species takes flight. Yet interspecies transformation here, and the metaphorical promise of racial transformation that it foreshadows, occurs *at the expense of* the Black female figure. While both entities "progress" into other states of being, the host cyborg body, unlike the butterfly, is left exposed, bleeding, and vulnerable. The emerging butterfly—a sign of positive metamorphosis—initiates a detrimental bond between insect and cyborg body, not beauty or desirable transformation. Instead of expressing fear and concern at what is to come, the cyborg as vessel appears unmoved; her facial expression is one of submission, of indifference. These dysfunctional relations and affective registers between species permeate Mutu's later works. Just as her protagonists model a new ethics of non-relationality at the level of the individual, so do the artist's collages of alien mothers, families, and multiracial kin networks.

The amalgamations in *The Evolution of Mud Mama from Beginning to Start* of 2008 and *Family Tree* of 2012, wrought of disorder and disfigurement, repel the promise of multiracial mutualism that has become lingua franca in twenty-first-century American discourse. Both bodies of

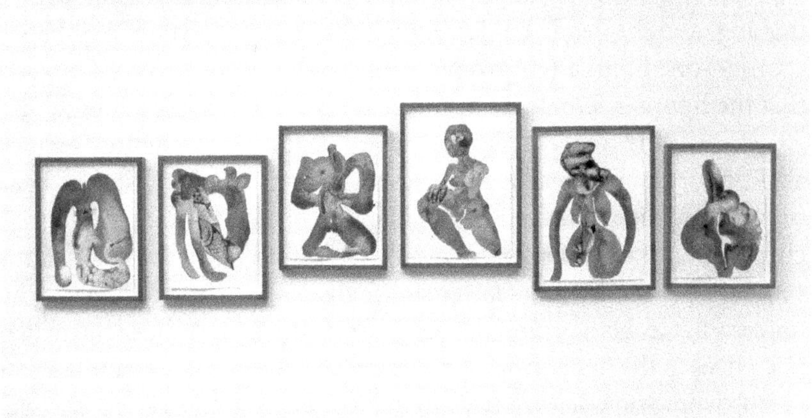

Figure 2.4. Wangechi Mutu, *The Evolution of Mud Mama from Beginning to Start*, 2008. Watercolor, ink, and collage on paper. Six parts: 19 1/2 × 75 in (49.53 × 190.5 cm) overall. Courtesy of the artist and Vielmetter Los Angeles. Photo credit: Robert Wedemeyer.

work were made in the years leading up to and during Barack Obama's two-term presidency, a historical event that mobilized old anxieties within American social consciousness about race mixing and new anxieties about the origins of Blackness.[93] From left to right, the six portraits in *The Evolution of Mud Mama* form a narrative and visual arc of racial and gender kinship. The collage-and-watercolor series pictures ovular, anthropomorphic shapes painted in various hues of red and blue, approximating life-giving organs such as uteri, lungs, and other internal organs. Photo fragments depicting the anatomies of birds and other animals are present, too. A crane's neck and a fleshy, speckled tube containing white blood cells form the center of the far-left image. Here, a small egg is nestled into the tip of the downward sloping appendage near the image's left edge, its exterior attachment a sign of arrested development, or *atrophy*.[94]

In addition to renderings of female reproductive organs and the process of human and nonhuman evolution, the figures themselves seem to evolve as they progress from left to right. Of all the images, the fourth and fifth in the series most directly correspond to human bodies and their anatomy. In the fourth, the figure sits upright in profile with its right hand—a gorilla hand—placed on its right knee. Its left arm is missing, and the head of a parrot replaces its face. A pair of misshapen breasts—one human (cut from a magazine), one watercolor—suggest that the figure is female, but there is no genitalia to substantiate this. As a result, the image denies the identification of the figure's sex just as the figure's multicolored skin cannot be attributed to a single racial or ethnic identity. In the fifth, the figure's breasts droop between the curving contours of its long arms. An upturned pair of macaws at the center splits the figure's teal-green thighs, as a photo-fragment of an unidentifiable, black-colored animal forms the figure's face. The ovular references in the final image, twin watercolor forms that resemble a pair of embryonic sacs, harken back to the first image in the series. The sacs share two stems, one at the bottom composed of paint and the other a folded leg wearing fishnet stockings at the top, as a pair of green apples hover at the right outer edge of the rounded form.

Family Tree of 2012 elaborates on the limits of hybridity and multiracialism by directly addressing the peculiar evolution of Blackness—its location and its origins—vis-à-vis filial ties. Made specifically for the artist's 2013 traveling survey show, *Family Tree* is a set of individually framed collages of various sizes presented as a genealogical chart. Appropriated imagery from a variety of sources, namely *El cuerpo del hombre*, a colonial Spanish publication of anatomical prints published in 1843, iconic African photography books, and motorcycle magazines, as well as hand-drawn and painted elements comprise the thirteen composite images. Drawn lines connect the characters in the collages: an original ancestral pair, their three offspring (two of whom have partners), and six grandchildren. The primordial ancestral pair Original Sky and Original Land sit side-by-side at the top of the family tree, joining the celestial with the terrestrial. Original Sky is an amalgam of human, animal, tree, and mechanical parts. Its head is a large egg-shaped, porcelain-colored cowry shell from which flayed forearms and hands hang. A bird's feathered wing protrudes from the back of the shell, and a muscular chest forms the figure's torso. The figure's lower half is made of a hornet's nest, motorcycle parts, a white telephone and its cord, and a pair of pale breasts for knees. Its slender, long-reaching sinewy arms are drawn, not collaged. A totem composed of tree bark, a snapping turtle claw, interlocking metal cogs, and hair dangle from the figure's left hand.

Original Land is a behemoth of stone, draped fabric, straw, and pearls set against a painted background of blue, white, grey, purple, and gold. For the head, a portion of *Surma Bride*, a photograph printed in the 2002 version of Carol Beckwith and Angela Fisher's controversial book, *African Ceremonies*, is layered atop the profile of a white, European, aristocratic male. A toucan bird perches at the center of the figure's forehead, and sunrays made of cut triangles of wood paneling extend from behind the figure's head. A tree limb forms the figure's spine, bisecting the image down the middle and rising up to jut across the figure's collaged face. The next generation of figures situated just below the ancestral pair to the right and left displays features of their forebears. First Hoofed Spawn on the right side of the tree is a composite figure of cut-out bird heads, voluminous feathers, clothes, a human baby, the portrait of an aristocratic white male, mechanical joints, and hand-drawn lines that demarcate a humanoid female figure. The figure's body is covered in silver foil patches in a pattern reminiscent of the stone torso at the center of Original Land. "Stabbed spouse," the partner of First Hoofed Spawn, is pictured in profile, turned toward her partner. The figure's face and upper body are a mix of disparate parts: the upper half of a Black woman's face, hand-drawn fangs, a hand, lips, a tarsier, and blonde hair that cascades down the figure's neck and upper back. A small tree branch with colorful bird feathers attached to its end punctures the red-and-blue, hand-drawn veins at the back of the figure's neck, creating a festering wound.

Ruptured bodies, wounds, and blood spatter mark the progeny of First Hoofed Spawn and Stabbed Spouse. Red and pink paint stains the lower right corner of Blue Lips, and dismembered body parts float at the left edge of Guts Smile. The main figure in Guts Smile looks grotesque and diseased; a picture of a digestive tract and uneven red and pink splotches of paint cover its face and neck. In both Blue Lips and Guts Smile, the simulated blood is not only a sign of injury or illness, but also an intergenerational transfer of trauma and rupture (of bodies, of organs, of bloodlines) that arises from the zones of contact—between races, species, cultures, and materials—in the series. Most importantly, the visualization of this transfer of trauma in *Family Tree* is asymmetrical. On the left side of the tree for instance, Second Snake Spawn, Lung Spouse, and their three offspring appear almost centered and balanced in their compositions, even as they register the zones of disjointed contact and violent relatedness unique to collage and racial belonging at the core of Mutu's practice. Meanwhile, Prodigal Sun Daughter on the far-left side of the tree reveals the perverse undesirability at the heart of the artist's project.

Estranged from the group, Prodigal Sun Daughter is the descendant of Original Sky, the last independent collage of the series to be completed, and the largest of the collages in *Family Tree*. She stands apart from her kin not just in size and distance; she is unique among her siblings in that she has no spouse, no offspring, and no line connecting her to a second parent. She is an outcast whose difference is amplified by vibrant color, a silver foil sun, and glitter, which gives her surrounding world a luminosity and lavishness distinct from the generally sparse white backgrounds of her kin. Her estrangement, her singularity, and the ways in which she defies the norms of reproductive futurity fulfilled by her siblings prefigure a broken genealogy—a natal alienation. This distinction illustrates what Kristine Stiles terms "eons of successive, dispersed generations of the broken genealogy of humanity" that "appear in each figure of *Family Tree*."[95] True to her name, the Prodigal Sun Daughter behaves recklessly in her apartness, in both collage form and in the anti-social gulf that exists between her and her prolific kin. Even as her eyes gaze up at her forebear, she shows no signs of returning home or repenting for whatever prodigal sin she has committed. Thus, rather than "a plurality that could lead to progressive forms of intercultural dialogue," as Stiles imagines, Mutu's collages posit violence, asymmetry, recklessness, and dismemberment as constitutive of filial and racial kinship.[96] From the prodigal sun daughter to the alien mother, the act of creation for Mutu is an act of alienation.

Ultimately, Mutu's cyborgs undermine normative notions of matter and reproductive futurity precisely *because* they are undesirable in their depictions of racial and gender embodiment *as* dismemberment. Her nameless, "inappropriate/d," fugitive, otherworldly racialized women carry with them a dangerous, inassimilable otherness while the compositional logic of her densely layered collages resists complete apprehension. Adding to the boldness of her art of refusal is the sociocultural critique embedded within it, a critique concerning the historical trauma of slavery and Black women's pathologies, which finds its suitable expression in collage: the medium refuses the potential for wholeness and coherence just as her pictures refuse to cohere within our field of vision.

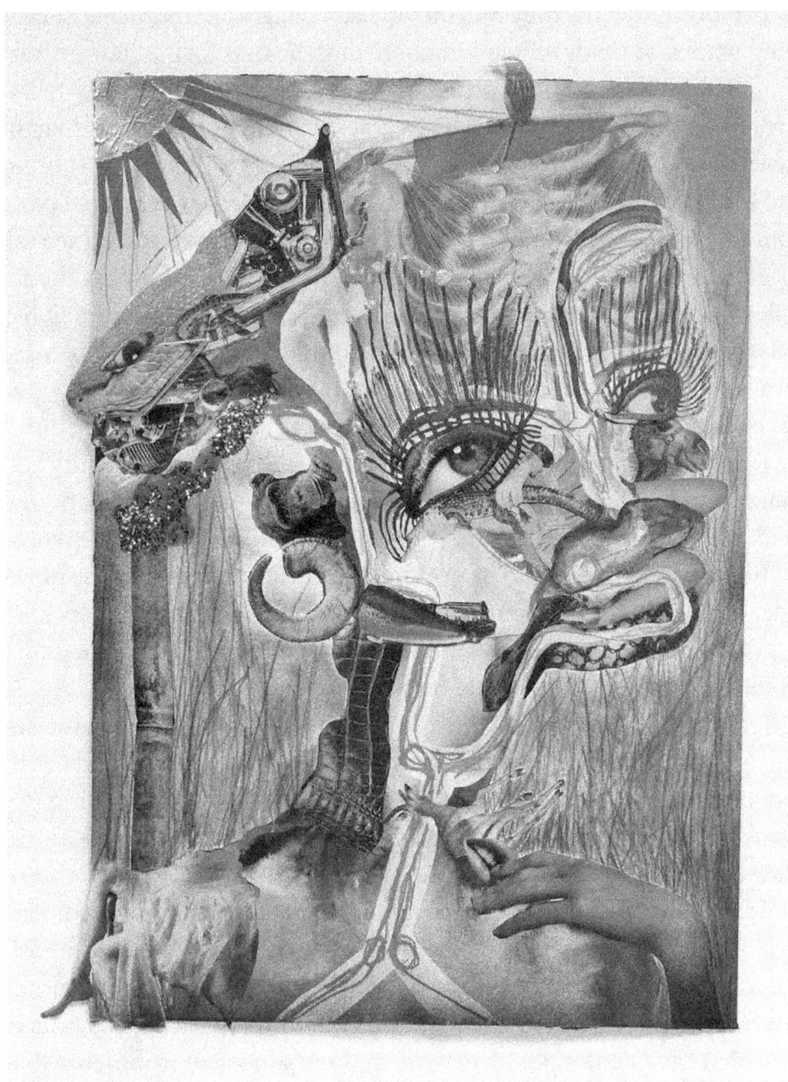

Figure 2.5. Wangechi Mutu, Prodigal Sun Daughter from *Family Tree*, 2012. Suite of thirteen, Mixed-media collage on paper, 16.25 × 12.25 in (41.28 × 31.12 cm). Collection of the Nasher Museum of Art at Duke University, museum purchase with additional funds provided by Trent Carmichael (T'88, P'17), Blake Byrne (T'57), Marjorie and Michael Levine (T'84, P'16), Stefanie and Douglas Kahn (P'11, P'13), and Christen and Derek Wilson (T'86, B'90, P'15). © Wangechi Mutu. Photo credit: Peter Paul Geoffrion.

"As composites," Courtney Martin writes, "collages are incapable of ever being whole, or made whole again. . . . In their new form, they are part of an unsolvable unit; the fracture of edges and angles giving way to fissures unsealed by glue or a cohesive background."[97] Indeed, as Martin suggests, even in the process of its making, collage is undone.[98] Thus, to read Mutu's collages properly, we must "first decompose the sutured parts from the composed whole," as Okwui Enwezor instructs, for "to see the images clearly, one has to strip the accreted parts, as if performing the act of decollage from the dense field of images."[99] Significantly, reading her collages *properly* entails acknowledging that the bodies they depict are always undone by acts of aggressive separation. The figures that populate the artist's collages do not naturally or predictably "come together;" they instead revel in the intervals between species, between identity and image, and between the individual racialized, gendered body and the collective. Consequently, Mutu's work suggests that Black female reproduction and reparation as the grounds for racial and gender kinship—indeed reproduction *as* reparation—are incommensurable. Repeated acts of dismemberment disavow bodily coherence, unity, and the future promise of social and historical transformation.

Both Walker and Mutu underscore the analogy between racism and speciesism, and the gender-based subjugation that subtends both phenomena. The Black female bottom and non-relationality vis-à-vis dismemberment recast human-nonhuman relationships during an era when digital imaging modalities, surveillance technologies, and forms of synthetic and machine-made media proliferate alongside Black women's visibility in popular culture and the art market. In this milieu, decomposition as rot, decay, planned ruin, and dismemberment emerges as a means and method for survival. Yet these Black feminist visions, the bodies on which they center, and the toxic and nebulous environments that surround them remain vulnerable and tenuous. In so doing, they shift the grounds and conditions for human and nonhuman entanglements and their attendant power dynamics away from an ethos of transcendence, enfolding viewers and critics into unruly and counterintuitive confrontations with the persistence of anti-Black racism and contemporary environmental crisis that refuses redemption and resolve. They also proffer performances of self-regard that pivot on self-disavowal, a strategy at the heart of both Xaviera Simmons and Narcissister's art that unsettles cohesive conceptions of Blackness and womanhood. What results is a politics without a program spurred by the aporias that Black womanhood's reproduction without futurity precipitates—a valuable and ethical undoing—that comes into view via opacity and race play in the following chapters.

3

Against Revelation

If the human body is the primary archive for the image state of photography, then what happens when the body is raced? If the epidermal signifier is read as a trace that race leaves on the body, then what kind of materiality is supposed by this interpretation? What is the "matter" of race?
—Alessandra Raengo

What possibilities of black subjectivity lie at the interstices of hypervisibility and disappearance?
—Krista Thompson

The pornographic grotesquerie, vivid imagery, and explicit perversion of undesirability and her sisters coalesce into an anti-redemptive ethics of representation and relation that stems from severing individual and collective attachments to the procreative promise of Black women's visual work. The artists in this book meet expectations of repair, salvation, social transformation, and womanhood itself with inscrutability at the level of celebrity, creativity, reproduction, wholeness, community building, and political participation. In so doing, they expand theories of intersectionality within the art world and the wider world. For Xaviera Simmons, who shares with Walker and Mutu an affinity for picturing Black female bodies in space, this inscrutability is material, metaphorical, and methodological. Like Mutu, Simmons engages origin stories—from extant allegorical artworks and their histories to identity myths—to consider the particular modes of reproduction and becoming that inhere in the photographic process.

Simmons's images combine performance and historical reenactment to destabilize narratives of the past narrowly constructed to privilege seemingly progressive aspects of the present, such as social transformation, democratic idealism, and racial comity. Deconstructing normative narratives is also a means for Simmons to interrogate cultural myths surrounding her own identity as a Black heterosexual female artist.[1] To do this she exploits photography's indexical properties by innovatively working between analog and digital photography. "Photography is about light and how your eye deals with light," she says, and her approach to making images is equally influenced by the materiality of film—"the (film) negative"—and digital processes, which she admits "are so [much] a part of our lives."[2] Whether shooting on film, hand printing her photographs in a darkroom, or relying on digital feed print, Simmons's process centers on the conditions of the photographic image and the historical space in which it is made. This focus extends to how Blackness functions as an index of both racial and gender belonging and becoming that is ultimately undone by her manipulations of the reproductive limits of photography and reenactment as a mode of (racial) performance. Consequently, her art demonstrates how photography's material conditions have and remain contingent upon Black female embodiment before and after the post-Black and digital turns. Her work also disrupts the assumed contiguity between photography and reality, as well as between Black skin and Black identity, in the new millennium.

Like Mutu's collages, Simmons's photographs destabilize how surface and depth, as well as rupture and repair, condition individual and collective acts of seeing and knowing Black female subjectivity. Her work, which critics have described as potent, unsettling, jarring, and elliptical, has been the subject of solo shows at David Castillo Gallery in Miami, the Kitchen in New York, and the Queens Museum in New York, as well as public art and group exhibitions that explore the meaning of freedom and justice in the new millennium.[3] Despite this attention, she differs from both Walker and Mutu in that there is a dearth of both arts criticism and scholarship on her expansive, multidisciplinary practice. In this way, she, along with Narcissister in the next chapter, occupies an alternate yet additionally minor position within this book in two ways: her art world 'status' and at the level of the artwork itself, where tensions emerge between hyper-visibility and invisibility.

Throughout her oeuvre, Simmons confounds viewers' ability to recognize various surfaces as themselves—land, objects, skin—by shape shifting between the genres of landscape and portraiture. In *Landscape (Two Women)* of 2007, two brown bodies, pictured in profile, hold each

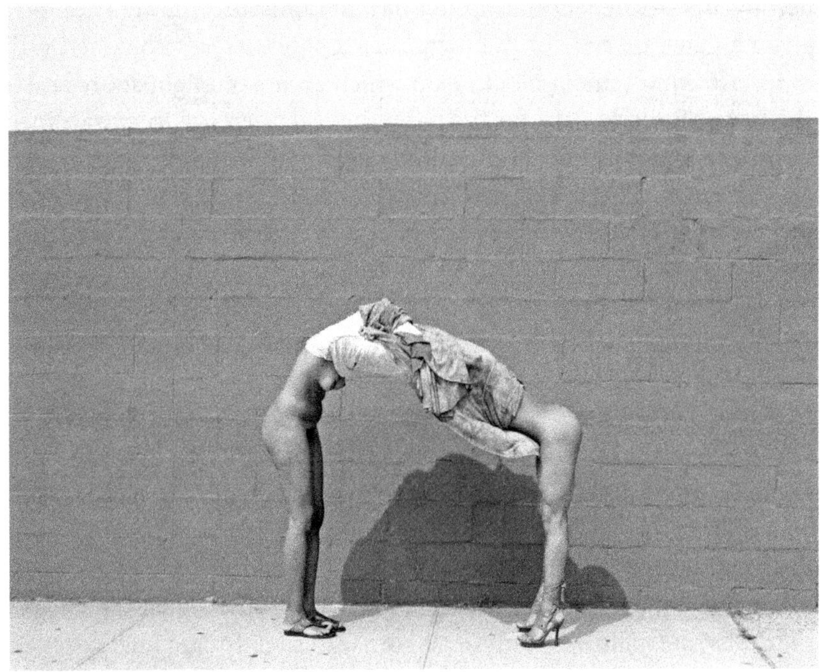

Figure 3.1. Xaviera Simmons, *Landscape (Two Women)*, 2017. Chromogenic color print, 30 × 40 in. Courtesy the artist and David Castillo. © Xaviera Simmons.

other as they bend forward at the waist with their garments flipped over their heads. Seen without pants, large portions of the figures' bodies appear nude, a stark contrast to their hidden faces. They are posed against a red block wall and seem to support one another, forming the shape of an arched bridge or any number of the red-rock formations found in the high-desert landscapes that pervade Simmons's oeuvre. The left-hand figure stands in flip-flops, toes curled up, breasts exposed. The other, slightly more covered, sports red stiletto sandals that wrap around the ankle.

Simmons's subjects join the other unruly "sisters" in this book in cultivating an alternative ethics of representation that obscures subjectivities and thwarts clear-cut interpretations of sisterhood and solidarity. *Landscape (Two Women)* pictures brown-skinned bodies in a bridge, a structure of support used to connect two points separated by distance and a word for reconciling conflict. But the anonymity of the scene betrays the covalent meaning that *bridge* connotes. Viewers are only given a general sense of the location—a sidewalk, a two-toned wall of interlocking cement blocks—on which an unseen light source casts shadows. Similarly, save for the parenthetical reference to two women in the photograph's title, limited amounts of physiognomic information are present such that viewers cannot confidently confirm the gender, or race, of the bodies pictured. Alternately, the figures see *each other* while viewers are not allowed "in" on that exchange. The bodies' shared exposed *surfaces*, therefore, are what connect them as "sister subjects" in the photograph. Yet their identities and location remain anonymous; they are nude and exposed but not known.

Just as *Landscape (Two Women)* draws the eye to various surfaces rather than to identity, *Beyond the Canon of Landscape (For Orhan. P, Zadie. S, Nia and Naima. M)* from 2008 withholds key physical features and information. In so doing, both photographs gesture beyond the body to complicate how self-fashioning in portraiture and landscape have come to mean and matter to Black female subjectivity in the digital age. *Beyond the Canon of Landscape* features a figure with slightly bent knees dressed from the waist down in an opaque black leotard and semi-opaque black tights. Although the figure's body is center frame, the image is slightly off kilter. In a room with a bright red wall, a white floorboard, and wood flooring, the body leans to the left, and the bottom of the image does not line up with the floorboard in the background. Symmetry is not the aim here, and the image is cropped such that viewers cannot see the subject's ankles and feet. From the waist up, a piece of cerulean-colored fabric covers the figure's face and most of the body. Pinned into the shape of a skirt that is flipped up as if held by a pair of hands out of frame or thrust into the air by a gust of wind from below, the fabric hides as much, if not more, than it reveals.

These two photographs demonstrate how bodies and subjects can remain radically opaque *despite* "visibility" (i.e., nudity or bold presence) at the same time that Simmons reconfigures reified genres within art history. In the history of art, pictures of figures—portraits—have been considered sources of self-fashioning and becoming where the expressivity of the face is seen to render the likeness and individuality of the subject at its center. Portraiture in this outmoded formulation functions as a narrative account, *an index*, of the figure's personality as well as the artist's acumen

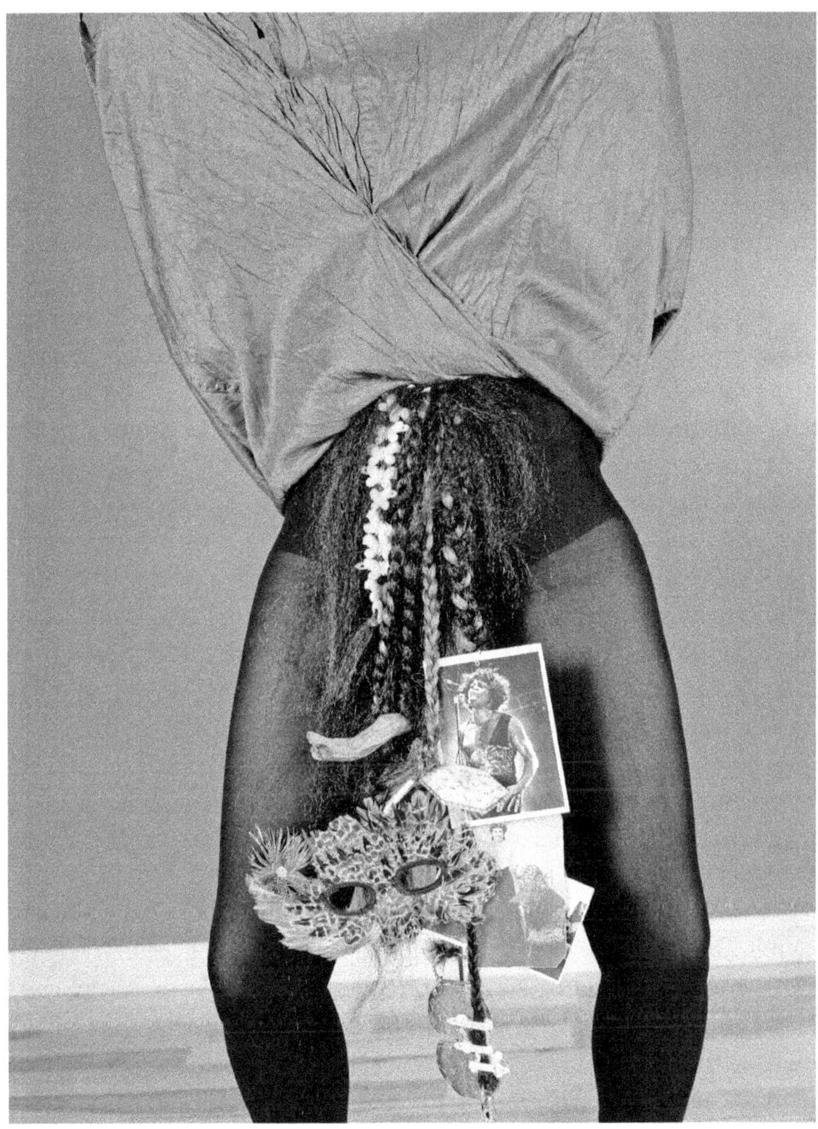

Figure 3.2. Xaviera Simmons, *Beyond the Canon of Landscape (For Orhan. P, Zadie. S, Nia and Naima. M)*, 2008. Chromogenic color print. Courtesy the artist and David Castillo. © Xaviera Simmons.

in conveying the subject's distinctive character. *Landscape (Two Women)* and *Beyond the Canon of Landscape* are early examples of Simmons's highly conceptual approach to Black portraiture, landscape, surface aesthetics, and historical reenactment. Combining her training in fine art and fashion photography with acting and directing, the artist enfolds genres and techniques into one another. "Portraiture, landscape . . . these words are interchangeable to me," she tells longtime art critic Paul Laster in a 2015 interview.[4] The artist also repeatedly centers the body and its gestures. As a result, her images exist somewhere between staged portraits, landscape photography, and performance documentation, an ambiguity that produces surface visual effects that are, on the one hand, undesirable and counterintuitive, yet on the other, profoundly compelling.

According to comparative race scholar Anne Anlin Cheng, the history of modernist surfaces is coterminous with the violent history of skin, gender, and race. The dream "of a second skin," Cheng writes, "of remaking one's self in the skin of the other—is a mutual fantasy, one shared by both Modernists seeking to be outside of their own skins and by racialized subjects looking to escape the burdens of epidermal inscription."[5] Simmons's depictions of second-skin-as-surface and her covering of key bodily features offer new, sensuous conditions of possibility for apprehending the complicated social and political life of minoritarian subjects. This is particularly true of the photographs and videos where she paints herself in blackface, a subversion of modernism's fetishistic relationship with Black skin, and Black women's bodies and skin, in particular. The obdurate "sisters" in Simmons's images and their second skins lie at the interstices of hyper-visibility and opacity, refusing legibility on the one hand and upending conventional narratives about the social good of art and togetherness on the other. They also disaggregate the affective pull that the materiality of the photographic portrait and the indexicality of Black skin hold for twenty-first-century understandings of transparency and authenticity. Rather than crafting images of fixed identities that reconcile the fissure between absence and presence, exterior and interior, the figures in Simmons's found and staged portraits are often grainy and obscured, with parts of the body—namely the face—totally hidden. Here she enacts the very process of becoming an image while also performing an obdurate subjectivity that refuses full disclosure. These acts, along with the techniques of masking and self-disavowal that the artist employs in landscape photography and portraiture, constitute a language of opacity that, in Uri McMillan's summation, declines to adhere or submit to "the interpretative demands of readability, certitude, and transparency so often expected of artists of color."[6] Likewise, her presentations of Blackness spotlight how racial intelligibility is immediately made manifest in perception as well as the assumptive logics that link Black presence and representation with collective well-being and progress.

Bridging the limits of visibility and racial and gender kinship with the right to be unruly and unbecoming, Simmons's play with surface and skin upends common-sense expectations about Black women's reproductive capacities, both biologically and creatively. Her output defies well-worn norms concerning Black image making as a means of (self)-representation while exposing the irreconcilable gaps between identity and image. Such gestures do not spur racial and gender solidarity and justice in the wake of trauma and upheaval. Rather, the unbecoming she stages prompts viewers and critics to face what happens when the sign that is meant to independently represent its object is deemed an object itself. In this schema of objectification, as outlined in the first half of this book and in the next chapter, the Black female body is excessively expressive and socially constructed as an outlaw capable only of reproduction without futurity. Within and against these conditions, Simmons's images transmute invisible yet hyper-visible "sisters" into visible yet illegible figures that transform how race and gender have been thought within genres of portraiture and photographic theory.

Since the medium's inception, the utility and effects of photography have been hotly debated. Early thinking on photography considered the medium to be indexical, that is, transparent and truthful, or, to put it another way, contiguous with the real.[7] In the latter half of the twentieth century, conceptual and post-conceptual photographers who became known as the Pictures generation exploited the contingent relation between presence and absence that inheres in the medium.[8] Doing so effected, per Douglas Crimp, an "unbridgeable distance from the original, from even the possibility of an original," and by extension, a referent.[9] Even though visual media producers, viewers, and critics now know better, questions concerning the referential, reclamatory, and emancipatory power of photographic images—both analog and digital—persist, especially within the current internet culture of selfies and deep fakes.

In "Objects of Affect: Photography beyond the Image," visual and historical anthropologist Elizabeth Edwards asks, "What are the material and affective performances through which photographs might become a form of history or engagement with, and reclamation of the past?"[10] Edwards's appeal to sensory effects beyond the visual represents a growing interdisciplinary interest in the impact and efficacy of new materialisms that animates the "post"-ness of contemporary art and identity throughout this book. Concurrent debates concerning authentic Blackness as a primary tenet of African diasporic identification have also gained more traction in the new millennium. Simmons's visual work addresses these issues head on by exacerbating the chasm between surface and depth that arises from photography's imbrication with the Black female body. Hiding more than they reveal, her images test the reproductive potential of photography and the Black female body as indexical objects of memory, as traces of absence, presence, and progress.

Additionally, during the years that Simmons has been active, calls for surveillance technology and government transparency have intensified both nationally and globally in response to various security crises. These calls are entangled with anti-Blackness and histories of what Black studies scholar Simone Browne calls "racializing surveillance—when enactments of surveillance reify boundaries along racial lines, thereby reifying race, and where the outcome of this is often discriminatory and violent treatment."[11] Demands for accountability often hinge on the presumption that emergent visual mediums, digital imaging, and the internet are race neutral and that increased visibility and transparency inherently create a more just and equitable world. The struggle for visibility and inclusion has also been the crux of Black representational space, a politics of racial reckoning that has been foundational to the study of Black diasporic visual culture at and after the turn of the twenty-first century. For Black British cultural studies scholar Stuart Hall, whose influence continues to permeate contemporary accounts of art of the Black diaspora and minoritarian aesthetic practice, the struggle to come into representation "was predicated on a critique of the degree of fetishization, objectification and negative figuration which are so much a feature of the representation of the black subject."[12] These concerns were "not only with the absence or marginality of the black experience but with its simplification and its stereotypical character."[13] This measure of Black self-determination links a drive for recognition to a politically viable and visible identity in individual and group terms.

Emblematically, *Beyond the Canon of Landscape* undermines its own generic codes as a container for selfhood and memory, even as the names between the title's parentheses read as an ode or a dedication. Between the figure's legs in the photograph hangs a hodgepodge of items: a black-and-white postcard featuring an image of James Brown singing, a feathered mask, a vintage portrait photograph of an unnamed woman, bundles of synthetic hair both loose and braided, and two vintage compact mirrors, among other things. All these bear some relation to constructing the self, whether through performance, masking, portrait photography, hairstyles, or the actual application of makeup and cosmetics, the topos of which has been used in art practice from the Renaissance onward.

Self-fashioning, a term introduced into literary criticism by Stephen Greenblatt in *Renaissance Self-Fashioning: From More to Shakespeare* (1980), generally describes the process of constructing one's identity and public persona according to a set of social norms.[14] This process presupposes a series of reveals in which a sitter's innermost being is not only discernible and accessible, but transparently so. Portraiture's "transparent visual rhetoric," according to art historian Joanna Woodall, "was broadly seen to privilege truth to the appearance of the subject over the [artist's] mediation," a logic that became the basis for photography as a means of self-representation.[15] Photography, in turn, buttressed the desire for transparent likeness, as the medium "was considered to guarantee an inherent, objective visual relationship between the image and the living model."[16] By this logic, capturing both the subject's likeness and trace in the form of a portrait imbues photography with the ability to capture and assert a kind of constant presence in the face of separation, absence, and death. This re-presentation subsequently produces "a unifying revelatory encounter between subject [the internal character of the sitter] and object [the faithful likeness of that person's external appearance]."[17] Simmons's staged portraits behave differently. Through various instantiations of refusal, reversal, withholding, and unbecoming, they work against revelation.

Although historians of Western art in the United States and Europe now question the validity of Greenblatt's concept of self-fashioning because of how it centers white maleness while ignoring the politics of the body, the practice is a vital feature of Black artistic production. The reciprocal relationship between portraiture and self-presentation takes on new dimensions when applied to the study of historically marginalized subjects and their self-imaging processes. As Gwendolyn DuBois Shaw tells us, artists produced dynamic images of Black sitters in efforts to create enduring symbols of self-possessed identity from the American Revolution to the Civil War into the Gilded Age.[18] Simultaneously, many of these portraits provide a window into cultural stereotypes and practices of their time because they picture generalized types rather than distinct, named individuals. By the middle of the nineteenth century, photography offered Black sitters an affordable and accessible way to fashion individual identities. In the case of Black artists creating art in their own images, portraiture is seen to record and assert a sitter's presence in the absence of adequate or culturally sensitive representations. In what art historian Richard J. Powell calls "cutting a figure," African Americans marshal a particular kind of self-conscious performance in photographic and painted portraits in the nineteenth and twentieth centuries to subvert the popular, stereotypical representations that emerged in the wake of slavery's constitutional abolition. By evincing such traits as self-composure, self-adornment, and self-imagining, Black subjects, according to Powell, were able to craft alternative images of their own making imbued with social capital and power that counterposed public misconceptions about Black identity and interiority.

Simmons's critiques of art history and Black diasporic kinship invite viewers and scholars to engage more decisively with how sociopolitical life informs artistic production that wrestles with the origins and effects of racial and gender difference. Her work also underscores shifting anxieties about photography's evolution, authorship, and authenticity. Here, attachments to the power of self-representation persist in light of claims concerning the particulars of post-identity, specifically humans as "post-human," Americans as "post-race," art as inhabiting a post-medium condition, and contemporary Black art as post-Black.[19] The "post" at the fore of all these terms evokes a sense of liberation from past constraints, tropes, and expectations, a juncture flanked by renewed interests in racial reparations (legally and aesthetically), on the one hand, and hopes concerning multiracialism and intersectional feminism in the new millennium, on the other. This milieu and Simmons's engagement with it is compelling for many reasons. For the past two decades, new technologies in the realm of digital imaging, biotechnology, and social media applications such as Instagram (now Meta) have impacted not only the circulation of images but also the authority of the photographer. Additionally, in a world where race and gender continue to be read on and through the surface of the body as traces, as exteriorizations of some kind of innate difference despite post-identity claims, Simmons's images defuse the idea that visibility and transparency—between perception and knowledge and between the state and society—are viable markers of both presence and progress.

This chapter explores how the hyper-visible yet illegible Black forms in Simmons's art function as enactments of opacity that upend the interpretive demands of transparency and authenticity so often expected of artists of the Black diaspora. Because of the ways they gesture beyond themselves and amplify various surfaces, the landscape photographs, "self"-portraits, performative reenactments, and hyper-black images discussed in the following pages bring new meaning to the "post"-ness of contemporary art. By troubling what is lost and gained from privileging visibility as a salve for racial and gender subjugation in the past and present, her practice of opacity and inscrutability redefines the contours of progress and empowerment in an era of new racial and gender meaning. Spotlighting how Black women artists self-consciously navigate the fraught terrain of Black image making and progressive politics in the new millennium, Simmons's visual work unravels widespread expectations that portraiture, landscape, and skin should evidence, much less recover and repair, historical experience. It also undermines the presumption that increased visibility and transparency can yield reparative justice.

Queering Form in Landscape and Portraiture

Simmons first developed her interests in photography, portraiture, and landscape as an undergraduate student at Bard College.[20] Nestled in New York State's Hudson Valley, the area surrounding Bard is the birthplace of the Hudson River school, a mid-nineteenth-century American painting movement. Thomas Cole, Thomas Doughty, Asher Durand, and other early members of the school painted detailed, idealized portrayals of human figures peacefully coexisting with nature, a kind of romanticism that served as a vehicle for transmitting such themes as discovery, exploration, and settlement. This propensity for picturing the American landscape as rugged, untouched, and vastly unexplored terrain on the one hand and as a sublime, pastoral setting on the other inspired Simmons to think about "the history of painting and photography and characters that didn't populate or own those spaces," to expand romantic notions of landscape to include characters typically missing from such scenes.[21]

Although she is often one of the subjects or the only subject pictured in her staged photographs, Simmons does not consider her images to be self-portraits. In this way, she builds on extant feminist genealogies of photography and performance that question the nature of self-representation and sisterhood. Her "pieces," she tells us, "are a little different than, say, Cindy Sherman's."[22] Widely recognized as one of the most influential contemporary artists, Sherman worked as her own model for the first thirty years of her career. To create her images, she assumes multiple roles—photographer, model, makeup artist, hairdresser, stylist, and wardrobe mistress—and plays various characters and caricatures found in mass media and art history, from screen siren to clown to unhappy housewife to aging socialite.

In questioning who has had access to both representation and freedom in art history and feminism, Simmons hews more closely to Carrie Mae Weems, Lorna Simpson, Renee Cox, and Deana Lawson.[23] All four artists make staged portraits of themselves or others performing characters and stereotypes in different environments. Yet by repeatedly turning away from the camera, appropriating and transmogrifying racist imagery, and deconstructing art history's Eurocentrism, these Black women artists use their practices to confront issues of race, gender, cultural work, and activism. As a peer, Lawson is a particularly relevant comparison for Simmons. She, too, has been investigating the limits of photographic language since the early 2000s. But she directs the medium and the camera to very different ends than Simmons.

Drawing on the family album, studio portraiture, staged tableaux, documentary pictures, and appropriated images for inspiration, Lawson meticulously poses her subjects—familiar acquaintances as well as strangers she meets on the street.[24] Her desires for control, her use of nude

Black female subjects, and her growing acclaim has made her the target of vitriolic criticism. Although she aims to cultivate intersubjective unions with her photographic subjects, the ways her images oscillate between social realism and exploitation have raised questions about what counts as ethical practice in the arts. Other concerns about authority, agency, authenticity, and racial and gender kinship have also emerged. "In a world where Black female bodies are continually exploited in real life and in art," Gwendolyn DuBois Shaw writes, "I am not sure there is true willing consent in Lawson's prurient nudes."[25] In a *Hyperallergic* op-ed review of the artist's 2021 exhibition at the Guggenheim Museum in New York, a celebration of Lawson's 2020 Hugo Boss Prize, Shaw evokes the language of sisterhood, class difference, and debasement to critique the artist's representations of sex work, consent, and "troublesome, pornotropic strategies of artistic mastery" on the part of the photographer.[26] For Shaw, the "glossy lighting and shiny skin" that structures many of Lawson's images result in a formal grammar that is "resoundingly commercial" and pornographic.[27] In the face of ongoing anti-Black violence, the art historian and critic worries that the artist's images do little to change how Black people, and Black women in particular—sisters in the collective sense and in the familial sense for Shaw—are seen in the space of galleries and museums.[28]

Simmons's unbecoming mobilizations of opacity and sisterhood as well as her use of photography and skin as technologies of light and power differ from Lawson's approach to hyper-visibility in crucial ways. While both artists amplify the surface aesthetics of Black skin, Lawson's compositions are highly orchestrated at the level of revelation, visibility (i.e., nudity), and commercial appeal. Alternately, she focuses on her subjects' gazes and faces, a method that curators and critics imbue with political import. As Shaw outlines, "the searing gazes of Lawson's subjects are often referenced as the method by which her images subvert or challenge the violence that photography has historically imposed on the Black body."[29] In a 2018 essay on the artist's work, art historian Steven Nelson argues that the stares of Lawson's subjects "place our focus not on their naked bodies or on the acts in which they may be engaged, but on their faces."[30] As a result, "Lawson's figures, aware of being seen, watch us watch them—and in doing so, our very right to look at them is called into question."[31] In addition to emphasizing hyper-visibility, Shaw and Nelson also underscore how theories of the face, gaze, and body continue to drive analyses of post-Black portraiture where showing too much skin poses a problem for the project of racial and gender kinship and empowerment.

This context makes Simmons's minor strategies of withholding and indirection in tandem with portrayals of hyper-black skin and other surfaces even more noteworthy. Her opaque and highly conceptual work *works* to disavow the reproductive capacities of the Black female body and photography in the digital age by gesturing beyond themselves to unsettle the integrity of artifice and its relationship to identity performance. One of the effects of this, in my view, is a subtle yet self-conscious critique of the rate at which Black-made images of Black figures flood the art market in the United States and abroad. Such images have become more than financial investments, doubling as fungible commodities and cross-cultural symbols of "wokeness" in the age of Black Lives Matter. Against this backdrop of cultural cache and institutional calls for visibility, diversity, equity, and inclusion, Simmons's measured productivity, her refusal to identify as the self in her portraits, and her formal and aesthetic maneuvers of withholding and unbecoming circumvent the gratuitous forms of surveillance and assault that Black women endure in the twenty-first century.

Many of the actions Simmons performs are new versions of poses, characters, and settings that already exist in image form, the sources for which come from the Western art historical canon of portraiture and landscape. For these images, Simmons uses a large-format 4×5 camera to capture images of herself standing and pointing or reading maps within unspecified locales. In *Canyon* (2010), for example, she stands at the edge of a cliff dressed in black with her hair in braided pigtails. Her brownish gold blazer compliments the earthen tones of the landscape, and behind her the steep slopes of two mountains form a V that further outlines her form. In *Maps*, also from 2010, a disheveled Black female traveler pauses before a backdrop of weathered red rock to read a map. She seems to have cut a path through the rough desert landscape, and her clothes show patches of red dirt and dust, indications of her arduous journey. A camera, a duffle bag, and some additional maps are strewn out on the ground beside her. Just above the map's lower corner, the word "Utah" is visible. Yet, as curator Jill Dawsey concludes, "this is not a photograph

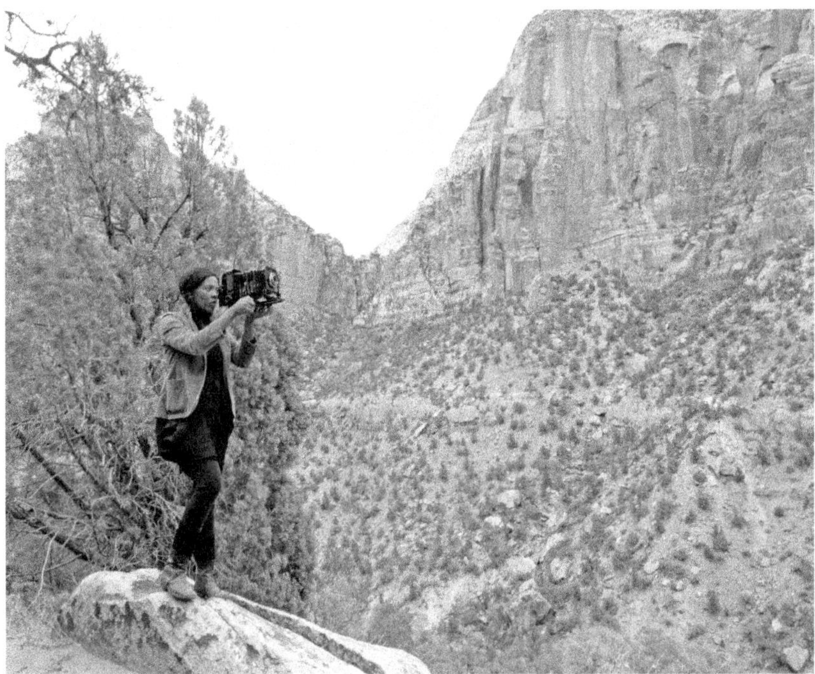

Figure 3.3. Xaviera Simmons, *Canyon*, 2010. Chromogenic color print, 30 × 40 in. Courtesy the artist and David Castillo. © Xaviera Simmons.

of Utah, any more than this is a portrait of Xaviera Simmons, who appears as the traveler holding the map."[32] It is a photograph of an idea, a desire that undergirds the genre of landscape. In a third image from 2010, *Composition One for Score A*, Simmons is a stately figure dressed in black. She stands in the foreground left of center among dusty desert weeds and cuts a silhouette against a pale gray sky. With one hand on her hip, she points into the distance with her other hand and arm outstretched, guiding the eye toward the ridges and plateaus behind her. Simmons repeats this gesture in most of her landscape photographs, a reference to the visual history of Manifest Destiny and a trope most associated with Western landscape painting.

Playing "the photographer" and inserting herself, a Black woman, into the canon contests histories of art wherein white men have almost exclusively occupied the role of landscape painter, photographer, and pioneer.[33] "Who, historically and traditionally," she asks, "gets to exist

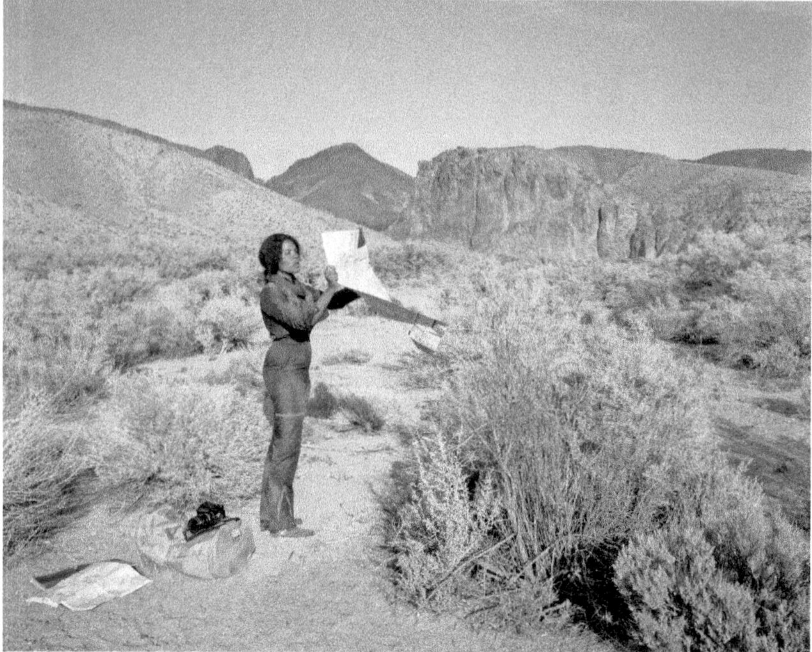

Figure 3.4. Xaviera Simmons, *Maps*, 2010. Chromogenic color print. 30 × 40 in. Courtesy the artist and David Castillo. © Xaviera Simmons.

in the sublime with regards to landscape photography and landscape painting?"[34] When landscape photographer Carleton Watkins made a portrait of himself in 1883, he posed as a gold miner, playing a character just as Simmons does. Likewise, landscape painters, such as those of the Hudson River school, occasionally inserted miniscule portraits of themselves into scenes to provide a sense of scale, to claim their place in nature, and to demonstrate their ability to transform the materials of nature into artful representation. Ansel Adams's many heroic portraits of himself positioned behind his large format camera in dramatic locales in the wilderness extend this legacy into the late twentieth century.

Beyond performances of selfhood, landscape photography and painting in American art have existed explicitly to embody an ethos of nationalism and supremacy. Constructions of the individual and collective self in this genre obfuscate the legacies of imperial violence that ground it across mediums, whereby the whiteness and maleness of its makers elide and supersede the racial and gender difference of the land's inhabitants. Manifest Destiny is part of this. Figures in the landscape, not unlike depictions of such explorers as Lewis and Clark, point and look toward uncharted terrain, shorthand for future imperialist expansion and, by extension, "progress." In this regard, figures in the foreground and midground of picturesque landscapes are conventionally seen as mediators between the depicted scene and viewers, aids that construct imaginary experiences of the land and conditions of personhood by representing the prospect of habitation and human presence in wild, unusual, seemingly inhospitable places.[35]

Simmons's performances of underrepresented, racially divergent characters—from photographers to nomads and migrants to willful travelers to fairytale characters—exceed the demand to correct this trope. Recent studies of landscape highlight how the genre functions as a cultural practice of coactivity between humans and nature, self and other. Landscape as representation reveals a certain kind of desire, whether that desire has to do with ownership, with beauty, with obfuscating previous occupants, or with the labor that goes into "making" landscapes. In this way, landscape acts "as space, as environment, as that within which 'we' (figured as 'the figures' in the landscape) find—or lose—ourselves," as visual studies scholar W. J. T. Mitchell proclaims.[36] Historically, landscape has been "a dynamic medium, in which we 'live and move and have our being.'"[37] It is "a process by which social and subjective identities are formed," a process of becoming.[38] Simmons instead positions landscape as an overlooked site for exploring Black and Indigenous histories and subjectivities, and her elliptical, unbecoming performances of opacity hold open, rather than reconcile, the gap between past and present, sign and signified, identity and image.

Her figures do not exist in relationship to their surroundings as small and featureless bodies dwarfed by immense vistas, a metaphor for a fledgling individual (and national) self potentially overwhelmed by the vast frontier. Simmons's depictions of figures in transit without a clear transportation plan or destination in sight invoke a queer sense of unbecoming that arises from inhabiting an undesirable state of being outside the established social order. They illustrate her preoccupation with placing underrepresented characters in the landscape to create what the artist calls "other characters, narratives, and geographies" that are not proxies for subliminal self-discovery.[39] These "other" characters undermine the American landscape tradition as a mode of knowledge production as well as the power of location and recovery by inviting viewers into encounters with anonymous places and figures. In these works, Simmons is often nowhere in particular, en route between departure and arrival, and looking at maps. Her fabulations consequently upend conceptions of landscape as an idealized setting, an inert background, and a site for accounting for and actualizing the rugged American explorer.

Defying genre specificity also happens on the level of the self in Simmons's work. By punning on both character acting and the art of cosmetology—making up the self—her compositions short-circuit how we see the Black body in portraiture as an index of Black identity more broadly and the value of Black women's lives and labors specifically. In a profile piece in *Modern Painters*, she declares, "I don't consider any of the images that I'm in as self-portraits. . . . My pieces are about nebulous narrative, or an unofficial narrative, or a nonlinear narrative."[40] Simmons's phrasing here orients us toward a mode of becoming that, for the artist, necessarily entails a deferral of identity, an unbecoming.[41] Regarding her approach to portraiture and photography, the artist admits, "I'm trying to combine parts of different artistic practices, to almost force the portrait onto the photograph even if the face is not there, even if the figure is not there."[42] Forcing the portrait while at the same time eliding its conventions is an example of what Kadji Amin, Amber Musser, and Roy Pérez call "queer form" in that it activates sensuous, affective modes of meaning-making unbridled by narrow, prefabricated narratives about what Black women's art can and should do. Her elisions and refusals at the level of the self constitute another layer of opacity that counteracts portraiture's ability to evidence selfhood as well as the potential for skin-as-surface to produce affirmative knowledge about Black female being in a marketplace that continually surveils and lustfully consumes the Black figure.

Simmons's other staged portraits, especially those that double as landscapes, likewise queer their form by disrupting the conventions of indexicality and reenactment. In the context of theater, dance, and visual art performance, a reenactment is like a citation, a reference to a preexisting text; it is the action of performing a new version of an older, often categorically "classical" or "master" work of art. Historical reenactments function similarly. Actors perform a role in an event that occurred at an earlier time, recreating the past both for themselves and for spectators with the hope of knowing and understanding history more fully in the present.[43] Both forms of reenactment engender revisionist possibilities, whether performers try to produce a new work that is as close to the original as possible or they intentionally alter recognizable details. The former leaves room for interpretation in the translation from past event to present enactment, and the latter becomes a way to critique and ultimately undermine the authority of the master text.

In bringing practices of photography and historical reenactment together, Simmons joins a cohort of contemporary artists and critics who call attention to how the past continues to inhabit, even haunt, the present through the photographic medium in contemporary art. In *Photographic Returns: Racial Justice in the Time of Photography* (2020), Shawn Michelle Smith traces how historical moments of racial crisis (and gender crisis for my purposes) come to be known photographically. The Black and non-Black artists on whom Smith focuses—Carrie Mae Weems, Lorna Simpson, Dawoud Bey, and Jason Lazarus among them—use nineteenth-century techniques to recreate iconic historic photographs that mediate the unfinished political project of racial justice in the United States. Because of her techniques, Simmons's work could easily be included in this cohort. Her reenactments foreground how central the photographic image is to the American cultural imaginary as well as how race and gender have been pivotal to constructions of the American self. Yet her reenactments also push against the idea that a more just future lays at the ready vis-à-vis recovering the past or being able to see and be seen. By masking the face and parts of the body as the points of accountability for photographer, subject, and viewer, Simmons transgresses aesthetic and social norms concerning the reparative ethos of Black portraiture.

Index/Composition elaborates on this tendency by expanding the strategies of denial and refusal—of working against revelation—expressed in *Beyond the Canon of Landscape*. Found images and artifacts, from postcards to braided hair to textured fabrics, such as raffia and lace, hang like totems from the waist of the body pictured in the series. But none of the items are easily identifiable, nor is the body. The upper half of the body is wrapped in fabric like a cocoon, creating two contiguous yet

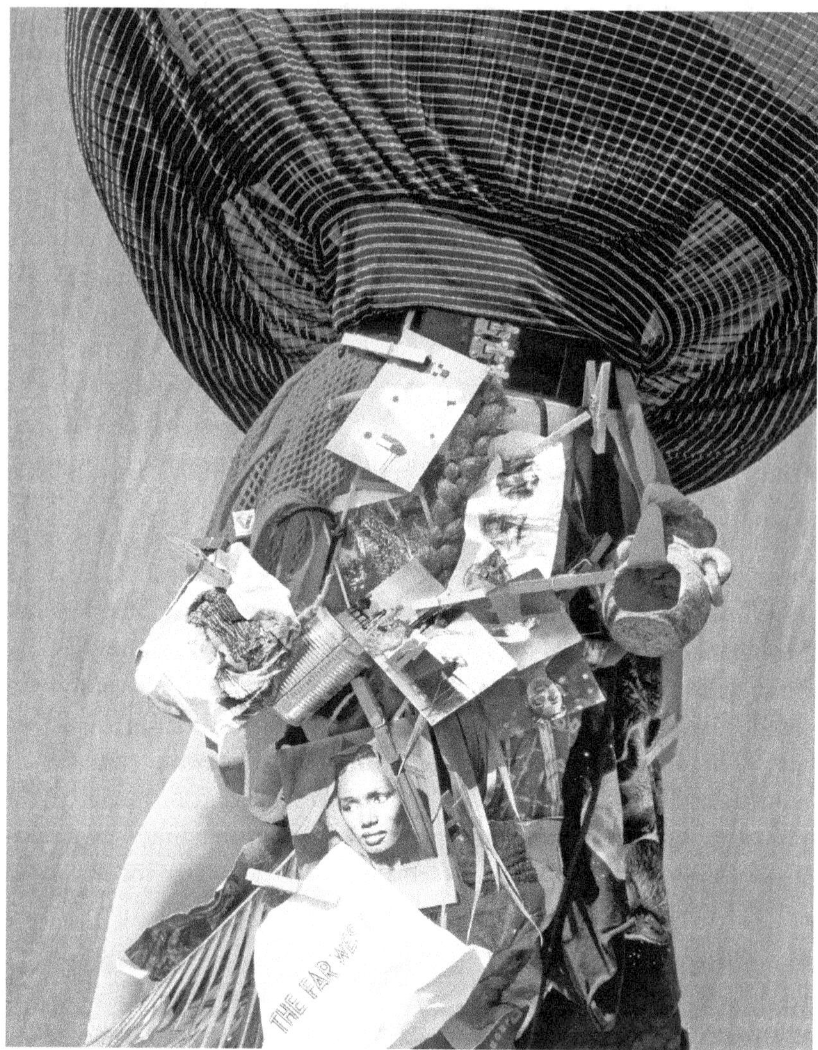

Figure 3.5. Xaviera Simmons, *Index Two, Composition Three*, 2012. Chromogenic color print, 50 × 40 in. Courtesy the artist and David Castillo. © Xaviera Simmons.

distinctly different object worlds that draw attention to the body's topography, its surface rather than its substance. The figures' fabric "skirts" are suspended overhead while the figures' middle and nether regions are exposed, playing a kind of peekaboo with the body's anatomy and expectations about its reproductive capacities.

Formally, the effacing, column-like arrangements in the *Index/Composition* series combine sculpture with the language of full-body portraiture. Theoretically, the series coalesces issues concerning photography, the index, and the self. In referencing sculpture, a medium fundamentally about space and its perception, Simmons employs an additive technique—the action of putting things together—that mirrors the act of composition itself as individual items are fastened to each other to create the larger work. Consequently, the body *becomes* a landscape through the process of accumulation, thus interchanging two genres that picture an imagined, or desired, reality meant to aestheticize space and ideals of selfhood. In some of the works, the body's skin color is visible; in most of the works, however, neither the body's race, its gender, nor its sex are easily discernible, a motif present in each iteration of the series. As the series progresses, the backgrounds for each new set of images, which range from wood paneling to black, white, and solid colors, remain fairly mundane. Meanwhile, the fabric patterns and totem configurations grow more sophisticated and complex. The focus of the series, consequently, is the body and its various states of concealment.

For one critic responding to Simmons's depiction of becoming in the series, "the body [acts] as a vessel and memory as the tangible object."[44] In this formulation, the body is a container of information that orders our senses of identity and spurs our ability to recollect past experiences. But Simmons's effacement of bodily surfaces, in my view, conveys a counterintuitive enactment of becoming—*an unbecoming*—that mirrors and, ultimately departs from, the one that critical theorist Gilles Deleuze describes in *A Thousand Plateaus*. Becoming, according to Deleuze, is not an evolution. Although it concerns alliance and coalition—"every becoming is a block of coexistence"—it is the continual production of difference initiated by a disruption of norms, a break or turning away from conventions, that makes said norms impossible to distinguish or see.[45] "To become," in other words, "is not to progress or regress along a series."[46] Becoming "is the movement by which the line frees itself from the point, and renders points indiscernible: the rhizome, the opposite of arborescence; break away from arborescence. *Becoming is an antimemory*."[47] In mathematics, and more specifically in graph theory, arborescence refers to a kind of data structure also known as a rooted tree, in which any two vertices are connected by exactly one directed path. In this formulation, branches of data spur and point away from the root, all the while maintaining their core attachment to it. This form of ordering information constrains certain possibilities for alternative modes of interpretation, of knowing, of being. As acts of unbecoming, Simmons's art turns away from coexistence and leans into non-disclosive subjectivity and sisterhood, thus proffering a different kind of relational model—a non-relationality—akin to the one that emerges in Mutu's work.

Along with withholding information, defiance and indirection are two other significant articulations of unbecoming and radical opacity on display in Simmons's work, and in *Index/Composition*, she once again folds one genre into the other, thereby defying their respective distinctions; a portrait becomes a landscape. Alternately, by covering the face and most of the body, the figure as a fully discernible "self" remains hidden, laden with totems and signs that are physically connected to the figure's body, but whose referents are irretrievable or out of view. Thus, instead of visual arguments that convince viewers of the ostensible reality and enduring presence of the subjugated self, Simmons's staged images punctuate the kinds of desire—namely, racial and sexual—that photography and its genres purportedly conjure. Her portraits, diasporic totems, and cloaked poses purposely do not reveal the "subject-self" pictured in them; they instead amplify surfaces—of disparate items, masked bodies, incongruous object worlds—that invite close looking, only to refuse access to any kind of interiority. Her images contest the very impulse to self-identify, and what lies beneath is ultimately unknowable.

The Opacity of Fact and Fiction

Similar to Walker's silhouettes that unsettle standards of etiquette at the meeting point between trace and race, Simmons's images trouble the index and its relationship to vision and value.[48] Portraiture and identity are not co-constitutive in her art, and she dismantles photography's ability to bear witness to past experience. Her pictures do not, as most portraits aim to do, provide information about the character, class, or vocation of the figures in them; and she adamantly refuses to specify both the self and the locations in her pictures. She also challenges how the medium—and its inherent reproducibility—is imbued with transformative, revelatory power. These activities force a distinction between the procreative capacities of

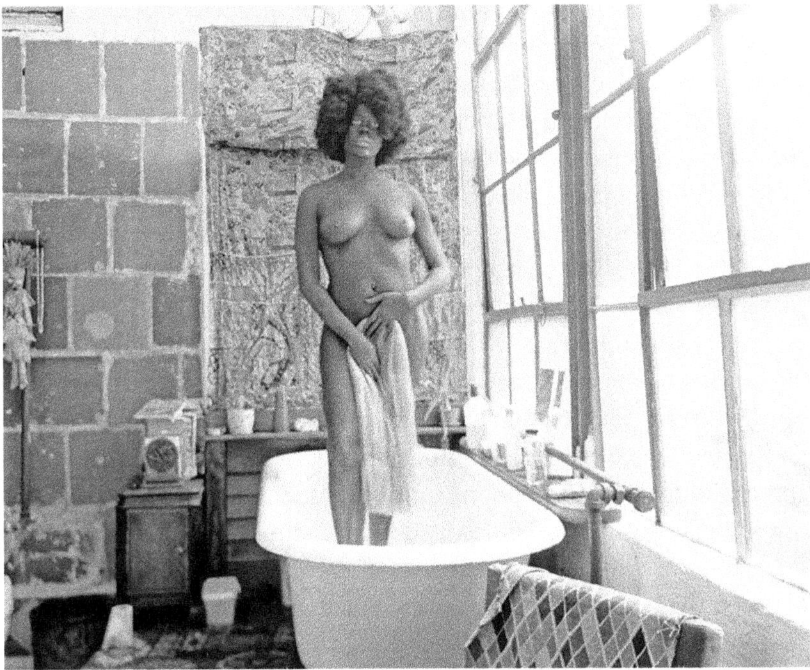

Figure 3.6. Xaviera Simmons, *Landscape (Home)*, 2005. Chromogenic color print, 30 × 40 in. Courtesy the artist and David Castillo. © Xaviera Simmons.

representation and the reproductive body as fixed, unchanging, mystical sites of memory work. Thus, rather than "photography as a public act of bearing witness and . . . as an expressive act of self-exploration," as Kobena Mercer puts it in his writing on Black diasporic portraiture, Simmons uses the photochemical imagination to different ethical ends.[49] She forges new pathways—transience, denial, indirection, and refusal—for seeing and evaluating Black portraiture and landscape.

Nowhere is this more apparent than in her hyper-black still and moving images that traffic in blackface imagery.[50] As discussed in chapter 1, mammy and minstrel stereotypes have been dismissed as negative and politically harmful within Black arts discourse. In the next chapter, Narcissister makes similar moves with her darkly humorous embodiment of the topsy-turvy doll—part of a lineage of Black visual satire where artists of African descent dispute history, matters of identity, viewer expectations, and the past and present currency of cultural and racial stereotypes. A groundswell of artists engaged with this type of production at and after the turn of the new millennium when post-identity discourse escalated. For Richard Powell, Black visual satire in twentieth and twenty-first-century America engenders anti-racist dissent and introspective critique that defuses the social power of art.[51] The sensuous quality of Simmons's opacity is equally disruptive.

Instead of gloss, bling, and shine, Simmons's hyper-blackness is dusty and matte. This difference unsettles the power of visibility and representation to signify and unify Black subjects in creative and collective struggle. Although her performative interventions are part of a genealogy of Black feminist citational practice advanced by artists like Josephine Baker and Grace Jones for whom manipulating skin-as-surface and opacity were critical, Simmons's matte hyper-blackness *withholds* shine.[52] Rather than amplifying luminescence as a mode of presence or unveiling, the resulting dullness and flatness directs attention not only to other objects and surfaces in the scene but also to the startling contrast between the body and the landscape where non-disclosing subjects refuse to accede to Black representational protocols regarding visibility, presence, authenticity, and revelation. The sequencing of the images also challenges group identity dynamics in relation to genre, racial, and gender unity. Not conceived as a series, Simmons's hyper-black images posit a different kind of relational structure that is bound by loose chronological proximity and the repetition of resonant imagery, not by sameness.

In *Landscape (Home)* of 2005, Simmons stands nude in a bathtub pressing a bundle of crimped, synthetic blonde hair to her body. Folded in half by her hands, the bundle of hair hangs between her legs to cover her pubic region, a citation of Botticelli's fifteenth-century Italian Renaissance painting *The Birth of Venus*. In *her* image, Simmons's Black female body replaces the idealized white female figure—a new millennium Sable Venus.[53] Here, the raced and gendered body is a character as well as a site and surface to behold. While the items around her comprise a typical bathroom scene—bottles of personal care products on the window ledge, a half-used roll of toilet paper on the floor—Simmons's body is what is out of place: her lips are painted bright red, she wears a large wooly Afro wig, and her already Black skin is painted black from head to ankles. Her eyelids droop as she stares blankly into the camera; her face is expressionless, and her actual Black skin peeks through the paint on her body.

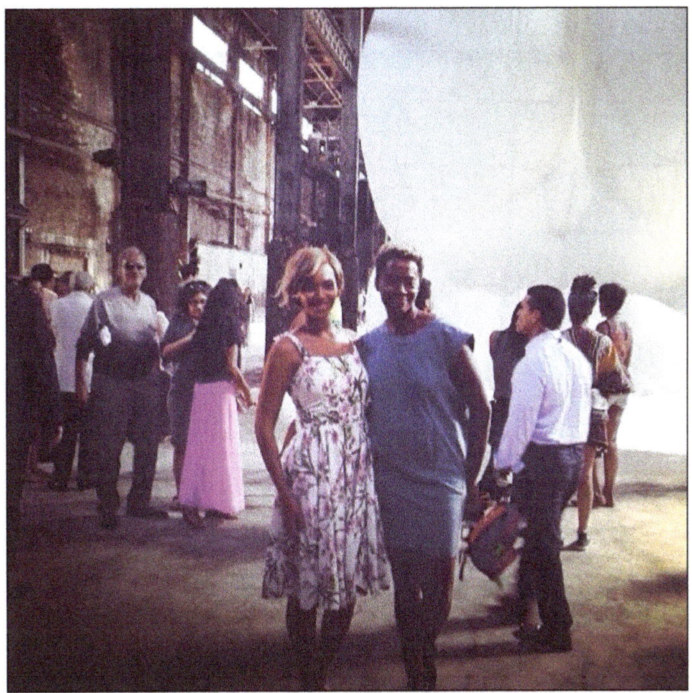

Plate 1. Photographer unknown, Digital color photograph, BeyLite Instagram, 2014, Fair Use. Beyoncé and Kara Walker stand close and pose together in front of Walker's large-scale sugar sculpture and installation *A Subtlety* in 2014 in Williamsburg, Brooklyn.

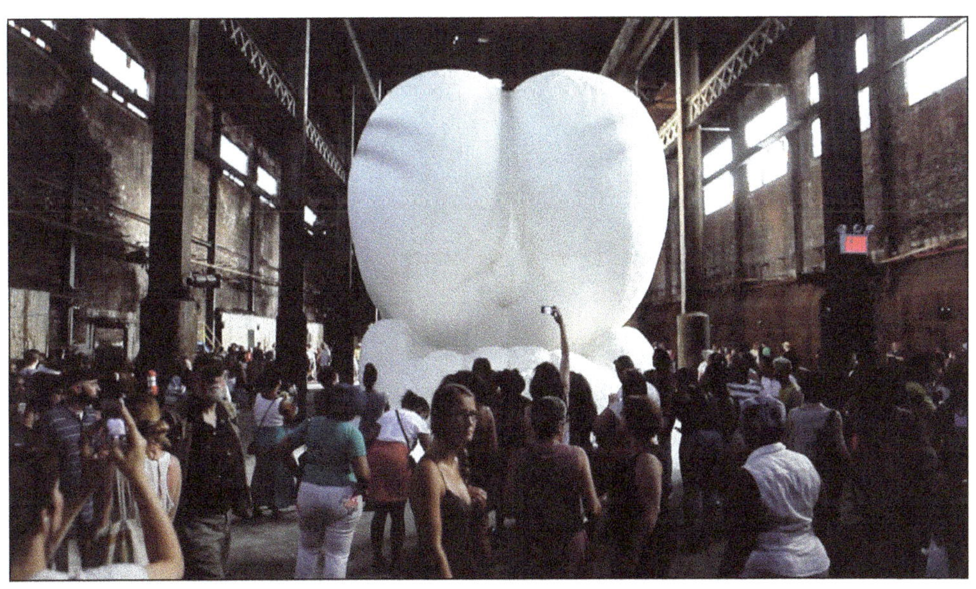

Plate 2. Kara Walker, film still from *An Audience*, 2014. Digital video with sound. Artwork © Kara Walker. Courtesy of Sikkema Jenkins & Co. and Sprüth Magers.

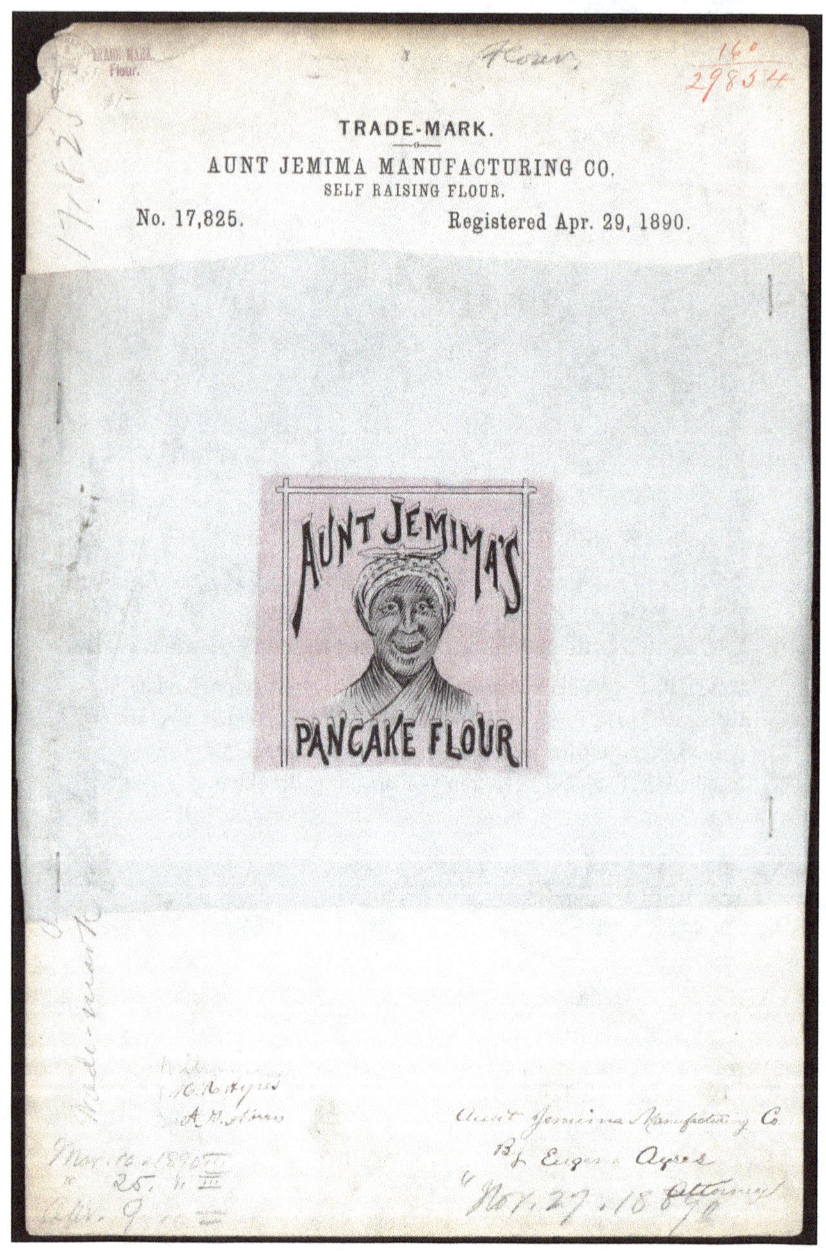

Plate 3. Trademark registration by Aunt Jemima Manufacturing Co. for Aunt Jemima's Pancake Flour brand Self Raising Flour, April 29, 1890. One item; sheet 26 × 29 cm, Library of Congress Prints and Photographs Division, Washington, DC, open access reproduction number LC-DIG-trmk-1t17825 (digital file from original, front) LC-DIG-trmk-2t17825 (digital file from original, underneath overlay on front).

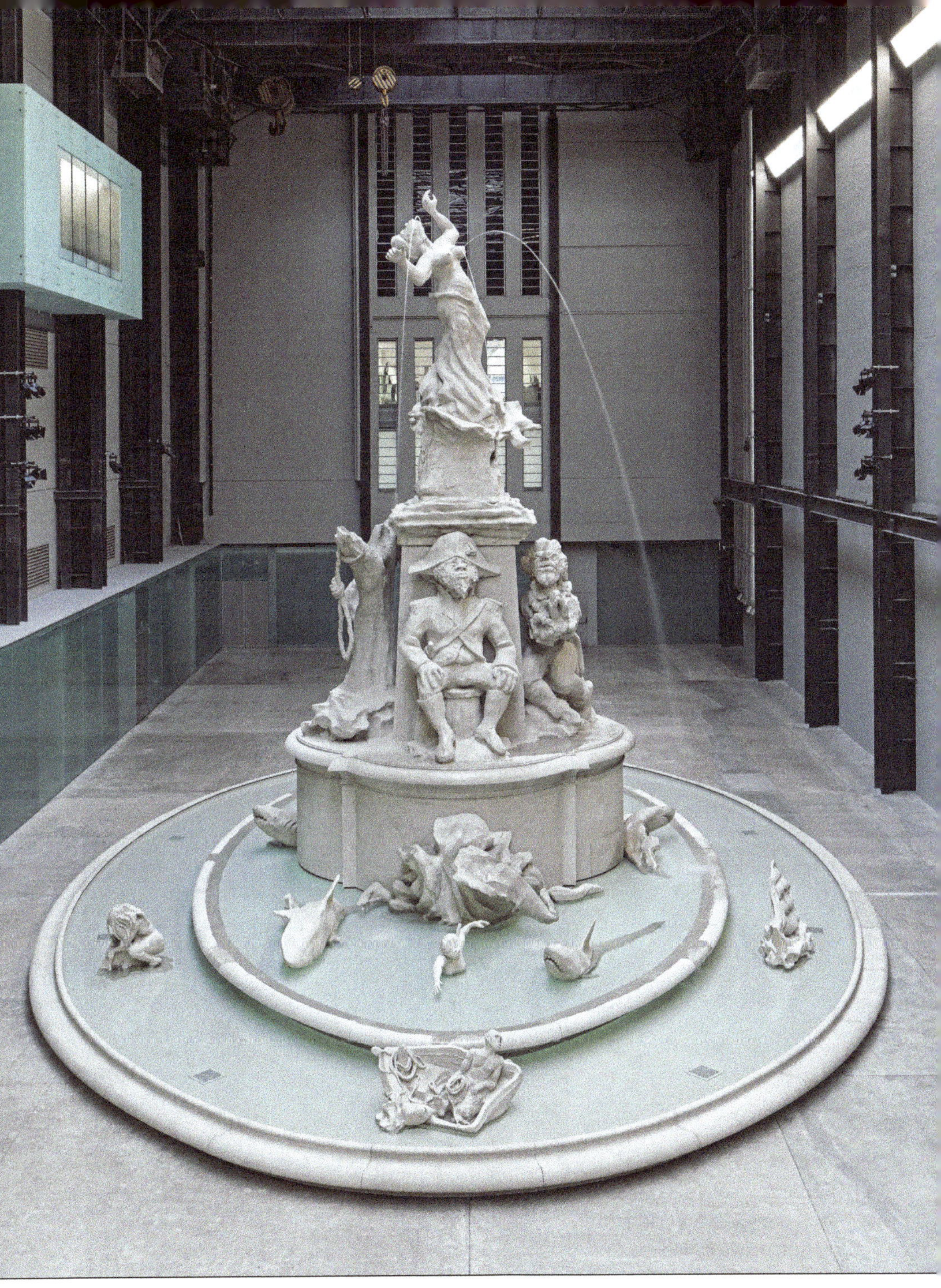

Plate 4. Kara Walker, *Fons Americanus*, 2019. Non-toxic acrylic and cement composite, recyclable cork, wood, and metal. Main: 73.5 × 50 × 43 ft (22.4 × 15.2 × 13.2 m). Installation view, 2019. Hyundai Commission: Kara Walker—Fons Americanus, Tate Modern, London, UK, 2019. Photo credit: Tate (Matt Greenwood).

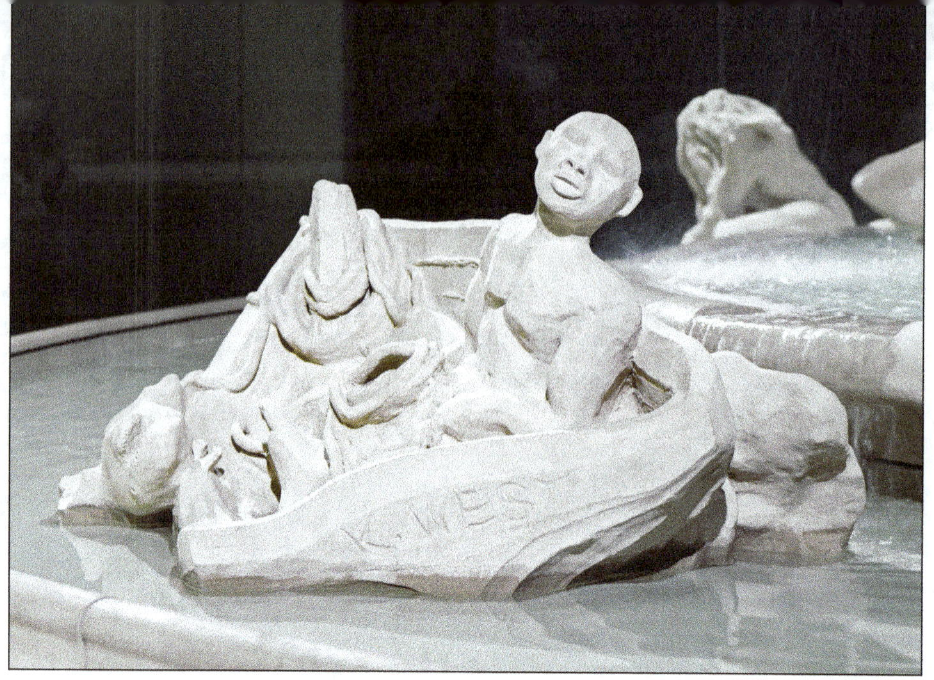

Plate 5. Kara Walker, detail from *Fons Americanus*. Non-toxic acrylic and cement composite, recyclable cork, wood, and metal, Main: 73.5 × 50 × 43 feet (22.4 × 15.2 × 13.2 meters). Installation view, 2019. Hyundai Commission: Kara Walker—Fons Americanus, Tate Modern, London, UK, 2019. Photo: Tate (Matt Greenwood).

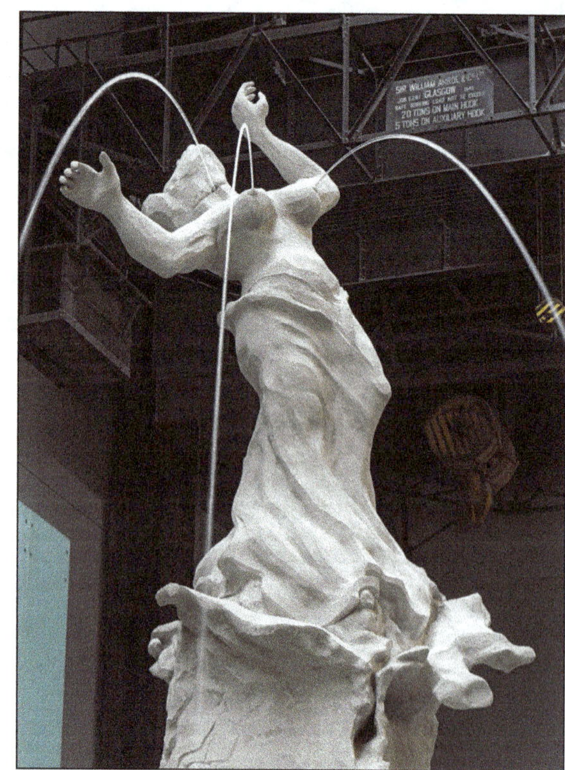

Plate 6. Kara Walker, Detail from *Fons Americanus*, Non-toxic acrylic and cement composite, recyclable cork, wood, and metal, Main: 73.5 × 50 × 43 feet (22.4 × 15.2 × 13.2 meters). Installation view, 2019. Hyundai Commission: Kara Walker—Fons Americanus, Tate Modern, London, UK, 2019. Photo: Tate (Matt Greenwood).

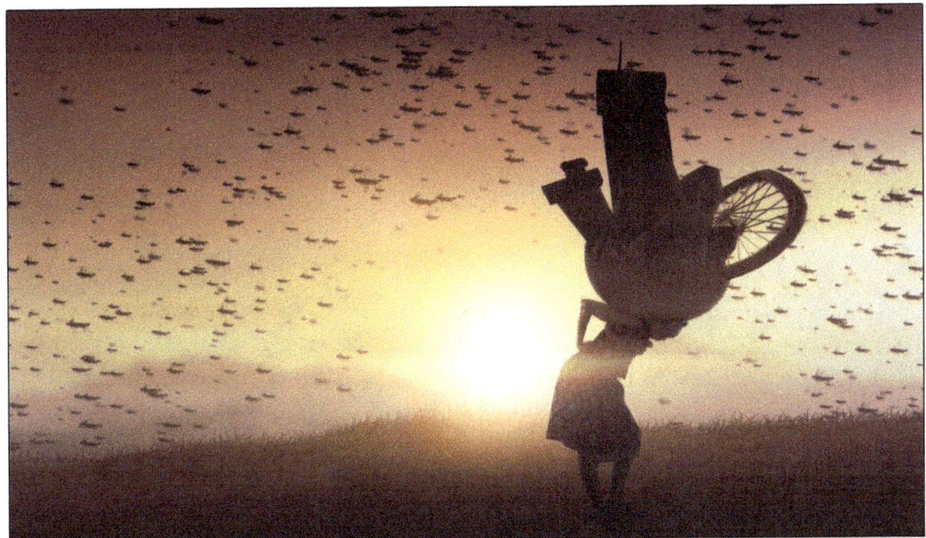

Plate 7. Wangechi Mutu, *The End of Carrying All*, 2015. Three channel animated video (color, sound), edition three of three, two AP. Courtesy of Gladstone Gallery, New York, Victoria Miro, London and Vielmetter Los Angeles.

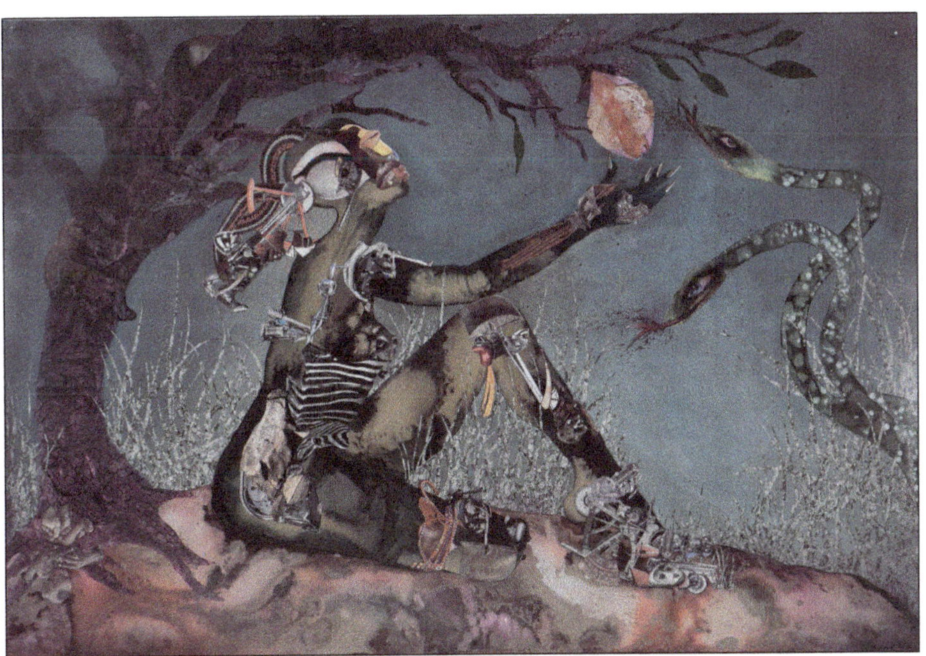

Plate 8. Wangechi Mutu, *Forbidden Fruit Picker*, 2015. Collage painting, 39 1/2 × 58 5/8 in (100.33 × 148.89 cm). Courtesy of Gladstone Gallery, New York, Victoria Miro, London and Vielmetter Los Angeles. Photo credit: Alessandra Chemollo.

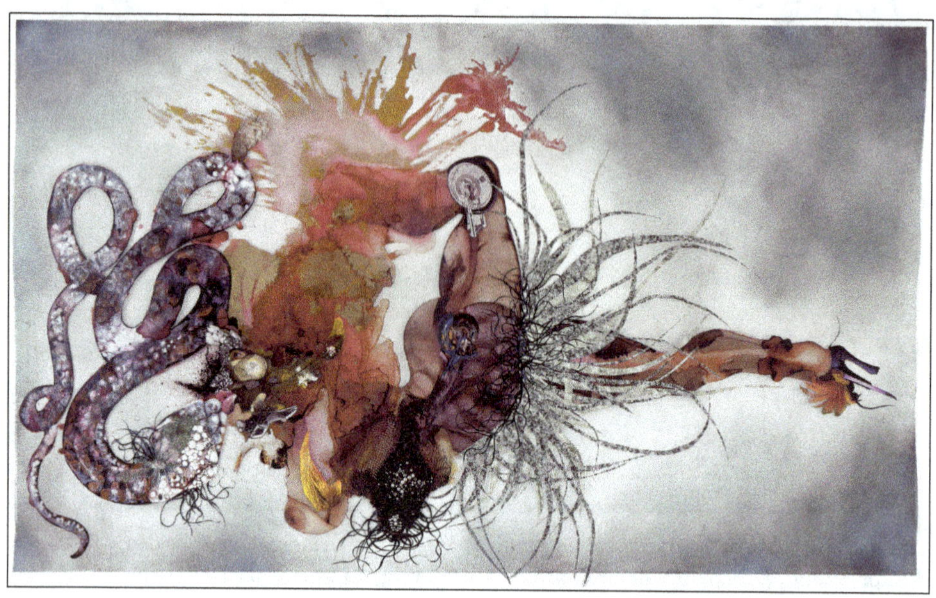

Plate 9. Wangechi Mutu, *Non je ne regrette rien*, 2007. Ink, paint, mixed media, plant material, and plastic pearls on Mylar, 54 × 87 1/8 in (137.16 × 221.31 cm). Courtesy of the artist and Vielmetter Los Angeles.

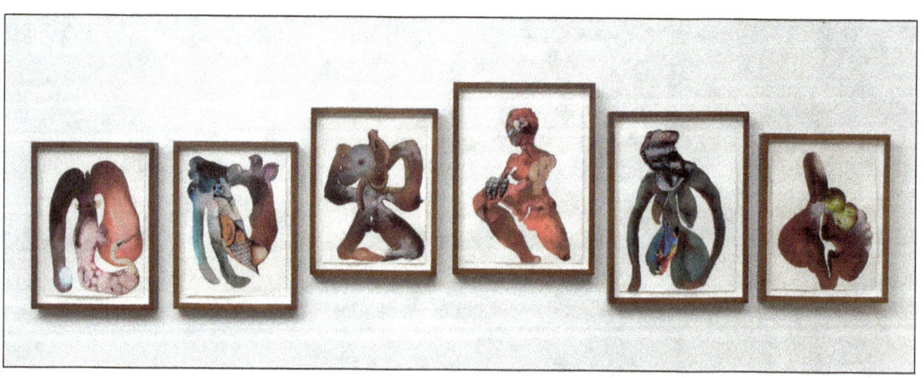

Plate 10. Wangechi Mutu, *The Evolution of Mud Mama from Beginning to Start*, 2008. Watercolor, ink, and collage on paper, six parts: 19 1/2 × 75 in (49.53 × 190.5 cm) overall. Courtesy of the artist and Vielmetter Los Angeles. Photo credit: Robert Wedemeyer.

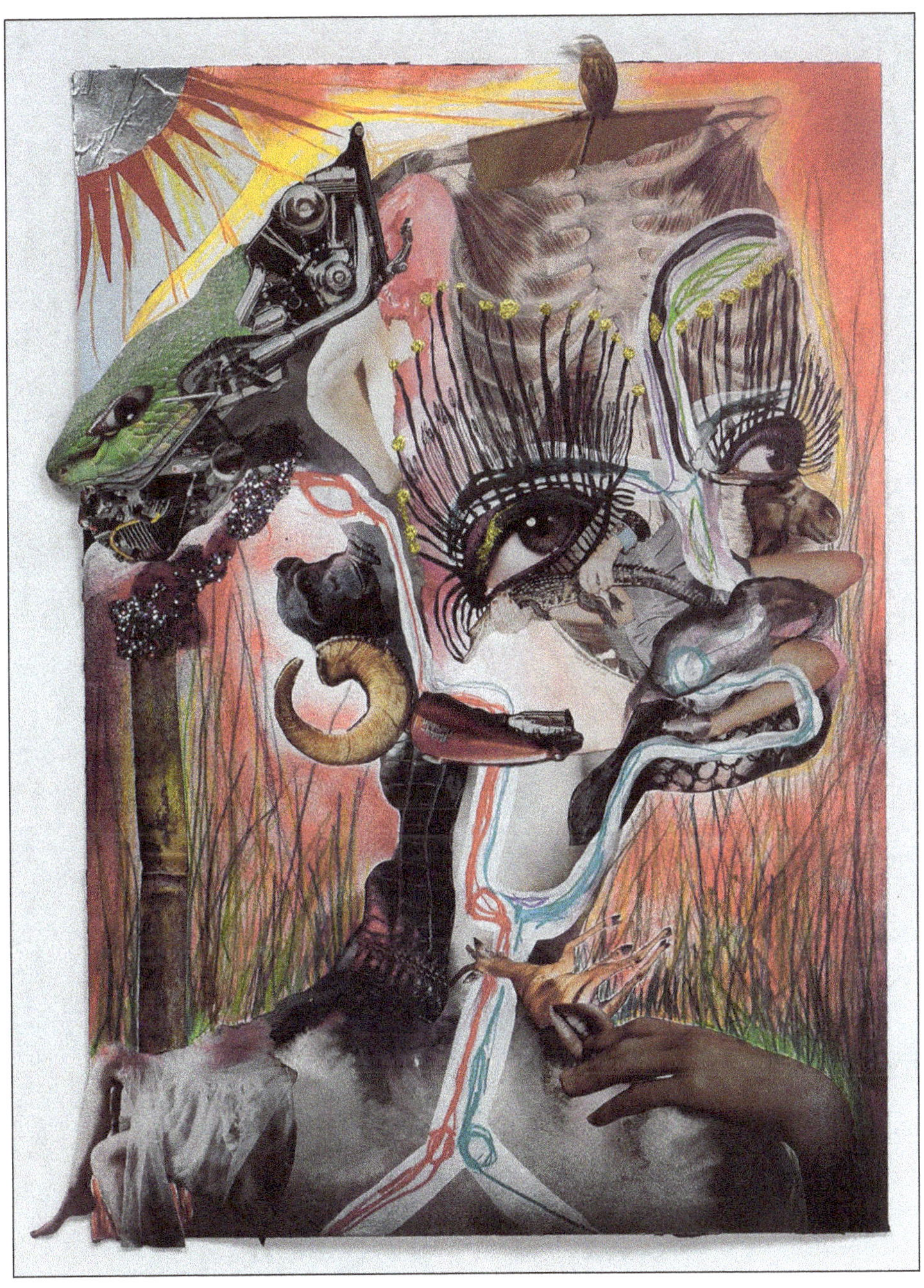

Plate 11. Wangechi Mutu, Prodigal Sun Daughter from *Family Tree*, 2012. Suite of thirteen, mixed-media collage on paper, 16.25 × 12.25 in (41.28 × 31.12 cm). Collection of the Nasher Museum of Art at Duke University, museum purchase with additional funds provided by Trent Carmichael (T'88, P'17), Blake Byrne (T'57), Marjorie and Michael Levine (T'84, P'16), Stefanie and Douglas Kahn (P'11, P'13), and Christen and Derek Wilson (T'86, B'90, P'15). © Wangechi Mutu. Photo credit: Peter Paul Geoffrion.

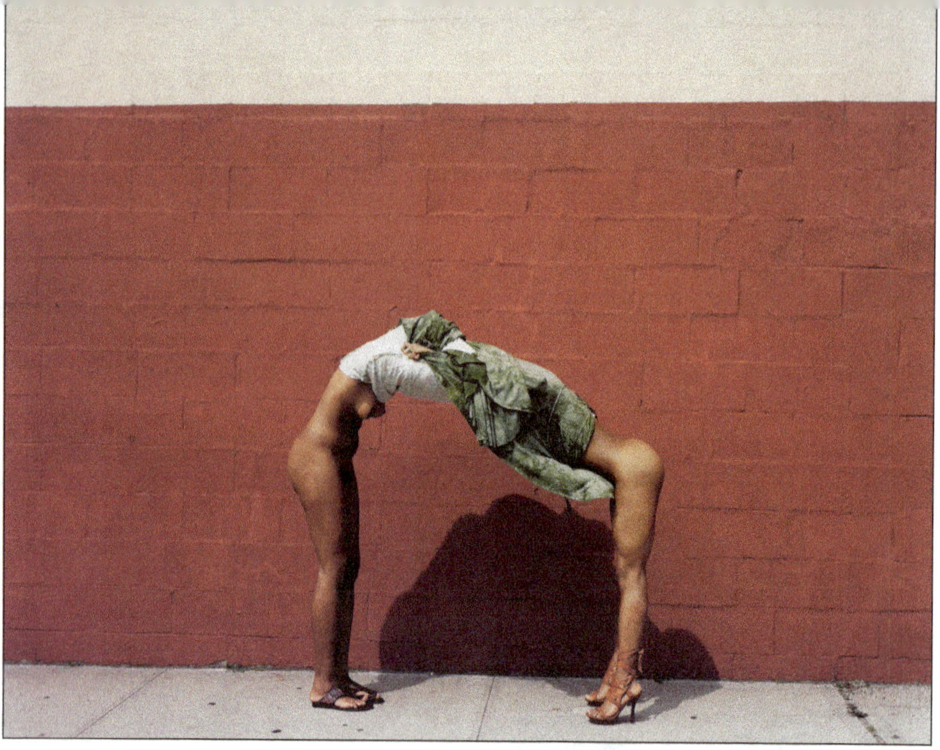

Plate 12. Xaviera Simmons, *Landscape (Two Women)*, 2007. Chromogenic color print, 30 × 40 in. Courtesy the artist and David Castillo. © Xaviera Simmons.

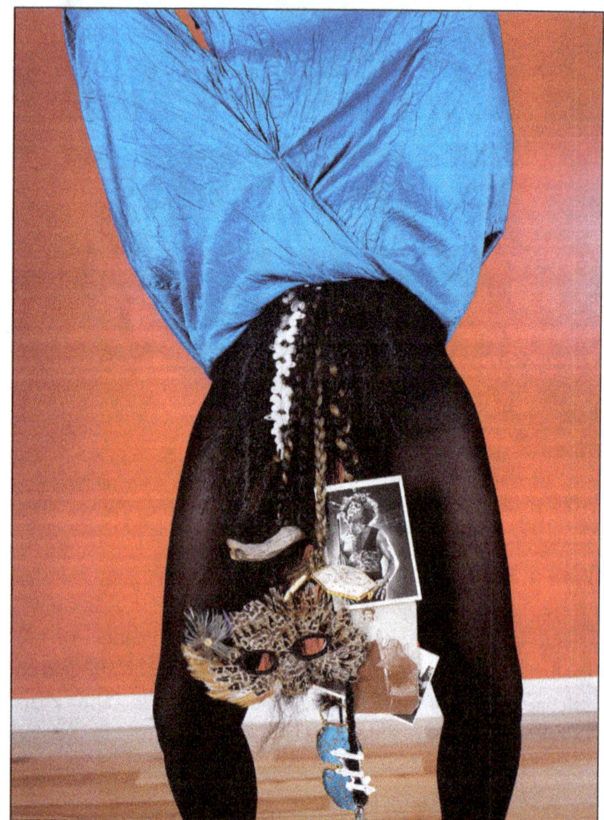

Plate 13. Xaviera Simmons, *Beyond the Canon of Landscape (For Orhan. P, Zadie. S, Nia and Naima. M)*, 2008. Chromogenic color print. Courtesy the artist and David Castillo. © Xaviera Simmons.

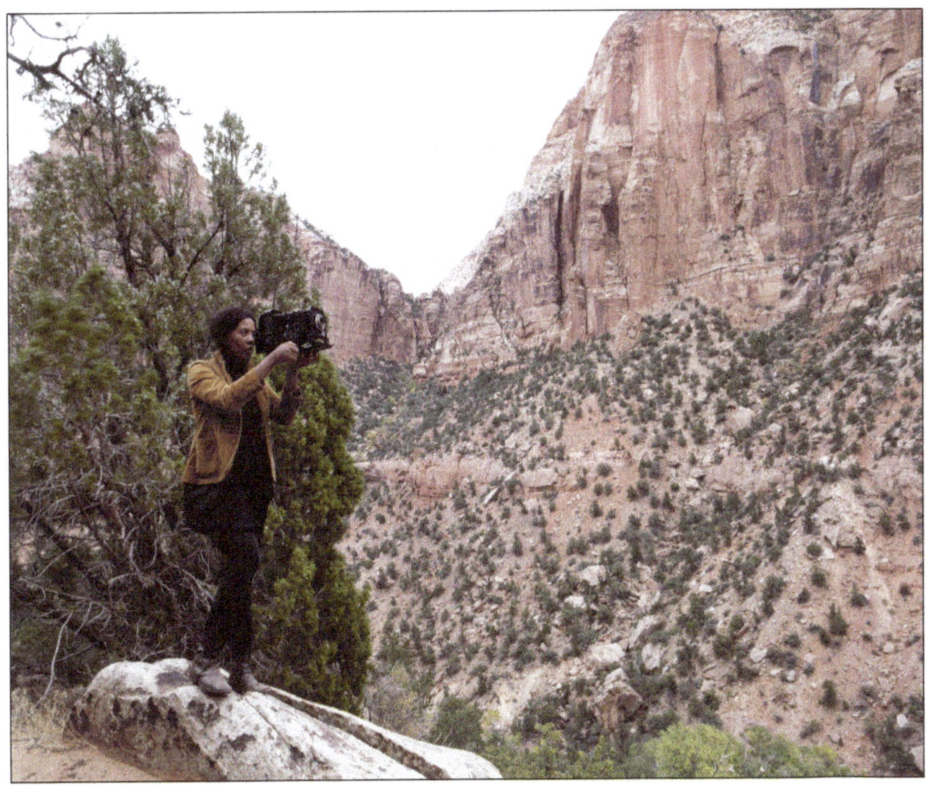

Plate 14. Xaviera Simmons, *Canyon*, 2010. Chromogenic color print, 30 × 40 in. Courtesy the artist and David Castillo. © Xaviera Simmons.

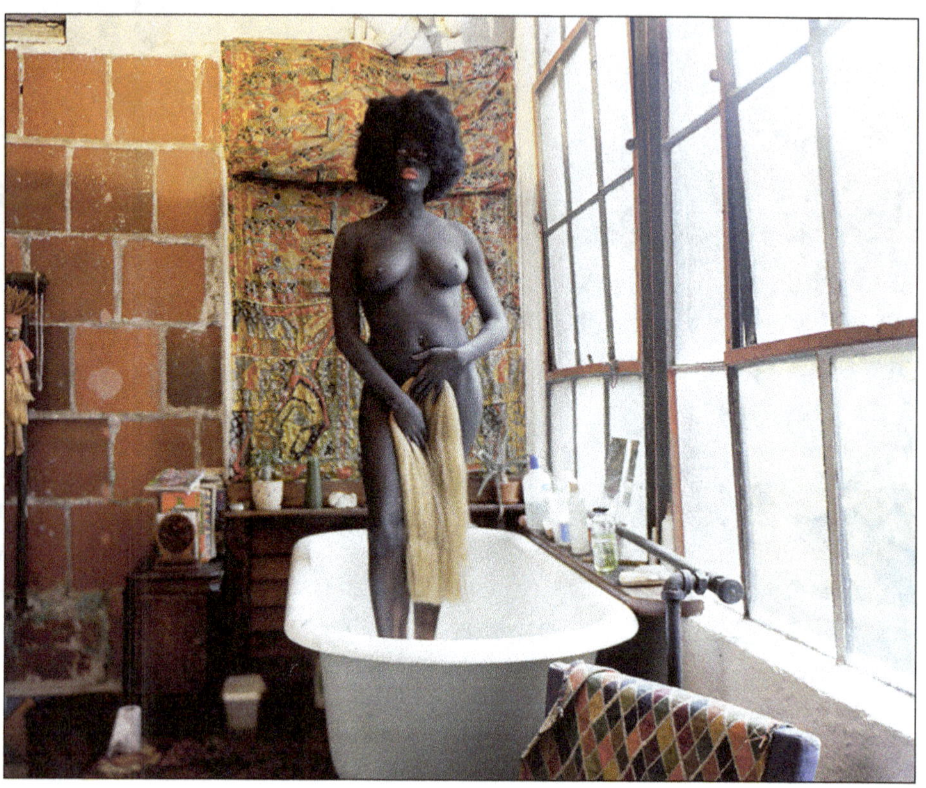

Plate 15. Xaviera Simmons, *Landscape (Home)*, 2005. Chromogenic color print, 30 × 40 in. Courtesy the artist and David Castillo. © Xaviera Simmons.

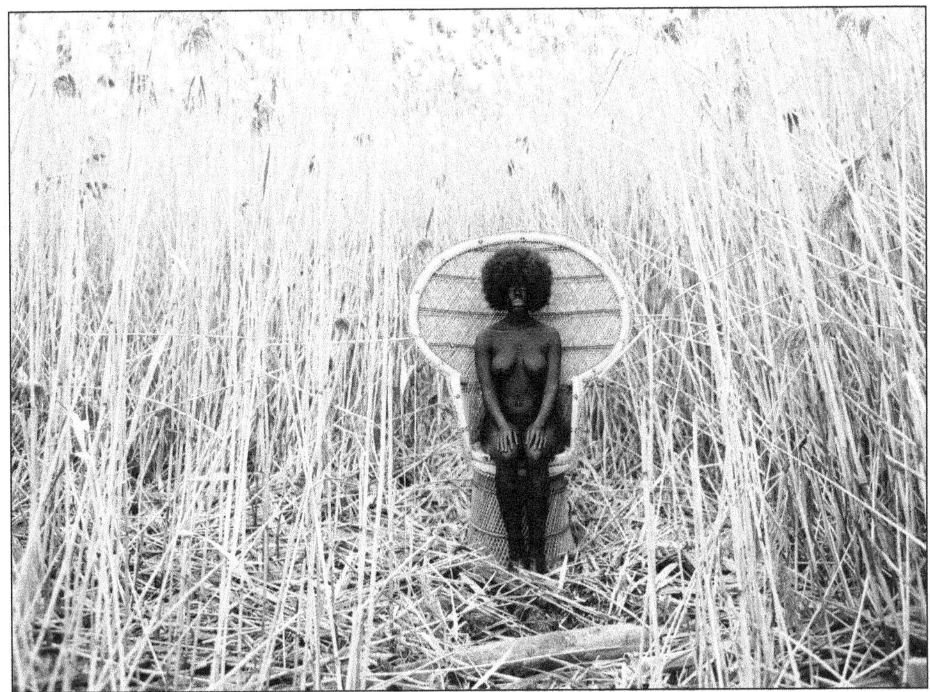

Plate 16. Xaviera Simmons, *One Day and Back Then (Seated)*, 2007. Chromogenic color print, 30 × 40 in. Courtesy the artist and David Castillo. © Xaviera Simmons.

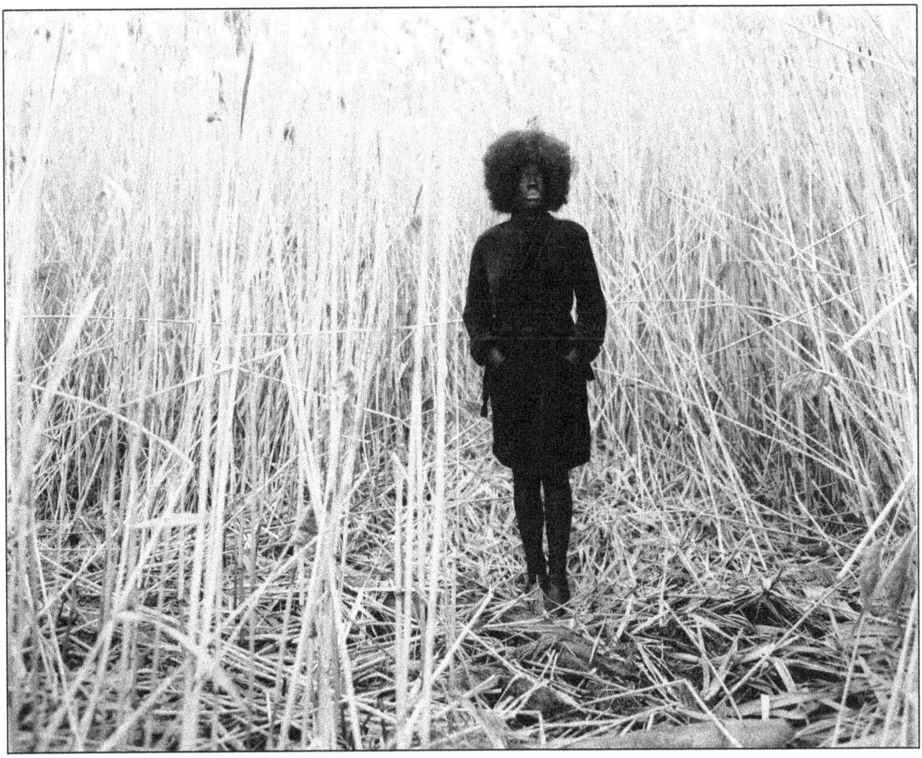

Plate 17. Xaviera Simmons, *One Day and Back Then (Standing)*, 2007. Chromogenic color print, 30 × 40 in. Courtesy the artist and David Castillo. © Xaviera Simmons.

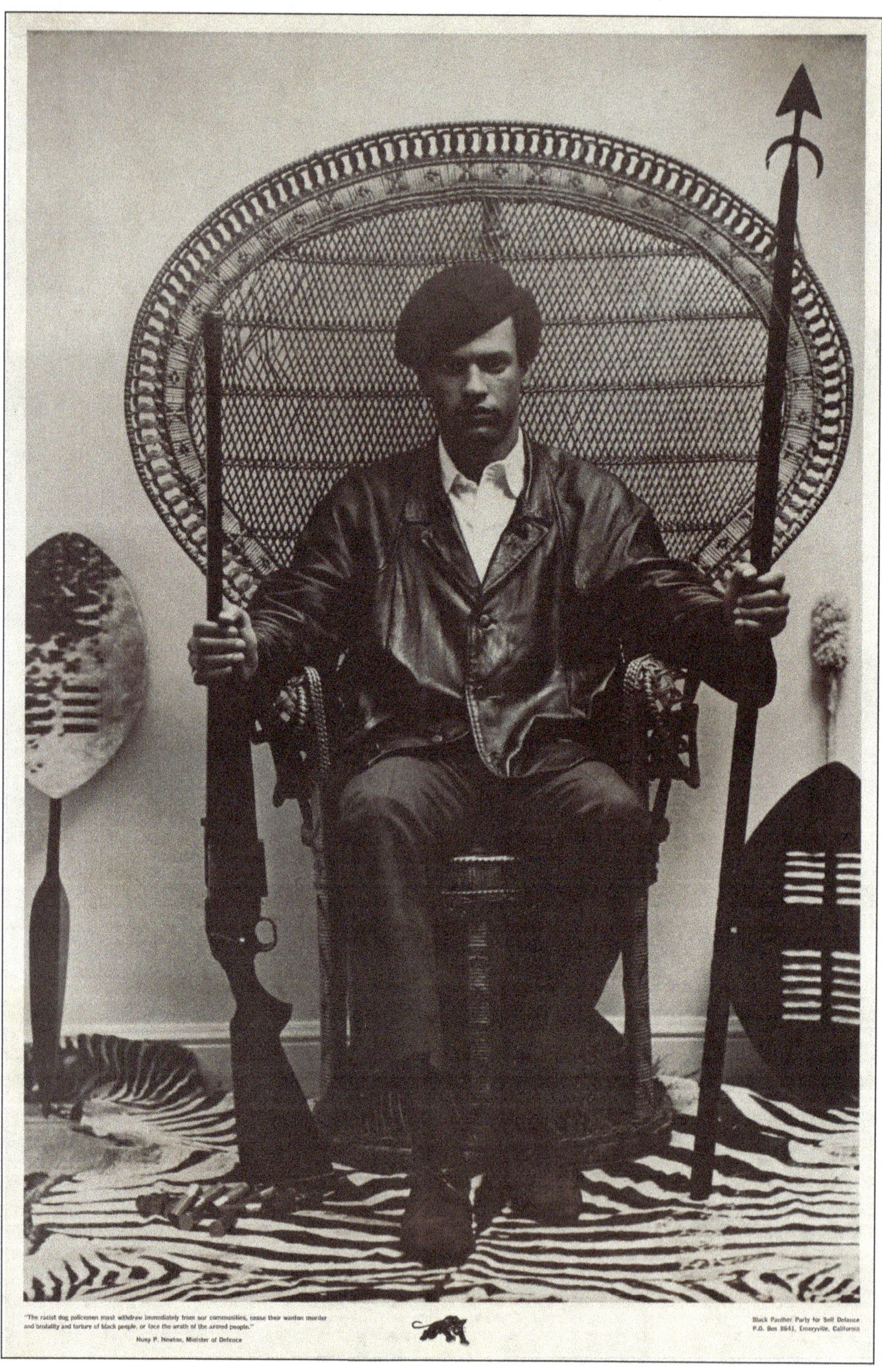

Plate 18. Blair Stapp and the Black Panther Party, *Dr. Huey P. Newton*, ca. 1967. Lithographic ink on paper (fiber product) and linen (material). Collection of the Smithsonian National Museum of African American History and Culture, Fair Use.

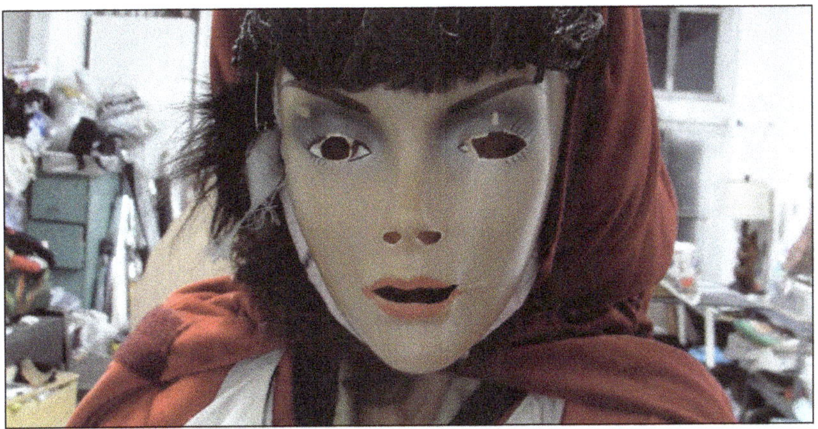

Plate 19. Narcissister, *Red Riding Hood*, 2014. Mixed media. Courtesy the artist. Photo credit: Narcissister.

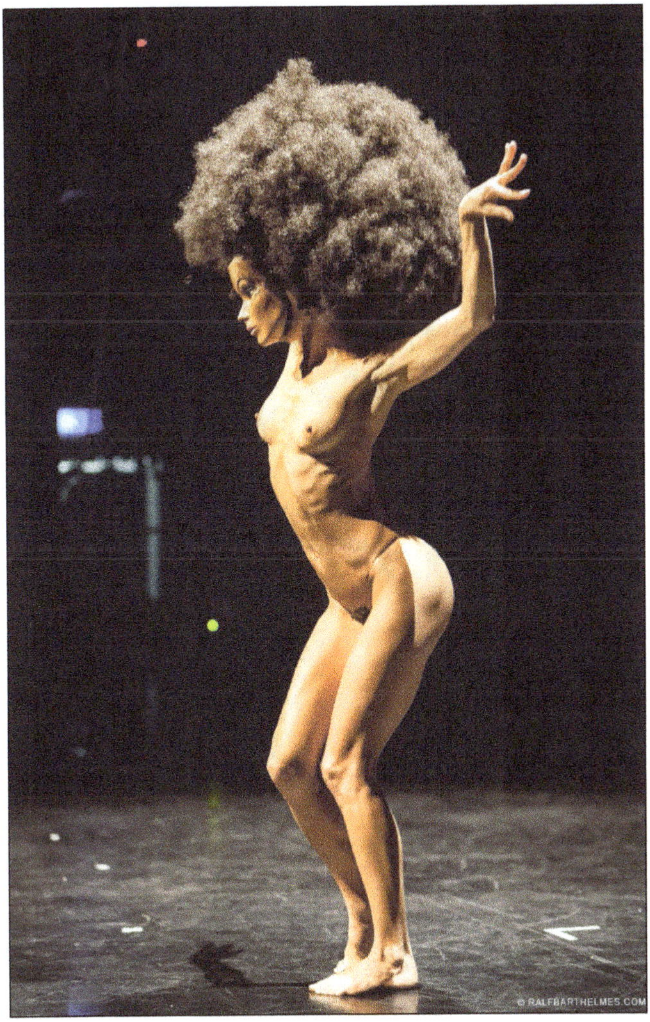

Plate 20. Narcissister, *Every Woman*, 2008/09. Photographic stills of Narcissister in a live 2013 performance in Frankfurt, Germany. Mixed media. Photo credit: Ralf Barthelmes.

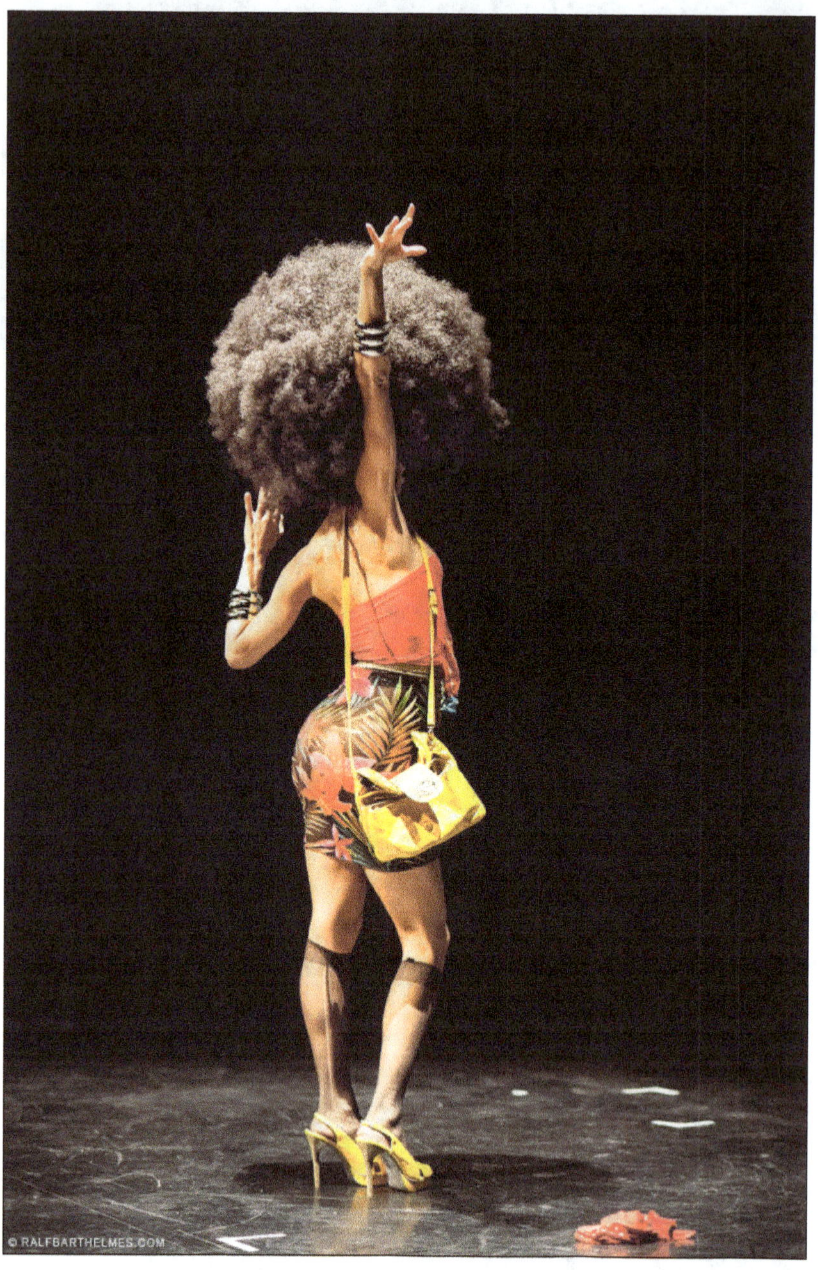

Plate 21. Narcissister, *Every Woman*, performance still, 2008/09. Mixed media. Photo credit: Ralf Barthelmes.

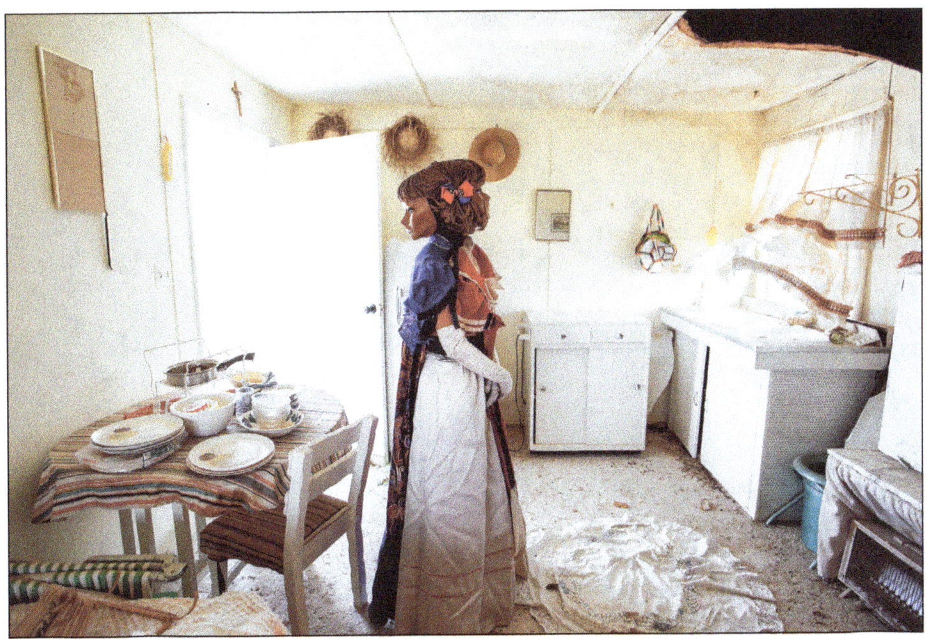

Plate 22. Narcissister, *Upside Down*. Performance still, mixed media, 2017. Courtesy of the artist. Photo credit: Sarah Lyon.

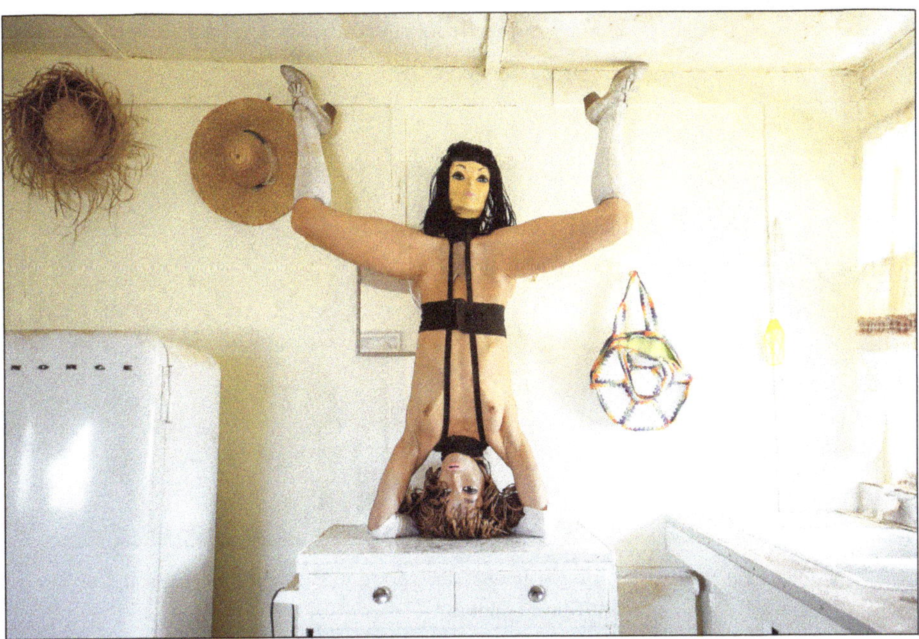

Plate 23. Narcissister, *Upside Down*. Performance still, mixed media, 2017. Courtesy of the artist. Photo credit: Sarah Lyon.

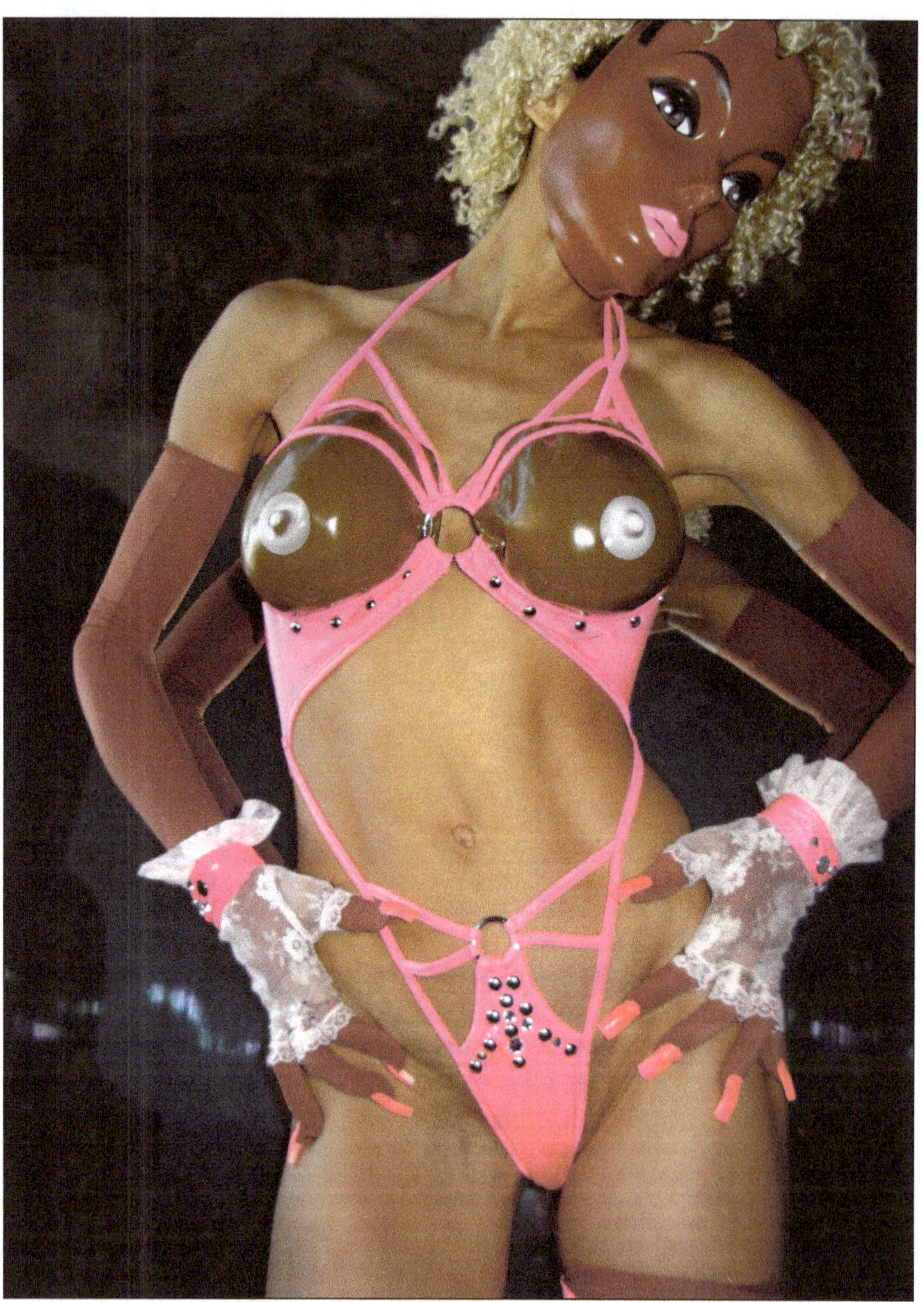

Plate 24. Narcissister, *Man/Woman*, 2007. Mixed media, color photograph. Courtesy of the artist. Photo credit: Tony Stamolis.

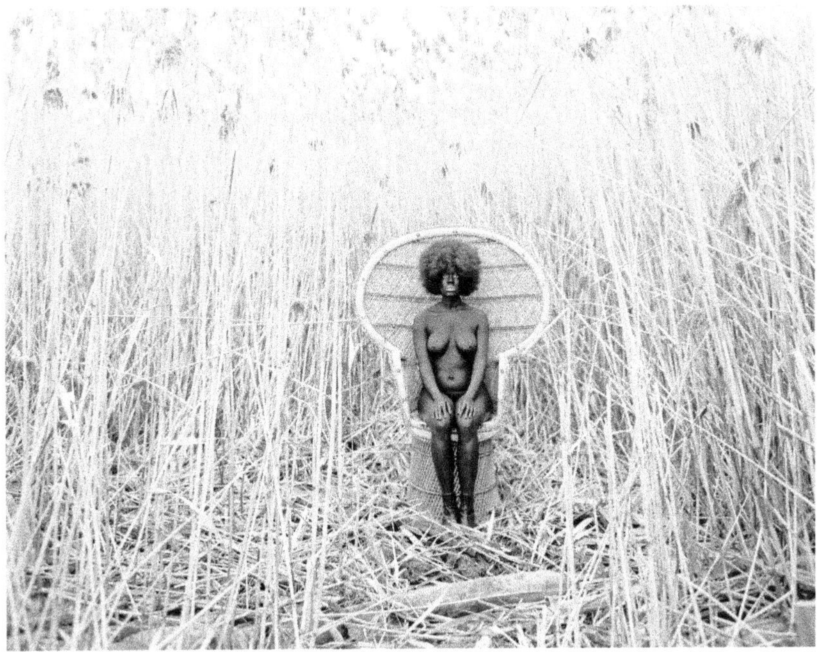

Figure 3.7. Xaviera Simmons, *One Day and Back Then (Seated)*, 2007. Chromogenic color print, 30 × 40 in. Courtesy the artist and David Castillo. © Xaviera Simmons.

That same year, Simmons produced another examination of the sociocultural implications of skin. In *Landscape: Beach (Density)*, an eleven-minute video, the artist lounges on a beach towel next to a white woman who is sunbathing. Sitting then standing, Simmons generously applies a near-black-colored tanning lotion to her medium-brown legs, torso, neck, and face. Although she is on a public beach, no one notices her exaggerated and altered appearance. The beach itself is picturesque yet generic; people walk by in the background, a lifeguard chair sits on the mound of sand, and waves ebb and flow. Near the end of the video, the artist puts on an Afro wig, adjusts it, and continues enjoying the sun. Against a partially overcast sky, the whirring sound of an airplane is the only audible noise.

One Day and Back Then (Seated) of 2007 pictures Simmons sitting nude in a wicker chair in an unruly field of sea reeds. Her hands rest on her knees. The chair's high-rounded back cuts across the vertically jutting reeds, framing the upper half of Simmons's body, while the reeds' thick

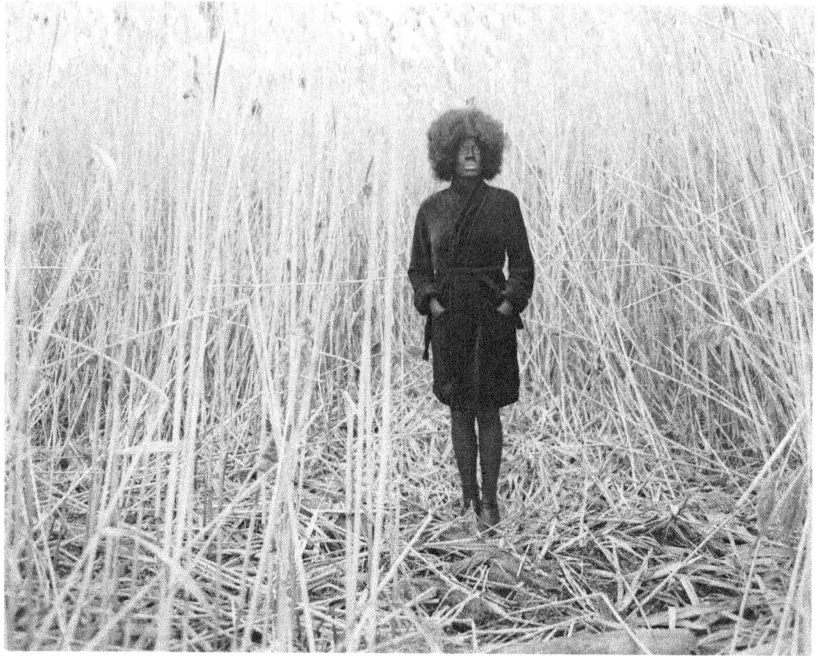

Figure 3.8. Xaviera Simmons, *One Day and Back Then (Standing)*, 2007. Chromogenic color print, 30 × 40 in. Courtesy the artist and David Castillo. © Xaviera Simmons.

cover obscures any discernible horizon line or view beyond the field and its edges. Despite her seated pose, the figure-ground delineation is unclear. There are no shadows. Other than its immediate features, the landscape is anonymous, as is the seated figure. The whites of her eyes accent her neutral, unaffected stare. Her lips are painted bright red, and her nude, medium-brown skin is again covered in black paint. Crowned by a thick, curly Afro wig, Simmons's appears blacker than Black.

(Seated)'s companion image, *One Day and Back Then (Standing)* also from 2007, depicts Simmons standing in an opaque, black, terrycloth robe that hugs the curves of her blacker than Black body. Her hands are tucked away in her coat pockets; the only skin on view is a small portion of Simmons's painted wrists and expressionless face, while her head tilts ever so slightly to the left. In both *One Day and Back Then* images, the artist is positioned slightly off center, and the labor she has taken to cut a path to sit and stand among the reeds is visible. Unlike *(Seated)*, in *(Standing)* Simmons appears closer, a kind of progression—or becoming—in the

visual field. But like her other counterintuitive enactments of becoming, not much is really revealed or resolved here. The image's compositional elements instead work to constrain vision, limiting what viewers can know and see. Despite the presence of exposed flesh, black paint, opaque clothing, and a self-imposed anonymity conceal her. The dense thicket of reeds blocks the view of the distance, and Simmons's expressionless face and the layer of black paint as artificial skin accentuate the surface of the body rather than its interiority. Closeness in this image does not lead to sensual intimacy or new knowledge. There is no vanishing point; all sightlines lead to the hyper-black figure in the landscape.

This body of work probes a specific relation between surface and depth that mediates Black representational practices as well as anxieties about racial difference in an era when Black bodies continue to endure unique forms of surveillance and scrutiny. With the apprehension of the horizon cluttered and blocked the way that it is, Simmons halts perspectival depth, directing the focus to the surface—the skin—of the image and the body. Alternately, the blondeness of the crimped hair and of the landscape against the artist's blacker-than-Black form produces a contrast so high that it repels rather than reconciles, forcing the eye to look elsewhere—to the canon of art history and to the color line—for meaning. For Simmons, the blackness and whiteness of the images evoke various states of forced migration, distress, and displacement that Black Americans have endured under white supremacist structures that have yet to be fully acknowledged and dismantled.[54] She thus gestures beyond herself, challenging viewers and critics to think deeply about who occupies the categories of oppressed and oppressor amid ongoing debates about power, vision, and racial and gender justice in the new millennium. The nowhereness of the landscape, her expressionless face under and against hyper-blackness, and the field's constraining thickness also incites psychological interest, the desire to know what is before, behind, and beyond the frame. But Simmons frustrates this drive by composing an image that depends on inscrutability. Identifying information, from the work's title to the figure to the locale, is withheld, as is the face and body's expressiveness. This is not merely obscurity or even the opposite of transparency; opacity, on all of these registers, is a form of refusal.

Caribbean philosopher Édouard Glissant theorizes opacity as a response to Enlightenment ideals about self-possession and Western colonial impulses upheld by desires for a world that opens itself to knowledge. These tenets result in a "lukewarm humanism, both colorless and reassuring."[55] Opacity, most importantly for Glissant, interrupts the desire for visibility and in so doing, resists total incorporation and inclusion. During the last decade, opacity has become a cornerstone of contemporary Black art criticism. Scholars of art history, queer studies, transgender studies, and ethnic studies have also expanded Glissant's thinking on opacity as a tactic of resistance. C. Riley Snorton, L. H. Stallings and Elliott Powell, Rizvana Bradley, Sampada Aranke, Jules Gill-Peterson, michá cardenas, Eric A. Stanley, Erica Rand, and David J. Getsy have argued that opacity directly responds to the violences that subtend physiognomic scrutiny and surveillance. They have also detailed how minoritarian artists' use of opacity counters how the discipline of art history has privileged Eurocentric, Enlightenment ideals as the grounds for visual interpretation and evidence.

My analysis of the mechanics of opacity and unbecoming in Simmons's hyper-black still and moving images builds on this wave of scholarship and its implications for how art historians and practitioners of Black and feminist study understand the value of surface aesthetics. Historically, a hermeneutics of the surface has situated photography and the body as reproductive mediums whereby Black women are read as exceptional commodities yet formidable subjects capable of fashioning identities that redress subjugation. This understanding of surface resonates with psychiatrist and philosopher Frantz Fanon's theorization of epidermalization, a disabling over-visibility to which Black skin and its function as a racial index are apposite. Drawing from his own confrontations with the colonial white gaze, he narrates "the fact of blackness," an enduring conception of race and its effects in an anti-Black world: "I am the slave not of the idea that others have of me but of my own appearance."[56] So deeply internalized is this perception that the Black subject becomes a slave *of*, and *to*, their own appearance. Epidermalization is "the most visible of fetishes," the intertwining of self-perception and the embodied experience of anti-Blackness, critical theorist Homi K. Bhabha argues.[57] This schism conditions and produces the Black subject's abject social position; it also spurs Blackness's intelligibility, which surfaces at the apex of translation from phenotype—namely skin color—into stereotype. "Skin," in feminist film scholar Mary Ann Doane's interpretation of Fanon, "becomes the locus of an alienation more acute to the extent that it is inescapable."[58] Black skin overdetermines and *is overdetermined* from without, a condition that must be overcome, Fanon asserts.[59] The primacy of vision gives rise to this inevitable condition, what in Fanon's view is a cancer on the bodies that must live in Black skins without ever being able to escape them. Skin and its color, in this schema, engenders racial intelligibility as well as social and moral degradation. As a result, Black skin functions as a racial signifier through which one's subjectivity "is turned inside out like a shirtcuff," as novelist and philosopher Charles Johnson puts it in his consideration of the Black body's phenomenology.[60]

Significantly, Fanon likens epidermalization to photography's ability to fix other black images: shadows. In this process, the "other" becomes fixed through the colonial white gaze and through its own "gestures and attitude, the same way you fix a preparation with a dye."[61] This reciprocal fixation is fundamental to the sense of presence and materiality that both Blackness and photography entail.[62] Just as "the photographic both chemically and metaphorically 'fixes' its ostensible subject quite literally as an object of vision . . . concretely [reproducing] the visible in a material process," media theorist Vivian Sobchack explains, Blackness imprints the body, externalizing the racialized subject and arranging—fixing—its contents into a visual effect to be seen and felt.[63] This process "results in a . . . form that can be objectively possessed, circulated, and saved," in terms of both the photograph as a material object and Blackness as a floating signifier.[64] Crucially, for Fanon, photography and the racial epidermal schema share a compulsion toward surface as the basis of one's perception in and of the world. "Seen from the outside by the other," Alessandra Raengo summarizes, "the body becomes 'epidermalized'; that is, fully externalized (to the other looking, but also the self who now sees himself from the outside) and deprived of interiority."[65] The Black body is thus all surface, and Simmons's mobilizations of opacity suggest that such a surface may yield more than identity categories.[66]

Recent interdisciplinary interventions on the role of surface in psychoanalysis, Black cultural studies, queer studies, literary studies, sensation and affect studies, and aesthetic theory have shifted this critical dialogue to consider Black skin as a vital, overlooked site of sensory knowledge. Anthropologist and art historian Christopher Pinney first used the term surfacism in 2003 to describe how western African and

South Asian artists manipulate photography to reject narrative, perspective, and detachment in favor of "a world of surfaces and materiality that reach out to their embodied viewers."[67] By emphasizing texture, embodiment, tangibility, and shine, these practices, Pinney explains, build on Baroque pictorial traditions to counter Cartesian ways of thinking about perspective and depth that favored a detached observation of the world-as-picture.[68] Art historian Krista Thompson's writing on Black diasporic shine in painting and photography turns away from the Eurocentric latencies of Pinney's ideas, underlining "how the representation of black figures and modern slavery at times literally provided the background and formed the flesh against which the surfacist aesthetics could be staged."[69] Still, according to Kadji Amin, Amber Musser, and Roy Pérez, situating skin within the sensorium as a nexus of queer form resists "the violences of interpretation that prematurely fix the meaning of minority artistic production within prefabricated narratives."[70] More still, minoritarian subjects' myriad enactments of surfacism and shine vis-à-vis skin and its manipulation produce representational flatness, refusals of depth, blinding hyper-visibility, and new relational intimacies that deflect a dominant gaze that seeks mastery over a knowable, intelligible racial and gendered subject.[71]

While much of the writing on surface aesthetics sees the sensory capacity of skin as one defined by liberation, cross-cultural connection, and self-determination, Simmons's images—where skin is the primary surface that invites prolonged looking—make Blackness a matter of exteriority, of epidermalization a la Fanon, *not* one of interiority or self-actualization. The opacity of her hyper-black still and moving images takes many forms—nondisclosure, illegibility, dissemblance, unrecognizability, excess—that point to the limits of art's liberatory, revelatory power. Advancements in visual technologies in the biotechnical domain amplify the urgency of Simmons's deployments of opacity in the new millennium. From X-ray photography to direct-to-consumer test kits that analyze one's DNA and antibodies, "Today skin is no longer privileged as the threshold of either identity or particularity," Paul Gilroy declares in his polemical study of twenty-first-century racial politics beyond the color line.[72] Whether imposed or insurgent, Gilroy renounces race and racial thinking because, in his view, they impede the human, cosmopolitan project of freedom. Indeed, visual signifiers of race, and gender for that matter, are increasingly mediated and transmitted through digital means, from emails to Google searches to avatars to memes to tweets. Because of this, racial phenotypes in the digital age, subtended by colorblind rhetoric, have been declared absent or invisible even as anti-Black violence persists.

Submitting to the digital realm and its allure of immateriality, however, overlooks how skin and screens have become conflated. As Lisa Nakamura, Ruha Benjamin, and Wesley E. Stevens outline, online environments accentuate identity's performative nature.[73] Although the internet "allows users to obscure the body due to the digital medium," Stevens explains, "race is still constructed online, often replicating the racist logics and stereotypes that exist offline."[74] Within this matrix, "culture and technology have become inextricable from one another, rendering Black identity intelligible through digital and discursive means."[75] For present-day confirmation of this phenomenon, one need only look to the popular, online, multiplayer video game *Fortnite* where users can choose which characters (also known as *skins*) they want to "embody" during play within the world of the game.[76]

Concurrent debates concerning the material and affective dimensions of authentic Blackness as a primary tenet of African diasporic identification have also circulated, gaining more traction with the phenomenon of blackfishing. Blackfishing names the process by which non-Black artists, celebrities, and social media influencers, most often women, appropriate Afrocentric hairstyles, clothing, language, and skin color to build their personal brands and secure lucrative endorsements. In parroting the aesthetics of Blackness, blackfishers mine Black identity for its cultural and economic value without the burdens of *being* Black. This act of appropriation draws upon the facets of Blackness and its depiction that are desirable, and thus, profitable.[77] Meanwhile, social media platforms have also become vital spaces for marginalized subjects, particularly Black women, to communicate, advocate, and mobilize.

Within this context, the focus on matte exteriority vis-à-vis skin and its color, and Simmons's alterations of it in her hyper-black images, upends what literary critic and art historian Harry Berger, Jr. calls "the fiction of objectivity," the presumption that "character [or selfhood] may be inferred from [an] image" and that the face acts as "the index of the mind."[78] Her hyper-black images are not an objective record of what is in front of the camera and viewers. Portraiture does not amount to self-representation, and the body's surface does not readily open itself to transparent knowledge. Relatedly, Simmons's animation of the fiction of objectivity vis-à-vis blackface imagery emphasizes literary studies scholar Sianne Ngai's account of animatedness as a stereotypical attribute of surplus liveliness historically attached to Black bodies in American popular culture. This liveliness—"the exaggeratedly emotional, hyper-expressive, and even 'overscrutable' image"—is meant to function as a sign of the racialized body's natural, authentic faculties on the one hand and its expressiveness on the other.[79] These perceptions reinforce "the notion of race as a truth located, quite naturally, in the always obvious, highly visible body."[80] Under this articulation of signification, Black bodies are seen as excessively and effusively expressive.

Simmons's use of digital photography, its immateriality a challenge to indexicality's contiguity with the real, is especially important here because it exposes how "the index as trace . . . has most strongly been mobilized to secure a closure of the visual field—a folding of the real onto visual representation," as Alessandra Raengo puts it.[81] This transposition "has paradigmatically occurred at the expense, and on the ground, of the black body because the 'truth' it displays on its surface is supposedly connected, like an indexical trace, to the 'truth' of its genetic makeup."[82] The Black body becomes the photographic object par excellence, doubling "in a different scale," Raengo continues, "the photographic map of the visual; that is, the sense of a phantasmatic and affective continuity between essence and appearance, inside and outside, identity and image."[83] Like Walker, Simmons stages Black intersectional unbecoming as *antimemory*, a progression towards incompletion. Her elliptical images fail to spur reconciliation by holding open the gap between past and present, sign and signified, identity and image.

Extra-Visual Effects and Affects

The grammatical ambiguities in the titles for Simmons's hyper-black photographs—one day and back then, seated and standing—extend the artist's acts of refusal at the same time that they punctuate her enactments of unbecoming. *One Day and Back Then* recalls critical theorist and semiotician Roland Barthes' formulation of the photographic index as the conjunction between the here and the formerly, the having-been-there, the presence of the image as evidencing the referent and the past event. But which day, how far back then, and what is the precise spatial location of the Black body pictured therein? A forking happens in Simmons's hyper-black photographs in three ways. The first is when the figure *seated* in the past and the figure *standing* in the present point in both directions temporally. A similar forking happens on the level of genre. The images exist somewhere between staged photography and performance documentation. Yet there is no evidence of theatrical lighting, make up (other than black paint), or elaborate direction. Simmons instead reorders the photographs' causal links to reality and past events by concealing openly recognizable staging efforts. Thus, even as her images approximate portraiture and performance, they undo this relationship. The performance is not a staged event per se; the performance is Blackness (both hers and the social construction) itself.

The third forking occurs as the result of Simmons's performance of racial excess—painting her phenotypically Black skin black. Beyond demonstrating how racial imagery in photography and film has shaped what constitutes Americanness and African Americanness, her hyper-black images make plain the role that artifice and color have played within both visual culture and modern and contemporary racial thinking. The minstrel circuit in the West shares a lineage with the innovative applications of paint used in the dramatic arts of the Renaissance era, which made color and skin indices of racial reckoning.[84] American blackface, however, further conflated racial appearance with racial essence for white and Black actors as well as viewers. On stages across the United States and Europe, minstrel performers used burnt cork and black greasepaint to blacken their skin and Black vernacular dialect to blacken their speech to amplify racial difference and delineate popular notions of Black deficiency. Considered intercultural performance, cross-dressing, and an act of love and theft in scholarship on the topic, blackface performance is a combination of gag, slapstick, and racial excess.[85] Moreover, blackface minstrelsy is often dismissed as an unfortunate occurrence within histories of Black self-representation. Black blackface performers are generally assumed to have taken on the minstrel form without troubling its racist tropes, providing the perfect spectacle for non-Black audiences. But as dance and theater studies scholar Amma Y.

Ghartey-Tagoe Kootin states in her study of Fred McClellan's blackbody minstrelsy school of the early 1900s, "Blackface minstrelsy was the ultimate counterfeit. Conceived in the minds and through the bodies of white men," she continues, "it was the paradoxical conflation of white theatrical construction and black authenticity" that turned on the signifying power of skin.[86]

Simmons's images that traffic in blackface imagery present surfaces that insist on being looked at while also defying immediate understanding, thereby challenging the presumed transparency of photography and racial authenticity. The streaking in these images is crucial here because it makes two elements visible: first, Simmons's application of black paint fails to evenly coat her body, and second, the black paint layered on top of her Black skin is not the same color. That is, the blackness of the paint does not coincide with the Blackness of the body. By privileging the visual effects and minor affects of hyper-blackness rather than the document itself, her manipulations of surface also force distinctions between visual essence and racial appearance, as well as between personhood and thingness. This "historical ontology" borne from slavery, as thing theorist Bill Brown calls it, made Black bodies and their labor exchangeable with property, collapsing the distinction between person and thing.[87] In so doing, slavery spurred one of the greatest paradoxes; it occasioned a physical and imaginative vision that disregarded the signs of personhood for the African slave's body but also relied on the slave's subjectivity—the quality of its existence in the (white) imagination as being *in* but not *of* the external world—as the basis for its function as a form of economic return.[88] As a result, value became both embodied and visible on the surface of the body, a social contract that attempted to fix the value of Blackness's materiality. Blackface further inflates this chiasmus by drawing into relation the counterfeit with the authentic "nature" of racial Blackness, a crossing that both elevates "blackness to the function of the money commodity," Raengo intimates, and attaches the history of visuality and its slavery roots to the history of capital.[89]

Following Brown's repackaging of Heidegger's writings on being and thingness, the value of an object's materiality cannot be acknowledged until it breaks, at which point its objectness becomes clear. In this context, Simmons's haphazard application of black paint to her phenotypically Black body makes light of Blackness's arbitrariness while also pointing out its uselessness as an index of racial authenticity. Instead of pointing beyond the pictorial frame as she does in other photographs, the uneven use of black paint points toward the value of Blackness itself, towards the thingness of Blackness as a manner—and a matter—of appearance that exceeds color and symbol. Thus, Simmons's play with second-skin-as-surface "vertiginously confounds," as Uri McMillan argues, "our all too simple binary logics—between interior and exterior, essence versus covering, a superficial surface and a fleshy invisible depth—while also," McMillan continues, "gesturing toward the emergence of alternative, even illegible, forms of representation and personhood."[90] Additionally, Simmons's painted Black skin in *Landscape (Home)* appears dusty and grey whereas in her *One Day and Back Then* images, the color appears densely saturated but likewise lacking in shine. These differences suggest that performance is immanent to Blackness, bringing blackface and the U.S. entertainment complex to bear on the problem of the Black figure as aesthetically pleasing and open to exploitation at a time when the Black image is rapidly consumed and policed.

When Simmons coats her already Black skin with black paint, she puts on a mask that is "phenomenologically tangible, intimate, and carnal because it adheres to the skin," as Raengo puts it in her discussion of blackface as face value.[91] This performance challenges "the fact that skin pigmentation, understood as the index of race, tends to remain the unchallenged starting point of the signifying chain."[92] It also confirms Michelle Ann Stephens's arguments about visibility's failure to drive progress. At the turn of the twentieth century, blackface trained white audiences "to see black corporeality reductively, as meaningful only in terms of its epidermal surface."[93] When Simmons substitutes an outward property—a boundary—of the body with paint, she exchanges a face for a mask, all to suggest that they are each other's conditions of impossibility.[94] The artist's already Black body further complicates this arrangement. "A black body is already marked as black," visual and performance studies scholar Tina Post elucidates in her study of Bert Williams's black-body minstrelsy, "at least in the ongoing dynamics of racialization that set the scene for minstrelsy in the antebellum United States, and that continues to this day. If a black body already signifies a black figure," she goes on to note, "what becomes of the effort to imitate blackness through the application of blacking?"[95] In the case of Simmons's hyper-black images, the effort to imitate is precisely to contest, rather than affirm, the figurative capacities of Blackness as a veritable expression of racial difference, on the one hand, and selfhood and sisterhood on the other.

At first glance, Simmons's excessive display of Black expressivity seems to diminish any appreciable distance between the artist's phenotypical Blackness and the prosthetic blackness of racial impersonation. Paint as pigment appears exchangeable with paint as skin. Her individual, anonymous Black body undermines this potential conflation, however, as it shows through the paint, displaying the mechanism of racial performance itself while avoiding the tendency to reduce Black identity to either verifiable essence or mere artifice. Rather than an ideal or intrinsic embodiment of Blackness, in other words, Simmons's visually dissonant and doubled racial appearance disrupts the continuity of racial essence just as her performance of blackface shows how *unlike* Blackness it actually is. Her blank stare, almost lifeless, bolsters the Black female body's disturbing presence; her face, quite literally, refuses to express.

These deployments of opacity and unbecoming against revelation amplify the political value of Simmons's appropriation of Black power iconography and her role as artist. Her pose and the wicker chair in *(Seated)* reference the iconic sepia-and-white photograph of Black Panther Party leader Huey P. Newton staged by Eldridge Cleaver and taken by Blair Stapp circa 1967. The image of Newton brandishing a spear in one hand and a rifle in the other became a widely circulated poster and an emblem of the Black liberation struggle in the United States and abroad. Simmons's large Afro alternately signifies Black Power, a material symbol celebrated and later adopted as a racial trope within Blaxploitation films of the 1970s.[96] Relatedly, Simmons's stance and terrycloth trench recalls characters like Shaft that became synonymous with a hypermasculine form of Black cool. To sport an Afro, within Black expressive culture, is an act of emulation that represents Black resistance and racial belonging; it means Black style, Black authority, and Black solidarity.

The raison d'être of such imagery—the Newton photograph and the Afro—was to elevate Black people as worthy of recognition, beauty, respect, and authority. The slogan "Black is Beautiful" and the Afro emerged alongside the rise of Black Nationalism among grassroots separatist organizations of which the Black Panther Party is but one yet significant faction. This era of Black Nationalism, also expressed in Blaxploitation

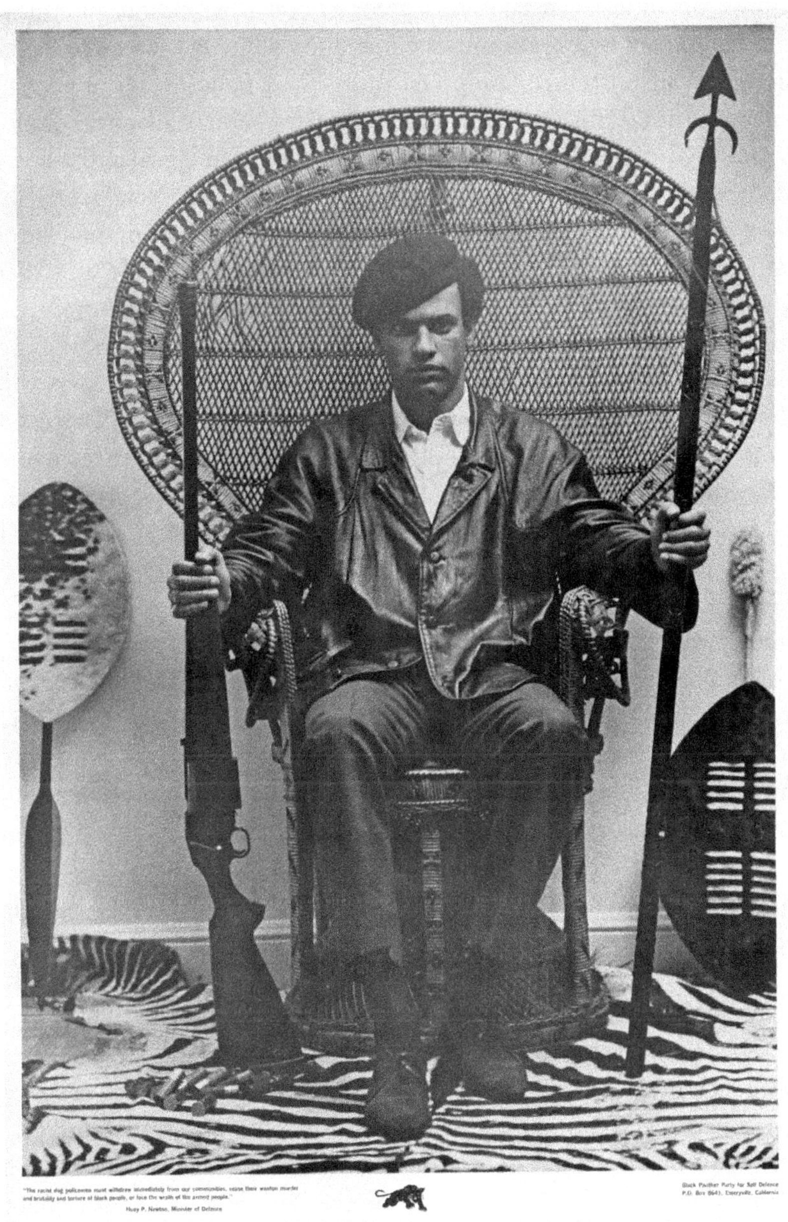

Figure 3.9. Blair Stapp and the Black Panther Party, *Dr. Huey P. Newton*, ca. 1967. Lithographic ink on paper (fiber product) and linen (material). Collection of the Smithsonian National Museum of African American History and Culture, Fair Use.

films at the time, has been criticized for its overly masculine, monolithic construction of Blackness and its obfuscation of the Black female leadership on which it relied. Simmons's nude Black female body appears to intervene in this history, offering an alternate vision of Black revolution on the level of gender and sexuality, a twist on what visual and cultural studies scholar and curator Nicole R. Fleetwood terms racial icons. But what is most striking about these images is neither the props, nor the citations, nor the feminist critique latent within each picture. It is their opacity, their denial of skin color as an index for racial truth beyond demands for group affiliation and solidarity across time and space.

The identification of Newton's image, and alternately the Afro, with the struggle for Black liberation are what Joanna Woodall terms "a contemporary twist on the old idea of the exemplar," figures whose exceptional qualities and achievements merit emulation in portrait-making traditions.[97] Within this schema, individual subjectivity is sacrificed for imitation, whether emulating a preexisting image or racially collective ideals. According to Woodall, "processes of emulation [presume that] identity [is] produced through resemblance to a potent prototype," a process that Simmons extends to racial resemblance as the grounds for a radical Black politics.[98] From this angle, her displays of Black power and Blaxploitation iconography imitate figurative types whose qualities and likeness elicit racial emulation. Thus, when Simmons paints her already Black skin black, she brings into view the complex problems of subjectivity and sociality that concentrate in the figure of the radical "sister" artist in the wake of intersectionality's mainstream appeal and the post-Black turn.

Her minor, multivalent enactments of Black female unbecoming complicate what Darby English calls "the representationalist, collectivist black-ideological norm."[99] This is not a scene of reverent homage where the Black revolutionary, the Black intellectual, and the Black artist are presented as the apotheoses of racial personality.[100] Instead, Simmons's excessive Blackness disrupts the venerated act of emulation by emphasizing how exemplary Black personae are elevated to a racially collective ideal in ways that ultimately hinder progress and systemic change. Moreover, rather than a mark of racial resemblance, Simmons's painted skin does not reveal some discernible essence that connects her Blackness with that of Newton, the Black Panther Party, or Blaxploitation characters. In these images, racial appearance is not requisite to racial essence, and Simmons breaks open representational identity politics by enfolding the cutting edges of anonymity, celebrity, iconicity, and notoriety back in on themselves.

In forcing a distinction between appearance and essence, identity and image, Simmons's visual work calls attention to how the epistemological, phenomenological, and affective force of photographic vision always already depends on its imbrication with race and gender. Significantly, Barthes's own conceptualizations of photography's affective power is mediated through touch and skin; photography is a carnal medium that produces "a skin [he] share[s] with anyone who has been photographed," and the index is an "umbilical cord."[101] Even more crucially, photography's embodied materiality and the awakening and circulation of desire that inheres in the *punctum*—one of the most discussed features of photographic theory—spring from displacing the Black maternal figure. Barthes locates the essence of photography in a picture of his deceased mother because it pricks him, inviting him into a particular kind of space, its bosom (by his account). For Barthes, photography is a vehicle for both necrophilic encounters and a return to the inside of the mother's body, a womb. Here, he explores photography's ability to connect rather than represent, and Blackness occupies a spectatorial position—as a mode of interaction, as enclosed space (womb and bosom), and as death.[102]

Despite the punctum's potential to move viewers emotionally, and its ability to migrate from one photograph—and body—to another in Barthes's account, the understanding of photography and Blackness as traces that point inward to their respective meanings and truths persists even after the digital turn. This turn assumed the loss of indexicality and its promise of existential and material continuity with reality.[103] In its wake, and regardless of the technological mode of production, the photographic image has occasioned two different logics—a photochemical logic in which the indexical exudes a fantasy of referentiality, and a digital logic invested in resemblance and computational equivalences.[104] These two logics, according to Raengo, "articulate changing notions of indexicality, materiality, and embodiment" that center on an in-between state of the image, a type of passage that counteracts the volatile effect of the trace, of photography as the art of *fixing* shadows.[105] The digital, in this arrangement, offers the fantasy of immateriality.

Simmons's hyper-black images answer the art of fixing shadows and photography's ability to ossify the otherness—indeed the undesirability—of Black female being and becoming, with opacity. Her visual language is one of holding viewers at bay, thus obscuring and upending expectations concerning the relation between recognition and discipline, representation and power. Her hyper-black images turn away from calls to self-identify—to stand up and be counted, to use Walker's words—at the level of aesthetics, race, and sisterhood. Her face refuses to communicate her mind and her subjectivity, and the inconsistencies of her painted skin as a form of blackface interrupt her actual skin's ability to animate and affirm minoritarian struggle and unity. Here, paint is not the embodiment of expressivity. The materiality of the Black female body—its physical presence, its place in the landscape, and its reproduction in the photograph—contrasts the materiality of black paint. Performance, therefore, allows Simmons to appropriate a racial persona that is historically resonant, but ultimately distinct from her own.

The subject's innermost self is hidden—behind an expressionless face, a mask of paint, and the artist's own self-effacement, her dissociation, in her portraits. In this way, Simmons's opacity rhymes with the distinctions Mutu draws between African Blackness and American Blackness. The presumption of racial intelligibility that Simmons's Black skin carries is further undone by the self-repudiation that adheres in both the depersonalized titles of her images and her refusal to identify herself as the subject of her portraits. Performance for Simmons, then, facilitates self-disavowal. It offers the artist the opportunity to play a role or a character, to *dissociate* from previous models of Black self-representation and to dissolve the boundaries between herself as "art maker," in her words, "in relation to the passerby, the potential participant, the viewer and the various landscapes" she engages.[106] As a result, she occupies a space between the constructedness and materiality of intersectional subjectivity that turns on a surplus layer of blackness, starkly transmogrifying what it means to be Black and woman in the new millennium.

Simmons's use of blackface imagery and black paint obscures her bodily form all the while outlining it, defining its contours. The blackness of the paint is superficial, to be sure, and a fabrication, a counterfeit Blackness presented as a manner—and a matter—of appearance, a visual effect.[107] The artist's denial of portraiture's norms gains more currency here precisely because of her performance of Blackness and its various states of unbecoming as object, as aesthetic practice, as thing, and as a language of desire. While she masks her body with black paint and refuses to disclose her identity, she gains a "face," so to speak, by "blackening up," a face whose value is nonetheless inherently unstable.[108] Still, Simmons's practice does more than confound binary logics concerning rupture and repair and exterior and interior.

In addition to troubling photography and blackface as technologies of seeing, witnessing, and performance, the artist's counterintuitive self-fashioning practices destabilize the privileged position of the human in relation to landscape. Her deployments of opacity prompt an extra-visual theorization of all these practices not only in terms of what they refuse and disrupt but also in terms of how obdurate forms of subject formation and selfhood extend subjectivity beyond the human with regard to the project of progress and futurity. Her work, like Narcissister's in the next chapter, demonstrates how bodies and subjects can remain radically opaque despite "visibility," as various forms of cover for the most disrespected and neglected. Simmons's critique of normative assumptions that link art as a social good to uncomplicated forms of mutuality underlines the coexistence of systems of signification and valuation that operate alongside, yet remain self-consciously and strategically inaccessible to, dominant ones. It is a practice of refusal to submit to demands for readability, certitude, and transparency in the art world and the wider world that is productive in its embrace of negativity.

Ultimately, Simmons's hyper black images are depictions of black skin and how it *acts* on the artist's own Black skin, under different sources and amounts of light, within the art historical canon, and in relation to demands for racial and gender reckoning in the digital age. In these images, Black skin performs myriad forms of cover: protection, concealment, territory, and surface that consolidate a non-relational, non-disclosive subjectivity unbound by public and private desires for security, accountability, and even solidarity. In the next chapter, Narcissister mobilizes similar practices of masking in the context of racial performance. Like Narcissister's topsy-turvy live artworks, the obvious excess of black paint on Simmons's medium-brown face and body mobilizes perverse forms of racial nostalgia on both sides of the color line. In so doing, the artist prompts a consideration of the *matters* of

Black female being in the past and as an enduring phenomenon that structures social relations in the present. Her use of opacity denies accountability, similar to Walker's refusal to be counted in chapter 1, in an era when emergent digital-imaging modalities, calls for transparency, and unprecedented forms of Black visibility not only proliferate but are also marshaled in public discourse as civic duty and as evidence of racial and gender progress.

By presenting opacity as integral to depictions of selfhood and sisterhood in contemporary visual culture, Simmons's art undoes what constitutes identity and loss in the new millennium. Her work models how to contend with what literary studies scholar Kevin Quashie calls "the impasse of history and Blackness," wherein no progress is possible because Blackness is and remains readily and literally indexed to dispossession and death.[109] In repeatedly staging illegible and illegitimate forms of representation and subjectivity against accepted norms, her work locates Blackness in other sensory registers—other surfaces—beyond the realm of the visual. Portraits become landscapes, bodies refuse identification, nomadic characters are seen nowhere in particular en route from one place to another, and performances of Blackness do not coincide with the Black female body on which they are staged. In the process, she actuates novel, counterintuitive embodiments of selfhood and sisterhood that are equal to new millennial challenges ushered in by socially constructed desires for transparent, positive, mutually beneficial, and equitable coactivity between individuals and collectives, humans and nonhumans, technology and progress, and visual media and its makers.

A Double Refusal of Memory

Whether defying medium distinctions, cloaking bodies, cutting pathways, or performing personas that do not coincide with her own identity, all of Simmons's photographs invite viewers to think not only about the character being portrayed, but also about how the figure is physically placed in and by the landscape. As she sits or stands in each of the scenes that appear across her practice, Simmons illustrates how Black bodies, and contemporary racial and gender politics more broadly, animate digitally processed mediums, geographies, and transhistorical discourses concerning power, reproduction, and representation. Her centering of racial fetishism as a problem inherent to the index also situates embodied materiality and the refusal to collapse the gap between Blackness and the body, individual and collective, as important frameworks for understanding racial and gender otherness in the new millennium. These counterintuitive enactments of becoming result in forms of (racial and gender) appearance that are at once self-effacing *and* something to be taken at face value.

By privileging surface and superficiality—indeed opacity—Simmons likewise raises ethical questions about the ends of representation, particularly for Black female subjects who continue to endure unique and violent forms of physiognomic scrutiny and subjugation that undermine the matter and mattering of Black lives. In art historians Cheryl Finley and Deborah Willis's view, elements of self-fashioning such as idealized poses, style, and dress work together in the Black portrait to present a sense of place and identity in visual form. Self-fashioning in this context redresses "the experiences of a people who have been caricatured through much of visual history, particularly in nineteenth-century anthropological and colonial photography."[110] For Finley and Willis, self-fashioning in photography endures as a reparative act of creativity and a celebrated aesthetic quality of Black portraiture.[111] During the first two and a half decades of the twenty-first century when post-racial aspirations and progressive identity politics collide with anti-Black animus, this amounts to "visual testimony of a collective memory" in "an age where black lives matter."[112] By invoking the Black Lives Matter movement, Finley and Willis make Black portraiture and activism correlative forms of Black resistance during moments of social upheaval. From this perspective, art is quite literally reparative justice. Especially evident in this framing is Black portraiture's status as a substitute for social relations routinely invoked by politics: portraits, in other words, function as proxies for individual and collective selfhood. Simmons's visual work, by contrast, short-circuits both the sociocultural import of Black women's image making and its capacity to reckon with racial and gender becoming at the edges of collective trauma and crisis. In so doing, she fashions a new kind of Black portraiture that comprises negativity and ennui consistent with the challenges of our time.

Up to now in this chapter, I have been winding my way through Simmons's oeuvre in a mode similar to the nomadic characters that appear in her work. Part of my reasoning for employing this method is to underscore the radical disjunctions her work poses to photography, to the indexical properties of Blackness and being, and to the social and aesthetic expectations of racial reconciliation often thrust upon women artists of African descent. My other reason for choosing this method—a counterintuitive practice of looking that her work likewise demands—is to enact reversal as an aesthetic strategy of repulsion that emerges in Simmons's early formation as an artist and in the work of Narcissister discussed in the next chapter.

The Interfaith Pilgrimage of the Middle Passage, a walking tour that retraced the transatlantic slave trade in reverse, is one of Simmons's earliest projects and a precursor to her rebuffs of the politics of recognition and visibility that structure Black representational space. The *Interfaith Pilgrimage of the Middle Passage* began in 1998 as a twelve-month-long trek through the United States, the Caribbean, Brazil, West Africa, and South Africa. Convened by Sister Clare Carter, a Buddhist nun of the Nipponzan Myohoji order based at the New England Peace Pagoda in Leverett, Massachusetts, and performance artist and activist Ingrid Askew, the walk was envisioned as a mobile site of multiracial dialogue, mutual understanding, and healing. Adopting the ritual practice of the pilgrimage as a journey of atonement and self-discovery in religious and racial terms was an effort to liberate participants, and the greater, global public, from racial strife. "The idea," according to Askew, "was to begin a process of healing the wounds of slavery, looking at racism, which is the legacy of slavery."[113] In moving backward along the route of the transatlantic slave trade, the conveners and participants hoped to symbolically and geographically reverse the direction of slavery and its injuries.

Along the route, participants of different religious and racial backgrounds that numbered between fifty and seventy-five walked eight to fifteen hours a day, visiting sites associated with the history of slavery. These sites included former slave quarters in Virginia, stations on the Underground Railroad, and villages that had been raided in Africa. They chanted and meditated while they walked, offering a "living prayer of the heart, mind, and body for the sons and daughters of the African Diaspora."[114] They also conversed nightly about their experiences and slept in tents, on church pews, and at truck stops among other locales. A mobile memorial to those held in bondage and those who resisted, the pilgrimage was intended to redress individual and collective psychic wounds inflicted by encounters with slavery and its afterlife.

The interfaith pilgrims had a variety of reasons for joining the march. Many shared utopian goals of healing slavery's injuries by physically encountering a history seldom taught or discussed in public. Some wanted to be part of an adventure. Some were at a crossroads in their own lives. Simmons, who grew up in a Buddhist household, took on the sojourn at a crucial time in her artistic development. Of the journey she says, "I was an assistant to photographer Walter Chin, and happy with the job, but I left it and a boyfriend to go on the journey. I was a year-and-a-half with the monks and then I hitched throughout the east coast of Africa with a friend for another year. We walked eight hours a day, everyday. It was a walking meditation."[115]

Apart from the organizers' lofty aspirations for repairing the trauma of slavery through multiracial coalition, the pilgrimage highlights how traversing landscape is a spatial practice that distinguishes and arranges bodies, identities, and Simmons's own self-conception. "It ended 14 years ago," she says in a 2016 interview, "but it was such an epic experience that there are aspects of it that I'm still uncovering."[116] She continues,

> The main thing that I learned was how to share resources and live communally, which I later realized was not the way I want to live. It was an experience to think about faith and about each step you take as a meditation. . . . Each moment has an impact. Each parcel of land has a history. You're thinking about the consequences of European history, the consequences of American history, the consequences of the Native Americans, the consequences of the slave trade, the consequences of the immigrants that came through Ellis Island and the consequences of the Civil Rights movement because you're having nightly conversations, which roused so many raw emotions.[117]

These remarks reveal why surface and memory work are so central to her practice. For Simmons, marking the land with her steps, an indexical act, gave rise to questions of the self. She acknowledges the impact of the walking tour on her thinking about history, her own being in the world, and ultimately her artistic motivations. Significantly, Simmons rejects communal living as a result of her experience and reflects on landscape as a fraught site of national and racial becoming.

Within the context of the walking tour's official history, Simmons enacts a forking similar to the one that happens in her *One Day and Back Then* images by pointing in two directions at once; respectively, in her participation and her recollections, she points toward her own identity as well as toward a social desire to reconcile the ongoing trauma of slavery beyond the event. But this forking is fraught with material conditions of deferral and failure. Other than the artist's biography and memory, reports of her participation in the pilgrimage are scarce: she goes unnamed in the official accounts that exist, identified only as a documentary filmmaker in anthropologist Peter Sutherland's published ethnography. Moreover, the film she shot during the tour has been lost.

The walking tour's mobilization of reversal mirrors the chiasmus in representation and reckoning, in reproduction and repair, that Simmons undoes across her practice. Despite its utopian conceit, the walk became a microcosm of vexed race relations in the United States. By the time the group arrived in New Orleans, racial tension among the participants had become so deeply felt that some chose not to continue. Two types of movement deployed in the pilgrimage doubled the irony—the forward motion of walking, processional ritual, and progress, on the one hand, and tracking the slave trade in reverse, on the other. Instead of racial healing or transcendence, the participants' prolonged proximity to one another inspired a wellspring of racial discord, which was exacerbated by the interfaith ethos of the pilgrimage. In Peter Sutherland's summation, "Interfaith pilgrimages are by definition symbolically incoherent . . . Given the 'interfaith' conception of the Middle Passage pilgrimage, cultural coherence was neither proposed nor possible."[118] Reversal in this frame is multivalent. Walking the slave trade route backward *and* the resulting racial regression that occurred internally not only fold into each other with regard to the project of racial healing and communal becoming. Reversal also inverts both the pilgrimage's insistence on moving forward in space and its ethos of making multiracial progress *together*. This form of historical reenactment, then, ultimately undercuts idealistic narratives about America's racial present and future, namely that forward motion and multiracial hope are or can be the means for relieving and moving beyond slavery's debilitating grip on contemporary (Black) social life. In spite of the group's aspirational efforts, reversal in the end thwarts the participants' hopes of retracing the land, of recovering the past, and of racial reparation.[119]

Simmons's various acts of refusal and unbecoming—her turns away from shared living, photography's norms, and the Black female body as affirmative trace—rhyme with her self-effacing performances of Blackness. In privileging surface rather than indexicality and interiority, the artist presents Blackness, and by extension slavery, not as historical phenomena, as events that occurred in the past and have attained closure, but rather as ontologies that bifurcate the particularities of the past and present, of person and thing, and of identity and image. Thus, the value of Black female (un)becoming is that of visual interruption, an aesthetic strategy of repulsion that, much like the proliferation of transgressive dismemberment in Mutu's collages, refuses to reconcile the space between 'others.' Put differently, to embrace opacity is to refuse the desire to be accounted for, to reject the historical demands for Blackness's persistent visualization, and to defy the impulse to recover and reconcile trauma. It is to be unassimilable, undesirable.[120]

By enfolding viewers into encounters with Black womanhood that slip between occlusion and hyper-visibility, Simmons asks viewers and critics to consider the costs and means of progress and historical transformation. That "photographs are always, and only," in art historians Diarmuid Costello and Margaret Iversen's summation, "depictions of whatever was before the camera at the moment of exposure," and, as such, occupy the correct "causal relation to the resulting image," is continually frustrated in her work.[121] Obscured figures and grainy images, citations of canonical poses and artworks, self-effacing performances of Blackness, and participation in spatial practices meant to redress slavery do not lead to transparent meaning, feelings of wholeness, or racial repair. Alternately, her portraits do not progress or regress along a series nor do they engender kinship, even as her photographs are produced *as sets of related images*. They instead deny specificity and definition by dissolving genre boundaries, just as her refusals and opaque performances of Blackness as a visual effect dispense with an affirmative tie between the image and its subject and vice versa. The result is loosely connected series where ideas, narratives, subjects, and selves migrate between media and loop back on themselves.

Thus, the adjoining yet disparate image worlds that comprise Simmons's non-revelatory practice engender a process of unbecoming that is against direct associations, the retrieval of the past, and norms concerning the (Black female) body as a reproductive medium. Most importantly, the opacity that emerges in her practice is not at odds with or merely oppositional to hyper-visibility. In their unbecoming, her photographs depict multiple ways to hide in plain sight vis-à-vis camouflage and masking, withdrawing and withholding, all of which confront viewers with a lack of straightforwardness in both action and progress. The destabilizing, dispossessive force of this counterintuitive plurality expands and condenses, unbound by secured meaning. In so doing, her work models how extra-sensuous ways of knowing and being can exceed the visual as well as how bodies function as markers of territories, whether known or unknown, under and against the transparent, immaterial lure of digital capture. Ultimately, her subjects relish the ability to be anonymous and undesirable—or momentarily sovereign—outside of the grid of identity and representation. By disrupting assumed continuities between reproduction and reparation, perception and knowledge, they evacuate the desire for visibility and inclusion to function as ethical imperatives that mandate belonging and togetherness as social goods in the twenty-first century. In this space, new forms and formations of Black expression and being are possible precisely because they are extra-visual and fugitive, in but not of this world.

Performance artist Narcissister, the subject of the next chapter, explores similar questions of selfhood and solidarity. Where the other artists in this book specifically interrogate the origins of Blackness and the impossibilities of historical recovery, Narcissister transmogrifies the cultural currency of multiracialism in the new millennium. The artist brings the language of narcissism—pathological self-desire—as an aesthetic and political strategy to bear on progressive discourses concerning contemporary multiracial representation and feminist practices of art and activism. She is known for wearing an eerie Barbie mask, a kinky-haired merkin, and never revealing her identity. In titillating yet repulsive displays of uncomfortable, abject sex that she performs on herself, Narcissister decouples reproduction and reparation by dramatizing the repulsions and reversals that proliferate throughout this book. In so doing, she transforms narcissism into something else altogether that, along with the other minor aesthetic strategies herein, coalesces into a new Black feminist ethics of representation and relation.

4

Masks, Mayhem, and Kink

Can perversion open up new modes of being in the world for black women while at the same time accounting for the historical bondage (literally and symbolically) associated with black women's bodies?
—Ariane Cruz

As a performance persona rooted both in an aesthetic practice and political strategy, Narcissister draws from the Greek myth of Narcissus, the god who fell in love with his own reflection. This mythological story provides the namesake and source for the present-day disorder known as narcissism in psychoanalysis. The artist's own suggestive moniker derives from this cultural history, while her perverse enactments of self-sex tether such obsessive self-love to the history and memory of racial and gender subjection, and, more recently, feminist performance art. Her acrobatic choreography and costumes often mimic topsy-turvy dolls, a toy made popular in the United States during the antebellum and postbellum periods. From behind multiracial masks, Narcissister subjects herself to erotic spankings and penetration with sharp objects. In bringing all of these elements together, she dramatizes mixed-race relations and self-objectification, stimulating new modes of thinking and being that account for the fraught relationship between Black women's bodies and bondage.

Narcissister's embodiment of taboo characters and kinky choreography defies categorization. Her perverse mix of highbrow and lowbrow genres and forms sits between fine art and entertainment, an attribute that has relegated her to the minor edges of the art world. Like Simmons, there is minimal academic scholarship on her work, and she has received a dearth of major exhibition opportunities. A self-identified "sister" of African American and Moroccan-Jewish descent, Narcissister's

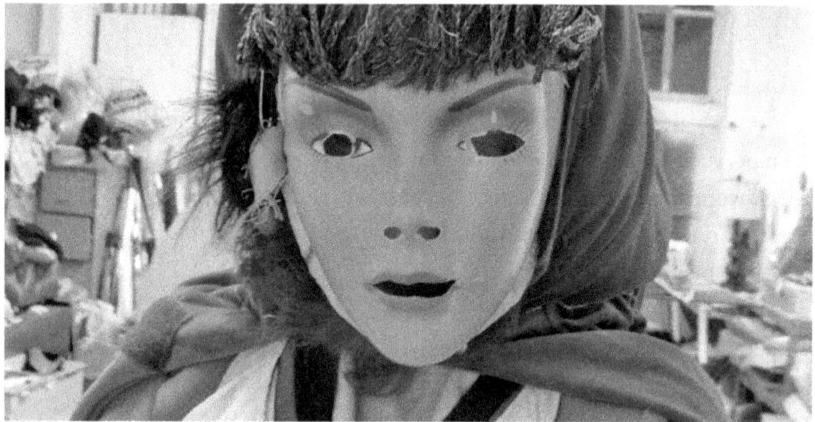

Figure 4.1. Narcissister, *Red Riding Hood*, 2014. Mixed media. Courtesy the artist. Photo credit: Narcissister.

world consists of racialized dolls, mannequins, autoerotic sex play, and remarkable yet anticlimactic performances of constructed identities.[1] She strips, flips upside down, spreads her legs to reveal multiracial doll heads nestled in her crotch, and plays with herself as she frenetically rubs the masks and heads attached to her body. While inserting and pulling items from her mouth, vagina, and anus, the artist moves quickly and gracefully. One blink and you might miss something, like a swift costume change or the climax one might expect from such a titillating display. She is known for wearing an expressionless Barbie mask, wigs, and a kinky-haired merkin, all while concealing her "real" identity. Her solo performances thus contain all the makings of psychosexual disorder: multiple identities, kinky sex, and self-objectification.

In the prevailing analysis of narcissism from 1914, Sigmund Freud characterized narcissism as a sexual perversion wherein romantic attraction is directed exclusively toward oneself.[2] This twisted form of self-centering, typically understood as an extreme, pathological form of self-desire, is thought to lead to self-affirmation and reassurance. Narcissists, in this formula, love the self-image they project onto others, and when others reflect the projected image back, the narcissist's own sense of self is reaffirmed. In this cyclical exchange, narcissists are reassured both of their existence and of the boundaries of their ego, a reflexive process that blurs all distinctions between reality and fantasy.

Beginning in the 1970s, art critics saw in narcissism a novel approach to understanding performance art, even while the framework was hotly debated along gender lines. The question was, Who exactly could or was allowed to put oneself on display? As critic and curator Lucy Lippard outlines, white, second-wave feminist performance artists who used their own bodies in live and video art were held to a different standard than men who also used their own bodies as the primary vehicle for artmaking:

> Men can use beautiful sexy women as neutral objects or surfaces but when women use their own faces and bodies, they are immediately accused of narcissism. . . . Because women are considered sex objects, it is taken for granted that any woman who presents her nude body in public is doing so because she thinks she is beautiful. She is a narcissist, and [Vito] Acconci, with his less romantic image and pimply back, is an artist.[3]

Lippard's lacerating comments underscore how (white) women artists often have had to contend with the uneasy tension between feminism, self-display, and the male gaze. White male artists, on the other hand, were afforded the unmitigated capacity and ability to be self-absorbed. In *Seedbed* of 1972, for instance, Vito Acconci masturbated as he hid underneath a gallery-wide ramp installed at the Sonnabend Gallery in New York while vocalizing into a loudspeaker his fantasies about the visitors walking above him.[4] Even with his pimply back and crude performance, Acconci and his white male contemporaries making conceptual video and performance art in the 1960s and 1970s were considered creative and radical by the art world establishment. In response, women artists and their critics claimed performance and narcissism as self-affirming sources of creative agency and self-representation to counter white male privilege and its perceived links to creative genius, radicalism, conceptual art, and narcissism.

Extending Lippard's critiques of whiteness and masculinity, later feminist art scholars have responded to a lack of analysis about the strategies of self-display that BIPOC (Black, Indigenous, and people of color) artists employ in their work. For Amelia Jones, narcissism is a radical practice, especially when enacted by marginalized subjects, namely women artists, queer artists, and artists of color. In her analysis, narcissism has the capacity to break down the self-other, mind-body split that subtends prevailing conceptions of modern subject formation in the West. These binaries often characterize culture and the mind as masculine and nature and the body as feminine. Self-centeredness shatters these reductive binaries, and in so doing, Jones explains, becomes empowering rather than perverse. Centering the self can, in other words, elevate queer and BIPOC artists, thereby expanding narrow understandings of feminism and art's social dimensions.[5]

Narcissister complicates the above discourses by performing undesirable selfhood and subjectivity through a persona of her own creation. Her repulsive spin on classical dance, BDSM (shorthand for bondage/discipline, dominance/submission, sadism/masochism), and feminist art exposes how various forms of movement typically associated with free expression and self-fulfillment become conduits for disciplining the racialized female body. Often, while dancing a mix of simple jazz and burlesque choreography comprising hip rolls, raised arms, and pantomimed hand gestures that indicate a woman's curves, she performs the extraordinary feat of storing a whole outfit in her private parts. Her recent art features dolls with crudely assembled body parts, cut-up masks of various skin tones, dysfunctional and ill-fitting costumes, and oversized props that often thwart the artist's seamless execution of a choreographed step or cue. By staging such feats and failures, Narcissister participates in a Black feminist performance art tradition set forth by Lorraine O'Grady, whose work also explored lived experiences of duality in a world structured by difference and inequity. O'Grady challenged the fixed positions of self and other as a self-proclaimed insider-outsider, a famed conceptual artist, a Black feminist provocateur, and a person marked by racial hybridity—her family histories connect the Caribbean, Africa, Europe, and the United States. Her work also highlights art historical omissions and institutional failings related to the creative agency of historically marginalized artists. Under the name of Mlle Bourgeoise Noire, a French Guianese pageant winner and O'Grady's former alter ego, the artist disrupted art openings in New York in the early 1980s by publicly whipping herself with a cat-o'-nine-tails while spewing poetry. Dressed in a gown and cape made of white gloves, she decried work by Black artists that pandered to market demands ("No more bootlicking . . .") and censured the art world's racial and gender makeup.

In similar ways, Narcissister's racially marked body is central to her expansions of feminist art and critique as well as racial and gender kinship. She alters the conventions of burlesque, African American concert dance, women's work as craft (quilt making and collage), and camp (she hand-makes her props and costumes from discarded materials) by combining these elements with the visual histories of Black subjugation and sexual transgression. While her work operates on multiple registers, Narcissister highlights how the two latter phenomena, enmeshed since the eighteenth century, remain entangled in the new millennium amid renewed interests concerning racial reconciliation and the promise of multiracial feminism.[6] Her visual work, like that of Walker and Mutu, also illustrates how non-relationality haunts conceptions of women-of-color sisterhood within Black feminist praxis. She further builds on Walker's depictions of the Black female bottom by playing in the bottom register, a body part and social sphere commonly associated with both Blackness and queerness. Bottomness for Narcissister often surfaces in her choice of archetypes and forms of dance as well as in the use of her own anal cavity.

In *Every Woman* (2008/9), her best-known work that has live and video versions, the artist reorders the striptease—a lowbrow form of entertainment where performers generate visual pleasure through sexual play, pole-dancing, and the removal of one's already-skimpy clothing—by performing it in reverse. The quality of the video, a kind of home-movie aesthetic, is also notable. At the start of the video version of the piece, red curtains with gold lining and black tassels part to reveal a nude Narcissister facing away from viewers as the camera zooms to compress the frame and focus on the artist's backside. Wearing her signature mask, the artist revolves on a rotating platform similar to the kind that circus performers use, making her nude body, brown-toned Barbie face, and kinky-haired merkin visible from all angles. To Chaka Khan's "I'm Every Woman" (1978), she pulls clothing and accessories from her mouth, from between her legs, and from the oversized, kinky Afro wig she wears. Rather than revealing the artist, Narcissister's masking devices, similar to Simmons's enactments of opacity, ensure that she is never fully exposed, despite being, in some cases, almost completely nude. She instead presents an artificial construction—the flipside of Chaka Khan's lyrics, "Anything you want done baby/I do it naturally."[7]

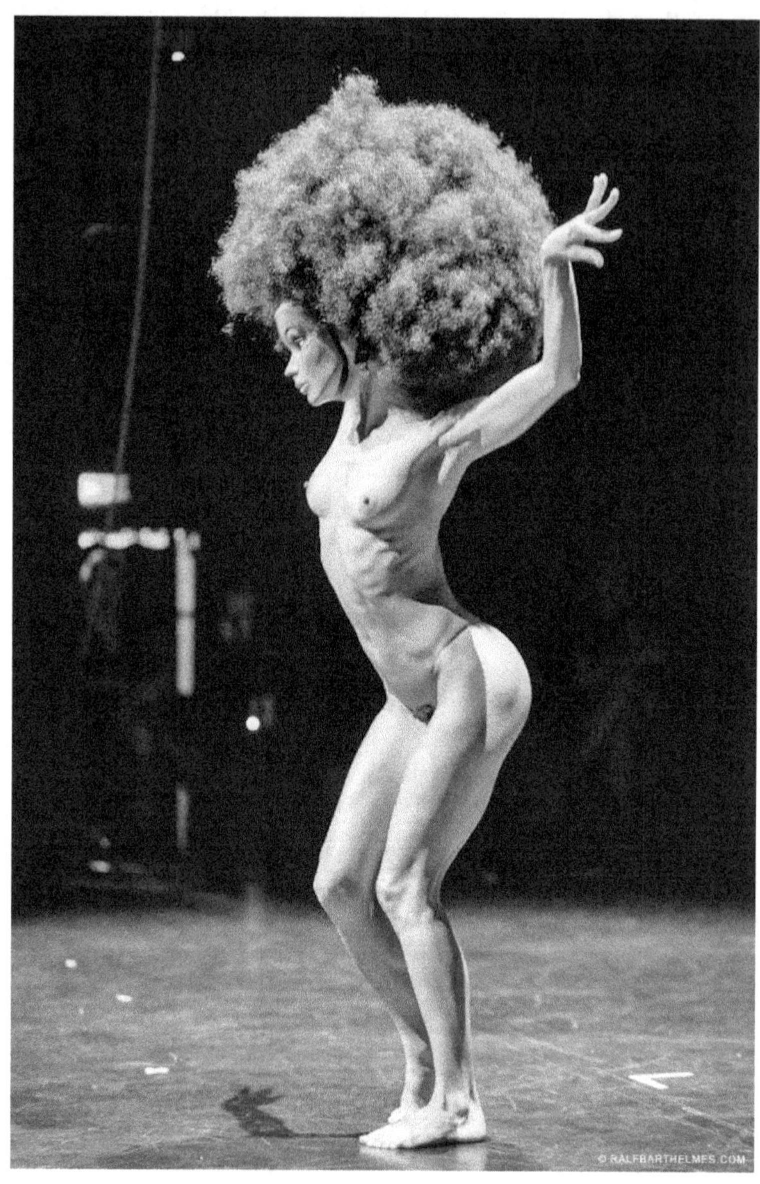

Figure 4.2. Narcissister, *Every Woman*, 2008/9. Performance still, mixed media. Photo credit: Ralf Barthelmes.

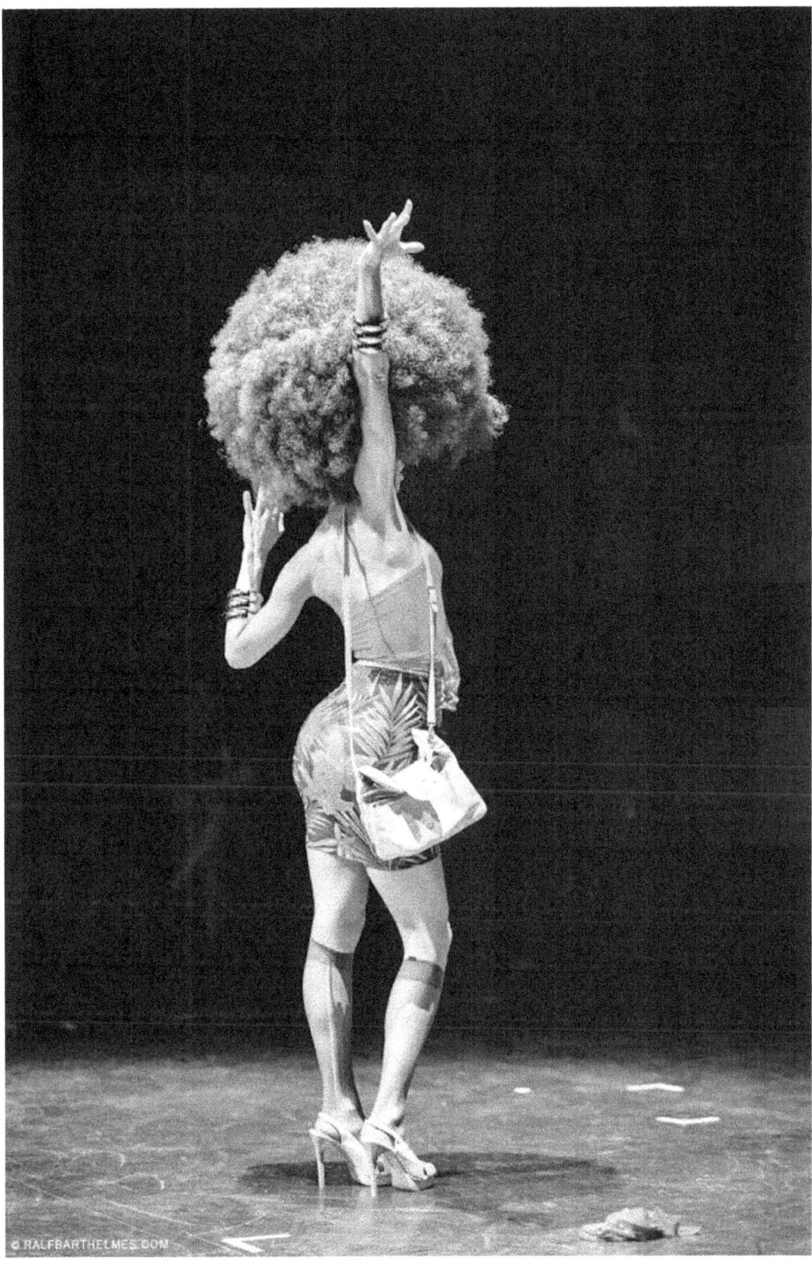

Figure 4.3. Narcissister, *Every Woman*, 2008/9. Performance still, mixed media. Photo credit: Ralf Barthelmes.

Just as *Every Woman* reverses the norms of burlesque, the work also contests media fictions and fantasies associated with Black women's sexual desires and performance prowess. The Afro wig and pop song function as signifiers that recall the self-objectifying racial fictions of the Blaxploitation film genre and racialized pornography of the 1970s and 1980s, the Golden and Silver Eras of erotic film, respectively. During this time, Blaxploitation and erotic films trafficked in exaggerated depictions of Black women doing "it"—sex and sexuality—both exotically and "naturally," as Chaka Khan sings. The voluptuous, lustful Black woman kicking ass in a huge, weapon-storing Afro and low-cut, impossibly tight clothing—Pam Grier as Coffy in the 1973 film of the same name, for instance—is a recognizable and recurring stereotype in the former. In the latter genre, lascivious Black women who possess special "skills" and enjoy being racially subjugated during sex evince such fantasies. Narcissister's simulations of self-sex in *Every Woman* and elsewhere in her practice, however, do not lead to self-affirming ecstasy; instead the orgasm is routinely displaced, frustrated, or quite literally fabricated in her work. Rather than mastery, incompletion—of sex, race, and reproduction as well as dance-based virtuosity and fully knowable identities—is the acme of her art.[8] Her choreographed failures to climax, which appear as various forms of reversals and refusals across her practice, overturn early twenty-first-century expectations that identity performance be legible and discernible vis-à-vis the body and self-representation. Narcissister's kinky art also challenges the exceptionalism attached to multiracial figures and futures in the American imaginary.

Like Mutu's collages of interracial, interspecies, and intermedia relations, Narcissister's art satirizes the myriad ways that American public discourse valorizes multiracialism—one of the greatest hopes and myths of the new millennium. Often referred to as the browning of America, attachments to multiracialism and its potential to transform the social and political body of the United States into a majority-minority society stems from the country's present and future demographic changes. As population growth slows among aging white populations, the numbers of Latinx, Asian, and multiracial Americans are rapidly increasing. African Americans and other non-white groups are also experiencing moderate growth, so much so that by 2044, the Census Bureau predicts no one racial group will comprise the majority of the country. This browning is cultivated in the private, intimate arenas of sex, family, and friendship, bridging issues of race and ethnicity with those of gender, reproductive futurity, and kinship. While some see these new racial demographics as a good thing—an explosion of diversity and an answer to anti-Blackness—others see it as a threat to historical demands for racial justice.[9]

In contemporary American media, desirable images of multicultural figures, especially those with one Black parent and one white, are everywhere, from reality shows to make-up commercials to primetime televisions shows such as ABC's *Mixed-ish*. Some of this media depicts multiracial protagonists as mired in painful confusion; others equate them with progress, as the embodiment of a post-racial utopia.[10] Both portrayals hinge on the racist notion that Blackness is a deficit that must be overcome through whiteness. On the covers of magazines such as *Ebony* and *Vogue*, mixed-race celebrities like Jesse Williams, Kendrick Sampson, Colin Kaepernick, Zendaya, and Amandla Stenberg have been featured as the faces of twenty-first-century activism and social change. Zendaya and Stenberg have also been touted as icons of present-day Black feminism in and after the age of Obama, a figure whose own mixed-race heritage sparked public debates about the origins and boundaries of Blackness during what many hailed as the most progressive era in the United States in recent years. The fervor surrounding Vice President Kamala Harris's multiracial identity and performance of Blackness during her 2024 presidential campaign from the right and the left further underscores America's infatuation with mixed-race exceptionalism.

Within the academy, critical mixed-race studies has emerged as a new field of inquiry for scholars interested in the historical and present-day significance of race mixing, hybridity, collective identity, transracial adoption, and the persistent problem of the color line.[11] Writing on the American public's embrace of interracial coupling in terms of policy preferences and cultural trends, communication studies scholar Catherine R. Squires observes, "Promoting tolerance and cross-racial intimacy at the dawn of the twenty-first century is much better than the hysteria over race mixing that ushered in the twentieth. . . . That the mainstream press is declaring a consensus that interracial marriage is a social good is no small change."[12] By Squires's account, this embrace moves away from centuries-old angst about race mixing to promote tolerance; it affirms the promise and possibility of coalitional politics and celebrates cross-racial intimacy as a form of social advancement. Following this media trend, multiracial bodies are now seen as harbingers of racial harmony rather than racial degradation, and this development is "evidence of some progress."[13] These putatively progressive concepts are punctuated by the gains and failures of Obama's 2006–8 presidential campaign and his 2009–17 occupation of the White House, important years for Narcissister's artistic development. Yet while representations of hybridity and multiplicity recur throughout her oeuvre, she repeatedly distorts idealized images of the mixed-race figure by performing its shortcomings.

With her name, multicolored masks, and performances of stereotypes such as the everywoman, topsy-turvy, and the mammy, the artist plays with the polysemy of gender and racial affinity to redefine collective imaginings of community and solidarity. Instead of romantically revering the browning of America, her work challenges the reparative viability of interracial intimacy within identity-based art and performance, contemporary theories of feminism, and coalitional politics. Her combination of self-loving absorption with "sisterhood, especially among women of color" recalls legacies of activism from the 1960s to the present that oppose gender and racial discrimination.[14] Within these restorative justice movements, formal political power leads to equity, and positive self-representation repairs injuries borne from oppressive violence. Narcissister, however, burlesques her own mixed-race heritage as a site of undesirability where self-objectification functions as the limit of intersectional feminism and multiracial promise. In so doing, her work compels viewers and critics to interrogate the pitfalls of inclusive theorizing that have emerged in the wake of intersectionality's mainstream popularity, from shared identity categories such as race and gender to shared national memory. At the limits of the contemporary art world and multiracial, intersectional feminism, her live performances occupy an uneasy relationship to a marketplace that categorizes and trades physical art objects as commodities. They also fail to mobilize a sisterhood that is organized around racial and gender solidarity and sameness. Her topsy-turvy, kinky art consequently upends how individual and collective attachments to the language of commonality and coherence mask and occlude the messiness of subjectivity and difference.

Routinely disrupting expectations of self-mastery and multiracial exceptionalism, Narcissister transmutes self-loving absorption by adding a little kink to the mix. Within modern studies of human sexuality, kinkiness encompasses non-conventional sexual concepts, practices, and fantasies. The term derives from the idea of a "bend" in one's sexual behavior that contrasts "straight" or "vanilla" sexual mores and proclivities, attributes that likewise equate normativity with whiteness. Narcissister's kink expands the term's racial framework. Her performances of perversion span crude forms of self-sex; curly wigs and merkins; choreographic flaws and failures; and sociocultural entanglements of Blackness and whiteness, gender, and sexuality. From thick, curly hair to sexual fetishes, her kink epitomizes undesirability and the aesthetic strategies of repulsion that populate this book. The artist's performances of racialized stereotypes within and beyond the body also contest the limits of Black female subjectivity and solidarity in light of her own racial identifications as a "sister," a woman of color. Her kink, therefore, bends the (inter)racial boundaries of intersectional feminism by animating how positions of dominance and subordination, privilege and oppression, can co-constitute minoritized women's experiences of selfhood.

Narcissister's kinky brand of self-objectification undercuts social mores about sexual agency with repeated acts of self-inflicted discomfort, stalled orgasms, and bodily harm, progressing not toward mastery, but toward a kind of incompletion that corresponds with Simmons's unbecoming portraits. Rather than work that culminates in glorious—orgasmic—ends, the artist draws attention to the journey of self-realization and its perils. Although she possesses the talent, skill, and flexibility, she is thoroughly uninterested in a presentation of mastery. Instead, Narcissister tarries in self-neglect and frustration, a baseness that stems from racialized abjection but that also gives rise to perverse forms of value in and of themselves. Her Afro wig and choice of soundtrack for *Every Woman* are particularly important here because they both elucidate how kink, from myths about Black women's hair to their sexual prowess, circumscribes Black female embodiment in the recent past and present. Significantly, the year Khan released "I'm Every Woman" was a pinnacle year for disco, a genre of dance-pop music lauded as a democratized, multiracial form of cultural production that held the power to foster togetherness, love, and new freedoms for historically marginalized subjects. "Before commercial success twisted the music into a polyester perversion of itself," music journalists Bill Brewster and Frank Broughton reminisce, "disco was the hottest, sexiest, most redeeming and most deeply loving dance music there has been."[15] For Brewster and Broughton, disco engendered hope for minoritarian subjects during the post–civil rights era when attitudes and policies about racial equality and sex dramatically changed. Sex, in the age of disco, was "for enjoyment, not procreation."[16]

This framing, popular music scholar Brittnay L. Proctor explains, obscures the labor of Black femme performers like Gloria Gaynor and Sylvester who created and popularized beloved disco anthems such as "I Will Survive" and "You Make Me Feel (Mighty Real)" (both also from 1978).[17] Queer white male subjects, Proctor convincingly argues, have recruited these tunes as conduits for coming out and to affirm interpersonal connection as a way to allay feelings of isolation and otherness.[18] Narcissister's bodily contortions and song choices across her practice draw attention to a similar matrix of difference, self-fashioning, cover, revelation, and intimacy. But her use of covers, in terms of masks and costumes, not popular music (she always performs to originals), repels commonplace expectations concerning the reproductive, liberatory capacities of dance, dance music, intersectionality, and racialized women's work. Khan's anthem celebrates female empowerment, and Whitney Houston (a Black femme diva in her own right) remade the song in 1992 to popular acclaim. In sticking to the original, Narcissister transports viewers and listeners back to the moment of conception for Khan's version, a reversal and backward glance that tethers Black women's creative labors to a queer futurity not contingent on procreation or forward motion. In so doing, *Every Woman* destabilizes the notion of a universal or every 'woman' as well as the idea that Black women's bodies are 'naturally' or solely sites of strength, reproduction, repair, and transcendence in service to the future care and well-being of both the nation and humankind.

Inserting and expelling items from her genitalia and other sexual orifices as well as exploiting minor sociopolitical positions like being in the middle and at the bottom are other important ways the artist destabilizes Blackness and the body as sites of resistance and reproductive futurity. The disturbing displays of penetration and versions of "the pullout method" that she performs on herself comingle with a multiplicity of characters and fictions typically considered taboo. In mixing edgy sex acts with kitschy soft porn archetypes, topsy-turvy dolls, and mammies, Narcissister crafts complex, insider-outsider, dominant-submissive images of racialized gendered embodiment that also contest two widespread stereotypes about twenty-first-century mixed-race African Americans. These stereotypes, the "new millennium mulatta" and the "exceptional multiracial," inscribe mixed-race African Americans as tragic figures whose Blackness predestines them for misfortune in the case of the former and rewards mixed-race African Americans for successfully erasing their Blackness in the case of the latter.[19]

Narcissister's background in African American concert dance, her training in Black feminist craft and performance, and her participation in exhibitions solely comprising artists of African descent is especially important here as is her use of the mask and various racial and sexual stereotypes typically ascribed to Black women's bodies. Bridging her own complex racial and ethnic heritage with her artistic influences and practice, the artist refracts narcissism's sexually perverse origins to focus on how pathologies of race, and specifically Blackness, continue to energize the liberal imagination. Her onanistic acts of incomplete performance upend normative notions of mastery, on the one hand, and the present and future value of Black women's reproductive labor, on the other. She is the ultimate outlaw who turns away from both sexual pleasure as a remedy to racial and gender subjugation as well as biological and artistic reproduction as the grounds for progress. Narcissister's visual work also underscores the myriad ways in which the visual economy of race and phenotype appears to be inherently sexual and libidinal.

This mode of moving—between the conceptual and the kinetic—is novel, especially in terms of kink. In her discussion of kink as perversion, Black gender and sexuality studies scholar Ariane Cruz writes:

> My conjuring of a politics of perversion relies on the plural and polymorphous resonance of the term perversion. A corruption itself, the politics of perversion recognizes the subversive, transformative power of perversion as the alteration of something from its original course, and the kink—the sexual deviance—that perversion evokes. In theorizing the politics of perversion I mine the multivalence of the word pervert itself,

> defined as (verb) "to alter (something) from its original course, meaning, or state to a distortion or corruption of what was first intended; lead (someone) away from what is considered right, natural, or acceptable;" and (noun) "a person whose sexual behavior is regarded as abnormal and unacceptable."

Narcissister's kink is both verb and noun. But it also expands on the term's more sensuous arenas with regard to *movement* in ways that suggest a different mode of refusal. Her kink does not defer to stasis, which is where most of the recent projects devoted to mapping various practices of refusal stop. By centering failure and incompletion, she instead stages the very process of adhering to the grammars of choreography, embodiment, work, and a lack of fixity as *destabilizing* and *dispossessive*. From life-sized dolls and doppelgängers to becoming "every woman," the artist dispenses with easy formulas for creating and enacting selfhood and sisterhood. In her performances, twenty-first-century aspirations for racial and sexual transcendence as culturally compensatory exercises are untenable, thus unsettling the reparative expectations of contemporary art, feminist activism, and multiculturalism.[20]

Unmaking Blackness in Dance

Narcissister began developing her perverse brand of racial performance as an undergraduate at Brown University. During her junior year she studied abroad at the Sorbonne in Paris, where along with French-African literature courses toward her Afro-American studies major, she took a number of dance classes. Because her body was still new to rigorous dance training, she tore a ligament in her ankle, and in the spring of 1992, she returned home to Southern California to recover. During her rehabilitation, she completed a semester of coursework at the University of California, San Diego, where she studied with legendary African American artist-activist Faith Ringgold. Ringgold is best known for her "story quilts," which bring together high art and craft by integrating painting with quilt making and storytelling. In the 1970s, Ringgold founded and participated in a number of anti-racist, feminist organizations. She cofounded the Ad Hoc Women's Art Committee with artists Poppy Johnson and Brenda Miller and critic Lucy Lippard and protested the

Whitney Annual for its exclusion of women artists and artists of color.[21] She was also a founding member of "Where We At" Black Women Artists, Inc., a New York-based collective associated with the Black Arts movement that promoted Black art's role in building community.

Of her time with Ringgold, Narcissister remembers, "I made my own contemporary quilts. I got so interested in the idea of incorporating unusual objects into wall pieces. All of that makes its way into my work as Narcissister—the fabrication of my costumes and unusual elements. Also the politics. She combined craft with racial politics. That made a huge impression."[22] Ringgold interwove artistic representation and political representation into the fibers of her work. Her images of the Black family and portraits of figures confronting racial strife as redress to Black subjugation reflect this philosophy. Her art also promoted inclusion, recognition, and racial and gender equality. By contrast, Narcissister's unwieldy combinations of perversity, artmaking, and racial and gender politics, filtered through the negative use of her own virtuosic body, transmogrifies aspirational and affirmative images of racial integration. Her training in African American studies, craft, dance, fine art, and window dressing, moreover, opens up new terrain for interrogating the bodily metrics of Blackness. Upon rehabilitating her ankle injury and graduating from Brown, she moved to New York City to pursue a performance career. In 1993, she was awarded a fellowship to train at the school for the renowned Alvin Ailey American Dance Theater (AAADT), started by dancer-choreographer Alvin Ailey in 1958. While there, the artist was immersed in Ailey's distinctive brand of dance making and technical training.

As a fellowship student, Narcissister was invited to perform one of Ailey's signature works, *Memoria*, which she counts among her professional highlights. Choreographed in 1979 as a tribute to Ailey's friend and colleague Joyce Trisler, *Memoria* is performed every year during the company's four-week winter season at New York's City Center Theater and features student performers hand-selected from the school. Divided into two sections, "In Memory" and "In Celebration," the twenty-six-minute work is Ailey's "grandest mature choreographic achievement," according to dance historian and Ailey scholar Thomas DeFrantz.[23] Set to jazz pianist Keith Jarrett's "Runes" and "Solara March," the dance begins with a woman in a pale lavender shift dress standing center stage. Throughout the first half of the piece, the solo woman treads the stage, often isolated even while surrounded by her two male attendants and other pairs of dancers who intermittently enter and exit the space. The mood of the second section appears to transcend the isolation and somber tenor of the first section. Amid upbeat music, multicolored costumes, turns with high parallel arms that transition into arabesques, and a mass of bodies that encircle and eventually lift the solo woman as she reaches her arms to the sky, the piece resolves in a joyous crescendo.

Aspirational narratives wherein communal experiences of joy and ascendance conquer racial strife define Ailey's signature dances.[24] Drawn from what he called "blood memories," his dances enfold African American expressive culture into high modern dance. *Memoria* and other masterpieces such as *Blues Suite* and *Revelations* also mediate the sociocultural climate at the time of their premiere. In its early years, the Ailey Company was comprised exclusively of Black dancers, one of the first of its kind in the predominantly white world of modern dance. But in 1963, Ailey chose to integrate the company due to mounting concerns about reverse racism and Black artists' social responsibility during the civil rights era. "I feel an obligation to use black dancers because there must be more opportunities for them, but not because I'm a black choreographer talking to black people," he admitted in a 1973 interview with Ellen Cohn in the *New York Times Magazine*.[25] "[I've] met some incredible dancers of other colors who could cut the work. Also, we were running into reverse racism. On our Asian tour in 1962, people kept saying about my pieces and Talley Beatty's piece—'Oh, they're wonderful, but only black people can do jazz.'"[26] By integrating his dance company, Ailey aligned AAADT with the civil rights agenda at the time. The company also undercut racist assumptions about what Black dance could be as well as what Black and other dancing bodies should do, thus transcending the color line of modern dance. In response, many patrons and critics saw Ailey and his dancers as ambassadors of cultural understanding.[27] Ultimately, Ailey used his company as a platform for racial integration and inclusiveness to speak back to the predominantly white dance profession's idealization of physical perfection and virtuosity.

According to DeFrantz, Ailey's dances are "clear intimations of socialization" represented by technical and expressive mastery, a combination that "intertwined [Ailey's] aesthetic and political aspirations."[28]

In addition to aspirational choreography and racialized virtuosity, key elements of the Ailey aesthetic include an emphasis on ballerina body types and dramatic expressivity. Ailey valued "the line and technical range that classical ballet gives to the body" as well as "the expressiveness that only modern dance offers, especially for the inner kinds of things."[29] The Ailey School's broad range of classes and performance opportunities reinforce this focus, marrying the rhetoric of racial uplift with virtuosic, well-trained bodies. The training is meant to grow "outstanding students as professional dancers by offering a diverse . . . curriculum of the highest caliber," a mission sustained by "a professional faculty of exceptional teachers, musicians, and guest artists."[30] From students to faculty, outstanding, exceptionally trained bodies are paramount to the school's philosophy.

When Narcissister began training at the Ailey School in 1993, principal dancer Desmond Richardson had become the poster child for the tenets of discipline and virtuosity that characterized the Ailey aesthetic at the time. Although virtuosic performance was elemental to the Ailey aesthetic from its beginnings, Richardson inaugurated a new brand of racialized virtuosity. According to Ariel Osterweis, dancer, scholar, and Narcissister's dramaturg, Desmond Richardson's "dancing was the prototype for those studying at the AAADC in the 1990s, and Narcissister's relationship to modern dance is grounded in this era and aesthetic."[31] This new era of artistic achievement occurred after Ailey's death in 1989 when former AAADT principal dancer and muse Judith Jamison succeeded Ailey as the company's artistic director. The racialized virtuosity that Richardson ushered in under Jamison's direction was a mix of athletic strength, muscularity, and extreme flexibility, "as his legs seemed to extend higher than others and his technique spilled over into hyperability," Osterweis declares.[32]

But where "Richardson's combination of virtuosity and charisma . . . draws people in," making viewers privy to both exceptional ("superhuman") skill and perceived access to his soul, Narcissister forecloses this possibility by wearing a mask.[33] Both the soul and the mask are popular tropes within Black expressive culture that have come to represent how people of the Black diaspora navigate the divide between the sacred and the secular to craft individual and group identities across time and space. Dance historian Brenda Dixon Gottschild further locates the place of "soul" in American and African American concert dance as a quality derived from the Black dancing body. She writes, "Soul represents that attribute of the body/mind that mediates between flesh and spirit. It is manifested in the feel of a performance. It has a sensual, visceral connotation of connectedness with the earth (and the earth-centered religions that distinguish West and Central African cultures) and, concomitantly, a reaching for the spirit."[34] Narcissister's masking, on the other hand, disallows viewers' apprehension of the dramatic expressivity and soul-affirming redemption expected of Ailey-trained dancers. Her eyes and face, plastic and expressionless, confound expectations that Black dancing bodies aspire to bare their souls and emotion for both the audience's pleasure and a higher spiritual power.[35] Osterweis calls this an active disavowal of dance-based virtuosity that, contrary to a complete denial, nonetheless results in a striving toward excellence.[36] "In disavowing the kind of virtuosity that has come to be expected of the black dancing body in the United States," Osterweis surmises, "Narcissister strips technical bravura of emotional affect, and pivots presentation away from charisma."[37] This disavowal in my view extends to sex—its biological purpose and its pleasures, especially when it comes to orgasms and climax. Narcissister's enactments of self-objectification upend both the aspirational ethos of Black concert dance and the potency assigned to multiracial bodies in the twenty-first century. Flipping back and forth between the dominant and submissive partner in racialized scenarios of uncomfortable sex disrupts the technical virtuosity, dramatic expressivity, and disciplinary scripts associated with Ailey dancers. Alternately, her art gestures beyond the bodily limits of racial and gender identification and coalition within inclusive theorizing and women-of-color feminist praxis. Rather than the seamless attainment of an ideal self as the source for empowerment, or the masterful execution of choreography and climaxes, her photography, videos, and live performances portray crude, abject, and unfinished scenes and actions that fail to reach desirable ends.

Unmasking Sex

Narcissister's simulations do not lead to self-affirming ecstasy; they instead routinely displace and frustrate the orgasm and feign climax, short-circuiting the desire for the completion of sex and self. *Vaseline*, from 2010, expresses this mode of being, a motif that, like Simmons's language of opacity, declines to reconcile the gap between crudeness and mastery, constructed self and ideal image. The video piece inverts the racial and gender valences of *Every Woman*, confronting viewers with a white male rockabilly character that dons pumps, a leather jacket, and a shiny oversized pompadour made of black plastic that resembles Elvis Presley's famous hairdo. Smeared on Narcissister's hairpiece and packed in her anus, Vaseline the substance creates both surface shine and lubricant, an invitingly viscous cover that repels visual and physical attachment much like her mask does. The video also features key elements of the artist's practice—concealed identities, oversized props, and stalled orgasms—that figure Black women's sexual organs as *the* site of imagined difference, dense and full, a space from which things disappear and emerge.[38] The undesirable function of her internal cavities and the items they store and collect challenge staid notions of Black women's reproductive capacities.

In *Vaseline*, the artist strips to Elastica's 1995 Britpop song about the need for lube to ease uncomfortable sex: "When you're stuck like glue/ Vaseline/When you need some goo." Narcissister then reaches her hand into a tub of thick cream-colored gunk atop the trashcan next to her and smears it over her hands and plastic hair. Next, with flair she snaps off her pants and the camera zooms in on the rubber dildo and balls hanging from the beige cloth that covers her private parts. She stuffs her pants into a slit in her trash-bag hair, detaches the sex toys, and slides the lubed dildo into her merkin-covered vagina. When she hears a noise emanating from the trashcan, she pulls a knife from her pompadour to defend herself against what she discovers is a harmless plush toy cat. With no use for the knife, she inserts it into her gunk-filled vagina to join the rubber dildo already there, activating the lyrical content of the song—the need for lube to ease uncomfortable sex. Then she unsnaps her sideburns, which become the hair of her merkin, and her shirt, which she stuffs into her mouth. Dangling at the end of the shirt is a piece of cut mask with a nose and a mouth that she attaches to the sides of her face where her sideburns used to be, her stuffed mouth now covered and doubled.

Next, Narcissister faces more fictive danger: a plush rabid dog that escapes from her trash-bag hair. She restrains the dog with the chain she swirls around her neck as the camera zooms in on her bouncing breasts. After defeating the second soft threat, she reaches for the cigarette pipe behind her ear to celebrate her triumph. But her long, fake, red fingernails foil her attempt to brandish this symbol of power; she struggles to strike a match to light the pipe. When she finally sparks a flame, this alone does not satisfy her desire. She turns, bends over, and slips the hot pipe into her lubed anus for a culminating moment that is also short-lived. In the video's final scene, her foot gets caught in the remnants of her trash-bag hair now sprawled on the floor. She stands, slumps her body, and shakes her head in frustration.

Vaseline's crudeness is distinct from her live performances, collages, photographic portraits, and other videos in two ways.[39] Contrary to the rehearsals that Narcissister undertakes to cultivate seamless, physical virtuosity for her live acts, extreme forms of obscenity, incomplete performance, gunky lubricant for aberrant pleasure, and abject sex leads to frustrated ends in *Vaseline*. Props misfire, and faulty fasteners prevent the artist from accomplishing her goals. Stymied choreography and not-so-seamless costume changes add to the lewdness, especially considering that contemporary artists have the option to reshoot ad infinitum with digital video. Second, *Vaseline* displaces the orgasm as an affirmative culmination of erotic pleasure, and instead zooms in on uncomfortable sex play and exasperation. These features of failure and the camping of normative sex more broadly across her practice place her work within a queer strain of experimental video and filmmaking "too crude, too live, too disinterested in an aesthetic polish and concerned more with blending moving image and performance strategies," as curator Bradford Nordeen describes.[40] She lets moments of failure remain instead of redressing them, even when she has the means to do so. More importantly, where many media portrayals of sex show perfectly synced orgasms, the dispossessive force of Narcissister's performance derives from her fabrications of stalled orgasms and other depictions of awkward, uncomfortable, undesirable sex.

Scholars of feminist art and performance have taken special interest in the queer, nonnormative nature of Narcissister's visual work because of her self-sex radicalism and transgressive deployments of the racialized female body. To Osterweis and performance studies scholar Barbara Browning, her performances are acts of reclamation and self-care that counteract images of Black women as degraded subjects.[41] As Browning puts it, the masturbatory quality of Narcissister's visual work is akin to feminist conceptual art of the 1970s and 80s that thematically presents "women taking care of themselves."[42] Arts and culture critic Priscilla Frank has called the artist a "queer feminist superhero," while art critic Katie Cercone has likened Narcissister to a post-racial feminist icon.[43] From these angles, the artist's creative endeavors recover the racialized, gendered self—restoring the historically subjugated body to some sense of wholeness and strength—through narcissistic sexual play.

These conclusions rely on an incongruent understanding of sex radicalism initiated by white second-wave feminists who used their lived experience as the basis for their conceptions of sexual freedom. These feminists, however, failed to address both their whiteness and how social categorizations intersect to reproduce racial, gender, and sexual oppression. On this model, indulging in or performing racial fictions results in an inversion of power that allows the artist to assert agency by reclaiming degrading stereotypes. This approach to feminist self-care takes for granted that all women experience pleasure in the same ways or that all women access power evenly. It likewise assumes that women of color are necessarily, and homogenously, interested in redressing demeaning stereotypes, and that inversions of power and racial repair are not only possible, but are in fact desirable and edifying.

Within this schema, the artist's mixed-race identity functions as a sign of progress. For Osterweis, the artist's refusal "to linger in any one character or style" yields self-affirming pleasure for viewers and the artist herself.[44] Osterweis claims that Narcissister's multiracial masks and performances of racialized dolls allow spectators, Black and non-Black alike, to escape feelings of shame, disgust, and debasement, "ultimately drawing attention back to herself, yourself."[45] Her multiple masks, characters, performance styles, and mixed-race identity in this view are mutable entities that engender opportunities for viewers to feel a sense of affinity that can then be used to build community. *Vaseline* in particular, Osterweis writes, "presents slippery transitions of costume, gender, and species, such that Narcissister consumes her own dick and balls, only to be replaced by merkin and a canine threat, ready to pounce."[46] This animation of self-objectification and otherness, outfitted in black-and-white checkered clothing and performed by a body racially marked as Black and white, is an "exploration of transgender and trans-genre," she continues, "haunted by America's ghosts, the brutality of racialized laws of segregation and miscegenation."[47] For Osterweis, Narcissister's art transmogrifies situational violences that arise at the socially constructed boundaries between male and female, Black and white.

In my view, *Vaseline* and Narcissister's other live and video works do not reveal or redress knowable truths about race or gender, nor do they build to sexual release or satisfaction. They are essentially plastic, anticlimactic, self-effacing acts of race play.[48] This form of kinky sex at once relishes yet exceeds erotic fetishism and fulfillment, and it materializes in the ways Narcissister flips in and out of costumes, multiracial masks, and abject sexual scenarios. Race play participants experience pleasure from recreating racist and xenophobic situations drawn from history, such as Nazi-Jew interrogations, master-slave relationships, and public displays in which white interlocutors grease up and sell Black bodies on the auction block.[49] Another dimension of race play is becoming aroused by the use of racist epithets and physical force to demean one's partner. Race play, then, is a kind of psychological theater that gains appeal from its associations with any combination of the following: the desire to abandon responsibility, the desire to be humiliated, self-hatred, the impulse to redress childhood trauma, or even to find or mimic spiritual connection. Moreover, latent within Narcissister's race play is a social critique of the art world and its role in gatekeeping how, why, and when which bodies, and bodies of work, are marketable and desirable. Curiously, people of color *do* engage in race play. But more often than not, the consumer base is generally white, not unlike the art world.

Under the sign of women-of-color sisterhood, Narcissister's race play complicates feminist art histories of self-display and Black feminist studies of pornography. Black feminists have critiqued race play and pornography because each practice has "been imagined to make explicit the exploitation that representation already inflicts on black women," Jennifer Nash writes.[50] This view positions popular culture media as injurious and delineates disempowering images as sources of violation for Black women. "Indeed, if dominant visual culture objectifies black female bodies," Nash adds, "racialized pornography is imagined to be particularly demanding in its incessant exposure of black female flesh and its insistence on black female sexual excess and alterity."[51] In order to redress the ways that visual images victimize them as degraded subjects, Black women must not only be invested in reparative imaginative labors; their self-pleasure is also inherently affirmative. Narcissister's art, by contrast, traffics in debasement. For her, freaky, undesirable expressions of pleasure arise from embodying demeaning images.

In addition to erotic fetishism, Narcissister's race play exceeds narrow understandings of Blackness and its embodiment. In contemporary art history and performance studies literature, uses of one's body such as Narcissister's are typically read as a way to heal racial pain and injury. This understanding of performance assumes that it "offers a substitute for something else that preexists it," making the performing body a proxy "for an elusive entity that it is not but that it must vainly aspire both to embody and to replace," in theater historian and practitioner Joseph R. Roach's interpretation.[52] Performance, therefore, functions as a process of substitution, of standing-in for something preexistent, lost, or elusive. In this process, the performing body is an effigy, cultural historian Robin Bernstein tells us, "as it bears and brings forth collectively remembered, meaningful gestures, and thus surrogates for that which a community has lost."[53] Rather than affirmative self-love or redress, Narcissister's antiredemptive enactments of self-sex bridge race play with Freud's pleasure principle, the instinctual seeking of pleasure and avoidance of pain in order to satisfy biological and psychological needs.[54] Freud locates pleasure and pain on a spectrum, and Narcissister's self-effacing, abject sex acts are situated at the point where pleasure and pain meet. But her "self-serving" practice of racialized BDSM changes the terms of pleasure *and* pain as they relate to power—domination and submission—and histories of racial and sexual subjection. In so doing, she troubles well worn theories of Black performance in the visual field that emphasize wholeness, positive self-representation, and the need to focus on reproduction and futurity as part of the recovery process for subjugated Black female bodies. Narcissister's race play exceeds any attempt to redress the trauma of racialized gender subjugation in the past and present, like Kara Walker's silhouettes engaged in freaky business from chapter 1. It also lampoons the intersectional idealism and privilege—the exceptionalism—that has become attached to mixed-race subjects and their progeny.

Undoing Multiracial Promise

Of all her pieces, *The Dollhouse* (2011), also known as *Upside Down*, most poignantly alters the promise of multiracial exceptionalism. Narcissister's body and movements in *The Dollhouse* highlight not only how heteronormative, interracial coupling continues to energize the American racial imaginary in the new millennium; as enactments of kink and race play, they also challenge the myths of happy "coexistence" and post-racial futurity in a society where racial others are inexorably dominated, enslaved, and violated. *The Dollhouse* has been performed at various lengths and at a variety of venues from The Box, a neo-burlesque nightclub in New York City, to America's Got Talent, a primetime television variety show that airs on NBC.[55] As a result, Narcissister has garnered a cult following that spans queer nightlife and club culture, experimental film and performance, TV, and the high art world. Like her audiences, *The Dollhouse* also crosses genres, underscoring the modes of interracial desire that imbibe Hollywood musicals and mainstream film, popular music, and material culture. At times preceded by a video featuring the artist's hands manipulating a topsy-turvy doll to the tunes of an eerie lullaby in a multilevel wooden dollhouse, *The Dollhouse* opens with Narcissister wearing a brown-toned mask, a brown bob-style wig with bangs, and a red sailor dress. She is cloaked in a floor-length, blue velvet hooded cape reminiscent of fairy tale characters such as Cinderella and Little Red Riding Hood with long white gloves covering her hands and forearms. A large dollhouse prop is positioned upstage and center.

To the lyrics of "At the Crossroads," a song about a girl coming of age from the 1967 Hollywood musical *Dr. Dolittle*, Narcissister twirls, raises her gloved hands to the sky, and slowly kneels as if praying. Her gestures mirror the lyrics of the song: "Here I stand at the crossroads of life/ Childhood behind me/The future to come/And alone/Nothing planned at the crossroads of life." She reaches far to the left and brings her hands to cover her masked eyes, her upper body contracting and releasing in an action that resembles crying. She yearns for something: romantic love and a certain future.

Then the music switches to a spare disco interlude, and Narcissister turns to face upstage. She pulls her hood down to reveal another brown-faced mask attached to the back of her head. Her dress also has a dual

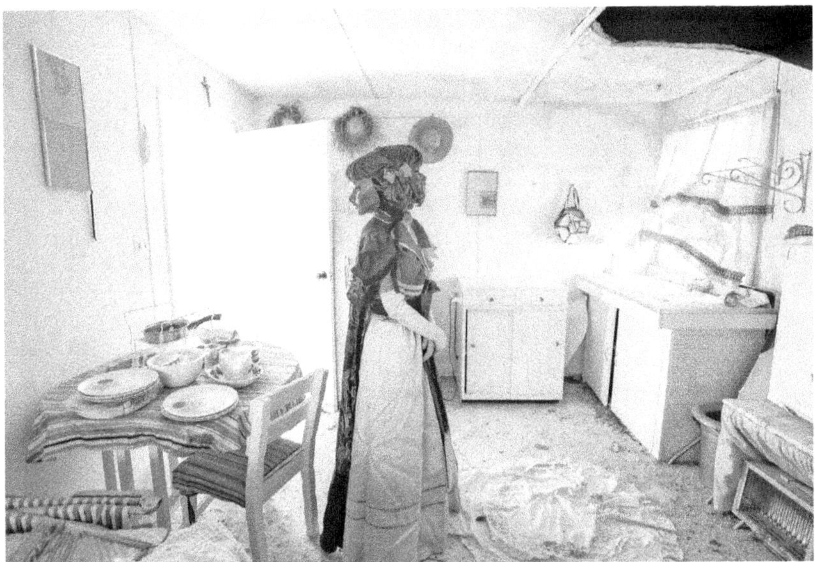

Figure 4.4. Narcissister, *Upside Down*, 2017. Performance still, mixed media. Courtesy of the artist. Photo credit: Sarah Lyon.

identity, red sailor in the front and blue and brown paisley print in the back. She bends and disrobes before her two-headed "self" skips and prances across stage, eventually transitioning into another costume change that takes place while she is upside down. Foreboding music signals that something strange is afoot, and Narcissister delivers on cue as she bows her head to the floor and slowly rises into a headstand, pointing her feet. She pauses and then splits her legs dramatically to reveal a brown dress and a third head, white with a black bob and bangs, between her thighs. Her legs are now arms and her white knee-high stockings are now gloves. She spirals her torso, places her feet behind the doll head, and contracts her torso front and side. To stand, Narcissister rolls out of a backbend, thrusts her pelvis to the audience, plays with her third "self," and jumps into a series of quick hip rolls.

The score changes to "Upside Down," Diana Ross's 1980 pop disco hit about a woman's disorienting, self-effacing experience of romantic love, and Narcissister performs a dizzying sequence of acrobatic choreography.[56] She flips in and out of handstands, strips topless, and turns to face the audience. Suddenly aware of her exposure, she covers her

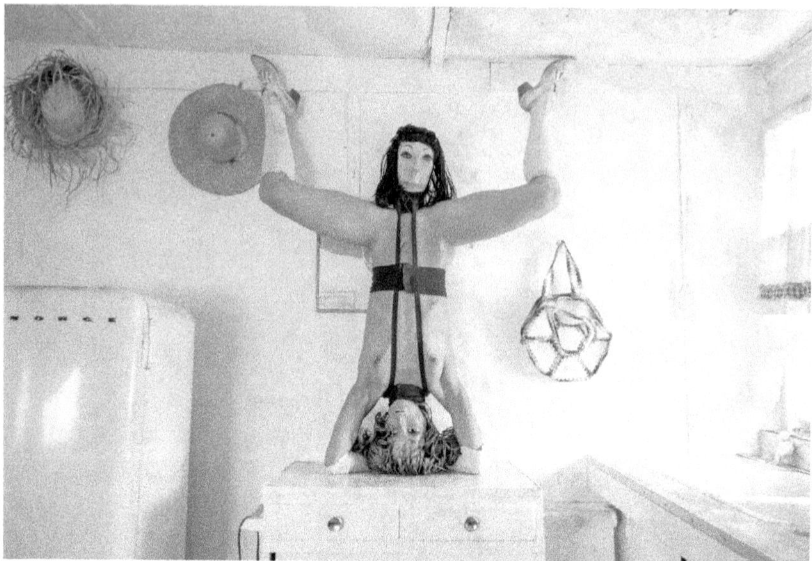

Figure 4.5. Narcissister, *Upside Down*. Performance still, mixed media, 2017. Courtesy of the artist. Photo credit: Sarah Lyon.

bare chest with her skirt as the music changes to a synth version of "At the Crossroads." She scurries upstage and kneels as "Just the Two of Us" (1980), a more promising love song than "Upside Down," blasts through the speakers.[57] Her feet walk up the dollhouse prop, and she is once again in a handstand, this time with her back facing the audience. Her skirt tumbles to the floor to reveal a black and gold embroidered dress and yet another white mask erect between her legs.

Flipped upside down and inside out, she is now a two-sided, four-headed, topsy-turvy doll. Thought to have originated as an act of resistance and a product of Black female slave labor in the antebellum South, the topsy-turvy doll became a symbol of miscegenation and a low-tech tool for preparing young Black female slaves for "a life devoted to nurturing two babies: one black and one white," as African American studies scholar Kimberly Wallace-Saunders historicizes.[58] It simultaneously emblematized racial fusion, cross-racial intimacy, racial hierarchy, and sexual violence.[59] The two halves of the doll share a waist and a skirt, and when the doll is flipped, the arms and face of either the white or black side are visible, a playful act of appearance and disappearance that Narcissister deploys in *The Dollhouse*. These actions contain within them the ideas of racial flip-flops and hidden identities, the promise or threat of total racial transformation—white to Black and vice versa—as the result of racial concealment. As Robin Bernstein explains, "If one side of the topsy-turvy doll is exposed, the other side lurks, waiting, beneath the skirts."[60] Although the flip of the skirt invites play, "the thing determines that [the doll's black and white] poles never interact, and that one character always obliterates the other," making racial union both contingent yet impossible—a kinky entanglement.[61]

In animating and embodying a life-sized topsy-turvy doll, Narcissister eschews common understandings of multiracialism that uphold heterosex and romantic intimacy as sites where racial conflict, even estrangement, can be suspended or dissolved.[62] Critical theorist Jared Sexton, author of *Amalgamation Schemes: Antiblackness and the Critique of Multiracialism*, explains how multiracialism and normative sexuality co-constitute and structure contemporary social relations. Sexton tells us that promoting multiracialism as a cornerstone of progressive social change misrecognizes the violent legacies of slavery and its afterlife to which race mixing is tethered, namely the sexual violence endured by Black female slaves at the hands of slave owners. Despite being heralded as the post–civil rights answer to racial strife, multiracialism bolsters anti-Black sentiment and sexual norms by evoking long-standing tenets of US racial formation while purporting to alleviate Black subjects' marginalization. Historically in the United States, offspring from interracial sexual reproduction assume the lower status of the Black (typically maternal) parent. Termed hypodescent, this automatic assignment of racial status is the basis of the one-drop rule ("one drop" of Black blood), a social and legal principle that evolved during the nineteenth century and was codified into law in the twentieth. Racial classification based on blood quantum gave rise to phenomena such as racial passing, racial purity, and moral panic over maintaining that purity in the antebellum and postbellum periods.

While interracial marriage is now legal, Narcissister's topsy-turvy performances illustrate that anxieties about race mixing persist in the present, despite melting pot metaphors and affirmations of America's so-called browning. Most importantly, her use of multiple masks and the varying phenotypes they visualize highlight the uncertain promise of post-racial integration. Narcissister crudely choreographs fantasies of miscegenation in order to thwart them, thus caricaturing the mythos of self-love and self-discovery that organizes prevailing visions of the future. Interracial intimacy cannot exist in her visual world without the brutal, undesirable histories that accompany it, even amid the rhetorical and physiological attempts to transcend these realities. This facet of the artist's performance practice typically eludes her critics. In Katie Cercone's review of *The Dollhouse*, Narcissister "is the integrated self. . . . She is swiveling, wheeling; a beguiling icon of a raceless, genderless, classless future feminism to come."[63] This neoliberal assessment echoes the reparative undercurrents of civil rights and white feminist discourse, which Cercone extends to a post-racial, post-gender, post-class future. While Walker's topsy-turvy aesthetics trouble how viewers see the intersections of race, gender, sexuality, and class, Narcissister's embodied version of the topsy-turvy doll ultimately refuses racial integration. Keeping the masks adjacent yet separate and apart, she joins the failure to achieve self-realization through sexual ecstasy with racialized gendered imperatives to biologically reproduce.

Narcissister's mixed-race sexual dancing body is the doll—*the thing*—that prevents the two poles and four faces from coming (and cumming) together. There is no racial harmony here, and it is on and through her body that racial union, or miscegenation, is foiled. While she is temporarily excited by the myriad options available to her, her frenetic costume changes, acrobatics, vaudevillian trickery, and multiracial dummy faces do not culminate in anything resembling integration, racial utopia, or a satisfying sexual union. Neither she nor the desires of her plastic, multiracial doppelgängers personified by Benson's lyrics—"just the two of us/we can make it if we try"—are fulfilled.

The artist's chosen props—dolls, masks, and double identities—further undo hopes for a post-identity future by putting undesirable animations of race and gender at the center of Freud's psychoanalytic theories of the "double" and the uncanny.[64] Narcissister's mobilization of the double and the uncanny generates feelings of revulsion in response to things and notions of identity that are familiar, but slightly off. For Freud, the uncanny's mixture of the familiar and the eerie confronts subjects with their own unconscious, repressed impulses.[65] Alternately, dollhouses, dolls, and the gendered play they inspire are signs that promote aspects of human development. Dolls, specifically, he explains, are imbued with living qualities, and as children, we treat dolls as if they are alive. Through interactions with such objects, children receive information about social relations and cultural norms concerning adulthood and domestic life. Additionally, doppelgängers in Western art and its histories have represented the divided self, allowing artists to explore myriad personas and express experiences of otherness and crisis.[66] Narcissister upsets this progressive arc and assumptions about the ends of racial mixing and sex by animating a facet of queer procreation—reproducing not children, but rather kitsch and multiracial plastic masks that do not find themselves in blissful union. Furthermore, her self-objectification—performing as a masked dancing doll that both mirrors and *animates* the props and effigies she employs—troubles the boundary between Black and white, person and thing, as well as the line between pleasure and pain.[67] By transposing narcissism from self-loving absorption to self-objectification, she abandons normative conceptions of identity, objecthood, and, ultimately, humanness. This abandonment applies to the role that whiteness plays in American social consciousness as well.

Although interrogating the boundaries of Blackness is the fulcrum of Narcissister's artistic practice, whiteness is not off limits. In *Conditions of the White Mask*, as in *The Dollhouse*, she comingles Blackness and whiteness as signs for interracial intimacy with a difference: she refracts the themes explored in *The Dollhouse* through the lens of white womanhood, expanding the scope of race play in her oeuvre. Included in Just Like a Woman, a festival co-presented by Abrons Arts Center on October 24, 2015, *Conditions of the White Mask* circles back to the doll as an object of terror, racial fusion, and pleasure. But rather than an outright refusal of cross-racial intimacy, the performance event sets in motion an intimate relation between whiteness and Blackness that Ariane Cruz argues is vital to racialized women's enactments of BDSM and erotic fantasy.[68]

Conditions of the White Mask troubles the currency of multiracial feminism in contemporary art. Rather than idealizing the racialized virtuosic body, the live work transmutes perverse performances of multiracial, intersectional exceptionalism to embodied ambivalence toward both multiracialism and white womanhood. *Baby Lady (Forever Young)*, set to Alphaville's "Forever Young" (1984), depicts the phases of (white) womanhood from birth to death.[69] On her knees, a white-faced Narcissister scuttles out from under a suitcase dressed as a bassinet. The bassinet holds a white baby doll, and a blonde, toddler-size girl doll in a white lace dress is attached to her face. Abruptly, Narcissister stands, turns, and pulls the doll down for a quick change. A bigger doll with crimped curls is fastened to her back, which now faces the audience. Next, she is an older version of the doll, wearing pigtails and a pink dress bloodstained in the back. Between character changes, she inserts dance moves—an arabesque turn, a *chassé*—gracefully transitioning from one phase of womanhood to the next. She plays softball in overalls. She marches down an imaginary aisle, first in a black graduation gown, then in a pink wedding dress and veil. "Next comes baby and the baby carriage," as the saying goes, and this is where things get kinky.

She strips to breastfeed, and after placing the doll back in its buggy, she pushes it away and pulls two gray braided pigtails from her anus. The gray pigtails replace the blonde ones as she slips into a different pink dress, circles the stage, and stops to "birth" a wrinkled mask from her vagina, which she fastens to her already masked face. She is now an elderly white woman, dropping her pigtail sideburns for the wrinkled face. To finish, she crawls back under the suitcase and reveals its contents to the audience—her gray-haired doppelgänger in a satin-lined coffin—before resetting the suitcase to the bassinet.

In the complementary set of works about sex, race, reproduction, and romantic love that follow *Baby Lady*'s depiction of white womanhood, Narcissister's body subverts conventional narratives associated with human development and cross-racial intimacy. *Man/Woman* (2009) stars a frustrated white fanboy. "Photograph," Def Leppard's 1983 pop-metal rock ballad about a sex symbol akin to Marilyn Monroe who is just out of reach, plays in the background.[70] But Monroe is not the fanboy's fantasy in Narcissister's video. In his cramped, cluttered bedroom, the fanboy flips through *Black Tail*, an adult fetish magazine specializing in photographs of Black women's backsides. On his already porn-covered wall he hangs a centerfold poster of his chosen piece: a curly blonde Narcissister in a dark-brown mask with matching plastic breasts.

The white fanboy caresses the image of Narcissister and excitedly pulls out his silicone penis to stroke and pleasure himself. In the act, he discovers a dark layer of skin and long pink nails underneath his own white "skin." Then the live Narcissister emerges, turning the props meant to

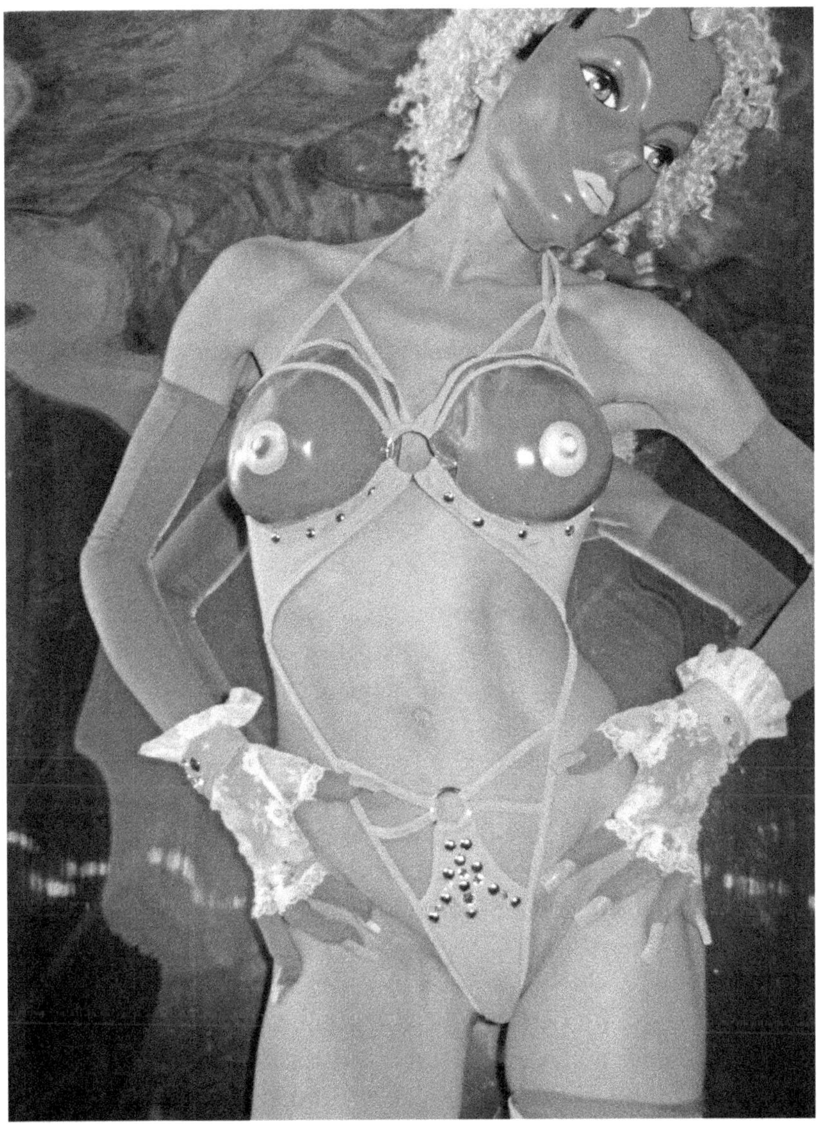

Figure 4.6. Narcissister, *Man/Woman*, 2007. Mixed media, color photograph. Courtesy of the artist. Photo credit: Tony Stamolis.

signify the white fanboy's person from the inside out and rearranging his clothing, hair, face, and chest on the bed. Wearing the mask, wig, and breasts from the poster along with a white strap-on over a pink G-string, the "real" Narcissister wildly rides the fanboy's remnants—dildo and all—to no avail. His parts do not hold up under her rigorous grinding; they literally fall apart, thus failing to satisfy her. Feigning disappointment, in silence she discovers her image in two facing pages of *Black Tail* and performatively masturbates to herself using the fanboy's detached, silicone member, climaxing and leaving him behind. In the next video, *18 Heads*, Narcissister is a double-headed Marie Antoinette searching for her other half. She tries on multiple heads that run the gamut from a green monster mask to the head of a woman carrying a basket of fruit on her head. Following the fate of the infamous queen of France, those that do not fit Narcissister's standards are guillotined. Finally, she finds the perfect mate to complete her: a matching Marie Antoinette head of a slightly darker hue.

In the final piece of the evening, *Unforgettable*, the artist dances in a tuxedo to Nat King Cole's eponymous ballad from 1951 before stripping down to black lingerie.[71] Next, she stages what appears to be a romantic tale of boy-meets-girl using two pale-colored puppets; the male is dressed in a top hat and tuxedo jacket, the female in a silver blouse. Her scantily clad body becomes a table where the puppets dine and admire one another to the sounds of Rihanna's "Birthday Cake" (2011).[72] To create a romantic atmosphere, the artist inserts a long-stem candle into her vagina before the puppets smooch and embrace.

Taken together, the various elements of *Conditions of the White Mask* expose not only the sexual dimensions of race, but also how multiracialism is imbued with heteronormative pronouncements such as love, romance, family, marriage, and reproductive futurity. Conceptions of multiracial figures "cannot help but imply a production of race in the field of heterosexuality, nominating, more specifically, the reproductive sex act as the principal site of mediation for racial difference itself," Jared Sexton explains.[73] Within this schema, the fruits of amalgamation become part of a reformist agenda where the future multiracial child is recruited to recuperate a traumatic past marked by unique forms of racial terror, paving the way for a racially transcendent future. By contrast, Narcissister burlesques her own mixed-race heritage as well as public debates concerning the biopolitics of interracial intimacy and its transformative potential when, instead of babies, she pulls a wrinkled mask from her vagina and synthetic braids from her anus in *Baby Lady*. Alternately as a table, as a candle stand, as sparkling entertainment for the doting puppets, and as a sex freak for the audience in *Unforgettable*, self-objectification *is* the limit of multiracial promise for Narcissister.

Instead of an imagined community of boundary-crossing hybrids who redeem the trauma of Black subjugation in the past, present, and future, Narcissister performs against the prospect of a multiracial future, resulting "in a representational space that is both black and, in a specific sense, negative," as Tavia Nyong'o puts it.[74] This black, negative space "cannot spell out a set of instructions on how to conduct ourselves in the present, but can only instruct against the presumption that its stories lie at the ready to be told."[75] Narcissister's non-procreative sex play short-circuits the rationales of both multiracial exceptionalism and the promotion of packaged family values vis-à-vis domestic coupling, two-parent households, and the nuclear family unit. This reveals two things. One is the true aspiration of multiracialism, which is the singularity of Blackness as a social identity, a political organizing principle, and an object of desire, to paraphrase Sexton. The other is a refusal of socially and aesthetically appropriate behavior pertinent to racial representation and sex in the twenty-first century.[76]

Thus, rather than "a deployment of sexual difference through which the seeming transgression of race mixing is resolved, first into the 'romantic complexity' of courtship and marriage, and then into the reproductive futurity of the 'mixed-race' child," as Nyong'o observes, Narcissister performs reproduction *without* futurity.[77] Her many "births" generate inanimate objects and fake adornments, not children, thus queering the racial and gendered dimensions of reproductive labor. The absence of men is also part of this queering; even when men are present, like the fanboy, they are empty signifiers of masculinity, not unlike the phallus itself. Her work, in other words, trades desirability for abjection, attraction for repulsion. In tethering narcissism to the history and memory of racialized gender subjugation, Narcissister's mobilizations of *undesirability*—her kink—animate how dominance and subordination, privilege and oppression, can co-constitute marginalized women's experiences of embodiment and selfhood.

Coda: Playing in the Bottom

Narcissister's perverse enactments of kink and race-play drastically alter the promise of multiracialism by transforming ego-loving self-absorption into undesirable self-objectification. In so doing, her reproduction without futurity in live performance and video, and her practices of inversion and repulsion more broadly, recalibrate the political and aesthetic value that art historians and critical theorists assign to marginality. In an era of new racial and gender meaning, her work highlights the pitfalls of celebrating and idealizing positions of social subordination, from being in the middle—the basis for multiracial exceptionalism—to looking to the bottom, a core feature of intersectional feminist methodology.[78] Within these theoretical frames, Black women, at once rejected and embraced, are both the source for claims to complex subjectivity as well as conduits for exposing the specters of racism and sexism. To this end, Nash writes, "black women's experiences are used as a theoretical wedge, designed to demonstrate the shortcomings of conventional feminist and anti-racist work."[79] Narcissister's manipulation and deployment of her own body, especially her orifices, upends myths about mixed-race figures as model minorities on the one hand and Black women as multiply marginalized subjects on the other. Furthermore, the way she plays in the specifically Black queer negative space of the bottom expands the boundaries of minoritarian aesthetic practice by parodying the capacity for perversion to redress Black women's historical bondage in the past and present. Where the bottom typically signifies submissive sex and the anus is generally regarded as the synecdoche for male homosex, Narcissister's art locates the Black female anus as a site of transgressive self-shattering. Her practice here becomes more than a disregard for the self and its care; it is a form of self-effacement that builds on the blacker-than-Black art of Walker and Simmons. The bottom for these artists is both a body part and a space of undesirable sexual and social subordination.

Organ Player from 2013, Narcissister's first evening-length live performance, further links female sexual expression with the anal opening. Presented as a work-in-progress at Abrons Arts Center in New York, *Organ Player* pivots on the artist's engagements with sexual and racial abjection, an important feature of her kink. The performance is also the basis for her feature-length experimental documentary released in 2018, which, in the artist's words, "explores how ancestral data is stored in our bodies, impacting the lives we lead. On the personal level, the film investigates how the artist's complex [mixed-race] family history compelled her to create [her] masked, erotic performance character."[80] As a preliminary script for the movie, the live performance likewise centers on the "birth" of Narcissister's performance persona. The image of the mother figure and the procreative acts presented in the live performance, however, activate a process of self-exploration that is much more offbeat than the family photographs and archival video footage that are featured in the film.

The whole of *Organ Player*—the perverse eroticism, the multiple expulsions of fluids and vital organs, "the me" eating the "not me"—is a metabolizing performance of self-abjection that shifts between expectorating and ejecting props and casting off bodily and social constructions of race, gender, and sex. At the performance's beginning, Narcissister appears onstage among set props—a table, a chair, a drinking cup, and a silver dome-covered meal—in her signature mask and brown curly wig, a pale pink suit dress, and a fur stole. She takes her seat, mimes the action of drinking, and prays over the meal before her. Alice Cooper's "I'm Hungry" (2008) blares through the speakers as she rubs her belly before removing the dome to reveal a lone lettuce leaf, a spare meal for such a hungry guest. After two large chews, Narcissister suddenly rises and spits out the lettuce, opting instead to eat, lick, and lift the items around her. Adding to the freakery, she balances the items on top of each other in her mouth like a circus performer and simultaneously strips and humps her props. Seconds later, Narcissister emphatically smacks her bare ass with the dinner plate then frantically rubs her merkin-covered vagina. With gusto, she pulls a white cloth napkin from her vagina to pat the corners of her mouth: another fake climax in a series of lonely, abject "endeavors that never seem to lead to prolonged satisfaction or ecstasy," as Osterweis puts it.[81]

Next, to a dissonant electronic soundscape Narcissister climbs a narrow cloth ladder into the mouth of a scrim that pictures a large signature Narcissister mask that acts as a kind of mother figure as the piece progresses. The mouth leads to a speckled cloth tube evocative of a birth canal, and as the lights fade to black she haphazardly shimmies down the tube, effectively giving birth to herself and expelling her body from her twin 'mother' figure. Following this ejection from the self-seeking maternal sphere, Narcissister appears in a braided wig and executes a series of stock stripper moves to Sisqó's "Thong Song" (2000). She twerks in front of a larger-than-life stage prop constructed in the shape of her bare backside before exiting the stage to push brown cloth turds through the prop's anus, the last of which becomes a covering for her own body.[82]

After writhing from the last brown casing, Narcissister arranges the remaining turds atop a round white tablecloth crowned by her dinner plate and silver dome in a setup that mimics that of the opening vignette. The next sequence, "Ass/Vag," which also exists in video form as a discrete work of art, features Narcissister as a cloth vagina.[83] With face covered, she contorts her body to make her labia move in front of her mother image and another larger-than-life cut-out of her backside with legs spread. To up the ante of self-stimulation, she pulls a bedazzled foam tongue from between the prop's cardboard legs and runs the tongue up and down her body. The sound score dictates her gestures; as the track of sexually suggestive moans speeds up, so do her movements. She pulls a long piece of white lace material from the dress's insides after repeatedly jabbing the center of it and writhes on the floor before she is carted off stage by a stagehand—another feigned climax.

In the final sequence and the most dancerly of *Organ Player*'s vignettes, Narcissister bursts from the prop puppet's chest in a heart costume to the croons of Billy Holiday's "Good Morning Heartache" (1946). After a series of stumbling, trembling movements, she descends to the ground while a heart-rate monitor beeps and she sheds her costume to reveal what has been animating the organ from the inside: another version of Narcissister as a nurse in a braided wig. Performing fan kicks, grand leg lifts, and a low arabesque turn to Toni Braxton's "Un-Break My Heart" (1996), nurse Narcissister repairs the gutted heart, reattaching it to the red-and-blue cloth tubes from which it has been separated. But instead of a seamless return to liveliness for both the object and its animator, resuscitating the heart triggers an identity crisis for Narcissister.

After returning the heart to the puppet's chest, nurse Narcissister unravels, frantically gesticulating and stripping down to a bloated prosthetic breastplate from which she rips a miniature version of the heart she has just revived. Narcissister looks perplexed as she starts to unmask and de-wig, lightly tugging at her artificial face and hair. After a firm yank, she is free and the set from the opening vignette returns. The original Narcissister places what remains of her dismembered self on the dining table. As she sits, Alice Cooper's sadistic lyrics blare again, and the "bad ideas eating [her] brain" materialize. The lights fade as she sinisterly rubs her belly, ready to satiate her hunger by eating her other self.

Organ Player ties abjection to subjection and the bottom vis-à-vis excrement, debasement, and excess, thus troubling the anus as a site for aberrant (homo)sex in general and the gendered and racialized dimensions of anal sexual pleasure in particular. Narcissister's onanistic sex acts approximate Leo Bersani's evaluation of male homosexuality and emphasize "the risk of the sexual itself as the risk of self-dismissal, of *losing sight* of the self."[84] Bersani's writings on male homosexuality and the stigmatization of gay men's imagined enjoyment of anal sex have been foundational to queer theorizations of desire and pleasure. Yet they neglect race as other scholars have pointed out. Darieck Scott builds on Bersani's work to examine how Blackness—as abjection—and the anus are conflated within libidinal economies of race and same-sex desirability. For Scott, the bottom is a pleasurable location, a site of Black debasement but also a locus of counterintuitive Black power.[85] The bottom, he writes, refers to "*both* the nadir of a hierarchy (a political position possibly abject) and . . . a sexual position: the one involving coercion and historical and present realities of conquest, enslavement, domination, cruelty, torture, and so on."[86] Bottoming, then, exceeds the realm of submissive (homo) sex. It is the anal opening, a channel for penetration, but it is also social subordination tethered to gratuitous acts of racial and sexual violence.

Like Walker's myriad articulations of the Black female bottom, Narcissister's performance fastens Black female sexuality to the anus. Centering this dynamic in contemporary Black women's art builds on Jennifer Nash's writing on Black anality. Furthering the discourse on bottomness and racialized abjection, Nash's formulation is an arresting argument not only because it allows us to dwell on the anal cavity in a mode that is separate from Bersani's focus on homosexuality and sameness, but also because it sutures anality to the spatial and sociocultural sphere. Black anality refigures the value of the bottom position in complex ways, specifically in relation to the ghetto, to dirtiness, and to mess, the latter two of which circulate throughout *Organ Player* as bad ideas, fecal matter, messy births, and rough self-sex. Most provocatively, this attention to anality's multiple dimensions and excess "pleasure" arises from the artist's own reckoning with her (self as a) mother figure. Here, she approximates what essayist Maggie Nelson terms a sodomitical mother, a concept first coined by Susan Fraiman to name the tension between queer resistance and female reproduction. In her genre-bending memoir *The Argonauts*, Nelson revises the term to describe mothers whose pleasures are perceived as threatening because they do not focus on their offspring, but on themselves. The sodomitical mother is an alternative to the obliteration of the self that stems from socially constructed fears concerning motherhood and the loss of self that could result from a mother's total devotion to her child. The sodomitical mother figure, by contrast, cultivates "nonnormative, nonprocreative sexuality" that exceeds "the dutifully instrumental" and the socially good.[87] Nelson's sodomitical mother is able to attach and detach herself to her child as a caregiver and as an individual seeking bodily pleasure. While driving her one-year-old son home from a vaccination appointment, for instance, she relates radio host Mary Roach's commentary about the anus being one of the most innervated parts of the human body to her interest in anal sex. Despite its alterity, however, Nelson's conception of motherhood and queerness, and the individual agency she reclaims as an act of self-identification in the face of potential loss, remains glaringly white.

Narcissister's anality, abjection, and masked performance of non-intimacy with the audience amplify how non-white mothers are socially constructed as engines of productivity but not necessarily reproduction. In birthing herself *for* and *to* herself in various scenes in *Organ Player*, she enacts a non-procreative form of sex—reproduction without futurity—that adds a kinky dimension to the Black feminist performance theories and practices she advances. Narcissister puts into motion and ultimately upends what performer and scholar Anna Martine Whitehead calls a "freak technique," an always already othered practice that sits at the intersection between Blackness, queerness, and embodied action. "First, appearing in the sixteenth century and deriving from the Old English [word] *Frician* [meaning] 'to dance,'" Whitehead writes, "the term *freak* was used by white Europeans with the power to name things to describe someone of 'capricious notion,' 'sudden turn of mind,' 'bold,' or 'gluttonous' disposition."[88] Whitehead uses the term "to suggest both a devastating lack of hegemonic protection and a legacy of sensuous and spirited cultural inventiveness."[89] As a creative strategy of survival, freak technique is one spur of "queer dance," an emergent style of performance that embraces downward movement, concaveness, and other minor forms of embodied expression to respond to, and even resist, capitalism as well as physical threats intrinsic to Black being. For Whitehead, these interventions—the mechanics of embodied resistance—also perform a kind of social recovery. Here, the get-down alchemizes Blackness and potential queerness, stealing movement away and transmuting it in order to get back up, to rise again, to overcome.

While Narcissister's extra-sensual inventiveness plays in the low registers of the body, aesthetics, and form, her merging of kink with the dance-based history of the freak ultimately turns away from any recuperative elements of performance. She is an artist who *works*, most certainly, but her labors do not fit into prescribed ideas of what is or would be socially reproductive, marketable, desirable, seamless, or good. The futility of her actions instead undermines virtuosity and exceptionalism as necessary elements for registering the radicalism behind her frustration. In combining desire with insatiability, the opening and final scenes of *Organ Player* also prefigure hunger as a minor state of being wherein one takes self-abasing pleasure in the incomplete. Her focus on incomplete climax and labor, rather than product, consequently initiates a different kind of value system. Masturbation without orgasm, for instance, is not essentially bad; nevertheless, the perversions that Narcissister performs fundamentally unsettle any framework that prioritizes orgasm as one space where we might imagine that the self gets made and remade. Her non-orgasmic displays thus refuse sexual and gender norms that emphasize procreativity and efficiency, both of which continue to impact organizational models and social relations in the new millennium. She stages inefficient actions that, in their failures to culminate in climax and integration, become potent forms of critique. These forms not only incite other ways of being in the world but an alternative understanding of pleasure as well.

In emphasizing abjection throughout, *Organ Player* demeans the seriousness of efforts to redeem the subjugated other. Its constellation of bottomness, racial difference, queerness, and self-effacement engenders a different kind of transgressive value by *not* rendering these entanglements as degrading or in need of repair. Pleasure, in other words, is not simply, or wholly, transcendent in Narcissister's world. It is mired in self-inflicted acts of torment that vacillate between race play and undesirable enactments of bondage. From uncomfortable sex and displaced orgasms to self-neglect and frustrated aesthetic ends, her visual work boldly galvanizes an anti-redemptive ethics of representation and relation that coalesces into a minor ensemble of rupturing shored up by her kinky occupation of the middle and the bottom.

At a time when reparation, harmony, and progress are the raison d'être of public discourse, Narcissister derives irreverent pleasure from upending racial fictions. From race and reproduction to dance-based virtuosity and fully knowable identities, her performances remain incomplete, open-ended, and nonlinear. In this way, her practice transmogrifies affirmative ideas about intersectionality, sisterhood, and art's liberatory potential in the digital, post-identity, selfie age. Her refusal to reveal her "real" identity or bare her soul, her use of parody and pastiche, and her performances of crude, anticlimactic sex consequently transform the ego-loving self-absorption of narcissism into something else altogether.

Unlike Narcissus, the center of the artist's affected narcissism is not a beautiful white male figure. In the story of Narcissus, the mythological anti-hero searches for a worthy object of desire, refusing all who court him. All his suitors fall short of his expectations, including Echo, who, cursed by Zeus's wife Hera, is unable to speak her love for the ill-fated hunter. When she reveals her identity and attempts to embrace him, Narcissus rejects her and she fades away; only her voice remains.[90] Eventually, Narcissus "finds himself" when Nemesis lures him to gaze into a pool of water in a secluded, dark meadow. In his reflection he discovers the love object for which he has been longing: himself. Transfixed by his own image, Narcissus stares at his reflection until he realizes his love can never be reciprocated, whereupon he commits suicide.

Though arrogance and vanity ring true of narcissism, *misrecognition*, not merely self-loving absorption, leads Narcissus to choose himself as a love object. In endeavoring to consummate his joining of himself to his love-image, he forgets himself entirely, foregoes relations with others, and ends his life. In so doing, Narcissus eschews culturally determined forms of sociality by forestalling a self-affirming future conventionally secured through romantic love, coupling, and procreation. This non-relational, anti-social thrust is at the heart of Narcissister's performance practice. But the artist's irreverence also propels narcissism and the concept of non-relationality into new territory.

In queer theory, non-relationality and anti-relationality emerge from queer, white, cis-masculine critiques of heteronormative injunctions that center on having children. Here, biological reproduction determines and evidences one's output and social value. That is, one's productivity—individually and collectively—is linked to one's reproductive capacities, and political possibility is tied to building a better world for future generations. For Lee Edelman, author of *No Future: Queer Theory and the Death Drive*, this logic of "reproductive futurism" presupposes three things. It suggests, first, that the future has "unquestioned value and purpose"; second, that we can improve it; and, third, that the future is emblematized by the child.[91] As such, reproductive futurism renders unthinkable all alternatives to kinship and solidarity.

Scholars of critical race theory and performance studies such as Amber Musser, Roderick Ferguson, Tavia Nyong'o, and José E. Muñoz have found fault with this line of thinking, arguing that queerness is neither counter to hope nor solely the domain of white cis men.[92] For these authors, racialized subjects, and Black subjects in particular, are always already against or outside the normative social order. Because of this positioning, minoritarian subjects cannot afford to turn away from the political possibility of communal world making. Queerness in this schema engenders utopian forms of being and belonging in the present that produce, according to Muñoz, "a type of affective excess that presents the enabling force of a forward-dawning futurity."[93] Minoritarian subjects, in other words, not only need hope and alternative configurations of futurity; they forge them in order to persist and thrive under and against oppressive forces.

Narcissister's art moves beyond the need for hope and futurity into a world where dissociation and disaffection are preconditions of Black female embodiment and being. Her work animates the racial valences of abjection, while also highlighting how the Black female body is expelled from the body politic, on the one hand, yet remains a barometer for measuring sexual deviance and desire in the public imaginary, on the other. The artist's self-identification and kinky performances of race, gender, and sex make this provocative and necessary shift more complex. Neither her creative labors nor her brand of self-objectifying narcissism can be extricated from her racial identification and women-of-color feminism because they are both circumscribed and complicated by multiracialism's problems and pitfalls. In the end, she mirrors back to viewers their own fragmented and upside-down projections of otherness, abjection, and Black womanhood.

Narcissister's donning of multiple selves, then, is more than mere performance meant to repair racial and gender wounding. Her performances bring into focus the pornotropic fields—of vision, of theory, and of marketplace capitalism in the art world and the wider world—that constrain her body and her artistic practice. The artist's non-procreative sex play upends prevailing ideas about what comprises value and desirability in the new millennium's present and future by demonstrating how racialized characters, and mixed-race figures in particular, continue to function as ciphers for social and sexual relations in the public sphere. Most importantly, her work foregrounds how a sexual act is always inevitably fraught with race and that self-objectification can constitute self-love and cross-racial intimacy, sometimes necessarily so. She is, simply put, a truly kinky artist.

Conclusion

We might use our position at the bottom, however, to make a clear leap into revolutionary action.
—The Combahee River Collective

In mining Black women's minor aesthetic strategies, *Undesirability and Her Sisters* models an interdisciplinary form of theory and criticism that troubles art historical norms as well as Black and feminist study's preoccupations with the reparative potential of representation. While other scholars frame Black women's cultural production as sites of recognition, resistance, healing, and pleasure, this book urges viewers and readers to see the speculative, irreconcilable, irreverent, and ambivalent ways of Black women's visual work as sources for political consideration and social critique. As I have outlined throughout, visual work refers to the creative act as a form of reproductive labor that has aesthetic, political, and monetary value. The phrase also emphasizes how Black women's visual and embodied otherness works on and in the US social imaginary, vitalizing the need for more robust, more ethical ways of knowing, seeing, and being when putatively progressive ideas about race, gender, sexuality, and class fail to yield equitable progress and protection. Undesirability as a method and framework is one such way.

Black women's reproductive labor is key to assessing the negative aesthetics and ethics of undesirability's messy terrain and its against-the-grain relationship to this new era of racial and gender meaning and reckoning. Through self-conscious engagements with Black women's minority status—their visual and embodied histories of marginalization and abjection—Walker, Mutu, Simmons, and Narcissister have developed equally minor aesthetic strategies in their lives and work that have major implications for the practice of art history, Black and feminist study, and their respective futures. These artists pry open the gaps that constitute the past, identity, and difference, cultivating discursive places in which to revel in a certain lack of mastery and power. This is not to discount the violence and trauma that constitutes Black female being in the past and present. On the contrary, *Undesirability and Her Sisters* takes seriously such ongoing violence and what it produces both aesthetically and politically.

Walker, Mutu, Simmons, and Narcissister spotlight how Black women's analogous relationship to systematic negation and dispossession serves as the grounds for divergent enactments of racial and gender belonging in the new millennium. Their aesthetic strategies undermine the idea that togetherness and transcendence are morally "good"—for Black and non-Black individuals, for their communities, for the nation, and for global humanity. But their visual work is more than a mere rejection of good or respectable representation and behavior. These artists' animations of undesirability and her sisters underscore the futility of looking for reparation and the shortcomings of efforts to redeem the racially and sexually subjugated self under and against unyielding structures of containment. Such acts of refusal elaborate on not only the queerness that fortifies undesirability, but also the sexual perversion that recurs as a pivotal component of Black women's visual work. This minor ensemble of rupturing, in my view, emerges and runs concurrent with a queer negative turn in Black feminist theorizing.

This book began with Beyoncé to foreground the messy terrain of race, gender, class, and sexuality with which Black women contend and the need for a new analytical framework for writing about Black women's art outside of a binary of trauma and repair, of woundedness and high-stakes achievement. Feminist attachments to Beyoncé—Black feminist attachments most potently—I argue, necessitate a broadening of intersectionality's conceptual and theoretical frames and impact as the most ethical kind of feminist and anti-racist work. Such broadening unmasks and unseats how Black and non-Black protocols of representation, interpretation, and self-making continue to hem Black women in *as subjects*, even and especially when done under the guise of celebrating Black feminism. Starting with the "major" and the "popular" to get to the "minor" contours of high art and the canon troubles the binary logics that undergird high-low categorizations, a system based on outmoded and erroneous white supremacist value hierarchies. This move also unsettles various close looking and reading conventions that haunt Black feminism and

Black visual culture as objects of theoretical inquiry in art history, Black and feminist study, and popular discourse. What results is a confrontation with the intimacy between personhood and objectification that emerges at the conjunction between celebrity, desirability, and racial and gender difference.

Undesirability and Her Sisters considers for the first time how Black women's triple otherness—*an alterity* at the intersection of race, gender, and sexuality—spurs negative aesthetics and ethics of representation and relation within contemporary art history. Following from discursive revolutions in identity-based art, its exhibition, and its histories since the 1980s to present, these strategies are concurrent with a negative turn in Black feminist theorizing. In bringing these threads together, this book builds on Black visual and cultural studies scholarship on the queerness of Blackness by way of refusal and sensation in the recent past and present, from the writings of the Combahee River Collective, Sylvia Wynter, and Hortense J. Spillers to those of Amber Jamilla Musser, Kaiama Glover, Jennifer C. Nash, Rizvana Bradley, Saidiya Hartman, Tavia Nyong'o, Tina Campt, Uri McMillan, and others. Perversity—not flawlessness and resilience—is one way contemporary Black women artists challenge representational protocols in the new millennium, from two of the most well-known living Black women artists to two artists that are differently situated in the art market. Iterations of this perversity show up in so-called high art that behaves badly as well as genres of photography and performance that defy categorization because of the works' inscrutable kinkiness.

The Black women artists in this book rattle the racist and sexist status quo of the art world and the wider world by modeling alternative conditions of being, raging in their own ways against structures of containment that relegate them to subhuman status. In so doing, they put on display the costs and burdens that Black women in the geo-historical space of the United States continue to bear in the new millennium, especially when such a woman says "no" to communal obligations that constrain her own being and becoming. The figures and environments they craft do not easily fit within the categories of "surrogate victim," "healer," "activist," "superwoman," "heroine," or even the "everywoman." Like the self-telling Black Caribbean women literary characters that Kaiama Glover analyzes, Walker, Mutu, Simmons, and Narcissister and their undesirable figurations of Black womanhood "are neither righteous nor even generous, at least not with any real consistency. They stand outside of communities with whom they ordinarily would be expected to identify, alongside [and] for whom they ordinarily would be expected to struggle."[1] This vantage point produces a different kind of orientation toward the social—a politics without a program—that demands sustained engagement with the conditions of subjugation and the crisis of participation and consent it precipitates over and over again. The ways that Walker, Mutu, Simmons, and Narcissister fail to exorcize the past, to nurture wholeness and healing, and to generate stable and transparent meaning are precisely the places that render art and Black female being not only worthy of analysis but ethically vital to realizing a more just world and, potentially, freedom. As Anne Anlin Cheng proposes, "Sometimes it is enough and downright crucial just to acknowledge what is in order to understand what will be. In short, we may have to risk the aporia of political uncertainty in order to reinvent the possibilities of the social."[2] Centering Black women's visual and embodied alterity thus brings a much-needed lens to critical theory and its norms. Grounded in disgust, dismemberment, opacity, and self-shattering objectification, undesirability precipitates modes of failing and unknowing that unravel, from the inside out, positivist, affirmative accounts of racial and gender progress in the art world and the wider world. Undesirability in this schema emerges as a forceful and productive instantiation of the antirelational ethics of seeing and being that Black women's queer negativity affords and demands. This framework is best exemplified by Walker, Mutu, Simmons, and Narcissister, artists who eschew both Eurocentric and intraracial beauty standards and collectivities by embracing errant, filthy, unstable, and disjointed aesthetic strategies that exist and thrive outside of the boundaries of respectable sociability and kinship.

Methodologically, my analysis merges the visual with the structural to outline an ethics of representation and relation that moves beyond the symbolic and didactic to a political economy where contemporary Black women's art necessarily reorders the logics of entertainment, education, subversion, and abjection precisely because of the social positions its makers occupy. *Undesirability and Her Sisters* not only reorients how we *look* at art by Black women at and after the turn of the twenty-first century; it models a novel historiographical approach that comprises the bottoming and negativity that stems from Black women's triple otherness. Social and aesthetic norms concerning reproduction and futurity energize this concept of otherness, yet the artists in this book dispense with the teleological underpinnings of reproductive futurity to model and embrace opaque and precarious forms of kinship that materialize at the threshold between Blackness and queerness as more than identity politics and sexual practice. As bookends to this study, Walker's and Narcissister's myriad interventions coalesce an anal ethics that expands the undertheorized possibilities of the Black female bottom within queer theory and intersectionality. Their "power dances" and acrobatic inversions vis-à-vis embodied enactments of topsy-turvy figures and mammies likewise repudiate present-day desires for racial integration and multiculturalism. Dispensing with well-worn notions of Black women's visual work as sites of wholeness and healing, their work presents the Black female bottom and race play as locations of transgressive self-shattering.

The repulsive, toxic, dismembered, wasteful, and perverse bodies in the art of Walker, Mutu, Simmons, and Narcissister upend positive accounts of Black women's bodies and art to register disenchantment with white, patriarchal, heterosexist narratives of sisterhood. These nonnormative figures instead lean into negativity and nihilism to urge viewers and critics to reconsider what racial comity, Black skin, and sexual pleasure mean and yield in a world obsessed with consuming Black women's cultural products while repeatedly championing progress at their expense. This paradigm shift matters now because it engenders a critique of the unwavering faith in "good behavior" and the pursuit of progress vis-à-vis moral and aesthetic redemption that drives mainstream understandings of success and wellness in contemporary social life. Of *A Subtlety*, Walker tells us, "If I've done the job well, then she gains her power by upsetting expectations one after the other."[3] Walker, Mutu, Simmons, and Narcissister meet the demands of reproduction and futurity with bottoming and anality, homogenous abjection with unruly sensual excess and inscrutability, and racial reconciliation with self-objectification. Such inversions incite viewers, scholars, and critics to take seriously what kinds of cultural knowledge emerges in the gap, the break, and the void.[4]

Walker, Mutu, Simmons, and Narcissister are not alone in producing knowledge in the gaps of the past, identity, and difference. The anxiety inducing, discomforting, destructive, deskilled, and glitchy art of Autumn

Knight, Caitlin Cherry, and Mandy Harris Williams remind audiences that redemptive multiculturalism and frictionless modes of togetherness are fantasies. In *Here and Now* (2017), for example, Knight gathers visitors for a group therapy session of sorts. Instead of bringing the diverse array of museum visitors together through conversations that sooth and empower viewers, the artist creates an uncomfortable and awkward environment that results in fragmented relationships and self-conscious disquiet born from the audience's confrontation with the artist's performances of satire as social critique and power.

The questions at the heart of *Here and Now*, scholar-artist Sandra Ruiz outlines in her writing on Knight, are, "How do we account for the unconscious properties of our flesh? That is, how do we negotiate the internal residue of race, gender, sexuality, and those power dynamics that mitigate difference in the space of any institution? . . . Who do we become in this space of aesthetics, with and against our own feelings, alienations, and unspoken biases?"[5] Undesirability, here, destabilizes the audience's senses and expectations of positive, affirming narratives of togetherness and consciousness that structure white patriarchal modes of belonging and becoming. Knight, whose work *WALL* (2014–16) is the first live performance artwork to enter the Studio Museum in Harlem's permanent collection, punctures the museum's illusions of intimacy and kinship by ushering visitors into a state of discomfort and disorienting otherness that fractures and unravels reality. She does not cultivate the kind of group therapy and community setting that participants expect. Rather, she enfolds them into a series of berating exercises that produce feelings of destabilization and alienation. In so doing, she reconstitutes the audience's relationship to power in the museum by inverting the source of control. More recently, Knight presented a series of performances that investigated the pleasures and possibilities of nothingness—of feeling in the void.

Caitlin Cherry paints layered, large-scale portraits of Black women that blur the lines between figuration and abstraction. Iridescent and visually dissonant by design, her most recent works are inspired by glitches that occur in LCD screens, a phenomenon she first noticed when, looking at her laptop from the side at a slant, the colors onscreen would invert. This process, known to photographers as solarization, changes the color of the figures onscreen to the hue most its opposite on the color wheel. Cherry's play with inversion builds on the aesthetic strategies outlined in this book and is materially tied to Black women's social position. "Black women have never sat comfortably in an idea of what femaleness is," she declares.[6] "Even if they don't realize," she continues, "they are playing by a set of queer politics."[7] For Cherry, this set of politics partially inheres in language as a structure of containment. In her 2020 oil painting *69 Syntax City*, syntax refers to grammar and composition—how sentences are formed and expressed—while 69 describes a sexual act that turns the relationship between tops and bottoms on its side. A widely adopted colloquialism, 69 is a sex position where two people align themselves so that each person's mouth is near the other person's genitals. From this mutually inverted position, each partner can simultaneously perform oral sex on the other. The title of the painting, then, names new value paradigms that digital space makes possible—a horizontal frame of pleasure that upends hierarchies with erotic words and acts that become memetic and transgressive as they travel through chat rooms, social media platforms, urban dictionary, and the everyday lexicon of subjects otherwise unaware of their meanings for Black women.

Cherry argues that just as iridescence forces people to move around her paintings and explore how they change under the casting of light, her works reorient viewers' perspectives on Black women as "systematically devalued in our society" but whose "aesthetics have filtered into popular beauty culture."[8] Whether "you're up close or far away," she reflects, she is "trying to figure out a way to disperse or reorient our society's relationship to Black femininity—and a very specific type of Black femininity that is both *underrepresented* and a part of everyday aesthetics, to the point that it is *almost never associated with high culture*."[9] In theory and in practice, Cherry interrogates Black women's undesirability—the condition of being historically marginalized yet hyper-visible in popular culture—and its relationship to subhuman, suprahuman, posthuman, and partially human forms. In terms of technique, the artist bridges digital codes and moiré patterns as the basis of her paintings to layer and ultimately obscure the found photographs she uses as source material. Her subjects as a result, many of whom are cabaret dancers and sex workers, simultaneously appear overexposed and underexposed. Such techniques permit the artist to create optical illusions that obfuscate and interrupt not only the pictorial space of the picture plane but also the status of her subjects and herself as minor characters and disempowered objects that circulate as commodities in the art world and everyday life. In so doing, she invites viewers and critics to question Western orders of aesthetic and political value that demand Black women's persistent authentication, subjugation, visualization, and vulnerability. Pulling from the latest movies, celebrity culture, TV, music videos, award shows, memes, and other social media content, the artist's source material, technique, and aesthetic choices in paintings such as *Video Killed the Painting Star*, *Czarists and Androids*, and *Proton-Enhanced Nuclear Induction Spectroscopy*, all from 2022, highlight the pornographic limits of visibility and self-transformation through the deployment of bottomness and baseness.

Mandy Harris Williams's practice is also deeply invested in the limits of Black women's desirability and self-determination on the internet and on social media. She is a proponent of algorithmic justice and a self-avowed "critical caption essayist" whose minimalist, text-based fine art objects, live performances, and sound art pieces disentangle technology's imbrication with white supremacy. Instagram, for Williams, along with independent radio and publishing—she is also a highly sought-after DJ—are the primary means by which she intervenes into the impacted structures of anti-Blackness. Her auto-critical methods yield confrontations with bottomness and baseness that stem from the artist's self-conscious engagements with Black women's social and structural queerness within the art world and the wider world. Through provocative passages of text on Instagram under the #BrownUpYourFeed hashtag, she argues that the white neoliberal attraction to representation is not only insufficient, but also an impediment to racial and gender progress. Only explicit anti-racism, she proclaims, can deprogram what she calls American fascism.

By reflecting on the terms that govern our attachments to racial and gender progress, the artists and artworks in *Undesirability and Her Sisters* constitute an epistemic rupture that expands our understanding of art's capacity to mediate trauma, history, and intersectional identities. Rather than a desire to become woman or become human, the perverse Black female figures in this book reinvest in the racial itself to invert its meanings by playing with the value judgements that provide a foundation for it. In so doing, they recalibrate how everyday viewers as well as humanities scholars and art world tastemakers understand the radical promise of Black women's creative labors. Undesirability thus serves as a powerful lens onto Blackness and its persistent visualization with implications that go beyond the field of contemporary art. The unruly Black female figures that populate this book proffer a relational strategy that finds purpose not in an essential and essentializing bond that stems from reproductive futurity but in its own self-conscious reckoning with subjection's ongoing permutations. Out of this reckoning, the propensity for abhorrence, revulsion, and nihilism abounds. Embracing negativity in this way occasions an altogether different, and more radically ethical, engagement with art and social life that is equal to the racial, gender, sexual, environmental, and economic challenges of our time.

ACKNOWLEDGMENTS

My mother's drawings and paintings of Black female figures were my first encounters with art and art history. Like most artists, my mother studied the masters. But having come of age during the Black Arts movement, she longed for figures and a canon that reflected her own experiences and identity. So she made her own, infusing her work, and her parenting, with aspirational narratives about the right and wrong ways to picture and perform Blackness. As I grew older, I began to question aspirational representations of the Black body. My undergraduate training at Fordham University/The Ailey School in New York crystallized these questions for me and set me on my path to graduate school. Through dance, in all its forms, I studied and practiced the dynamism and expressivity of identity, embodiment, and lived experience. It taught me that cultural production plays an important role in making place and meaning. Furthermore, I see dance as both a visual and an embodied medium that models how to think deeply about representation, power, value hierarchies, and how bodies move in space—in the studio, on stage, and in galleries and museums.

These formative moments fortify my scholarly pursuits as well as my practice as a curator and critic. My research, teaching, and curatorial practice bridge the disciplines of art history and Black studies to center lived experience as a source for theorizing encounters with visual culture. Looking closely at art and media, and the sociocultural contexts from which they emerge, can spur new ideas about the world, political possibility, and contemporary Black social life. Additionally, as my mother modeled for me, Black women ask questions of social and aesthetic norms in ways only they can and will. This book is a culmination of all of these forces.

I am so proud of this book, and I am grateful for everyone who has supported its development and me. These acknowledgments chart my intellectual lineage, from my family to the academy, and I am honored to be in such amazing company. First, my family. To my late grandfather, Albert McKinley Martin, affectionately known as Pete and Poppy, thank you for everything. Your adventurous, jolly, curious, critical, and scholarly spirit is in me and in these pages. I hope I have made you proud. To my mother, Debra E. Martin-Barber, and my late grandmother, June E. Martin, with whom I share my middle name and a family history of teaching, thank you for your endless encouragement, inspiration, and uplift. I remember going to my mother's office for Take Your Daughter to Work Day when I was a child, and I was in awe of all that she did to make a life for us. Now I get to take my mother to work with me, to conferences, on research trips, to art openings—I am so lucky. This book is for you, Nana, our cousin Stacey Holman whose Harlem apartment has been a respite and haven for me for decades, and all of the amazing Black women in our family line, those known and unknown. To my brother, Jonathan McKinley Barber, thank you for being a light for our family. You make the world brighter and better, and I am so excited for where your art and vision will take you.

I began shaping *Undesirability and Her Sisters* into a book when I was a 2016–18 predoctoral fellow at the University of Virginia's Carter G. Woodson Institute for African-American and African Studies. At the Woodson, I sat in on lectures about Black feminist projects on refusal and counterintuitive self-regard in their early formations by Kaiama Glover, Amber Musser, Tera Hunter, and others whose work has inevitably shaped my thinking and the arguments that course through the pages of this book. And there is the work of my cohort, many of whom have already published the books they were working on during our time at the Woodson. To Lyndsey Beutin, Petal Samuel, Julius Fleming Jr., Tony Perry, Xavier Pickett, Dionne Bailey, Ashleigh Greene-Wade, Chinwe Oriji, Seth Palmer, Ebony Jones, Ashley Rockenbach, and Corey Hunter, I have the fondest memories of our time in Charlottesville. Thinking with you all out loud about the limits and possibilities of Black study are still some of the most energizing and transformative conversations I have had to date. I am grateful to be among this elite group of scholars whose work is at the cutting edge of Black study, and I am deeply indebted to the institute's director at the time, Deborah McDowell, who mentored me and gifted me the title for this book. Your sharp intellect, fierce advocacy and leadership, impeccable style, and grace continue to be a model for me. Thank you to Alessandra Raengo and Amber Jamilla Musser who graciously served as guest critics for my manuscript workshops at the institute. The following pages are infused with your detailed notes and critical care. I am especially grateful to Amber for ongoing support, friendship, and fashion tips. What a treat to bask in your brilliance.

To the late great Douglas Crimp whose critical eye and mentorship first steered this book's focus and direction, I wish you were here to see and read where our many conversations have landed. Every word of this manuscript was written and rewritten with you in mind. You taught me how to use formal analysis to make arguments about objects without denying or dismissing my subjectivity and the broader importance of cultural context. You introduced me to Narcissister's art and knew that it was crucial to this book's formation long before I understood why. Now I know, and I am honored to have been your last student and to be a part of your rich legacy. To Stephanie Li, your leadership and influence has and continues to be a balm. You and I have organized symposia and developed classes together. You are one of my favorite thought partners, and every book you have authored (and there are many) has shaped my thinking in some way. Thank you for believing in me and advocating for me at and beyond the University of Rochester. I am so fortunate to call you colleague, mentor, and friend.

This book would be nothing without my developmental editor and the motley crew of writing buddies who sprinted with me to the finish line. To Alicia Inez Guzmán, you are one of the most brilliant people I know. You are a gift and this book is stronger because of your creative, critical eye. To the fierce thinkers and makers across the United States and Europe who continue to be my intellectual sounding boards and comrades, thank you for pushing my thinking to new heights. These include Adrian L. Burrell, Jerome P. Dent, Jr., Charisse Burden-Stelly, Alexandria Smith, Justin Dunnavant, Thomas Lax, Douglas Flowe, Tobias Wofford, Jenny Sorkin, C. Ondine Chavoya, Rebecca VanDiver, Teresita Fernandez, Angela Naimou, Laura Helton, Mireille Miller-Young, Sheena Sood, Gavriel Cutipa-Zorn, Sandy Placido, Anwar Uhuru, Takiyah Harper-Shipman, Banah Ghadbian, Brian Kwoba, Laura Helton, Janine de Novais, celeste doaks, Nora Khan, Alecia McGregor, Sarah Jackson, Gwendolyn DuBois Shaw, Jessica Horton, Mariola Alvarez, Jason Hill, Leah Modigliani, Delia Solomons, Erin Pauwels, Sarah Wasserman, and

DJ Lynnée Denise. If I have forgotten anyone, please charge it to my head and not my heart.

I am a social thinker, so I benefit from writing and thinking in community. To everyone who has invited me to workshop and deliver early versions of this manuscript as drafts and talks, I am forever in your debt. Your comments and generosity have transformed the arguments I present in these pages. These folks include Elliott Powell, Terrion Williamson, Jasmine Nichole Cobb, Franklin Sirmans, Heather Campbell Coyle, Karen Rapp, Chandra Frank, Anne Bray, Adrienne Childs, Lisa Uddin, Michael B. Gillespie, Melanee C. Harvey, Jeffrey McCune, Will Rawls, Tanisha C. Ford, P. Gabrielle Foreman, Lauren Cross, Jacqueline Francis, Jillian Hernandez, Erica Wall, Tanya Sheehan, and Cherise Smith, whom I am lucky to count as a mentor, advocate, Sagittarius sister, and friend. To J.T. Roane and the *Black Perspectives* editorial board for publishing my coedited series *New Black Surrealisms*; Deborah Willis, Cheryl Finley, Joan Morgan, and the Black Portraitures conference attendees who always offer informative feedback; my colleagues at the International Society for the Study of Surrealism; Robin D. G. Kelley for welcoming me to UCLA; and everyone who has advocated for my work, privately and publicly: thank you for unprecedented opportunities to expand the reach of my scholarship nationally and internationally. To Mike Williams, Raven Ferguson, and Marco Robinson of the National Humanities Center, my deepest gratitude for inviting me to speak at the 2023 Teaching African American Studies Summer Institute. To Reynaldo Anderson, John Jennings, Sheree Renée Thomas, Philip Butler, Zaika dos Santos, and my Black Speculative Arts movement fam, thank you for being my intellectual and political organizing home for all things Black futures. In 2021, I presented my research-based curatorial work on the value of Afrofuturism in times of crisis to a virtual panel and audience organized by Sandra Bradley at the American Council of Learned Studies. Kathy O'Dell and Safiyah Cheatam also invited me to present my work on Afrofuturism on a virtual panel of international artists and scholars at the University of Maryland, Baltimore County, in 2022. I have also presented this work and my writing on Wangechi Mutu at the Metropolitan Museum of Art in New York and at Negra Fest in Medellín, Colombia. I am honored and humbled to be doing this work for and with my community.

Prestigious fellowships and awards have provided uninterrupted time and resources for me to develop this book. In addition to the Woodson, I completed a 2021–22 postdoctoral fellowship at the Getty Research Institute. At the University of Delaware, where I was assistant professor of Africana studies and art history before joining the faculty at UCLA, the Gerald J. Mangone Young Scholars Award and a Faculty Research Award from the Department of Women and Gender Studies were instrumental sources of support early in my career. While at UCLA, I have received a Faculty Career Development Award, a Bunche Center Faculty Fellowship, and a Center for the Study of Women Research Grant. I am also a 2024–25 UCLA Hellman Fellow. To my colleagues at UD and UCLA, thank you for your continued engagement with my work and ideas.

Collegiality has been foundational to the development of this project. My time at the 2022 Writing Well retreat, founded by Jasmine Abrams, and the 2024 together retreat, organized by Joshua Myers, nourished my commitment to this project and my own well-being as a Black woman scholar. Workshopping a portion of this book's first chapter out loud with Josh, Kimberly Monroe, and Jewell Humphrey at the together retreat affirmed the multidisciplinary significance of this project during the copyediting phase. I am so moved by the attention and care that my colleagues, friends, family, and students have given this book. Additionally, portions of the fourth chapter of this book were published in a 2020 peer-reviewed article in *Art Journal* that won the Smithsonian's 2022 National Portrait Gallery Director's Essay Prize.

To my besties and framily Alicia Piller, Jerome P. Dent, Jr., Sam C. Tenorio, Michael Cooper, celeste doaks, Michelle Brugal, Shola Adisa-Farrar, Nicole Pollard, Sarah Williams, Kimberly Diane Jacobs, Anishika Sun, Jimmika Mika, Maxx Passion, Maya Taylor, Suede, Tina Farris, Seth Parker Woods, and Jean-Jacques Gabriel, thank you for holding me up when I needed it most. This book and our respective bonds have survived a pandemic and many moves across the country! You are all my mirrors; many of you are also my go-to thought partners and collaborators in all things life, love, and career. Celebrating milestones and making memories with each of you brings me deep and profound joy.

Prodigious student researchers Dajah White-Dumpson and Mali Collins at the University of Delaware and Joan Choi, Kahlila Williams, Mal Meisels, and Racquel Bernard at UCLA have helped me sharpen and refine the arguments in this book so that it might be a resource for future generations of students. Special thanks to Mal for assisting me in readying *Undesirability and Her Sisters* for production and publication. My deepest and sincerest gratitude for your attention to detail, your unbridled enthusiasm for this project, your editorial suggestions, and your skill and professionalism in securing the rights and permissions for the images reproduced. This book would not exist without you!

I am beyond excited to publish my first book with New York University Press and the Minoritarian Aesthetics Series. The press and series editors have offered invaluable feedback and stewardship along the way, from book proposal review to production and publication. Sandra, Uri, and Shane—wow. I am truly honored to be in your orbit and to have had your unyielding support throughout this process. Your feedback and cheerleading have transformed this book and me. I am so grateful! To Eric and especially Furqan, thank you for walking me through the twists and turns of the academic publishing world with care and vision. To the editing, design, marketing, and production team, specifically Valerie and Richard, you have given this book a striking face and presence. I am thrilled to be in such illustrious company and for NYUP to be the intellectual home for my first book.

Last but certainly not least, to the artists whose pathbreaking and challenging work spurred this book's interventions, thank you for granting me access to your studios and your practices. Kara, Wangechi, Xai, and Narcissister—your art has intoxicated and confounded me since my first encounters with it. Your willingness to share your processes and ideas with me has made this book an absolute pleasure to write.

NOTES

INTRODUCTION

Epigraphs: Malcolm X, "Who Taught You to Hate Yourself?," Lecture, Statler-Hilton Hotel, Los Angeles, CA (May 5, 1962), https://worldhistoryarchive.wordpress.com/. Malcolm X delivered this speech at the funeral for Ronald X Stokes, Nation of Islam member and temple secretary for Mosque 27 (which Malcolm established in 1957). Los Angeles Police Department officers murdered Stokes on April 27, 1962.

Chanda Prescod-Weinstein first tweeted this statement when Democrat Doug Jones defeated Republican Roy Moore in Alabama's highly contested special Senate election of 2017. The link to the tweet (https://twitter.com/IBJIYONGI/status/940963114589310978) is no longer active. But Prescod-Weinstein continues to tweet about media representations of the mammy in popular culture. Prescod-Weinstein also writes on issues of labor for Black women in the academy (with an emphasis on STEM) and in the public sphere, using the mammy stereotype as a point of departure to critique misguided, whitewashed diversity efforts. See Chanda Prescod-Weinstein, "How to Talk to Minorities, Part 2," *Medium*, July 1, 2015; and Chanda Prescod-Weinstein, "Don't Make Them Serve the Diversity," *Medium*, February 5, 2016.

1 The vulnerability of Black women and girls has been the subject of numerous scientific studies, sociological studies, blog posts, opinion pieces, grantmaking organizations, student writing, and single-authored academic books in the new millennium, especially in relationship to *Lemonade* and the Malcolm X quote. See Stewart M. Coles and Josh Pasek, "Intersectional Invisibility Revisited: How Group Prototypes Lead to the Erasure and Exclusion of Black Women," *Translational Issues in Psychological Science* 6, no. 4 (December 2020): 314–24; Deja Grissom, "Feminism Failed Black Women, Womanism Is the Solution," *Howard Community College Times* (2021); Christine Emba, "Black Women Deserve Better," *Washington Post* (January 9, 2019); Grantmakers for Girls of Color, https://g4gc.org/; and Trimiko Melancon, "'Left Exposed to View!': Black Women and Sexualized Violence," *Black Perspectives*, May 11, 2018, www.aaihs.org/. See also Moya Bailey, *Misogynoir Transformed: Black Women's Digital Resistance* (New York: New York University Press, 2021); and Zeffie Gaines, "A Black Girl's Song: Misogynoir, Love, and Beyoncé's Lemonade," *Taboo* 16, no. 2 (Fall 2017): 97–114.

2 For sources on the restorative justice process, see *Repairing Communities through Restorative Justice*, ed. John G. Perry (Lanham, MD: American Correctional

Association, 2002); Declan Roche, *Accountability in Restorative Justice* (Oxford: Oxford University Press, 2003); and Dennis Sullivan and Larry Tifft, eds., *Handbook of Restorative Justice: A Global Perspective* (London: Routledge, 2006).

3 "Freedom" contains three musical samples: Puerto Rican psychedelic funk band Kaleidoscope's "Let Me Try" (1969), written by Frank Tirado; "Collection Speech/ Unidentified Lining Hymn" (1959), recorded by ethnomusicologist Alan Lomax and performed by Reverend R. C. Crenshaw; and "Stewball" (1947), recorded by Alan Lomax and John Lomax Sr. and performed by Prisoner 22 at Mississippi State Penitentiary at Parchman.

4 For a recent journalistic take on this featuring many of today's prominent Beyoncé studies scholars, see Maria Sherman, "Kamala Harris Is Using Beyoncé's 'Freedom' As Her Campaign Song: What to Know about the Anthem," Associated Press, July 25, 2024, https://apnews.com.

5 For an extended discussion about the connection between the personal and the political in Beyoncé's *Lemonade*, see Tiffany E. Barber and Salamishah Tillet, "Close Up: Beyoncé: A Conversation with Salamishah Tillet," *Black Camera*l 9, no. 1 (Fall 2017): 205–16.

6 *Lemonade*, according to music critic Jillian Mapes, "proves Beyoncé to also be a new kind of post-genre pop star." See Jillian Mapes, "Beyoncé: Lemonade," *Pitchfork*, April 26, 2016. See also Robin Hilton, Ann Powers, Rodney Charmichael, and Sidney Madden, "The 2010s: 5 Ways Beyoncé Defined the Decade in Music," *NPR*, October 15, 2019, www.npr.org.

7 Although I use *Black feminism* as a primary phrase and lens throughout this book, the ethos of positive metamorphosis and repair that *Lemonade* mobilized also resonates with Alice Walker's pathbreaking conception of womanism and her own cultural production in the new millennium. See Alice Walker, *The World Will Follow Joy: Turning Madness into Flowers; New Poems* (New York: New Press, 2013).

8 For an overview of Black feminist theories on *Lemonade* and the national and international emergence of Beyoncé studies more broadly, see Adrienne Trier-Bieniek, ed., *The Beyoncé Effect: Essays on Sexuality, Race and Feminism* (Jefferson, NC: McFarland, 2016); Omise'eke Natasha Tinsley, *Beyoncé in Formation: Remixing Black Feminism* (Austin: University of Texas Press, 2018); Kinitra D. Brooks and Kameelah L. Martin, eds., *The Lemonade Reader* (London: Routledge, 2019); and Christina Baade and Kristin A. McGee, eds., *Beyoncé in the World: Making Meaning with Queen Bey in Troubled Times*, (Middletown, CT: Wesleyan University Press, 2021).

9 Candice Marie Benbow, "*Lemonade* Syllabus," *issuu*, May 6, 2016.

10 Benbow, "*Lemonade* Syllabus." Emphasis mine.

11 For a resonant discussion of triple otherness and the kind of consciousness it produces in Black women artists, see Adrian Piper, "The Triple Negation of Colored Women Artists," in *Out of Order, Out of Sight*, vol. 2, *Selected Writing in Arts Criticism 1967–1992* (Cambridge, MA: MIT Press, 1996), 161–73. Piper argues that

the ideological conceit of postmodern discourse is to repress and exclude women artists of color from the Western art canon, which she calls the Euroethnic mainstream. Within this purview, women artists of color, or CWAs (colored women artists) in Piper's terms, become threatening and necessarily repressible bodies.

12 Uri McMillan, *Embodied Avatars: Genealogies of Black Feminist Art and Performance* (New York: New York University Press, 2015), 205. Here, McMillan draws on Jennifer C. Nash's extended discussion of the politics of Black female representation and pleasure in *The Black Body in Ecstasy: Reading Race, Reading Pornography* (Durham, NC: Duke University Press, 2014).

13 In 2022, Beyoncé herself titled her seventh studio album, her first solo release since *Lemonade*, *Renaissance*. For more on the New Black Renaissance in recent art and culture writing, see Ibram X. Kendi, "Ibram X. Kendi: This Is the Black Renaissance," *Time*, February 3, 2021; Folasade Ologundudu, "Art Historian Darby English on Why the New Black Renaissance Might Actually Represent a Step Backwards," *artnet news*, February 26, 2021; Bertrand Cooper, "Who Actually Gets to Create Black Pop Culture?," *Current Affairs*, July 25, 2021.

14 See Monica A. Coleman, *Making a Way Out of No Way: A Womanist Theology* (Minneapolis, MN: Fortress, 2008); and Monica A. Coleman, "Sacrifice, Surrogacy and Salvation: Womanist Reflections on Motherhood and Work," *Black Theology* 12, no. 3 (2014): 200–12.

15 Huey Copeland and Krista Thompson, "Perpetual Returns: New World Slavery and the Matter of the Visual," *Representations* 113, no. 1 (Winter 2011): 6.

16 Jennifer C. Nash, "Re-thinking Intersectionality," *Feminist Review* 89, no. 1 (2008): 9.

17 Nash, "Re-thinking Intersectionality," 4.

18 In 1987, civil rights activists Audley Moore, Callie House, and James Forman along with Walter R. Vaughan, a Confederate veteran who believed that reparations would be a stimulus for the South, formed the National Coalition of Blacks for Reparations in America (N'COBRA). Moore was also responsible for founding the Reparations Committee of Descendants of United States Slaves in 1955, a possible template for N'COBRA. In January 1989, John Conyers Jr., a representative for Michigan's thirteenth congressional district (which includes Detroit), introduced the Commission to Study Reparations Proposals for African-Americans Act (HR 40). Conyers has continued to bring the bill before Congress, unsuccessfully, every year since its first introduction. Charles J. Ogletree Jr., a professor at Harvard Law School and cochair of the Reparations Coordinating Committee, has pursued reparations claims in court, putting forth what he calls a "litigation strategy [for] fully address[ing] the legacy of slavery in a spirit of repair" and remedying past wrongs (Charles J. Ogletree Jr., "Litigating the Legacy of Slavery," *N ew York Times*, March 31, 2002). Internationally, chattel slavery and the transatlantic slave trade were declared crimes against humanity at the 2001 United Nations World Conference against Racism, Racial Discrimination, Xenophobia, and Related Intolerance. For more on this history, see Ta-Nehisi Coates, "The

Case for Reparations," *Atlantic*, June 2014; and Martha Biondi, "The Rise of the Reparations Movement," *Radical History Review* 87 (Fall 2003): 5–18.

19 Amber Jamilla Musser, "Toward Mythic Feminist Theorizing: Simone Leigh and the Power of the Vessel," *differences* 30, no. 3 (2019): 65.

20 Sharon Holland, *The Erotic Life of Racism* (Durham, NC: Duke University Press, 2012), 66, quoted in Musser, "Toward Mythic Feminist Theorizing," 65–66.

21 Holland quoted in Musser, "Toward Mythic Feminist Theorizing," 65–66.

22 See Hortense J. Spillers, "Mama's Baby, Papa's Maybe: An American Grammar Book," Diacritics 17, no. 2, Special Issue, "Culture and Countermemory: The 'American' Connection" (Summer 1987), 64–81; David Marriott, *On Black Men* (New York: Columbia University, 2000); and Roderick J. Ferguson, *Aberrations in Black: Toward a Queer of Color Critique* (Minneapolis: University of Minnesota Press, 2003).

23 In a footnote, Zakiyyah Iman Jackson offers a rich explanation of how Spillers's prescriptions in "Mama's Baby, Papa's Maybe" spearhead a groundbreaking consideration of the intersection of Blackness, gender, sexuality, and rupture that guides my thinking on undesirability and the critical potential of embracing abjection: "Hortense Spillers offers a theory of black gendering at the limit of the subject. . . . Spillers describes a state of injury that makes gendered and sexual normativity possible, and argues that this predicament presents an opportunity for an ethical disinvestment in heteropatriarchy." See Zakiyyah Iman Jackson, "Waking Nightmares—on David Marriott," *GLQ* 17, no. 2–3 (April 2011): 359, 363.

24 Jackson, "Waking Nightmares," 360.

25 Scholars working across abjection and incompletion in aesthetics via Brownness offer a roadmap for studies in Black aesthetics that push against the colonial grammars of facile constructions and the traps of representation. Like my work, Black feminist theorizing motivates these interventions regarding Brownness as well. For such studies, see José Esteban Muñoz, *The Sense of Brown*, ed. Joshua Chambers-Letson and Tavia Nyong'o (Durham, NC: Duke University Press, 2020); Deborah R. Vargas, *Dissonant Divas in Chicana Music: The Limits of La Onda* (Minneapolis: University of Minnesota Press, 2012); Antonio Viego, *Dead Subjects: Toward a Politics of Loss in Latino Studies* (Durham, NC: Duke University Press, 2007); Leticia Alvarado, *Abject Performances: Aesthetic Strategies in Latino Cultural Production* (Durham, NC: Duke University Press, 2018); and Joshua Javier Guzmán and Christina A. León, "Cuts and Impressions: The Aesthetic Work of Lingering in *Latinidad*," *Women & Performance* 25, no. 3 (2015): 261–76.

26 For a succinct and insightful overview of these concepts and intellectual blind spots, see Uri McMillan, "Introduction: Skin, Surface, Sensorium," *Women & Performance* 28, no. 1 (March 28, 2018).

27 See Naomi André's back matter blurb for *Beyoncé in the World: Making Meaning with Queen Bey in Troubled Times*, ed. Christina Baade and Kristin A. McGee (Middletown, CT: Wesleyan University Press, 2021). She writes, "The lyrical writing in these essays combines the classic intersections of race, gender, and sexuality with themes of international fandom, celebrity activism, and construction of

colorism. This collection about Beyoncé illustrates the new Black feminist cool; it is central to any discussion about music and popular culture."

28 Stephanie Li, "Introduction: Who Is Beyoncé?," *Black Camera* 9, no. 1 (Fall 2017): 107.

29 See Omise'eke Natasha Tinsley and Caitlin O'Neill, "Beyoncé's 'Formation' Is Activism for African Americans, Women and LGBTQ People," *Time*, February 8, 2016; and Leigh Cuen, "Fans Hail Beyoncé's 'Formation' As Black Lives Matter Anthem," *vocativ*, February 8, 2016.

30 Music critics, scholars, and even the artist's husband have publicly denounced the fact that Adele and Taylor Swift have repeatedly garnered Album of the Year Grammy awards over Beyoncé and her record-breaking, best-selling albums.

31 *Swarm*, the 2023 comedy-horror television series about a Beyoncé-obsessed serial killer, satirizes this phenomenon.

32 Wesley Morris, "The Morality Wars," *New York Times*, October 3, 2018.

33 Morgan Jerkins, "'Lemonade' Is about Black Women Healing Themselves and Each Other—It's Beyoncé's Newest Feminist Statement," *Elle*, April 26, 2016.

34 Darlene Clark Hine, "Rape and the Inner Lives of Black Women in the Middle West," *Signs* 14, no. 4 (Summer 1989): 915.

35 Benbow, "*Lemonade* Syllabus."

36 See Stephen M. Best, "On Failing to Make the Past Present"; and Stephen M. Best, *None Like Us: Blackness, Belonging, Aesthetic Life* (Durham, NC: Duke University Press, 2018).

37 Sublimation is the cornerstone of social life in Sigmund Freud's view and the basis of widespread endorsements concerning the affirmative relationship between art and life in histories of modern and contemporary art. Freud believed sublimation to be a sign of mature cultural development, of civilization, in which socially unacceptable primal instincts, such as sex and sadism, are displaced to achieve non-sexual, socially useful ends. Sublimation, in this frame, is a practice of reckoning, a psychosocial defense mechanism that transforms unacceptable libidinal impulses into socially desirable behaviors that contribute to the greater good. "[It] is what makes it possible for higher psychical activities, scientific, artistic or ideological, to play such an important part in civilised life," Freud explains in "Civilisation and Its Discontents" (79–80). Consequently, erotic energy converts to creative energy: libido is transferred to artistic output as an act of social acceptability and duty. See Sigmund Freud, "Civilisation and Its Discontents" (1930), in *The Standard Edition of the Complete Psychological Works of Sigmund Freud—The Future of an Illusion, Civilization and Its Discontents, and Other Works*, trans. James Strachey (London: Hogarth, 1961).

38 Leo Bersani, *The Culture of Redemption* (Cambridge, MA: Harvard University Press, 1990), 97.

39 According to Saidiya Hartman, Black bodies in nineteenth-century America were excluded from "traditional notions of the political and its central features: the unencumbered self, the citizen, the self-possessed individual, and the volitional and autonomous subject." She also notes, "The slave is the object or the ground

that [made] possible the existence of the bourgeois subject and, by negation or contradistinction, defines liberty, citizenship, and the enclosures of the social body." Saidiya Hartman, *Scenes of Subjection: Terror, Slavery, and Self-Making in Nineteenth-Century America* (Oxford: Oxford University Press, 1997), 61, 62.

40 Thelma Golden, "Post . . . ," *Freestyle*, exhibition catalog, eds. Christine Y. Kim et. al. (New York: Studio Museum of Harlem, 2001), 14. *Freestyle* was presented at The Studio Museum in Harlem in 2001 and featured work by twenty-eight contemporary Black artists. The first in an ongoing series of survey exhibitions of contemporary Black art at the Studio Museum under Golden's direction, *Freestyle* has since been followed by *Frequency* (2005), *Flow* (2008), and *Fore* (2012). It is important to note that there is at least one instance in which the term *post-Black* enters art historical and scholarly discourse prior to Golden's proclamation. In "Afro Modernism," a September 1991 *Artforum* review of *Africa Explores: 20th Century African Art*, Robert Farris Thompson writes, "A retelling of Modernism to show how it predicts the triumph of the current sequences would reveal that 'the Other' is your neighbor—that black and Modernist cultures were inseparable long ago. Why use the word 'post-Modern' when it may also mean 'postblack'"? See Robert Farris Thompson, "Afro Modernism," *Artforum* 30 (1991): 91. While Thompson's review appears to be the first published use of the now pervasive term, his use of *post-Black* differs from current iterations of the term.

41 Touré, *Who's Afraid of Post-Blackness? What It Means to Be Black Now* (New York: Free Press, 2011), xiv.

42 Brandi Wilkins Catanese, *The Problem of the Color[blind]: Racial Transgression and the Politics of Black Performance* (Ann Arbor: University of Michigan Press, 2011), 27. I insert reparative here to acknowledge the student comments that Catanese includes in her account of the class discussion she facilitated about the uniqueness of the televised broadcast of Obama's inauguration. When asked what made the 2009 US presidential inauguration so special, one student replied, "There's a lot of excitement that a new administration will help to repair America's standing in the world community by taking us in a new direction" (26). Moreover, the students avoid discussing Obama's Blackness as a possible explanation for the media attention his inauguration receives—an indicator of the era's post-racial order.

43 David Hammons quoted in Deborah Solomon, "The Downtowning of Uptown," *New York Times Magazine*, August 19, 2001.

44 Thelma Golden quoted in Sarah Valdez, "Freestyling," *Art in America* 89, no. 9 (September 2001): 138.

45 For proof of this, see Derek Conrad Murray, *Queering Post-Black Art: Artists Transforming African-American Identity after Civil Rights* (London: I. B. Tauris, 2015). Post-Blackness, Murray writes, has "paradoxically become the most talked about and debated issue in contemporary African American art" (1).

46 Darby English quoted in Folasade Ologundudu, "Art Historian Darby English on Why the New Black Renaissance Might Actually Represent a Step Backwards," *artnet news*, February 26, 2021, https://news.artnet.com.

47 Darby English quoted in Ologundudu, "Art Historian Darby English."
48 Golden, "Post . . . ," 15.
49 Jennifer C. Nash quoted in Emerald Rutledge, "After Intersectionality: A New Book on Black Feminism," *Black Perspectives*, February 22, 2019, www.aaihs.org/.
50 Claire Hemmings, *Why Stories Matter: The Political Grammar of Feminist Theory* (Durham, NC: Duke University Press, 2011), 3.
51 Hemmings, 4.
52 Hemmings, 4.
53 Hemmings, 4, 106.
54 Hemmings, 5.
55 Amber Jamilla Musser, "Toward Mythic Feminist Theorizing: Simone Leigh and the Power of the Vessel," *differences* 30, no. 3 (2019): 65.
56 See Carole S. Vance, ed., *Pleasure & Danger: Exploring Female Sexuality* (London: Routledge and Kegan Paul, 1984). See also Mary Douglas, *Purity and Danger: An Analysis of Concepts of Pollution and Taboo* (New York: Praeger, 1966), a point of departure for Julia Kristeva's work that received renewed attention during the AIDS crisis of the 1980s and 90s.
57 Julia Kristeva, *Powers of Horror: An Essay on Abjection*, trans. Leon S. Roudiez (New York: Columbia University Press, 1982), 15.
58 Kristeva, *Powers of Horror*, 4.
59 In addition to extending the work of Hortense Spillers, David Marriott, Roderick Ferguson, and Zakiyyah Jackson, undesirability aligns with "low theory," a recognition "that alternatives," in J. Halberstam's words, "[also] dwell in the murky waters of a counterintuitive, often impossibly dark and negative realm of critique and refusal." See J. Halberstam, *The Queer Art of Failure* (Durham, NC: Duke University Press, 2011), 2. Halberstam adapts the phrase "low theory" from Stuart Hall's Gramscian concept of theory as a "detour en route to something else," Walter Benjamin's notion of the stroll, and the Situationist concept of the dérive. Amanda Anderson's "bleak liberalism" and Lauren Berlant's "cruel optimism" are other theorizations for the contemporary political economy from which my concept of undesirability springs, as is the work of the Practicing Refusal Collective. Formed in 2015 by Tina Campt and Saidiya Hartman, the Practicing Refusal Collective is an international Black feminist forum dedicated to initiating new dialogues on Blackness, anti-Black violence, and Black futurity in the twenty-first century. Responses to this political economy are also reflected in recent writings on anarchism, negative ethics, queer temporality, and failure. See David Graeber, *Fragments of an Anarchist Anthropology* (Chicago: Prickly Paradigm, 2004); José Esteban Muñoz, *Cruising Utopia: The Then and There of Queer Futurity* (New York: New York University Press, 2010); Lee Edelman, *No Future: Queer Theory and the Death Drive* (Durham, NC: Duke University Press, 2005); as well as Frank B. Wilderson III's and Jared Sexton's writings on Afropessimism.
60 Stephen Best, "On Failing to Make the Past Present," *Modern Language Quarterly* 73, no. 3 (September 2012), 456.

61 Tom Perez, "Black women are the backbone of the Democratic Party. I'm so proud of our candidates for their historic victories and I'm committed to a more fully representative and inclusive party." *Facebook* (November 10, 2017), www.facebook.com/TomPerez/posts/black-women-are-the-backbone-of-the-democratic-party-im-so-proud-of-our-candidat/742635782589312/. See also Rebecca Savransky, "DNC Chair: Black Women are the 'Backbone' of the Democratic Party," *The Hill*, December 13, 2017.

62 Vanessa Williams, "'Democrats Take Them for Granted': Black Women Call Out Party Leaders on Post-Election Strategy," *Washington Post*, June 1, 2017.

63 Tom Perez (@TomPerez), *Twitter* (July 31, 2018), 3:06 p.m., https://twitter.com/tomperez/status/1024370823782719489?lang=en.

64 Nash, "Re-thinking Intersectionality," 8. "These assertions, while useful for problematizing the notion that black women's experiences can be reduced solely to marginalization," Nash writes, "ultimately romanticize and idealize positions of social subordination and reinstall conceptions that black women's bodies are sites of 'strength' and 'transcendence' rather than complex spaces of multiple meanings" (8).

65 Kara Walker quoted in "Creative Time," *Tumblr*, June 25, 2014, https://creativetime.tumblr.com/post/89879126868/i-didnt-want-a-completely-passive-viewer-art.

66 Wangechi Mutu quoted in Soraya Murray and Derek Conrad Murray, "A Rising Generation and the Pleasures of Freedom," *International Review of African American Art* 20, no. 2 (2005): 8. For more on Wangechi Mutu's view of her figures as protagonists, see her commentary in the promotional video for her solo exhibition, *Wangechi Mutu: A Fantastic Journey*, curated by Trevor Schoonmaker at the Nasher Museum of Art at Duke University. The exhibition opened in March 2013 and traveled to the Brooklyn Museum and the Museum of Contemporary Art, North Miami, before closing at the Mary and Leigh Block Museum of Art in December 2014. The video, published on April 24 2013, can be found at www.youtube.com/watch?feature=players_embedded&v=Q-x9mdk13ds.

67 Wangechi Mutu quoted in Murray and Murray, "A Rising Generation," 8.

68 For an expanded treatment of this relation, see Tiffany E. Barber, Angela Naimou, and Wangechi Mutu, "Between Disgust and Regeneration: An Interview with Wangechi Mutu," *ASAP/Journal* 1, no. 3 (September 2016): 337–63.

69 Douglas Crimp, "The Photographic Activity of Postmodernism," *October* 15 (Winter 1980), 94.

1. THE BLACK FEMALE BOTTOM

Epigraph: Leo Bersani, *The Culture of Redemption* (Cambridge, MA: Harvard University Press, 1990), 1. Emphasis mine.

1 Kara Walker quoted in Jessica Kramer, "Kara Walker Addresses Art and Controversy at the Newark Public Library," *Huffington Post*, March 13, 2013.

2 Sarah Brophy, "The Stickiness of Instagram: Digital Labor and Postslavery Legacies in Kara Walker's 'A Subtlety,'" *Cultural Critique* 105 (2019): 23.

3 Jarvis C. McInnis, "Black Women's Geographies and the Afterlives of the Sugar Plantation," *American Literary History* 31, 4 (Winter 2019): 759–60.

4 For instructive accounts on the censoring of Kara Walker's *The Means to an End*, see Pamela Newkirk, "Controversial Silhouette," *ARTnews* 98 (September 1999): 45; Gwendolyn DuBois Shaw, "Censorship and Reception," in *Seeing the Unspeakable: The Art of Kara Walker* (Durham, NC: Duke University Press, 2004), 103–24; and Phillip Vergne et al., *Kara Walker: My Complement, My Enemy, My Oppressor, My Love* (Minneapolis: Walker Art Center, 2007).

5 David Penney quoted in David Lyman, "Exhibit Causes a Fuss at the DIA," *Detroit Free Press*, November 23, 1999, 7.

6 David Penney quoted in Lyman, "Exhibit Causes a Fuss at the DIA," 7.

7 Campbell Gibson and Kay Jung, "Table 23. Michigan—Race and Hispanic Origin for Selected Large Cities and Other Places: Earliest Census to 1990," in "Historical Census Statistics on Population Totals by Race, 1790 to 1990, and by Hispanic Origin, 1970 to 1990, for Large Cities and Other Urban Places in the United States," *Population Division: Working Paper No. 76* (Washington, DC: US Census Bureau, February 2005), www.census.gov.

8 See Anne M. Wagner, "Kara Walker: 'The Black-White Relation,'' in *Kara Walker: Narratives of a Negress*, exhibition catalog, ed. Ian Berry, Darby English, et al. (Cambridge, MA: MIT Press, 2003), 90–101. See also Gwendolyn DuBois Shaw, *Seeing the Unspeakable: The Art of Kara Walker* (Durham, NC: Duke University Press, 2004).

9 Whether Kara Walker's work successfully lambasts racist and sexist stereotypes or perpetuates them, particularly within a predominantly white art market, has been the subject of debate since Walker emerged on the art scene. See the unsigned editorial titled "Extreme Times Call for Extreme Heroes," *International Review of African-American Art* 14, 3 (1997): 2; Michael D. Harris quoted in "The Past Is Prologue but Is Parody and Pastiche Progress? A Conversation," *International Review of African-American Art* 14, 3 (1997): 25–27, and Howardena Pindell's "Diaspora/Reality/Strategies," paper delivered at the October 1997 Johannesburg Biennale symposium titled "Trade Routes, History, Geography, Culture: Toward a Definition of Culture in the late 20th Century," published in *N. Paradoxa* 7 (1998) and updated with new postscripts in 2002 and 2007. See also the entire issue of *International Review of African-American Art* 15, no. 2 (1998), which includes responses by Kara Walker and Michael Ray Charles; Michael D. Harris's *Colored Pictures: Race and Visual Representation* (Chapel Hill: University of North Carolina, 2006); Hamza Walker, "Nigger Lover, or Will There Be Any Black People in Utopia," *Parkett* 59 (2000): 152–65; Kymberly N. Pinder, "Missus Kara E. Walker: Emancipated, and On Tour," *Art Bulletin* 90, 4 (2008), 640–48; and Vergne et al., *Kara Walker*, which has an extensive bibliography on the artist's oeuvre and its reception.

10 See Christina Sharpe, *Monstrous Intimacies: Making Post-Slavery Subjects* (Durham, NC: Duke University Press, 2009). Sharpe devotes a chapter of her book to Kara Walker's silhouettes.

11 Kara Walker quoted in "Kara Walker Explains Her Interest in 'Demoted' Art Forms," San Francisco Museum of Modern Art, www.sfmoma.org.

12 Alessandra Raengo, *On the Sleeve of the Visual: Race as Face Value* (Hanover, NH: Dartmouth College Press, 2013), 147.

13 Here I draw on Alessandra Raengo's analysis of Kara Walker's silhouettes in *On the Sleeve of the Visua*. See also Anne W. Wagner, "The Black-White Relation"; and Mark Reinhardt's "The Art of Racial Profiling," in *Kara Walker: Narratives of a Negress*, exhibition catalog, ed. Ian Berry et al., (Cambridge, MA: MIT Press, 2003).

14 Johann Kaspar Lavater, *Essay on Physiognomy for the Promotion of the Knowledge and the Love of Mankind*, vol. 2, 90, quoted in John B. Lyon, "'The Science of Sciences': Replication and Reproduction in Lavater's Physiognomics," *Eighteenth-Century Studies* 40, 2 (2007): 262. See also Ida McLearn, G. M. Morant, and Karl Pearson, "On the Importance of Type Silhouette for Racial Characterization in Anthropology," *Biometrika* 20B, 3–4 (1928); and R. K. White and Carney Landis, "Perception of Silhouettes," *American Journal of Psychology* 42, 3 (1930).

15 Lavater, *Essay on Physiognomy*, 90, quoted in Lyon, "'The Science of Sciences,'" 262.

16 Alessandra Raengo, *On the Sleeve of the Visual: Race as Face Value* (Hanover, NH: Dartmouth College Press, 2013), 147.

17 Raengo, *On the Sleeve of the Visual*, 148.

18 For an account of the relationship between physiognomy and the racialization of the criminal as an archetype, see Allan Sekula, "The Body and the Archive," *October* 39 (Winter 1986): 3–64. Sekula illustrates how physiognomy became the basis for reading portrait photography, energizing the cataloguing processes by which criminal bodies were measured against ideal, respectable bodies within police and prison records.

19 Kobena Mercer, "Tropes of the Grotesque in the Black Avant-Garde," in *Pop Art and Vernacular Cultures*, ed. Kobena Mercer (Cambridge, MA: Iniva and MIT Press, 2007), 143. Mercer's discussion of the preexisting text of Blackness draws on Henry Louis Gates Jr.'s use of Barbara Johnson's definition of Black stereotypes as "already read texts." See Henry Louis Gates Jr., "The Trope of a New Negro and the Reconstruction of the Image of the Black," in "America Reconstructed, 1840–1940," special issue, *Representations* 24, (Autumn 1988): 148.

20 Evelynn Hammonds, "Black (W)holes and the Geometry of Black Female Sexuality," *differences* 6 (1994), 138.

21 Hammonds, 139.

22 Hammonds, 139.

23 Darby English also likens Kara Walker's work to landscape, comparing her sprawling silhouette scenes to the genre of nineteenth-century landscape painting. For this comparison, see Darby English, *How to See a Work of Art in Total Darkness* (Cambridge, MA: MIT Press, 2007).

24 As an anti-monument, *A Subtlety* is loosely based on Mississippi senator John Williams's unrealized 1923 proposal to honor the "memory of the faithful colored mammies of the South." For more on this history, see Joan Marie Johnson,

"'Ye Gave Them a Stone': African American Women's Clubs, the Frederick Douglass Home, and the Black Mammy Monument," *Journal of Women's History* 17, 1 (Spring 2005): 62–86.

25 For more on these criticisms, see Amber Jamilla Musser, "Riddles of the Sphinx: Kara Walker and the Possibility of Black Female Masochism," *New Directions in Black Feminist Studies* (February 5, 2015), www.youtube.com/watch?v=ma9JmtEi7VQ.

26 Tân Hoàng Nguyễn, *A View from the Bottom: Asian American Masculinity and Sexual Representation* (Durham, NC: Duke University Press, 2014), 14.

27 Nguyễn, *A View from the Bottom*, 2.

28 Jennifer C. Nash, "Black Anality," *GLQ* 20, 4 (2014): 439.

29 Nash, "Black Anality," 440.

30 For Jennifer C. Nash's full treatment of race pleasure, see Jennifer C. Nash, *The Black Body in Ecstasy: Reading Race, Reading Pornography* (Durham, NC: Duke University Press, 2014).

31 Darieck Scott, *Extravagant Abjection: Blackness, Power, and Sexuality in the African American Literary Imagination* (New York: New York University Press, 2010), 3.

32 Scott, 3, 165.

33 Scott, 265. Emphasis mine. For more recent theorizations of the bottom that align with my conception of the Black female bottom, see Zalika U. Ibaorimi, "The Bottom Dwellers: On Spiritual, Material, and Ontological Sites of Deviant Making," Black Women Radicals, streamed live on April 5, 2022, YouTube video, 1:32:49, https://www.youtube.com/watch?v=6kN6UysDZPs&t=1s; and Zalika U. Ibaorimi, "The Bottom Dwellers: On Spiritual, Material, and Ontological Sites of Deviant Making," Black Women Radicals, streamed live on April 5, 2022, YouTube video, 1:32:23, https://www.youtube.com/watch?v=9VTA2CC4uu4.

34 Amber Jamilla Musser, *Sensational Flesh: Race, Power, and Masochism* (New York: New York University Press, 2014), 154.

35 Bersani, *The Culture of Redemption*, 1.

36 Sianne Ngai, "Afterword: On Disgust," in *Ugly Feelings* (Cambridge, MA: Harvard University Press, 2005), 332. Ngai's work extends that of Hannah Arendt, William Ian Miller, and Theodor Adorno on disgust, Roland Barthes on jouissance, and Julia Kristeva on abjection. To this list, I would add Mikhail Bakhtin's theorization of the grotesque body given its relevance to the relation between Black bodies, excess, and inversion that is central to my conception of undesirability.

37 Carolyn Korsmeyer, *Savoring Disgust: The Foul and the Fair in Aesthetics* (New York: Oxford University Press, 2011), 9.

38 Korsmeyer, *Savoring Disgust*, 7, 9.

39 Tavia Nyong'o, "Racial Kitsch and Black Performance," *Yale Journal of Criticism* 15, no. 2 (Fall 2002): 371.

40 Nyong'o, "Racial Kitsch," 371. Emphasis mine.

41 Leo Bersani's critique of gay men's "uncontrollable identification with . . . the sacrosanct value of selfhood," which is ideologically reinforced by sanitized

narratives of heterosexual coupling that lead to "ill-practiced ideals of community and diversity," is instructive here. See Leo Bersani, "Is the Rectum a Grave?," in "AIDS: Cultural Analysis/Cultural Activism," ed. Douglas Crimp, special issue, *October* 43 (Winter 1987): 222. It offers a productive way of thinking about the political value of identity-based aesthetic practices that upend drives toward dignity, communal healing, and racial utopias. "What if we said," Bersani asks, "not that it is wrong to think of so-called passive sex as 'demeaning,' but rather that *the value of sexuality itself is to demean the seriousness of efforts to redeem it?*" (222). The value of sexuality, in other words, and its entanglements with the value of Blackness in contemporary art in my view, is its anti-redemptive thrust.

42 Nicholas Powers, "Why I Yelled at the Kara Walker Exhibit," *Indypendent*, June 30, 2014. Emphasis mine.

43 Supplements that further historicized the installation were included on Creative Time's website, which also hosted interactive components to encourage viewers to use the installation's custom twitter hashtag: #KaraWalkerDomino to create a "Digital Sugar Baby." Those writings included Haitian writer Edwidge Danticat's *The Price of Sugar* and illustrator and activist Ricardo Cortes's *The Act of Whitening*, See http://creativetime.org.

44 Kara Walker quoted in Carolina A. Miranda, "Kara Walker on the Bit of Sugar Sphinx She Saved, Video She's Making," *Los Angeles Times*, October 13, 2014.

45 The clip, originally published on *Vulture*, a web-based publication on arts and culture, has since been removed from the publication's website. See Rachel Corbett, "Kara Walker Secretly Filmed You Taking Selfies in Front of Her Sphinx," *Vulture*, November 19, 2014.

46 Kristin Iversen, "White People Problems: On Kara Walker and the Way White People Interact with Black Art," *Brooklyn Magazine*, June 9, 2014.

47 Nikita Richardson, "In Ruins: First Look at the Kara Walker Exhibit Every Brooklynite Needs to See," *Brooklyn Magazine*, May 9, 2014.

48 See Kara Rooney and Kara Walker, "A Sonorous Subtlety: KARA WALKER with Kara Rooney," *Brooklyn Rail*, May 6, 2014.

49 Lauren Berlant, "National Brands/National Body: *Imitation of Life*," in *American Comparative Identities: Race, Sex, and Nationality in the Modern Text*, ed. Hortense J. Spillers (New York: Routledge, 1991), 122.

50 Berlant, 122.

51 Berlant, 122.

52 Berlant, 113.

53 Berlant, 113.

54 Berlant, 114.

55 In this way, the mammy-faced surplus body and the overwhelming odor of the Domino Sugar Refinery and its contents run parallel in their excess and repulsive effects. As such, the force of *A Subtlety*'s undesirability was on par with the condition of the installation's temporary site itself; the refinery was ideal for Kara Walker's anti-redemptive art *because* it was in disrepair and slated for demolition

after the installation. This doubling, a characteristic found throughout Walker's oeuvre, also aligns with what Henry Louis Gates, Jr. identifies as "talking back," a riff on Mikhail Bakhtin's dialogical principles of the carnivalesque and grotesque. See Kobena Mercer's discussion of Gates and Bakhtin in Kobena Mercer, "Tropes of the Grotesque in the Black Avant-Garde," in *Pop Art and Vernacular Cultures*, ed. Kobena Mercer (Cambridge, MA: Iniva and MIT Press, 2007), 143–47. "Talking back" functions like the Black music tradition of call and response. It describes the formal moves and rhetorical devices that African American writers use to repeat and change "the preexisting text of blackness" as well as the largely white-male dominated American literary canon. Translating this to Black visual work, Kobena Mercer notes, "Black artists can be said to 'talk back' to depictions of blackness found in both fine art traditions and in popular visual culture." See Mercer, "Tropes of the Grotesque in the Black Avant-Garde," 144. Following Mercer, Walker's art reconfigures the silhouette, an eighteenth-century convention, as well as Black visual codes of respectability that became attached to post-Emancipation Blackness in the nineteenth and twentieth centuries. But her appropriation of the mammy differs from her earlier appropriations of the silhouette by emphasizing the corporeal excess of the nude Black female body in white coating, recontextualizing Bakhtin's notion of the material lower bodily stratum within grotesque realism. Bakhtin explains: "Grotesque realism imagines the human body as multiple, bulging, over- and under-sized, protuberant and incomplete. The openings and orifices of this carnival body are emphasized, not its closure or its finish. It is an image of impure corporeal bulk with its orifices (mouth, flared nostrils, anus) yawning wide and its lower regions (belly, legs, feet, buttocks and genitals) given priority over its upper regions (head, 'spirit,' reason)." See Mikhail Bakhtin, *Rabelais and His World*, trans. Hélène Iswolsky (Cambridge, MA: MIT Press, 1968), 9. Bakhtin does not address the racial and gendered undertones of the grotesque, but the racial grotesque finds expression in Walker's oversized, over-embodied mammy. Thus, the doublespeak of Walker's intervention into packaged, reparative understandings of Blackness—its histories, its signs, and its scripts—is not so subtle after all; it is protuberant, impure, and intoxicating in all senses of the word. "Scripts" here refers to the notion of disciplinary scripts as they relate to identity and struggles for freedom. Philosopher Kwame Anthony Appiah writes, "Demanding respect for people as black and gay requires that there are some scripts that go with being an African-American or having same-sex desires. There will be proper ways of being black and gay, there will be expectations to be met, demands will be made. It is at this point who takes autonomy seriously will ask whether or not we have not replaced one kind of tyranny with another." See Kwame Anthony Appiah, "Identity, Authenticity, Survival: Multicultural Societies and Social Reproduction," in *Multiculturalism: Examining the Politics of Recognition*, ed. Amy Gutmann (Princeton: Princeton University Press, 1994), 162–63. Walker's sphinx indeed therefore talks back, but not along the lines of Gates's formation;

it talks back in that it disobeys, misbehaves, and turns away from formal and social scripts concerning Black women's bodies.

56 Berlant, "National Brands/National Body," 112. For writing on the social media phenomenon that *A Subtlety* precipitated, see Stephanye Watts, "The Audacity of No Chill: Kara Walker in the Instagram Capital," *Gawker*, June 4, 2014; Jamilah King, "The Overwhelming Whiteness of Black Art," *Colorlines*, May 21, 2014; and Nicholas Powers, "Why I Yelled at the Kara Walker Exhibit," *The Indypendent*, June 30, 2014.

57 To understand the multiple refusals at play in *A Subtlety* and other artworks discussed in this book—aesthetic, visceral, ethical, and methodological—it is important to note that the integration that Kara Walker's work refuses at the level of cultural discourse extends to Black studies scholarship. To this point, the school of critical inquiry in which Henry Louis Gates Jr.'s formulation of "talking back" operates is generally identified with the integrationist paradigm of African and African American studies. This paradigm, in contrast to the Afrocentric paradigm, proposes the inclusion or integration of studies concerning aspects of Black life within "traditional" disciplines and canons of knowledge as recourse to the inconsideration and outright erasure of Black lived experience from Western historiographies. For more on the integrationist paradigm, see Ronald L. Taylor, "The Study of Black People: A Survey of Empirical and Theoretical Models," *Urban Research Review* 2, 2 (1987); and James B. Stewart, "Reaching for Higher Ground: Toward an Understanding of Black/Africana Studies," *Afrocentric Scholar* 1, no. 1 (May 1992): 1–63. While the integrationist and Afrocentric paradigms polarize Black studies discourse, there are other models. For this discussion, see Perry A. Hall, "African American Studies: Discourses and Paradigms," in *African American Studies*, ed. Jeanette R. Davidson (Edinburgh: Edinburgh University Press, 2010), 15-34.

58 Tavia Nyong'o, "Subtleties of Resistance: Sweetness and Violence in Kara Walker's *A Subtlety*," in *Kara Walker*, ed. Vanina Géré (Cambridge, MA: MIT Press, 2022), 168.

59 See Gwendolyn DuBois Shaw, *Seeing the Unspeakable: The Art of Kara Walker* (Durham, NC: Duke University Press, 2004).

60 Luis Garden Acosta quoted in *Toxic Brooklyn*, dir. Derrick Beckles, (Brooklyn, NY: VICE, 2009). Acosta, who died in 2019, founded the long-standing Williamsburg-based social and environmental justice organization El Puente along with his wife Frances Lucerna in 1982. El Puente is still active today.

61 Acosta, quoted in *Toxic Brooklyn*.

62 Kara Walker, quoted in *Art21 Exclusive*, 204, "Kara Walker: 'A Subtlety, or the Marvelous Sugar Baby,'" dir. Ian Forster, aired May 23, 2014 on https://art21.org/watch/extended-play/kara-walker-a-subtlety-or-the-marvelous-sugar-baby-short/.

63 Walker, quoted in *Art21 Exclusive*, 204.

64 For another example of this, see Andrea Fraser's *Untitled* (2003), an hour-long, single-take, silent video where she has sex in a New York hotel room with an unidentified white male art collector who paid $20,000 to participate in the artwork.

Fraser has said of the work that she wanted to investigate whether or not art is prostitution—"in a metaphorical sense, of course." See Andrea Fraser quoted in Praxis, "Andrea Frasier," *The Brooklyn Rail*, October 2004.

65 Bersani, "Is the Rectum a Grave?," 211.

66 See Doreen St. Félix, "After Her Sugar Sphinx, Kara Walker Is a New Kind of Public Figure," *Vulture* (April 2017).

67 Evelynn Hammonds, "Black (W)holes and the Geometry of Black Female Sexuality," *differencess* 6 (1994), 97.

68 Hammonds, "Black (W)holes," 97.

69 Janell Hobson, "Remnants of Venus: Signifying Black Beauty and Sexuality," *Women's Studies Quarterly* 46, 1/2 (2018): 105.

70 Hobson, "Remnants of Venus," 111.

71 Amber Jamilla Musser, "Queering Sugar: Kara Walker's Sugar Sphinx and the Intractability of Black Female Seuxality," *Signs* 42, 1 (2016): 170.

72 Musser, "Queering Sugar," 171.

73 Hortense J. Spillers, *Black, White, and in Color: Essays on American Literature and Culture* (Chicago: Chicago University Press, 2003), 157.

74 Spillers, 155.

75 Spillers, 156. Emphasis mine.

76 Zakiyyah Iman Jackson, "'Theorizing in a Void': Sublimity, Matter, and Physics in Black Feminist Poetics," *South Atlantic Quarterly* 117, no. 3 (July 2018): 617–48.

77 Musser, "Queering Sugar, 157.

78 Kara Elizabeth Walker, "Fons Americanus," in *Kara Walker: Fons Americanus*, ed. Clara Kim (London: Tate, 2019), 56.

79 Walker, "Fons Americanus," 58.

80 For a definition and discussion of refusal and negation as generative of disorderly power, see Tina Campt, "Black Visuality and the Practice of Refusal," *Women & Performance* 29, no. 1 (February 25, 2019): 79–87.

81 Jennifer C. Nash, "Black Anality," *GLQ* 20, no. 4 (October 2014): 439–60.

82 Walker, "Fons Americanus," 57.

83 J. Halberstam, *The Queer Art of Failure* (Durham, NC: Duke University Press, 2020), 128.

84 Walker, "Fons Americanus," 55.

85 Walker, "Fons Americanus," 56.

86 Paul Gilroy, *The Black Atlantic: Modernity and Double Consciousness* (Cambridge, MA: Harvard University Press, 1993).

87 Much of the work to date on empire and environment has focused on control. Drawing together critiques of colonialism, governmental reach and discipline, and profit, recent scholarship outlines how imperial systems of control and containment sought to collect, classify, and order human and nonhuman forms. Contemporary publications on this nexus also consider how, when, and where infrastructural development and extraction are deployed as forms of discipline to manage, engineer, contain, and destroy nature and various species through

hydraulic projects, land-use change, weather studies, and climate engineering. In this schema, projects that maximize, extract, and plant commercial resources are tied to profit.

88 The term *fabulation*, popularized by literary critic Robert E. Scholes, describes twentieth-century novels that do not fit the traditional generic categories of realism or romance and are written in a style similar to magical realism. Literary critic Saidiya Hartman extends Scholes's thesis to narrative interventions into the archive of slavery in history writing and fiction. Performance studies scholar Tavia Nyong'o further qualifies fabulation as a Black aesthetic mode in his articulation of Afro-fabulation. See Robert E. Scholes, *The Fabulators* (Oxford: Oxford University Press, 1967); *Structural Fabulation: An Essay on Fiction of the Future* (Notre Dame: University of Notre Dame Press, 1975); and *Fabulation and Metafiction* (Champaign: University of Illinois Press, 1979). See Saidiya Hartman, "Venus in Two Acts," *Small Axe* 12, no. 2 (June 2008): 1–14; and Nyongo, "Unburdening Representation," *Black Scholar* 44, no. 2 (Summer 2014): 70–80, for applications of Scholes's ideas to Black cultural production.

89 Walker, "Fons Americanus," 58.

90 Walker, 58.

91 Walker quoted in Doreen St. Félix, "After Her Sugar Sphinx, Kara Walker Is a New Kind of Public Figure," *Vulture* (April 2017). The article, which also discusses another of Walker's major public art commissions for the Prospect Biennial in New Orleans, first appeared in the April 17, 2017 issue of *New York Magazine*.

92 Walker, 55.

93 Walker, 55.

94 Emphasis in original.

95 Emphases in original.

96 See Thekla Morgenroth, Michelle K. Ryan, and Kim Peters, "The Motivational Theory of Role Modeling: How Role Models Influence Role Aspirants' Goals," *Review of General Psychology* 19, no. 4 (December 2015): 465–83. See also James W. Ainsworth, "Does the Race of Neighborhood Role Models Matter? Collective Socialization Effects on Educational Achievement," *Urban Education* 45, no. 4 (2010): 401–23; and Anat BarNir, Warren E. Watson, and Holly M. Hutchins, "Mediation and Moderated Mediation in the Relationship among Role Models, Self-Efficacy, Entrepreneurial Career Intention, and Gender," *Journal of Applied Social Psychology* 41, no. 2 (February 2011): 270–97.

97 See Joy James, *In Pursuit of Revolutionary Love: Precarity, Power, Communities*, (Brussels: Divided Publishing, 2023). See also Joy James, "The Womb of Western Theory: Trauma, Time Theft, and the Captive Maternal," in *Challenging the Punitive Society: Carceral Notebooks*, vol. 12, ed. Bernard Harcourt, Perry Zurn, and Andrew Dilts (New York: Publishing Data Management, 2016), 253–96; Joy James, *New Bones Abolition: Captive Maternal Agency and the Afterlife of Erica Garner* (Brooklyn: Common Notions Press, 2023); and Raw Wilcox, "At the Impasse of Revolution and Revolutionary Love," *Scalawag Magazine*, March 30, 2023.

98 See Kaiama L. Glover, *A Regarded Self: Caribbean Womanhood and the Ethics of Disorderly Being* (Durham, NC: Duke University Press, 2021). Concentrating on novels by Marie Chauvet, Maryse Condé, René Depestre, Marlon James, and Jamaica Kincaid, Glover reframes Caribbean literary studies by championing unruly female protagonists who challenge the primacy of the community over the individual and propose provocative forms of being.

99 Jennifer C. Nash, "Re-thinking Intersectionality," *Feminist Review* 89 (2008): 8.

100 Nash, "Re-thinking Intersectionality," 7.

101 For a thoughtful and thorough analysis of this phenomenon, see Nicole R. Fleetwood, *Troubling Vision: Performance, Visuality, and Blackness* (Chicago: University of Chicago Press, 2010).

2. ALIEN KIN

Epigraphs: Stephen M. Best, "On Failing to Make the Past Present," *Modern Language Quarterly* 73, no. 3 (September 2012): 465; Rizvana Bradley, "A Gathering of Aporetic Form," *e-flux* 105 (December 2019).

1 For an original treatment of the landscapes and environments that appear in Wangechi Mutu's art, see Chelsea M. Frazier, "Troubling Ecology: Wangechi Mutu, Octavia Butler, and Black Feminist Interventions in Environmentalism," *Critical Ethnic Studies* 2, no. 1 (Spring 2016): 40–72.

2 See Axelle Karera, "Blackness and the Pitfalls of Anthropocene Ethics," *Critical Philosophy of Race* 7, no. 1 (2019): 32–56.

3 For more on Wangechi Mutu's view of her figures as protagonists, see Mutu's commentary about her work in the promotional video for her solo exhibition, *Wangechi Mutu: A Fantastic Journey*, curated by Trevor Schoonmaker at the Nasher Museum of Art at Duke University. The exhibition opened in March 2013 and traveled to the Brooklyn Museum and the Museum of Contemporary Art, North Miami, before closing at the Mary and Leigh Block Museum of Art in December 2014. The video, published on April 24 2013, can be found at www.youtube.com/watch?feature=players_embedded&v=Q-x9mdk13ds.

4 Nancy Tuana, "Being Affected by Climate Change: The Anthropocene and the Body of Ethics," in *Ethics and the Anthropocene*, ed. Kenneth Shockley and Andrew Light (Cambridge, MA: MIT Press, forthcoming), 2, quoted in Axelle Karera, "Blackness and the Pitfalls of Anthropocene Ethics," *Critical Philosophy of Race* 7, no. 1 (2019): 34.

5 Famed curator Okwui Enwezor organized the 1997 Johannesburg Biennale, the second staging of the landmark event for a country that had theretofore been left out of global art conversations. Rather than a series of national pavilions, Enwezor collaborated with six international curators on a range of diverse exhibitions for the biennale. These curators included Kellie Jones, Gerardo Mosquera, Octavio Zaya, Hou Hanru, Colin Richards, and Yu Yeon Kim.

6 Isolde Brielmeier, "The Splendor of Our World," in *Wangechi Mutu: A Shady Promise*, ed. Isolde Brielmeier (Bologna: Damiani, 2008), 13.

7 Josée Bélisle, "The Anatomy of an Exquisite Horror: An Introduction to the Complex, Dazzling, Monstrous—and Moving—Art of Wangechi Mutu," in *Wangechi Mutu*, exhibition catalog, ed. Josée Bélisle, (Montréal: Musée d'art contemporain de Montréal, 2012), 61.

8 Kristine Stiles, "Wangechi Mutu's Family Tree," in *Wangechi Mutu: A Fantastic Journey*, exhibition catalog, ed. Trevor Schoonmaker (Durham, NC: Nasher Museum of Art/Duke University Press, 2013), 51–52.

9 Courtney J. Martin, "Fracture and Action: Wangechi Mutu's Collages, 1999–2010," in *My Dirty Little Heaven*, exhibition catalog (Deutsche Guggenheim Berlin; Ostfildern: Hatje Cantz, 2010), 50. Chelsea M. Frazier offers a compelling counterpoint to reading Wangechi Mutu's collages as metaphors for postcolonial identity. Mutu's "protagonists," she writes, "are illegible within the confines of anything resembling a nation-state," the politics of which are "irreducible to the language of citizenship, cultural particularity, and national governance as we currently conceive of it." See Chelsea M. Frazier, "Troubling Ecology: Wangechi Mutu, Octavia Butler, and Black Feminist Interventions in Environmentalism," *Critical Ethnic Studies* 2, no. 1 (Spring 2016): 42–43.

10 Transgressive dismemberment joins recent critical studies of ugliness, negation, failure, unbecoming, and repulsion within feminist, queer, and Black cultural theory. I apply these theorizations to Wangechi Mutu's collages in this chapter, adding Farah Jasmine Griffin's and Hortense J. Spillers's pivotal contributions to Black feminist thought in order to apprehend the value of Black female being that Mutu's work prompts.

11 This phrase appears in an untitled drawing featured in Kara Walker's 1996 interview with art critic Jerry Saltz, published in *Flash Art*. See Jerry Saltz, "Kara Walker: Ill-Will and Desire," *Flash Art* 29, no. 191 (1996): 82–86.

12 Amber Jamilla Musser, *Sensual Excess: Queer Femininity and Brown Jouissance* (New York: New York University Press, 2018), 9.

13 *30 Americans*, an exhibition of works by African American artists from the Rubell Family Collection in Miami, has been traveling to institutions across the United States for over ten years. The show includes thirty-one artists work by then-emerging talents like Rashid Johnson to established ones like Kara Walker and historical figures like Robert Colescott and Jean-Michel Basquiat. Like post-Blackness and the *Freestyle* exhibition, *30 Americans* expands the parameters of both African American art and American art beyond identity politics. One way it does this is by challenging where to locate Blackness in the United States. I see the inclusion of Wangechi Mutu's work as part of this mission.

14 Okwui Enwezor, "Weird Beauty," in *My Dirty Little Heaven*, exhibition catalog (Deutsche Guggenheim Berlin; Ostfildern: Hatje Cantz, 2010), 30.

15 Also known as the Garden of God in the Christian tradition, Terrestrial Paradise is the name popularly given to the Garden of Eden described in the second chapter of Genesis.

16 Wangechi Mutu quoted in Merrily Kerr, "Wangechi Mutu's Extreme Makeovers," *Art on Paper* 8, no. 6 (July/August 2004). *Art on Paper* was a bimonthly art magazine published from 1996 to 2009. Excerpts of Kerr's article can be found at www.saatchigallery.com.

17 In an interview with Robert Enright, Wangechi Mutu describes her use of print media as material for her collage: "You can tell what American mainstream culture is thinking by looking at a newsstand. For the most part, there's a lot of misogynistic material, and a few things that have to do with sports and cars. If you want to know what an animal's system is about, you look at its shit, like elephant dung. If you want to know where the animal has been and whether it's healthy, you sift through its stool. That's a little bit what it's like when I look at media; it's quickly processed, it's not the most high-end knowledge but it definitely gives you a cross-section of what is going on." Wangechi Mutu quoted in Robert Enright, "Resonant Surgeries: The Collaged World of Wangechi Mutu," *Bordercrossings* 105 (2008).

18 In addition to posthumanism, critics see Wangechi Mutu's work as examples of Afrofuturism in art because it joins racialized and gendered bodies with techno-mechanical parts. Reading Mutu's collages through the lenses of posthumanism and Afrofuturism, however, reveals redemptive conceptions of subjecthood relative to race, gender, and sexuality that run counter to Mutu's formal and aesthetic use of rupture. In the writings of Alondra Nelson, Kodwo Eshun, Nettrice Gaskins, and Ruth Mayer, Afrofuturism is a revisionist discourse in which racialized and gendered bodies in the past, present, and future use technology to reparative ends. Blackness is linked with notions of being alien and the historical experiences of colonization, displacement, and slavery in these works. The term *Afrofuturism* first appeared in the introduction to a series of interviews that cultural critic Mark Dery conducted with Samuel Delany, Greg Tate, and Tricia Rose. Dery coined *Afrofuturism* to describe literary works of science fiction written by African American writers that incorporate themes of abduction and alienation with images of "technology and a prosthetically enhanced future." Mark Dery, *Flame Wars: The Discourse of Cyberculture* (Durham, NC: Duke University Press, 1994), 180. Dery's essay and interviews originally appeared in *South Atlantic Quarterly* 91, no. 3 (1992), 501–23, a special issue on cyberculture. But Afrofuturism does more than reclaim the history of the past, according to science fiction studies scholar Lisa Yaszek; it is "about reclaiming the history of the future as well." Expressions of Afrofuturism mix African mythology and cosmology with technologically centered, speculative and science fiction tropes as a way to connect members of the Black diaspora with a lost ancestral past, to create community and imagine alternative futures. The term is now broadly applied to works of art that explore the complexities of Black identity and experience across genres and locales as a way to model and instigate social change. Lisa Yaszek, "An Afrofuturist Reading of Ralph Ellison's *Invisible Man*," *Rethinking History* 9,

no. 2/3 (June/September 2005): 297–313; and Reynaldo Anderson and Charles E. Jones, eds., *Afrofuturism 2.0: The Rise of Astro-Blackness* (Lanham, MD: Lexington Books, 2016). My analysis emphasizes the anti-redemptive force of Mutu's work and how such a reading might reorient the aims of Black women's art and its discursive currents.

19 David Moos, "*The Ark Collection*: Disjunctive Continuity," in *Wangechi Mutu: This You Call Civilization?*, exhibition catalog, ed. David Moos (Toronto: Art Gallery of Ontario, 2010), 17.

20 Aside from curator Okwui Enwezor's gloss of Wangechi Mutu's collages as examples of Afropessimism and writer Cinqué Hicks's designation of her works as picturing survival as "a form of erotic pleasure" instead of lamentation, the majority of critical accounts of Mutu's work imbue it with a redemptive function. Even Hicks wants to make the figures "totems of survival" despite characterizing them as uninterested in appealing to viewers' moral registers. See Enwezor, "Weird Beauty"; and Cinqué Hicks, "Review: Wangechi Mutu's Politics of Pleasure: A Fantastic Journey at the Nasher Museum of Art at Duke University," *Burnaway*, April 11, 2013.

21 Michael E. Veal, "Enter Cautiously," in *Wangechi Mutu: A Shady Promise*, ed. Isolde Brielmeier (Bologna: Damiani, 2008), 9–10.

22 Trevor Schoomaker, "A Fantastic Journey," in *Wangechi Mutu: A Fantastic Journey*, exhibition catalog, ed. Trevor Schoonmaker, (Durham, NC: Nasher Museum of Art/Duke University Press, 2013), 26.

23 Gwen Raaberg, "Beyond Fragmentation: Collage as Feminist Strategy in the Arts," *Mosaic* 31, no. 3, "The Interarts Project: Part Three: Representing Women" (September 1998): 153.

24 Raaberg, 153.

25 Raaberg, 154. In "Beyond Fragmentation: Collage as Feminist Strategy in the Arts," Gwen Raaberg traces the twentieth-century development of theories of collage as oppositional art within contemporary culture marked by postmodern fragmentation while challenging any essentialist basis for this development among women and racially marginalized artists. While Raaberg outlines the prevalence of collage for historically marginalized artists within contemporary art, she also critiques the assumption that marginalized artists have any essential relationship to collage. She additionally outlines the debates regarding collage's revolutionary potential, especially within feminist art production. She writes, "Current debates regarding the possibility of truly oppositional art, however, often involve a critique of collage, questioning assumptions about its revolutionary 'edge' and implicating it in concerns about the political limitations of any art embedded in postmodern culture. Allying feminist arts and agendas with collage would thus seem to pose a number of problems: insofar as the feminist arts assume a political stance and are directed toward a critique of contemporary culture, how can the practice of feminist collage be squared with the charge that collage is symptomatic of postmodern cultural fragmentation and that it is

incompatible with art as political critique?" (153). See Raaberg, "Beyond Fragmentation," 153–71.

26 In an interview with curator and art historian Lauri Firstenberg, Mutu states, "Of the artists you mentioned [Bearden, Höch, Fatimah Tugger, and Candice Breitz] I identify most with Bearden, his work strikes me as the least reactionary." Lauri Firstenberg, "Perverse Anthropology: The Photomontage of Wangechi Mutu, A Conversation with the Artist," in *My Dirty Little Heaven*, exhibition catalog (Deutsche Guggenheim Berlin; Ostfildern: Hatje Cantz, 2010), 42.

27 Kobena Mercer, "Romare Bearden, 1964: Collage as Kunstwollen" in *Cosmopolitan Modernisms*, ed. Kobena Mercer (Cambridge, MA: Institute of International Visual Arts and MIT Press, 2005), 125. For Romare Bearden's discussion of distortion, see Myron Schwartzman, *Romare Bearden: His Life and Art* (New York: Harry N. Abrams, 1950), 212–16.

28 Along with his collages, Romare Bearden produced a number of essays addressing these topics. See Romare Bearden, "The Negro Artist and Modern Art," *Opportunity*, December 1934, 371–72; and "The Negro Artist's Dilemma," *Critique*, November 1946, 16–22. See also "The Black Artist in America: A Symposium," *Metropolitan Museum of Art Bulletin* 27, January 1969, 245–61. This features a discussion between Sam Gilliam Jr., Richard Hunt, Jacob Lawrence, Tom Lloyd, William Williams, and Hale Woodruff that Bearden moderated.

29 Mercer, "Romare Bearden," 126.

30 For an early study on the relation between Dadaist and surrealist collage and critiques of war and the bourgeoisie, see William Rubin, *Dada, Surrealism, and Their Heritage* (New York: Museum of Modern Art, 1968).

31 Wangechi Mutu quoted in Firstenberg, "Perverse Anthropology," 42.

32 Wangechi Mutu quoted in Okwui Enwezor, "Cut & Paste: Interview with Wangechi Mutu," *Arise Magazine* 11 (2011). Originally a bi-monthly, international style magazine devoted to covering fashion, music, culture, and politics on the continent and in the African diaspora, *Arise Magazine* is no longer a hardcopy publication; it now exists only on social media platforms, namely Facebook, X, and Instagram. Wangechi Mutu's emphasis on invention in her *Arise* interview with Enwezor parallels Hortense Spillers's opening lines in "Mama's Baby, Papa's Maybe: An American Grammar Book." She writes, "Let's face it. I am a marked woman, but not everybody knows my name. . . . I describe a locus of confounded identities, a meeting ground of investments and privations in the national treasury of rhetorical wealth. My country needs me, and if I were not here, I would have to be invented." See Hortense J. Spillers, *Black, White, and in Color: Essays in American Literature and Culture* (Chicago: University of Chicago Press, 2003), 203. "Mama's Baby, Papa's Maybe" was first published in *Diacritics* 17, no. 2 (1987): 64–81. Mutu's distinctions concerning the historical experience of captive bondage and the Middle Passage slave trade from that of the experience colonialism on the African continent also suggests that racial slavery and colonialism are somehow separate phenomena. Recent studies by Achille Mbembe and Frank B.

Wilderson III, however, attest to racial slavery's intimacy with colonialism. For these studies, see Achille Mbembe, *On the Postcolony* (Berkeley: University of California Press, 2001); and "Necropolitics," *Public Culture* 15, no. 1 (Winter 2003): 11–40; and Frank B. Wilderson III, "Grammar & Ghosts: The Performative Limits of African Freedom," *Theater Survey* 50, no. 1 (May 2009): 119–25.

33 This phrasing is a riff on Christina Sharpe's articulation of Saidiya Hartman's claims in *Lose Your Mother* regarding loss, cross-racial kinship, and the impossibility of redress. In response to Dylann Roof's massacre of members of Emanuel African Methodist Episcopal in South Carolina, Sharpe writes, "Saidiya Hartman's concise articulation gets to the heart of the ways that chattel slavery continues to animate the present: transatlantic chattel slavery's constitution of domestic relations made kin in one direction, and in the other, property that could be passed between and among those kin. This is the ghost in the machine of contemporary U.S. life and politics." See Saidiya Hartman, *Lose Your Mother: A Journey along the Atlantic Slave Route* (New York: Farrar, Straus and Giroux, 2006); and Christina Sharpe, "Lose Your Kin," *New Inquiry*, November 16, 2016. Hartman's original claim, "Slavery is the ghost in the machine," first appears as a quote from the author in Judith Butler, "Is Kinship Always Already Heterosexual?," *differences* 13, no. 1 (2002), 14.

34 Derek Conrad Murray, *Queering Post-Black Art: Artists Transforming African-American Identity after Civil Rights* (London: I. B. Tauris, 2015), 3. Emphasis in original.

35 Paul Gilroy, *The Black Atlantic: Modernity and Double Consciousness* (Cambridge, MA: Harvard University Press, 1993), 73, quoted in Best, "On Failing to Make the Past Present," 456–57; Anne Anlin Cheng, *The Melancholy of Race: Psychoanalysis, Assimilation, and Hidden Grief* (Oxford: Oxford University Press, 2001); and Paul Gilroy, *Postcolonial Melancholia* (New York: Columbia University Press, 2005) are also exemplary in this recent resurgence of melancholic historicism, the origins of which Stephen Best traces to 1988. He writes, "I would nominate 1988 as an important turning point. In the advent of that year, significant works had appeared that placed the slave's narrative and habitus at the center of the symbolic order that Hortense J. Spillers would name the 'American grammar book': Henry Louis Gates Jr.'s *Signifying Monkey*, Houston A. Baker Jr.'s *Blues, Ideology, and Afro-American Literature*, Hazel V. Carby's *Reconstructing Womanhood*, Valerie Smith's *Self-Discovery and Authority*, and Spillers's own 'Mama's Baby, Papa's Maybe.' The paragon literary text of this moment was of course Toni Morrison's *Beloved*, which won the Pulitzer Prize in that year—about when the Schomburg Library of Nineteenth-Century Black Women Writers also began to appear. Soon after, Paul Gilroy's *Black Atlantic* (1993) promoted slavery to a unified field theory, which anchored the black experience of modernity in 'a continued proximity to the unspeakable terrors of the slave experience.'" See Stephen Best, "On Failing to Make the Past Present," 456–57.

36 Ashraf H. A. Rushdy, "Families of Orphans: Relation and Disrelation in Octavia Butler's *Kindred*," *College English* 55, no 2 (February 1993): 139.

37 Ron Eyerman, *Cultural Trauma: Slavery and the Formation of African-American Identity* (Cambridge, UK: Cambridge University Press, 2002), 2. On the connection between trauma, representation, and collective identity, Eyerman goes on to say, "As cultural process, trauma is linked to the formation of collective identity and the construction of collective memory. . . . In this sense, slavery was traumatic in retrospect, and formed a 'primal scene' that could, potentially, unite all 'African Americans' in the United States, whether or not they had themselves been slaves or had any knowledge of or feeling for Africa. Slavery formed the root of an emergent [post–Civil War] collective identity through an equally emergent collective memory, one that signified and distinguished a 'race,' a people, or a community" (60). This connection, spurred by a psychoanalytic understanding of traumatic repetition, also makes art responsible for recuperating the trauma of historical experience. Cathy Caruth's theory of trauma and memory is relevant here, too, for it is not the experience itself but the acts of remembering and forgetting that produce enduring traumatic effects. In this formulation, the aim of Black aesthetic production is necessarily to reflect on slavery as shared experience in order to instantiate communal bonds by reconciling a lost, traumatic past in the present.

38 Tavia Nyong'o, *The Amalgamation Waltz: Race, Performance, and the Ruses of Memory* (Minneapolis: University of Minnesota Press, 2009), 175.

39 Here I riff on Tavia Nyong'o's phrasing about the ways in which hybridity has repeatedly been enlisted as an antidote to racial strife in both utopian and dystopian scenarios. He writes, "This persistent projection of hybridity into a temporal and spatial elsewhere is itself a mechanism for resisting an awareness of the actual and ongoing mongrel past, a history which is neither a moral scandal nor a transcendental panacea, but an uneasy terrain of ordinary and difficult antagonism and conviviality." See *The Amalgamation Waltz*, 175.

40 Victoria Miro Gallery, *Wangechi Mutu: Yo.n.I* (2007), www.victoria-miro.com.

41 *Non je ne regrette rien* shares its title with a song made popular by French singer Édith Piaf, and alerts viewers to a politics of resistance, particularly to Algeria's postcolonial history. Piaf dedicated her 1960 recording of "Non, je ne regrette rien" to the French Foreign Legion. Charles Dumont originally composed the song in 1956 with lyrics by Michel Vaucaire, and at the time of Piaf's recording, France was engaged in the Algerian War of Independence (1954–62). The First Foreign Parachute Regiment, which was disbanded after backing a failed putsch by the French military against the civilian leadership of Algeria in 1961, adopted the song when their resistance was broken. Historian Alexander Harrison offers a brief discussion of the significance of Piaf's recording within French Foreign Legion history in *Challenging de Gaulle: The O.A.S. and the Counterrevolution in Algeria, 1954–1962* (New York: Praeger, 1989). Harrison's text outlines French colonization of Algeria and the roots of the counter-revolution, with chapters on the three abortive efforts to grant native Algerians their independence and the subsequent emergence of the Organisation de l'armée secrète (OAS, or Secret Armed Organization). Mutu's appropriation of Piaf's homage suggests a number

of meanings: French colonial history in Africa, the failure of the French Foreign Legion's role in a coup d'état, and the complex networks of alliance and dissent that eventually led to Algeria's independence from France. *Non je ne regrette rien* immediately registers fragmentation and dispersal, features of the so-called postmodern condition that are often mapped onto postcolonial nations and bodies. But to suggest that Mutu's collages signify a composite, postcolonial nationhood obscures the repulsion her work engenders. In my view, rather than making the process of collage and the fragmented (Black female) body repositories for postcolonial nations, Mutu's work defies systems of representation by which the Black female body has become, as David Harradine avers, "a locus for complex processes of ideological construction." These processes "materialise the body itself in and through discourse, and [reveal] the body as only the apparent base from which notions of 'identity' (such as 'race' 'sex' 'gender' 'class' or 'sexuality') can be read." See David Harradine, "Abject Identities and Fluid Performances: Theorizing the Leaking Body," *Contemporary Theatre Review* 10, no. 3 (2000): 69. In *Non je ne regrette rien*, the Black female body is excised as a privileged signifier and as the grammar by which Black female subjectivity is articulated. It is uneasy, undone.

42 Here, I refer to the gendered and sexual associations, including female sexual anatomy, ascribed to the symbolism of flowers in Aegean iconography, allegorical paintings of the Renaissance and late Renaissance era, Freudian interpretations of Georgia O'Keefe's modernist paintings, romantic poetry, and science and botany books from the 1500s to present. For various approaches to this topic, see Michael Juul Holm, Ernst Jonas Bencard, and Poul Erik Tojner, eds., *The Flower as Image*, exhibition catalog (Copenhagen: Louisiana Museum of Modern Art, 2004); Jack Goody, *The Culture of Flowers* (Wiltshire: Cambridge University Press, 1993); and Andrew Moore and Christopher Garibaldi, eds., *Flower Power: The Meaning of Flowers in Art*, exhibition catalog (London: Philip Wilson, 2003). For literal histories of Flora as a mythological goddess of flowers, see Ann B. Shteir, "Iconographies of Flora: The Goddess of Flowers in the Cultural History of Botany," in *Figuring It Out: Science, Gender, and Visual Culture*, ed. Ann B. Shteir and Bernard V. Lightman (Lebanon, NH: Dartmouth College Press, 2006), 3–27; and Joan Steigerwald, "Figuring Nature/Figuring the (Fe)male: The Frontispiece to Humboldt's *Ideas Towards a Geography of Plants*," in *Figuring It Out*, 54–82.

43 While a full consideration of the breadth of Wangechi Mutu's expansive oeuvre is beyond the scope of this chapter, I briefly analyze a selection of the collages she produced between 2001 and 2007 to gesture toward this perceived break. Although there is little to no scholarship or popular writing on this move from whole to more explicitly dismembered bodies in Mutu's collage practice, it is an observation I develop here to suggest a shift in the artist's practice that results in the ruptured figure that recurs throughout her later collages.

44 The stampede and mass rape of seventy-one female students in a Kenyan dormitory in 1991 have been cited as source material for Wangechi Mutu's early collages.

The disfiguring violence that miners incurred from the Sierra Leone "blood diamond" trade and its effects on women in war zones have also been identified as source material. For these references, see "Review: Wangechi Mutu's Politics of Pleasure: A Fantastic Journey at the Nasher Museum of Art at Duke University," *Burnaway* (n.d.), https://burnaway.org.

45 Donna J. Haraway, "A Cyborg Manifesto: Science, Technology, and Socialist-Feminism in the Late Twentieth Century," in *Simians, Cyborgs and Women: The Reinvention of Nature* (New York: Routledge, 1991), 180. Haraway first published "A Cyborg Manifesto" as "Manifesto for Cyborgs: Science, Technology, and Socialist Feminism in the 1980s" in *Socialist Review* 80 (1985): 65–108.

46 Haraway, "A Cyborg Manifesto," 181.

47 Donna J. Haraway, "Ecce Homo, Ain't (Ar'n't) I a Woman, and Inappropriate/d Others: The Human in a Posthumanist Landscape," in *Feminists Theorize the Political*, ed. Joan Scott and Judith Butler (London: Routledge, 1992), 86.

48 Haraway, "Ecce Homo," 91. See Trinh T. Minh-ha, "Introduction" and "Difference: 'A Special Third World Women Issue," *Discourse* 8 (1986/87): 3–10, 11–38.

49 Haraway, "Ecce Homo," 86–88.

50 Haraway, "Ecce Homo," 87. Haraway's objective here is similar to the retention of specificity that Leo Bersani calls for in his book *Homos* (Cambridge, MA: Harvard University Press, 1995).

51 Hip-hop scholar Tricia Rose brings a similar lens to the intersectional impasses of the cyborg in her interview with Mark Dery. See Tricia Rose quoted in Mark Dery, *Flame Wars: The Discourse of Cyberculture* (Durham, NC: Duke University Press, 1994).

52 Haraway, "Ecce Homo," 93–94. See also Hazel V. Carby, "Slave and Mistress: Ideologies of Womanhood under Slavery," in *Reconstructing Black Womanhood: The Emergence of the Afro-American Woman Novelist* (Oxford: Oxford University Press, 1987), 20–39; and Hortense J. Spillers, *Black, White, and in Color: Essays in American Literature and Culture* (Chicago: University of Chicago Press, 2003).

53 To be clear, during the era of slavery in the United States, white women did not legally own property, except in the rare cases that they inherited it from a male relative or spouse. But following Hazel V. Carby's writings on the Black female slave experience, I draw a distinction between Black and white women here to show how Black women's persons and subjecthood existed outside of the category of "woman." Special thanks to the students in my Fall 2013 Afro Future Females course at the University of Rochester, especially Quinlan Mitchell, for the illuminating discussions and responses that helped me finesse my thinking around this lineage of Black female cyborg identities.

54 Judith Butler, *Bodies That Matter: On the Discursive Limits of "Sex"* (London: Routledge, 1993), 31. Emphasis in original.

55 Social Darwinism formed a foundation for scientific examination of racial, gender, and sexual difference and spawned such studies as phrenology, physiognomy, and racial eugenics among others, which informed pictorial representations of

bodies in the United States, particularly in relation to practices of photography at the turn of the twentieth century. These modes of study are interwoven with a photographic history of producing subjects and stereotypes. See Elizabeth Edwards, *Anthropology and Photography 1860–1920* (New Haven: Yale University Press, 1994); and John Tagg, *Burden of Representation: Essays on Photographies and Histories* (Minneapolis: University of Minnesota Press, 1993). For an in-depth comparative study of how Black subjectivity throughout the African diaspora was constructed and subjugated through nineteenth-century American and European intellectual thought as well as contemporary counter-discourses, see Michelle M. Wright, *Becoming Black: Creating Identity in the African Diaspora* (Durham, NC: Duke University of Press, 2004).

56 See Janell Hobson, *Body as Evidence: Mediating Race, Globalizing Gender* (Albany: State University of New York Press, 2012).

57 Literary scholars Madhu Dubey and Sherryl Vint offer detailed discussions of how conventions of the genre of science fiction center on a Cartesian subjecthood rooted in wholeness. See Madhu Dubey, "Becoming Animal in Black Women's Science Fiction," in *Afro-Future Females: Black Writers Chart Science Fiction's Newest New-Wave Trajectory*, ed. Marleen S. Barr (Columbus, OH: Ohio State University Press, 2008), 31–51; and Sherryl Vint, *Bodies of Tomorrow: Technology, Subjectivity, Science Fiction* (Toronto: University of Toronto Press, 2007).

58 Wangechi Mutu quoted in "Wangechi Mutu by Deborah Willis," *BOMB Magazine*, February 28, 2014.

59 Spillers, *Black, White, and in Color*, 203.

60 For a compelling reading of the role of flesh within Black women's cultural production, see Nicole R. Fleetwood's *Troubling Vision: Performance, Visuality, and Blackness* (Chicago: University of Chicago Press, 2011).

61 Spillers, *Black, White, and in Color*, 207, 228. See also Nicole R. Fleetwood, "Excess Flesh: Black Women Performing Hypervisibility," in *Troubling Vision: Performance, Visuality, and Blackness* (Chicago: University of Chicago Press, 2010), 105–46.

62 Amber Jamilla Musser, *Sensual Excess: Queer Femininity and Brown Jouissance* (New York: New York University Press, 2018), 20.

63 Spillers, *Black, White, and in Color*, 215. Emphasis in original.

64 See Alexander Weheliye, "'Feenin': Posthuman Voices in Contemporary Black Popular Music," *Social Text* 20, no. 2 (2002): 21–47.

65 Kodwo Eshun, *More Brilliant Than the Sun: Adventures in Sonic Fiction* (London: Quartet Books, 1998), 005. See also Marlo David, "Afrofuturism and Post-Soul Possibility in Black Popular Music," in "Post-Soul Aesthetic," special issue, *African American Review* 41, no. 4, (Winter 2007): 695–707.

66 Axelle Karera, "Blackness and the Pitfalls of Anthropocene Ethics," *Critical Philosophy of Race* 7, 1 (2019): 48.

67 For an in-depth study of this phenomenon, see Zakiyyah Iman Jackson, *Becoming Human: Matter and Meaning in an Antiblack World* (New York: New York University Press, 2020).

68 Michelle Ann Stephens, *Skin Acts: Race, Psychoanalysis, and the Black Male Performer* (Durham, NC: Duke University Press, 2014), 2–3, quoted in Uri McMillan, "Introduction: Skin, Surface, Sensorium," *Women & Performance* 28, no. 1 (March 12, 2018).

69 Robert Crossley, "Critical Essay," in *Kindred* (Boston: Beacon Press, 1979), 274.

70 Octavia Butler quoted in Randall Kenan, "An Interview with Octavia E. Butler," *Callaloo* 14, 2 (Spring 1991): 498.

71 Grace McEntee, "Kindred," in *African American Women: An Encyclopedia of Literature by and about Women of Color, vol. 2, K–Z*, ed. Elizabeth Ann Beaulieu (Westport, CT: Greenwood, 2006), 524.

72 Pamela Bedore, "Octavia Butler's *Kindred*," in *Masterplots*, rev. 3rd ed., ed. Lawrence W. Mazzeno (Ipswich, MA: Salem Press, 2010), 3048–50. See also Pamela Bedore, "Slavery and Symbiosis in Octavia Butler's *Kindred*," in *Foundation* 84, no. 1 (Spring 2002): 73–81.

73 Ashraf Rushdy writes, "For Dana, the retrieving of the past in an act of what [Ralph] Ellison calls 'historical memory' costs her an arm, amongst other things." Rushdy also contends that "*Kindred* is most fruitfully seen as part of a movement in recent African-American fiction to produce the conditions of historicity by reconstructing the past to endow the present with new meaning." See Ashraf H. A. Rushdy, "Families of Orphans: Relation and Disrelation in Octavia Butler's *Kindred*," *College English* 55, no. 2 (February 1993): 135–38.

74 Rushdy, "Families of Orphans," 143.

75 Ruth Salvaggio, "Octavia Butler," in *Suzy McKee Charnas, Octavia Butler, Joan Vinge*, ed. Marleen S. Barr, Ruth Salvaggio, and Richard Law (Mercer Island, WA: Starmount House, 1986), 33.

76 Farah Jasmine Griffin, "Textual Healing: Claiming Black Women's Bodies, the Erotic and Resistance in Contemporary Novels of Slavery," *Callaloo* 19, no. 2 (Spring 1996): 521.

77 Saidiya Hartman, "Venus in Two Acts," *Small Axe* 12, no. 2 (June 2008): 4.

78 Octavia Butler, *Kindred* (Boston: Beacon Press, 1979/2003), 248.

79 Literary scholar Stephanie Li argues that in *Incidents in the Life of a Slave Girl* (1861), Harriet Jacobs's choice of a sexual relationship with Mr. Sands and her decision to hide in bondage to stay close to her children reconceptualizes agency, consent, freedom, and resistance. Although Jacobs chooses to remain in conditions of bondage, she experiences instances of freedom *within* this bondage. Her formulations of self are also constructed *intra*subjectively through her social networks, relations, and attachments rather than solely through a master-slave relation. See Stephanie Li, *Something Akin to Freedom: The Choice of Bondage in Narratives by African American Women* (Albany: State University of New York Press, 2011).

80 Individualism through mobility and flight as a means of escape to freedom are figured as gendered tropes in *Narrative of the Life of Frederick Douglass* (1845), *Narrative of William W. Brown, a Fugitive Slave* (1847), *Narrative of the Life and*

Adventures of Henry Bibb, an American Slave (1849), *Narrative of the Life of J. D. Green, a Runaway Slave from Kentucky*, and other male-centered slave narratives. Such pursuits of freedom through Emersonian self-reliance, by which male slaves have liberties to flee and visit other plantations that differ from female slaves who stay because of obligations connected to motherhood and other domestic roles or duties, requires a rejection or negation of family. See Ralph Waldo Emerson, "Self-Reliance," in *Essays: First and Second Series* (New York: Vintage, 1990). "Self-Reliance" was originally published in *Essays* (1841).

81 David Scott quoted in Best, "On Failing to Make the Past Present," 456.

82 Alondra Nelson develops the phrase "future text" after the character PaPa LaBas in Ishmael Reed's novel *Mumbo Jumbo*. Nelson writes, "LaBas believes that the next generation will be successful in creating a text that can codify black culture: past, present, and future. Rather than a 'Western' image of the future that is increasingly detached from the past or, equally problematic, a future-primitive perspective that fantasizes an uncomplicated return to ancient culture, LaBas foresees the distillation of African diasporic experience, rooted in the past but not weighed down by it, contiguous yet continually transformed." See Alondra Nelson, "Introduction: Future Texts," *Social Text* 20, no. 2 (Summer 2002): 8.

83 Nelson, "Introduction," 4.

84 Butler, *Kindred*, 264.

85 Walter Benn Michaels, *Our America: Nativism, Modernism, and Pluralism* (Durham, NC: Duke University Press, 1995), 141.

86 David Scott, *Conscripts of Modernity: The Tragedy of Colonial Enlightenment* (Durham, NC: Duke University Press, 2004), 50, quoted in Best, "On Failing to Make the Past Present," 471.

87 Hamza Walker, "Introduction: Domino Effect," in *Black Is, Black Ain't*, exhibition catalog, ed. Hamza Walker and Karen Reimer (Chicago: Renaissance Society at the University of Chicago, 2013), 12.

88 Orlando Patterson, *Slavery and Social Death: A Comparative Study* (Cambridge, MA: Harvard University Press, 1982), 7.

89 James Bliss, "Hope against Hope: Queer Negativity, Black Feminist Theorizing, and Reproduction without Futurity," *Mosaic: A Journal for the Interdisciplinary Study of literature* 48, no. 1 (March 2015): 85.

90 Bliss, "Hope against Hope," 86.

91 For a discussion of the instantiations of the primal scene in the 1979 film *Alien* and its implications in Freudian terms, see Barbara Creed, "Alien and the Monstrous-Feminine," in *Alien Zone: Cultural Theory and Contemporary Science Fiction Cinema*, ed. Annette Kuhn (London: Verso, 1990): 128–41. Creed's account, however, privileges white bodies and neglects the racial undertones of the film: the "other" and alienation, fear of contagion, and Blackness in terms of low-key lighting and the color of the alien creature itself.

92 In *Aliens* (1986), the human and nonhuman birth scene occurs in dream sequence. Ripley, the heroine played by Sigourney Weaver in each film of the *Aliens*

franchise, is detained in a hospital as she begins to convulse and writhe much like John Hurt's character in the preceding film. The alien that Ripley is carrying attempts to force its way out of her stomach. Frighteningly aware of the aggressively predatory creature that might emerge, Ripley would rather be killed than have the unwelcome alien "come to term," a fate she is unable to forego in the latter two films. Whereas the male body failed to fully realize parthenogenesis in *Alien*, by *Alien*[3] (1992), Ripley's female body has become the ultimate incubator for the opposing alien species; at the film's end, Ripley is pregnant with an alien queen, and she sacrifices herself to save humanity. The female body's compatibility with bearing offspring conceived asexually, which in turn inherits the parent's genetic material, is solidified in *Alien Resurrection* (1997), when both Ripley and the alien queen are cloned, sharing each other's DNA. In its regenerated form comprising alien and human parts, Ripley's (white) female body is solely responsible for the proliferation of a new human race.

93 Black and non-Black critics eager to identify who counts as Black in America were concerned with Barack Obama's cosmopolitan hybridity, as Tavia Nyong'o calls it, during his presidential campaign. Black conservatives in particular quibbled over whether Obama's Kenyan roots qualified him as Black enough within an American context since his ancestors presumably had little to no relationship to slavery, the defining attribute of African Americanness. This absence, scholars Stanley Crouch and Debra Dickerson surmise, permits the salving of the white American conscience. Put differently, embracing Obama's hybridity, or his partial Blackness (in both mixed-race and national terms), sidesteps a commitment to an authentic form of racial justice in which democracy is realized through the political and social integration of wholly Black figures. Meanwhile, reporters discovered that Obama does in fact have a connection to slavery—on the slaveholding side—and Obama's camp responded to interracial and intraracial fervor about his presidency with a simple story of redemption. Bill Burton, a spokesperson for Obama at the time, said, "It is a true measure of progress that the descendant of a slave owner would come to marry a student from Kenya and produce a son who would grow up to be a candidate for president of the United States." For more on this discourse, see Tavia Nyong'o, *The Amalgamation Waltz: Race, Performance, and the Ruses of Memory* (Minneapolis: University of Minnesota Press, 2009); Stanley Crouch, "What Obama Isn't: Black Like Me," *New York Daily News*, November 2, 2006; Debra Dickerson, "Colorblind: Barack Obama Would Be the Great Black Hope in the Next Presidential Race—If He Were Actually Black," *Salon*, January 22, 2007; Bill Burton quoted in Rachel L. Swarns, "Obama Had Slaveowning Kin," *New York Times*, March 3, 2007; and Jared Sexton, *Amalgamation Schemes: Antiblackness and the Critique of Multiracialism* (Minneapolis: University of Minnesota Press, 2008).

94 Atrophy has two meanings. One is the process by which body tissue or organs waste away, typically due to the degeneration of cells; the other is the arrested development or loss of a part or organ incidental to the normal development or life of an animal or plant, which I reference here.

95 Kristine Stiles, "Wangechi Mutu's Family Tree," in *Wangechi Mutu: A Fantastic Journey*, exhibition catalog, ed. Trevor Schoonmaker (Durham, NC: Nasher Museum of Art/Duke University Press, 2013), 53.

96 Stiles, "Wangechi Mutu's Family Tree," 54.

97 Courtney J. Martin, "Fracture and Action: Wangechi Mutu's Collages, 1999–2010," in *My Dirty Little Heaven*, exhibition catalog (Deutsche Guggenheim Berlin; Ostfildern: Hatje Cantz, 2010), 48.

98 Martin, "Fracture and Action," 48.

99 Okwui Enwezor, "Weird Beauty," in *My Dirty Little Heaven*, exhibition catalog (Deutsche Guggenheim Berlin; Ostfildern: Hatje Cantz, 2010), 30.

3. AGAINST REVELATION

Epigraphs: Alessandra Raengo, *On the Sleeve of the Visual: Race as Face Value* (Hanover, NH: Dartmouth College Press, 2013), 37; Krista Thompson, "The Sound of Light: Reflections on Art History in the Visual Culture of Hip-Hop," *Art Bulletin* 91, no. 4 (December 2009): 501.

1 In an interview with Katherine Brooks published in May 2016 on the website for the *Huffington Post*, Xaviera Simmons states in reference to *CODED*, her 2016 solo exhibition, "I will never understand why I as a heterosexual woman would not engage in topics that might be queer and homoerotic in their inspiration. Through my practice and especially with 'CODED' I want to enrich the language around the possibilities of looking, and find pleasure in bodies living and working through various poses." In another interview with Mallika Rao of the *Village Voice* published in December 2016, Simmons says in reference to the live performance portion of *CODED*, "I'm in a heterosexual relationship. . . . So that I guess classifies me, and I'm putting that in quotes, as being 'heterosexual.' But at the same time, I'm a New York female. I'm from here. I grew up in a New York that was very diverse. My mom's best friends in the Seventies and Eighties were queer and gay men." See Katherine Brooks, "How Performance Art Questions the Way We Talk about Gender Today," *Huffington Post*, May 18, 2016; and Mallika Rao, "Xaviera Simmons Elevates Queerness," *Village Voice*, December 7, 2016.

2 Xaviera Simmons quoted in Tamara Warren, "Back to the Land," *Life+Times*, August 12, 2011.

3 See Vanessa H. Larson, "A View of Women's Bodies, by 12 Female Photographers, That Is by Turns Playful, Provocative and Profound," *Washington Post*, November 27, 2019; Adam Kleinman, "Do Artists Have 'Soft Power' To Create Political Change?," *Frieze*, November 28, 2019; and Seph Rodney, "Nowhere to Go in a Desert of Images," *Hyperallergic*, July 22, 2016.

4 Xaviera Simmons quoted in Paul Laster, "Beyond the Landscape," *FLATT*, December 2015.

5 Anne Anlin Cheng, *Second Skin: Josephine Baker and the Modern Surface* (Oxford: Oxford University Press, 2010), 13.

6 Uri McMillan, "Introduction: Skin, Surface, Sensorium," *Women & Performance* 28, no. 1 (March 12, 2018), www.womenandperformance.org.

7 The index, in the most general terms employed by semiotician Charles Sanders Peirce, refers to a sign that represents its object independent of any resemblance to it, a concept central to modern theories of photography. For Roland Barthes, whose *Camera Lucida* remains arguably the most influential account of the photographic surface and its effects, photographs, and portraits in particular, act as a sign of past happenings in the present, the "having-been-there" of the object. For Walter Benjamin, whose writing on the value of art in the face of its increasing technological reproducibility holds a similar place as Barthes's within Western art history and media theory, photography diminishes a work of art's essence, its originality. Photography and the technological processes of reproduction that make it possible also mediate the world and our perceptions of it. For both Barthes and Benjamin, the photograph is a document of reality and a window into the past. Furthermore, Barthes's and Benjamin's foundational writings on the medium position photography more broadly and portraiture specifically as sources of redemption within collective self-understanding. Redemption, in Barthes's writing, is a form of historical awareness that stems from an affective encounter with the punctum, the emotional stab of understanding that, while photographs bring the past into the present, what is visible in the photograph is irretrievably lost. Historical awareness underlies redemption in Benjamin's thinking as well, albeit in a more optimistic register. For Benjamin, photography opens up history; sharing reflections of the past with others—the point of writing—contributes to the collective redemption of humanity. See Justus Buchler, ed., *The Philosophical Writings of Peirce* (New York: Dover, 1955); and Charles Hardwick, ed., *Semiotics and Significs* (Bloomington: Indiana University Press, 1977). See also Roland Barthes, "The Rhetoric of the Image," in *Image-Music-Text*, trans. Stephen Heath (London: Fontana Press, 1977), 44. For more on Barthes and Benjamin's redemptive criticism concerning photography, see Tim Dant and Graeme Gilloch, "Pictures of the Past: Benjamin and Barthes on Photography and History," *European Journal of Cultural Studies* 5, no. 1 (February 2002): 5–23; and Kathrin Yacavone, *Benjamin, Barthes and the Singularity of Photography* (New York: Bloomsbury, 2012).

8 Conceptualism in art, and more recently postconceptualism, coincides with the groundswell of interest in Black portraiture that has surfaced during the past thirty years thanks to the work of Gwendolyn DuBois Shaw, Cheryl Finley, Deborah Willis, Kobena Mercer, Richard J. Powell, and the Harvard University Press series, *The Image of the Black in Western Art* (2010–17). Conceptualism focuses attention on the ideas behind art objects, ideas *as* art objects, and questions the traditional view of objects as conveyors of meaning. Artists working in this vein "dematerialize" the art object by producing time-based and ephemeral artworks. Although total dematerialization of the art object is impossible, conceptualism

challenges medium boundaries. Contra theorist Clement Greenberg's elevation of formalism, which linked artistic value to aesthetic experience as germane to modern art discourse, conceptual art foregrounds intellectual content and the thought processes it spurs *over* or *as* form. Consequently, conceptualism and its attendant theories trouble the status of the art object. The conceptual art object is flexible, a malleability that, coupled with the late-twentieth-century turn toward French post-structural thought, semiotics, and digital imaging technologies, resulted in postconceptual inquiries into the inherent value of art objects. See Peter Goldie and Elisabeth Schellekens, eds., *Philosophy and Conceptual Art* (Oxford: Oxford University Press, 2007) for a diverse collection of essays on these distinctions. For a thorough history of conceptualism in art, see Robert C. Morgan, *Art into Ideas: Essays on Conceptual Art* (Cambridge, UK: Cambridge University Press, 1996). In *Art after Conceptual Art*, Benjamin Buchloh points out that postconceptual art is already emerging in the late 1970s and early 1980s in the photo-based appropriation art of Martha Rosler, Louise Lawler, Cindy Sherman, Peter Nagy, Barbara Kruger, Sherrie Levine, Dara Birnbaum, and other artists of the Pictures generation. For Buchloh's thesis, see Benjamin H. D. Buchloh, "Conceptual Art 1962–1969: From the Aesthetic of Administration to the Critique of Institutions," *October* 55 (Winter 1990): 105–43; and Alberro and Buchmann, *Art after Conceptual Art*. Postconceptualism builds on conceptualism and further deflates autonomous notions of artistic form and authorship, prompting a controversial yet common view of contemporary art as against, or beyond, aesthetics. For more about post-conceptual art as a set of deflationary practices, see John Robert, *Revolutionary Time and the Avant-Garde* (London: Verso, 2015).

9 Douglas Crimp, "The Photographic Activity of Postmodernism," *October* 15 (Winter 1980): 94.

10 Elizabeth Edwards, "Objects of Affect: Photography Beyond the Image," *Annual Review of Anthropology* 41, no. 1 (September 2012), 230.

11 Simone Browne, *Dark Matters: On the Surveillance of Blackness* (Durham, NC: Duke University Press, 2015), 8.

12 Stuart Hall, "New Ethnicities," in *Stuart Hall: Critical Dialogues in Cultural Studies* (New York: Routledge, 1996), 442. See also Darby English's exposition of Black representational space in *How to See a Work of Art in Total Darkness* (Cambridge, MA: MIT Press, 2008); and Jennifer A. González's explication of the history and persistence of race as a form of visual hegemony in *Subject to Display: Reframing Race in Contemporary Installation Art* (Cambridge, MA: MIT Press, 2008).

13 Hall, "New Ethnicities," 442.

14 During the Renaissance, conduct books and religious iconography heavily influenced the norms of self-fashioning. In Stephen Greenblatt's summation, Renaissance-era subjects, typically male members of the noble class, met these norms by dressing in their finest clothing and participating in art, literature, and other exercises designated as virtuous. Commissioning self-portraits where these subjects appear carefully composed were also part of this cultural formation. As a

result, the relationship between self-fashioning and portraiture painting became a reciprocal one. The practice of constructing one's identity and concern for one's projected image was reflected in the portraiture of the time, making portraiture correspondent with self-representation. "Self-portraiture is a rhetoric of the self," Andrew Small explains in his comparative analysis of self-portraiture in early modern literature and visual art. "A self-portrait," he claims, "is self-descriptive because its discourse is auto-referential: the persona and events of the text reflect back to the self-portraitist, giving us a window into his or her life and personality." See Andrew Small, *Essays in Self-Portraiture: A Comparison of Technique in the Self-Portraits of Montaigne and Rembrandt* (New York: Peter Lang, 1996), 9.

15 Joanna Woodall, "Introduction: Facing the Subject," in *Portraiture: Facing the Subject*, ed. Joanna Woodall (Oxford: Manchester University Press, 1997), 7.

16 Woodall, 6.

17 Woodall, 13.

18 Gwendolyn DuBois Shaw lists Joshua Johnston's painting *Portrait of a Man* (ca. 1805–10) and the circa 1802 silhouette inscribed "Mr. Shaw's blackman," cut by the manumitted slave Moses Williams, as examples of Black sitters visualizing a self-possessed identity. For a consideration of portraiture and African American identity in the early republic and its significance for contemporary Black artists working at the intersection of portraiture and the archival turn, see Gwendolyn DuBois Shaw, *Portraits of a People: Picturing African Americans in the Nineteenth Century* (Seattle: University of Washington Press, 2006); and Jasmine Nicole Cobb, *Picture Freedom: Remaking Black Visuality in the Early Nineteenth Century* (New York: New York University Press, 2015).

19 See Jessica L. Horton and Cherise Smith, "The Particulars of Postidentity," *American Art* 28, no. 1 (Spring 2014): 2–8, for a concise overview of these claims and their articulations within the global context of contemporary art. Regarding post-Blackness, Xaviera Simmons's work was included in *Frequency* (2005), the second of The Studio Museum in Harlem's so-called "F" shows that extended Thelma Golden's 2001 post-Black provocation.

20 After graduating from Bard College with her bachelor of fine arts degree in 2004, Xaviera Simmons simultaneously trained as an actor at the Maggie Flanigan Studio and completed the Whitney Museum's Independent Study Program in Studio Art.

21 Xaviera Simmons quoted in Laster, "Beyond the Landscape."

22 Xaviera Simmons quoted in "Hot Shots: A Selection from Photography's New Guard," *Modern Painters*, November 2010, 54.

23 Describing her 2018 billboard for For Freedoms' 50 State Initiative, an artist-led public art project intended to get out the vote, Xaviera Simmons says, "The freedom of the female body—and the black body—is definitely not guaranteed." See Xaviera Simmons quoted in Yasmin Belkhyr, "Can Public Art Inspire Productive Political Conversations?," *TED*, July 4, 2019. Simmons's For Freedoms billboard features a signature landscape photograph of Simmons dressed in an all-black

ensemble, standing in a field and pointing beyond the frame of the image. Her black silhouette cuts a figure in the landscape.

24 In the online promotional text for her 2021–23 traveling exhibition that originated at the Institute of Contemporary Art in Boston, Deana Lawson states, "I photograph family, friends, and strangers, and I operate on the belief that my own being is found in union with those I take pictures of." See Deana Lawson quoted in Institute of Contemporary Art Boston, www.icaboston.org.

25 Gwendolyn DuBois Shaw, "The Many Problems with Deana Lawson's Photographs," *Hyperallergic*, September 23, 2021.

26 Shaw, "The Many Problems with Deana Lawson's Photographs."

27 Shaw, "The Many Problems with Deana Lawson's Photographs."

28 Gwendolyn DuBois Shaw appeals, "These women, who could be my sisters, had been directed to line up with their genitals brushing against a dirty rug in what appeared to be a dank basement room, arranged before the photographer and her assistants, the hot lights bearing down on them as the eye of the large format camera captured their vulnerability." See Shaw, "The Many Problems with Deana Lawson's Photographs."

29 Shaw, "The Many Problems with Deana Lawson's Photographs."

30 Steven Nelson, "Issues of Intimacy, Distance, and Disavowal in Writing about Deana Lawson's Work," *Hyperallergic*, June 4, 2018, quoted in Shaw, "The Many Problems with Deana Lawson's Photographs."

31 Nelson, "Issues of Intimacy, Distance, and Disavowal."

32 Jill Dawsey, *salt 4: Xaviera Simmons*, exhibition catalog (Salt Lake City: Utah Museum of Fine Arts, 2011), 2, http://centralpt.com/upload/417/18782_salt4_XavieraSimmons_essay.pdf.

33 As curator Jill Dawsey outlines, Xaviera Simmons's role as photographer in *Canyon* alludes not just to representations of landscapes of the past; it also recalls their makers. The artist also signifies on the ways photographers construct and collect their own images by playing a character Dawsey fittingly terms "the photographer," a figure that recurs in Simmons's oeuvre. See Dawsey's art historical analysis of Xaviera Simmons's citations of Watkins and Adams, which I replicate here. Dawsey, *salt 4*, 1–8.

34 Xaviera Simmons quoted in Hannah Southern, "Artist Spotlight," *National Museum of Women in the Arts*, January 8, 2020, https://nmwa.org.

35 For this history, see Joel Snyder, "Territorial Photography," in *Landscape and Power*, 2nd ed., ed. W. J. T. Mitchell (Chicago: University of Chicago Press, 2002), 194–95.

36 W. J. T. Mitchell, "Introduction," in *Landscape and Power*, 2nd ed., ed. W. J. T. Mitchell (Chicago: University of Chicago Press, 2002), 2.

37 Mitchell, "Introduction."

38 Mitchell, "Introduction," 1. In the history of art, pictures of figures—portraits—have also been considered sources of becoming. They are seen to render likeness and individuality, the affirmation of which are rooted in the expressivity of the

figure's face. Portraiture in this formulation functions as a narrative account, an index, of the figure's personality as well as the artist's acumen in conveying the figure's distinctive character, a formulation in tension with the Deleuzian becoming Simmons's activates in her practice.

39 Xaviera Simmons quoted in "Hot Shots: A Selection from Photography's New Guard," *Modern Painters*, November 2010, 54.

40 Simmons quoted in "Hot Shots," 54. Although her assistant clicks the shutter, Simmons insists she is the author of her images. She says, "I work with a 4 by 5 camera and therefore I make the images myself. I have an assistant . . . but I tell them exactly when I am ready when I am in the works." Xaviera Simmons, e-mail message to author, February 23, 2012.

41 Xaviera Simmons's insistence on not identifying her portraits as self-portraits contrasts the work of other feminist, postconceptual photographers such as Cindy Sherman, who depicts herself in many different contexts and as various imagined characters. Sherman's *Untitled Film Stills* series of seventy black-and-white photographs of herself performing feminine archetypes that proliferated in art house films and popular B-movies of the early-to-mid twentieth century is often considered to be the artist's career-defining work. Her work has since evolved to focus more on costuming, lighting, and facial expression.

42 Xaviera Simmons quoted in Laster, "Beyond the Landscape."

43 Historical reenactments play a special role in American culture. Folklorist and former director of the Middle Atlantic Folklife Association Rory Turner explains the significance of historical reenactments to American self-understanding, a focus of Xaviera Simmons's engagement with genres of landscape that I analyze in this chapter. Writing on reenactments of the Civil War, Turner states, "Reenacting presents the past, presents history as a usable symbolic resource. This resource is put to service not only in the representation and acting-out of cultural identity with varying agendas, but also in predications of personal identity that capitalize on the complex and emotionally resonant semantic field that the Civil War, as it was and as it has been culturally redefined, evokes." See Rory Turner, "The Play of History: Civil War Reenactments and Their Use of the Past," *Folklore Forum* 22, nos. 1–2 (1989): 54. See also James W. Fernandez, *Persuasions and Performances* (Bloomington: Indiana University Press, 1986); Richard Handler, "Dyssimulation: Reflexivity, Narrative, and the Quest for Authenticity in 'Living History,'" *Cultural Anthropology* 3 (1988): 242–60; and P. G. Davis, *Laying Claim: African American Cultural Memory and Southern Identity* (Tuscaloosa: University of Alabama Press, 2016).

44 Shana Beth Mason, "Xaviera Simmons, Open," *Miami Rail*, March 6, 2014.

45 Gilles Deleuze and Felix Guattari, *A Thousand Plateaus: Capitalism and Schizophrenia*, trans. Brian Massumi (Minneapolis: University of Minnesota Press, 1987), 292.

46 Deleuze and Guattari, *A Thousand Plateau*, 238.

47 Deleuze and Guattari, *A Thousand Plateaus*, 294. Emphasis in original.

48 For further reading on this history and the intersections between race, photography, the index, and Americanness, see Nicholas Mirzoeff, "The Shadow and the Substance: Race, Photography, and the Index," in *Only Skin Deep: Changing Visions of the American Self*, ed. Coco Fusco and Brian Wallis (New York: Abrams, 2003), 111–27.

49 Kobena Mercer, "Neo-Romantic, Afro-Atlantic: Rotimi Fani-Kayode's Aesthetic Singularity," in *Events of the Self: Portraiture and Social Identity*, exhibition catalog, ed. Okwui Enwezor (Göttingen: Steidl, 2010), 222.

50 *African Grape* (2004) demonstrates Xaviera Simmons's early interests in blackface performance and racial alterity. The photograph is tightly framed, and the scene is densely populated with household items. The work's name references the disparaging term for watermelon and the predilection that people of African descent are supposed to have for it, but Simmons's appropriation of racial stereotypes exceeds the photograph's titular citation. It is internal to the visual world of the image. Among a kitchen full of Americana kitsch, from the refrigerator magnets to the black-and-white checkered tile floor, the artist eats a slice of watermelon upside down in a midcentury, floral-patterned dining chair. She imitates with these gestures other, less pleasant forms of Americana kitsch placed near her throughout the kitchen scene such as a set of "mammy" and "Uncle Tom" salt-and-pepper shakers and posters featuring pickaninnies holding partially eaten slices of watermelon.

51 For a detailed history of this lineage, see Richard J. Powell, *Going There: Black Visual Satire* (New Haven, CT: Yale University Press, 2020). See also Tiffany E. Barber, "Dark Humor and the African American Image," in *Dark Humor: Joyce J. Scott and Peter Williams*, exhibition catalog (Towson, MD: Center for the Arts Gallery, Towson University, 2017), 8–16.

52 See Anne Anlin Cheng, *Second Skin: Josephine Baker and the Modern Surface* (Oxford: Oxford University Press, 2010) for this genealogy.

53 British painter Thomas Stothard (1755–1834) made an engraving that served as the frontispiece for the 1801 edition of *The History, Civil and Commercial, of the British Colonies in the West Indies*. British politician Bryan Edwards, a staunch supporter of the slave trade who published a number of books describing the economy and history of the West Indies, wrote the edition. In it, Edwards included Isaac Teale's poem "The Sable Venus: An Ode," which compares the Sable Venus to Botticelli's *Venus*. The image in the frontispiece has since become an iconic allegorical rendering of the transatlantic slave trade of the time. It has also been criticized for its romantic portrayal of Black women's experiences of sexual violence and its repression of the enormity of the slave trade. The engraving pictures an African woman who, like many images of Venus Anadyomene, stands on an opened half-shell. White cherubs surround Stothard's Black Venus who, urged by Triton, moves across the Middle Passage.

54 On the occasion of *Live Dangerously*, a 2019 exhibition organized by the National Museum of Women in the Arts in Washington, DC, Xaviera Simmons explains

one of the meanings behind *One Day and Back Then (Standing)*. She says, "Our collective narrative doesn't really account for the white people, their children, and so on across the country who oppressed negros for centuries, like till right now." See Xaviera Simmons quoted in Hannah Southern, "Artist Spotlight," *National Museum of Women in the Arts* (January 8, 2020), https://nmwa.org.

55 Édouard Glissant, *Poetics of Relation*, trans. Betsy Wing (Ann Arbor: University of Michigan Press, 1997), 111.

56 Frantz Fanon, *Black Skin, White Masks*, trans. Richard Philcox (New York: Grove, 1991), 116.

57 Homi K. Bhabha, *The Location of Culture* (London: Routledge, 1994), 78.

58 Mary Ann Doane, *Femmes Fatales: Feminism, Film Theory, Psychoanalysis* (London: Routledge, 1991), 223.

59 Fanon, *Black Skin, White Masks*, 116.

60 Charles Johnson, "A Phenomenology of the Black Body," *Michigan Quarterly Review* 32, no. 4 (1993), 606.

61 Fanon, *Black Skin, White Masks*, 89.

62 At the heart of what visual studies scholar Alessandra Raengo calls "the photochemical imagination" is an investment "in the indexicality of the photographic image facilitated by its analogy with the black body." This is so, she explains, because the photographic trace and Black skin as a racial signifier share similar processes of exteriorization; they are both conceived as continuous, transitive surfaces from which legible information can be discerned. Not only do photography and racial difference share a similar semiotic grid, Raegno tells us; they fortify each other: "Photography has lent materiality to race because it has provided a visual technology that has further sutured race to the body." See Alessandra Raengo, *On the Sleeve of the Visual: Race as Face Value* (Hanover, NH: Dartmouth College Press, 2013), 27. Following Raengo, my analysis of Simmons builds on a number of scholars who interrogate how photographic indexicality relates to race as equally indexical, turning the epidermis into a writing pad. See essays by Coco Fusco, Nicholas Mirzoeff, and Jennifer A. González in *Only Skin Deep: Changing Visions of the American Self*, exhibition catalog, ed. Coco Fusco and Brian Wallis (New York: International Center of Photography, 2003). See also Beth Coleman, "Race as Technology," *Camera Obscura* 24, no. 1 (2009), 177–207.

63 Vivian Sobchack, *Carnal Thoughts: Embodiment and Moving Image Culture* (Berkeley: University of California Press, 2004), 142.

64 Sobchack, *Carnal Thoughts*, 142.

65 Raengo, *On the Sleeve of the Visual*, 43.

66 Here I am inspired by Alessandra Raengo's citation of Gayle Salamon and the association between Frantz Fanon's theorizations and those of Maurice Merleau-Ponty: "The body Fanon describes is all surface." See Gayle Salamon, "'The Place Where Life Hides Away': Merleau-Ponty, Fanon, and the Location of Bodily Being," *differences* 17, no. 2 (2006), 101. See also Raengo, *On the Sleeve of the Visual*, 43.

67 Christopher Pinney, "Notes from the Surface of the Image: Photography, Postcolonialism, and Vernacular Modernism," in *Photography's Other Histories*, ed. Christopher Pinney and Nicolas Peterson (Durham, NC: Duke University Press, 2003), 218.

68 This mode of knowledge production stems from the pernicious historical linkage between early photography and European travel that came to define European modernity and reaffirmed European superiority.

69 Krista Thompson, *Shine: The Visual Economy of Light in African Diasporic Aesthetic Practice* (Durham, NC: Duke University Press, 2015), 38.

70 Kadji Amin, Amber Jamilla Musser, and Roy Pérez, "Queer Form: Aesthetics, Race, and the Violences of the Social," *ASAP/Journal* 2, no 2 (May 2017): 227.

71 For a more detailed expansion of this summary, see Gayatri Gopinath, "Seeing and Hearing the Thinking Voice," *Current Musicology* 102 (Spring 2018): 243–45.

72 Paul Gilroy, *Against Race: Imagining Political Culture beyond the Color Line* (Cambridge, MA: Harvard University Press, 2002), 47.

73 See Lisa Nakamura, *Cybertypes: Race, Ethnicity, and Identity on the Internet* (London: Routledge, 2013); Lisa Nakamura and Peter Chow-White, eds., *Race after the Internet* (London: Routledge, 2013); and Ruha Benjamin, *Race after Technology: Abolitionist Tools for the New Jim Code* (Cambridge, UK: Polity Press, 2019).

74 Wesley E. Stevens, "Blackfishing on Instagram: Influencing and the Commodification of Black Urban Aesthetics," *Social Media + Society* 7, no. 3 (July-September 2021): 2.

75 Stevens, "Blackfishing on Instagram, 2.

76 For a discussion of the performance of race and Fortnite from an art historical perspective, see Cherise Smith, "About the Black Skin We Live In," *Hyperallergic*, June 21, 2020.

77 Stevens, "Blackfishing on Instagram, 2.

78 Harry Berger Jr., "Fictions of the Pose: Facing the Gaze of Early Modern Portraiture," *Representations* 46 (Spring 1994): 103, 88.

79 Sianne Ngai, *Ugly Feelings* (Cambridge, MA: Harvard University Press, 2005), 93.

80 Ngai, *Ugly Feelings*, 95.

81 Raengo, *On the Sleeve of the Visual*, 32.

82 Raengo, 32.

83 Raengo, 32. See also Douglas Crimp, "The Photographic Activity of Postmodernism," *October* 15 (Winter 1980): 91–101, for another eloquent explication of the relation between the index, the aura, and photographic technologies of reproduction within postmodern discourse and performance. According to Crimp, presence is predicated on absence and an exemplary group of artists—Jack Goldstein, Robert Longo, Sherry Levine, and Cindy Sherman among them—who approach the question of representation through this relation.

84 As Europe's Black presence increased, Black characters became more prevalent in Renaissance portraiture and drama. How to render them in both image and text stimulated artistic experimentation at the time. According to Shakespearean actor

Richard Blunt, "The words used to describe blackened characters and the makeup used to create them changed[d] alongside the types of blackened characters being written and performed." See Richard Blunt, "The Evolution of Blackface Cosmetics on the Early Modern Stage," in *The Materiality of Color: The Production, Circulation, and Application of Dyes and Pigments, 1400–1800*, ed. Andrea Feeser, Maureen Daly Goggin, and Beth Fowkes Tobin (Burlington, VT: Ashgate Publishing, 2012), 223. In 2012, Blunt recreated two brown-face makeup recipes extant from the Renaissance and recorded his observations in the aforementioned essay titled "The Evolution of Blackface Cosmetics on the Early Modern Stage," a valuable resource for tracing the origins of blackface performance later practiced during the antebellum and postbellum periods. "Generally speaking," he writes, "Renaissance plays contain more highly developed characters than the emblematic ones seen in medieval plays; and more detailed and specific characters require a higher level of verisimilitude when wearing makeup. Correspondingly," he continues, "the recipes extant from the Renaissance are more sophisticated than the basic substances used to blacken faces in the medieval period" (223). Whereas masks, scarves, costuming, soot, and burned cork had been the norm for representing blackened characters in "true black color" before the 1600s, brown paint of various shades, most notably walnut, were used for more natural or realistic portrayals of African-derived characters by the seventeenth century. This material shift also precipitated a shift in cultural meaning; black-painted skin, whether on stage or in portraiture, now signified both moral *and* racial otherness. Blackened characters in morality plays, masques, and pageants during the Middle Ages were proxies for evil, folly, disease, and damnation. With the introduction of the blackamoor and the tawnymoor in Renaissance visual culture, however, black paint also became a sign for the exotic, dangerous, and morally questionable African-derived other. For these reasons, blackface as an act of bodily modification and racial masquerade carried a cultural stigma, one that sparked worry about racial and moral purity in the European imagination. Shakespeare scholar Katharine Maus notes, "The sense of discrepancy between 'inward disposition' and 'outward appearance' was unusually urgent and consequential," for the English public in particular. See Katharine Maus, *Inwardness and Theater in the English Renaissance* (Chicago: University of Chicago Press, 1995), 13. Anxieties about the skin as a fixed, yet permeable, membrane between a person's inherent qualities of mind and character (their essence) and their appearance were directly related to the effects of paint (color) as a device for depicting and ultimately containing racial sameness and otherness. Stage paint at this time was used to cosmetically transform actors' corporeal surfaces to account for a character's subject position and their ethical orientation. Paint *as* color was regarded as the embodiment of expressivity. By the end of the nineteenth century, the invention of photography decades earlier had revolutionized Western figurative painting in the areas of color, lighting, and subject matter just as ethnographic, racialized portraiture and the introduction of blackface minstrelsy transformed public life.

85 See Coco Fusco, "The Other History of Intercultural Performance," *TDR: The Drama Review* 38, no. 1 (Spring 1994): 143–67; Eric Lott, "White Like Me: Racial Cross-Dressing and the Construction of American Whiteness," in *Cultures of U.S. Imperialism*, ed. Amy Kaplan and Donald Pease (Durham, NC: Duke University Press, 1993); and Eric Lott, *Love and Theft: Blackface Minstrelsy and the American Working Class* (New York: Oxford University Press, 1993). See also Michael Rogin, *Blackface, White Noise: Jewish Immigrants in the Hollywood Melting Pot* (Berkeley: University of California Press, 1996); Stephen Johnson, *Burnt Cork: Traditions and Legacies of Blackface Minstrelsy* (Amherst: University of Massachusetts Press, 2012); and Catherine M. Cole and Tracy C. Davis, eds., *TDR: The Drama Review*'s 2013 special issue, "Routes of Blackface."

86 Amma Y. Ghartey-Tagoe Kootin, "Lessons in Blackbody Minstrelsy: Old Plantation and the Manufacture of Black Authenticity," *TDR: The Drama Review* 57, no. 2, (Summer 2013): 104.

87 See Bill Brown, "Reification, Reanimation, and the American Uncanny," *Critical Inquiry* 32 (2006): 175–207.

88 For an expanded discussion of this troubling occurrence, see Raengo's chapter "The Money of the Real" in *On the Sleeve of the Visual*, 87–128.

89 Raengo, *On the Sleeve of the Visual*, 99. Here, Raengo draws on Bill Brown's writing on the historical ontology of slavery to expand the idea of blackface as a kind of counterfeit first put forth by literary scholar Eric Lott. See Raengo, *On the Sleeve of the Visual*, 98–103. See also Brown, "Reification, Reanimation, and the American Uncanny"; Eric Lott, "Love and Theft: The Racial Unconscious of Blackface Minstrelsy," *Representations* 39 (1992): 23–50; Lott, *Love and Theft: Blackface Minstrelsy and the American Working Class*; and recent theorizations of Blackness as an analytic for new materialisms, namely Fred Moten, "The Case of Blackness," *Criticism* 50, no. 2 (Spring 2008): 177–218; and Huey Copeland, "Tending-toward-Blackness," *October* 156 (Spring 2016): 141–44.

90 Uri McMillan, "Introduction: Skin, Surface, Sensorium," *Women & Performance* 28, no. 1 (March 12, 2018), www.womenandperformance.org.

91 Raengo, *On the Sleeve of the Visual*, 101.

92 Raengo, *On the Sleeve of the Visual*, 102.

93 Michelle Ann Stephens, *Skin Acts: Race, Psychoanalysis, and the Black Male Performer* (Durham, NC: Duke University Press), 39.

94 Raengo, *On the Sleeve of the Visual*, 102.

95 Tina Post, "Williams, Walker, and Shine: Blackbody Blackface, or the Importance of Being Surface," *TDR: The Drama Review* 59, no. 4 (Winter 2015): 94.

96 See Angela Y. Davis, "Afro Images: Politics, Fashion, Nostalgia," *Critical Inquiry* 21, no. 1 (Autumn 1994): 37–45; and Leigh Raiford, *Imprisoned in a Luminous Glare: Photography and the African American Freedom Struggle* (Chapel Hill, NC: University of North Carolina Press, 2011).

97 Joanna Woodall, "Introduction: Facing the subject," in *Portraiture: Facing the Subject*, ed. Joanna Woodall (Oxford: Manchester University Press, 1997), 8, 3.

98 Woodall, "Introduction," 3.
99 Darby English, *1971: A Year in the Life of Color* (Chicago: University of Chicago Press, 2016), 11.
100 This phrasing follows Darby English's pronouncements concerning the impositions of representation within Black art. For English, the elevation of representation as the basis of Black cultural politics in the 1960s and 70s constrained Black modernists' self-understanding and accounts for the lack of attention to Black modernists in African American art history and the art historical canon more broadly, especially those working in abstraction and color painting. He writes, "Representation has been so imposing that nothing can displace it, least of all one person making sculptures or paintings. The priority given to representation and never substantially questioned practically demotes any experience that finds expression in nonrepresentational form. According to the prevailing logic, the black modernist perverts black nature. She effectively enlists *herself* in the well-circulated ledger of object lessons about how to get one's blackness wrong" (emphasis his). See English, *1971*, 25.
101 Roland Barthes, *Camera Lucida: Reflections on Photography*, trans. Richard Howard (New York: Hill and Wang, 1981), 81.
102 For explications of this relation, see Fred Moten, *In the Break: The Aesthetics of the Black Radical Tradition* (Minneapolis: University of Minnesota Press, 2003); and Raengo, *On the Sleeve of the Visual*. See also Carol Mavor, "Black and Blue: The Shadows of *Camera Lucida*"; Margaret Olin, "Touching Photographs: Roland Barthes's 'Mistaken' Identification"; and Shawn Michelle Smith, "Race and Reproduction in *Camera Lucida*," all in *Photography Degree Zero: Reflections on Camera Lucida*, ed. Geoffrey Batchen (Cambridge, MA: MIT Press, 2009).
103 For literature on the status of the index during and after the digital turn, see Frank Kessler, "What You Get Is What You See: Digital Images and the Claim on the Real," in *Digital Material: Tracing New Media in Everyday Life and Technology*, ed. Marianne van den Boomen et al. (Amsterdam: Amsterdam University Press, 2009); Antony Bryant and Griselda Pollock, *Digital and Other Virtualities: Renegotiating the Image* (London: I. B. Tauris, 2010); Raymond Bellour, "Concerning 'the Photographic,'" in *Still Moving between Cinema and Photography*, ed. Karen Beckman and Jean Ma (Durham, NC: Duke University Press, 2008); and Greg Hainge, "Unfixing the Photographic Image: Photography, Indexicality, Fidelity and Normativity," *Continuum* 22, no. 5 (2011): 715–30.
104 Here I draw on Alessandra Raengo's discussion of Roland Barthes's *Camera Lucida* and Mary Ann Doane's writing on "the photographic" and indexicality. See Raengo, *On the Sleeve of the Visual*, 37.
105 Raengo, *On the Sleeve of the Visual*, 38.
106 Xaviera Simmons, "Xaviera Simmons," Artist statement (Woodstock: Center for Photography at Woodstock, 2006), www.cpw.org.
107 For a related notion, see Alessandra Raengo's formulation of Blackness as a reality a(e)ffect. She writes, "Said otherwise, as the paradigmatic visual sign, as the sign

that wears its value on its surface and its ontological status on its sleeve, the black body is both product and trigger of an *effect* and *affect* of reality, a reality a(e) ffect" (emphasis hers). See Raengo, *On the Sleeve of the Visual*, 11, as well as notes 32 and 171.

108 Alessandra Raengo, building on Bill Brown, makes a similar claim in her compelling analysis of *Bamboozled*. The racist collectibles featured in the film, she writes, have to "blacken up" to gain a face, "a recognizable site of personhood." Raengo, *On the Sleeve of the Visual*, 109. My formulation here differs in that I argue that Xaviera Simmons's performance of Blackness in these images works to displace rather than recover personhood, or even the visual markers used to affirm race, for that matter.

109 Kevin Quashie, "A Flash of Life and Light," *Journal of African American History* (Winter 2021): 122. See also Kevin Quashie, *Black Aliveness, or a Poetics of Being* (Durham, NC: Duke University Press, 2021).

110 Cheryl Finley and Deborah Willis, "From the Editors: Black Portraiture[s]," *Nka* 38–39 (November 2016): 7.

111 Both Deborah Willis and Cheryl Finley have been active in bringing Black photographers to light within the Western art canon with their scholarship and as organizers of the biannual Black Portraiture[s] conference. See Deborah Willis, *Picturing Us: African American Identity in Photography* (New York: The New Press, 1994); and Deborah Willis, *Reflections in Black: A History of Black Photographers—1840 to the Present* (New York: W. W. Norton, 2000). See also Deborah Willis, Cheryl Finley, et. al., *Harlem: A Century in Images* (New York: Skira Rizzoli, 2010); and Cheryl Finley et. al., *Teenie Harris, Photographer: Image, Memory, History* (Pittsburgh: University of Pittsburgh Press, 2011). For more information on the Black Portraiture[s] conferences, see www.blackportraitures.info.

112 Finley and Willis, "From the Editors," 7.

113 Ingrid Askew, "Ingrid Askew on the Purpose of the Interfaith Pilgrimage of the Middle Passage," n.d., www-tc.pbs.org/thisfarbyfaith/transcript/ingrid_askew.pdf. This document is part of the archive of transcripts and supplemental materials that accompany *This Far by Faith: African-American Spiritual Journeys*, a television program coproduced by Blackside (*Eyes on the Prize*) and The Faith Project, in association with the Independent Television Service. It was presented in the United States on PBS (Public Broadcasting Service) and included six episodes. The final episode, "Rise Up and Call Their Names," was an exposé on the interfaith pilgrimage of the Middle Passage. Leslie D. Farrell produced it. For more information, see www.pbs.org/thisfarbyfaith/about/episode_6.html; and www-tc.pbs.org/thisfarbyfaith/transcript/episode_6.pdf.

114 Patsy Askew, *The Passion to Persist: A Woman's Story* (Raleigh, NC: Lulu, 2010), 94.

115 Xaviera Simmons quoted in Paul Laster, "Beyond the Landscape," *FLATT*, December 2015.

116 Simmons quoted in Laster, "Beyond the Landscape."

117 Simmons quoted in Laster, "Beyond the Landscape." Emphasis mine.

118 Peter Sutherland, "Walking Middle Passage History in Reverse: Interfaith Pilgrimage, Virtual Communitas and World-Recathexis," *Etnofoor* 20, no. 1 (2007): 49.

119 Many participants continued on the journey after the group split in New Orleans, though racial tension was present for the rest of the journey. Two other events that occurred during the course of the pilgrimage are worth noting in this regard. First, there were two pilgrimage groups originally, one that started in the United States, on that started in Europe. Both groups were scheduled to meet in Africa. However, the group walking in Europe did not believe the US group would make it, so they ended their journey in Europe. Second, the pilgrimage was supposed to culminate in a meeting with Archbishop Desmond Tutu, a leader in South Africa's post-apartheid Truth and Reconciliation Commission. However, Peter Sutherland reports that Tutu was unavailable to meet; he sent a congratulatory letter in his stead. Notably, Xaviera Simmons's account of the tour's culminating moment differs from the available records. In her 2015 interview for *FLATT* with Paul Laster, she recalls meeting Tutu. However, in the PBS transcript that accompanies the television special *This Far by Faith: African-American Spiritual Journeys*, the pilgrimage ends with a small group ceremony in a slave house located on Goree Island. For a first-hand account of the split from one of the pilgrimage participants, see Daniel A. Brown, "Walking the Talk: The Interfaith Pilgrimage of the Middle Passage," Authors' Den, 1998, www.authorsden.com/categories/story_top.asp?id=46016&catid=76. This account was first published in a December 1, 1998, issue of *Hampshire Life* magazine. See also reproductions of this account in Sutherland, "Walking Middle Passage History in Reverse," 51. For an account of the two pilgrimage groups, see Peter Sutherland, "Walking Middle Passage History in Reverse," 33–35. See also John W. Fountain, "Taking a Long Walk on the Slave Road," *Washington Post*, July 14, 1998. The PBS archive for the television special on the pilgrimage can be found at www.pbs.org/thisfarbyfaith/about/the_series.html.

120 For more on the covert, unassimilable possibilities of Black radical insurgency see Stefano Harney and Fred Moten, *Undercommons: Fugitive Planning and Black Study* (New York: Minor Compositions, 2013).

121 Diarmuid Costello and Margaret Iversen, "Introduction: Photography after Conceptual Art," *Art History* 32, no. 5 (December 2009): 825.

4. MASKS, MAYHEM, AND KINK

Epigraph: Ariane Cruz, *The Color of Kink: Black Women, BDSM, and Pornography* (New York: New York University Press, 2016), 10–11.

1 "[The name Narcissister] refers to that fact I'm a 'sister,'" she tells Joseph Keckler in a 2014 interview. Narcissister quoted in Joseph Keckler, "The Real Face of Narcissister: A Conversation with the Woman Behind the Mask," *VICE*, September 17, 2014. Narcissister was born to an African American father and a Jewish mother who grew up in Morocco. Her mother's Jewish ancestry is Sephardi, an ethnic division with roots in precolonial Spain, Portugal, and Northern Africa.

2 Sigmund Freud, "On Narcissism: An Introduction," in *Literary Theory: An Anthology*, ed. Julie Rivkin and Michael Ryan, 2nd ed. (Oxford: Blackwell, 1998/2004), 415–17. Freud's essay was originally published in 1914 under the title, *Zur Einführung des Narzißmus*.

3 Lucy Lippard, "The Pains and Pleasures of Rebirth: European and American Women's Body Art," in *Feminism-Art-Theory: An Anthology 1968–2014*, 2nd ed., ed. Hilary Robinson (Chichester: Wiley-Blackwell, 2015), 341.

4 Rosalind Krauss offers a different take on Vito Acconci's video works of the time, claiming that in pieces like *Centers* of 1971 Acconci used the video as a mirror. In so doing, he initiates a line of sight that begins at his plane of vision and ends at the eyes of his projected double. "In that image of self-regard," she writes, "is configured a narcissism so endemic to works of video that I find myself wanting to generalize it as *the* condition of the entire genre" (50, emphasis in original). See Rosalind Krauss, "Video: The Aesthetics of Narcissism," *October* 1 (Spring 1976: 50–64.

5 See Amelia Jones, "The 'Eternal Return': Self-Portrait Photography as a Technology of Embodiment," *Signs* 27, no. 4 (Summer 2002): 947–78. See also Amelia Jones, *Self/Image: Technology, Representation, and the Contemporary Subject* (London: Routledge, 2006), where she introduces the concept of parafeminism. Jones argues that feminism at the turn of the twenty-first century is undergoing revision. It is no longer tied to the debates concerning essentialism and anti-essentialism that characterized feminism's first and second waves. More importantly, parafeminism revives feminism, making it relevant beyond prescriptive bad-girl behavior and white middle-class theories of identity.

6 "Despite the importance of late-nineteenth-century medical and legal discourses, which founded theories of sexual perversion and punitive consequences," writes literary scholar Aliyyah Abdur-Rahman, "racial slavery provided the background—and the testing ground—for the emergence and articulation of {theories of sexual perversion}." See Aliyyah Abdur-Rahman, *Against the Closet: Black Political Longing and the Erotics of Race* (Durham, NC: Duke University Press, 2012), 27. Abdur-Rahman further elaborates on this history and its permutations in African American literature from slave narratives to early twenty-first-century fiction and visual culture.

7 Chaka Khan, "I'm Every Woman," recorded 1978, track 1 on *Chaka*, Warner Brothers Records.

8 Here I build on Ariel Osterweis's phrase "incomplete performance," which she uses to describe Narcissister's active disavowal of dance-based virtuosity. For Osterweis, Narcissister's work results in a striving toward excellence. Not a complete denial, "The focus shifts," she argues, "from virtuosity to aspiration: instead of fulfilling a sustained aesthetic of virtuosity, Narcissister stages through partial embodiment and incomplete performance no more than a striving toward excellence" (112). See Ariel Osterweis, "Public Pubic: Narcissister's Performance of Race, Disavowal, and Aspiration," *TDR: The Drama Review* 59, no. 4 (Winter

2015): 101–16. For my purposes, rather than the seamless attainment of an ideal body, or the perfect, masterful execution of choreography and climaxes, I consider Narcissister's photography, videos, and live performances to be portrayals of crude, abject, and unfinished scenes and actions that fail to reach desirable ends—an aesthetic practice of refusal.

9 For journalistic reports on this phenomena, see William F. Frey, "The Browning of America," *Milken Institute Review*, October 19, 2015, www.milkenreview.org; Domenico Montanaro, "How the Browning of America Is Upending Both Political Parties," National Public Radio, October 12, 2016, www.npr.org; and Ronald R. Sundstrom, *The Browning of America and the Evasion of Social Justice* (Albany: State University of New York Press, 2008).

10 For an in-depth analysis of these phenomena, see Ralina L. Joseph, *Transcending Blackness: From the New Millennium Mulatta to the Exceptional Multiracial* (Durham, NC: Duke University Press, 2012).

11 San Francisco State University's College of Ethnic Studies offers an undergraduate minor in critical mixed race studies.

12 Catherine R. Squires, *Dispatches from the Color Line: The Press and Multiracial America* (Albany: State University of New York Press, 2007), 180.

13 Squires, *Dispatches from the Color Line*, 180.

14 Narcissister quoted in Keckler, "The Real Face of Narcissister."

15 Bill Brewster and Frank Broughton, *Last Night a DJ Saved My Life: The History of the Disc Jockey* (New York: Grove, 1999), 126.

16 Brewster and Broughton, *Last Night a DJ Saved My Life*, 126.

17 Brittnay L. Proctor, "'I Am What I Am:' Disco, Queer Anthems, and Black Femme Labors," unpublished manuscript, February 1, 2021, typescript.

18 Proctor, "'I Am What I Am," 6, 8.

19 Ralina L. Joseph details how the persistence of these widespread stereotypes and negative assumptions about mixed-race African Americans pervade contemporary culture. See Joseph, *Transcending Blackness*. Joseph's study updates the tragic mulatto trope for the twenty-first century. The tragic mulatto is a mixed-race person assumed to be sad, or even suicidal, because they fail to completely fit into a racially divided world. The archetype emerged as a fictional character in American literature during the nineteenth and twentieth centuries after abolitionists, in an effort to represent slaves as more human, used the trope to cultivate sentimentality and empathy in white readers. In novels of the era, the character often meets an untimely end because there is no place in American society for one who is neither completely "Black" nor completely "white."

20 For an account of how these intersecting topics inform contemporary art and feminist performance practices, see Cherise Smith, *Enacting Others: Politics of Identity in Eleanor Antin, Nikki S. Lee, Adrian Piper, and Anna Deavere Smith* (Durham, NC: Duke University Press, 2011). Smith argues that by drawing on conventions such as passing, blackface, minstrelsy, cross-dressing, and drag, Antin, Lee, Piper, and Smith highlight the constructedness and fluidity of identity.

Ultimately, performance, Smith argues, offers a type of self-fulfillment for these four women artists.

21 For Faith Ringgold's description of this pivotal time and event, see Faith Ringgold, *We Flew over the Bridge: The Memoirs of Faith Ringgold* (Durham, NC: Duke University Press, 2005), 175–78.

22 Narcissister quoted in Keckler, "The Real Face of Narcissister."

23 Thomas F. DeFrantz, *Dancing Revelations: Alvin Ailey's Embodiment of African American Culture* (New York: Oxford University Press, 2004), 205.

24 *Memoria*'s revelatory arc typifies the choreographic ethos Alvin Ailey initiated when he formed AAADT on March 30, 1958, the result of an informal concert shared with Ernest Parham at the 92nd Street YMCA in New York City. In *Blues Suite* of 1958 presented that night, the staged fighting sequences, dramatized social dances, bright red flapper dresses, depression-era imagery, and suggestions of heterosex merge Ailey's West Coast theatrical training with stylized, wishful depictions of Black social life. In DeFrantz's words, the blues dancing in the production stands "for the ephemeral release from overwhelming social inequities suffered by African Americans." Choreographed in suite form, the dance establishes aesthetic qualities—suite sequencing, revelatory ends to despairing beginnings, and "the transformation of social and political rage into art"—that Ailey explores in subsequent dances. The most famous of these later dances is *Revelations* of 1960, a dance about Black struggle, spiritual redemption, and physical liberation. Permanently endowed by a generous gift from Donald L. Jonas, it is the most often performed work in the Ailey Company's repertory and the most widely seen modern dance work in the world. See Thomas F. DeFrantz, *Dancing Revelations: Alvin Ailey's Embodiment of African American Culture* (New York: Oxford University Press, 2004), 38, 39.

25 Alvin Ailey quoted in Jennifer Dunning, "Alvin Ailey, a Leading Figure In Modern Dance, Dies at 58," *New York Times*, December 2, 1989.

26 Dunning, "Alvin Ailey."

27 For one example of this characterization, see S. L. Miller, "A Tribute to Alvin Ailey," *Crisis* 98, no. 2 (February 1990): 6–8.

28 DeFrantz, *Dancing Revelation*, 240.

29 Alvin Ailey quoted in DeFrantz, *Dancing Revelations*, 136.

30 "History & Philosophy," The Ailey School (n.d.), www.theaileyschool.edu.

31 Osterweis, "Public Pubic," 110. See also Ariel Osterweis, *Body Impossible: Desmond Richardson and the Politics of Virtuosity* (Oxford: Oxford University Press, 2024).

32 Osterweis, "Public Pubic," 110.

33 Osterweis, "Public Pubic," 111.

34 Brenda Dixon Gottschild, *The Black Dancing Body: A Geography from Coon to Cool* (New York: Palgrave Macmillan, 2003), 223.

35 Osterweis, "Public Pubic," 113.

36 Osterweis, 112.

37 Osterweis, 113.

38 See Evelynn Hammonds, "Black (W)holes and the Geometry of Black Female Sexuality," *differences* 6, nos. 2–3 (1994), 127–45.

39 Crudeness as a motif recurs throughout the artist's practice, from early forays into feminist collage to lowbrow forms of dance to grotesque self-portraits. The artist's *Cut Mask Series* (2013–14), for example, consists of overlapping pieces of cut Narcissister masks, doll parts, and tangled wigs. Although they approximate reconstructed faces, the dizzying, three-dimensional arrangements are grotesque and violent, with parts that purposely do not cohere. These acts of cutting and disarrangement are applied to more than faces in her *Hungry Series* of 2014. In three of the images, flat, cutout photo-fragments of savory and sweet treats penetrate the three-dimensional masks and mouths of varying shades, sizes, and shapes pictured. In four of the images, microphones, pubic hair, a multicolored array of dildos, and a dismembered, bleeding dildo in one particularly disturbing composition replace the treats, juxtaposing symbols of pleasure and pain. The dildos disappear in the *Plastic Series* of 2015, but the dark, monstrous facial compositions remain.

40 Bradford Nordeen, *Check Your Vernacular: Dynasty Handbag + Narcissister + Colin Self + Chris E. Vargas*, exhibition catalog, ed. Bradford Nordeen (New York: Dirty Looks Press, 2014), 7. Bradford Nordeen is the curator of Dirty Looks, a roaming platform for queer experimental film, video, and performance. Following Nordeen's comments, Narcissister's art and the type of failure, grotesque humor, lowbrow pop, and camp that she performs share affinities with mid-twentieth-century American avant-garde filmmakers such as Kenneth Anger, Curtis Harrington, and Maya Deren. Deren combined her interests in the psychology of the self, dance, and the Afrodiasporic religion, vodun, to produce short surrealist, stream-of-consciousness films. Deren's explorations of the violent conflict between the self and the "other" through the use of doppelgängers, jump cuts, and her own image are a point of reference for Narcissister's art. Jack Smith's queer, underground filmmaking practice is another point of reference. Best known for low-budget films made from expired film stock, Smith's aesthetic sensibilities include camp, junk, kitsch, and drag. Narcissister and Smith, while active during different decades, share other affinities, too. Smith and Narcissister have amassed cult followings because of the performance practices they both honed in underground nightclubs in New York City's Lower East Side. Artists such as Karen Finley, Ann Magnuson, Carmelita Tropicana, and Vaginal Davis, whom Narcissister cites as an influence, are all part of this queer underworld, with countless others owing their starts to these early days of performance. For a compelling description of Jack Smith's use of knives and anal penetration that resemble Narcissister's work, see Michael Moon's account of Smith's *Blonde Cobra* and his other films of the 1960s in *A Small Boy and Others: Imitation and Initiation in American Culture from Henry James to Andy Warhol* (Durham, NC: Duke University Press, 1998). For a detailed description of Smith's iconic film *Flaming Creatures*, see Richard Dyer and Julianne Pidduck, *Now You See It: Studies in Lesbian and Gay Film*, 2nd

ed. (London: Routledge, 1990/2003). See also Jack Smith, "The Perfect Filmic Appositeness of Maria Montez," *Film Culture* 27 (1962): 28–36.

41 See Osterweis, "Public Pubic," 115; and Barbara Browning and Ariel Osterweis, "Dancing Social," *Theatre Survey* 53, no. 2 (September 2012), 270.

42 Browning and Osterweis, "Dancing Social," 271. Infused with postmodern theory, feminist conceptual art of the 1970s and 80s incorporated explicit images of lesbian sex, surgically and hormonally altered bodies, and women in drag to question the relationship between representation and monolithic constructions of gender and sexual identity in art and media. These performative strategies, later taken up and retooled by women, gender non-conforming, and queer artists of the 1990s when Narcissister began making art, aim to disrupt gender binaries and to reclaim the sexualized female image from a male-dominated visual field. For writings on this era and the artistic practices that emerged therein, see Laura Mulvey, "Visual Pleasure and Narrative Cinema," *Screen* 16, no. 3 (Autumn 1975): 6–18; Harmony Hammond, "Art, Contemporary North American," in *Lesbian Histories and Cultures: An Encyclopedia*, ed. Bonnie Zimmerman (New York: Garland, 2000), 63–66; Nayland Blake, Lawrence Rinder, and Amy Scholder, eds., *In a Different Light: Visual Culture, Sexual Identity, Queer Practice*, exhibition catalog (San Francisco: City Lights Books, 1995); SAMOIS, *Coming to Power: Writings and Graphics on Lesbian S/M* (San Francisco: Up Press, 1981); Jan Avgikos et. al., eds., *Coming to Power: 25 Years of Sexually X-Plicit Art by Women*, exhibition catalog (New York: David Zwirner Gallery, 1993); Pati Hertling and Julie Tolentino, eds., *I'm Still Coming: Ellen Cantor's Coming to Power 1993 & 2016*, exhibition catalog (New York: Capricious Press, 2016); and past issues of Heresies Collective's *Heresies: A Feminist Publication on Art and Politics* (1977–93).

43 See Priscilla Frank, "Narcissister Is The Topless Feminist Superhero New York Needs (NSFW)," *Huffington Post*, June 27, 2014; and Katie Cercone, "Lorraine O'Grady & Narcissister Do Future Feminism at the Hole," *Posture Magazine*, September 30, 2014.

44 Osterweis, "Public Pubic," 110.

45 Osterweis, "Public Pubic," 110.

46 Ariel Osterweis, "Vaseline," *Narcissister*, www.narcissister.com/vaseline.

47 Osterweis, "Vaseline."

48 This phrasing follows Thomas Waugh's analysis of classic American stag films, where he claims they fail to make visible "the unknowable 'truth' of sex." See Thomas Waugh, "Homosociality in the Classical American Stag Film: Off-Screen, on-Screen," in *Porn Studies*, ed. Linda Williams (Durham, NC: Duke University Press, 2004), 128.

49 For scholarly and popular literature on race play and the BDSM scenarios it entails, see Isaac Julien, "Confessions of a Snow Queen: Notes on the Making of *The Attendant*," *Critical Quarterly* 36, no. 1 (March 1994): 120–26; Daisy Hernandez, "Playing with Race," *Colorlines*, December 21, 2004; and Chauncey DeVega, "Race, Sex, and BDSM: On 'Plantation Retreats' Where Black People Go to Serve

Their White 'Masters,'" *Daily Kos*, August 14, 2012. Both Hernandez and DeVega reference the particular scenarios I list: Nazi-Jew interrogations and various master-slave dynamics and reenactments.

50 Jennfier C. Nash, *The Black Body in Ecstasy: Reading Race, Reading Pornography* (Durham, NC: Duke University Press, 2014), 2.

51 Nash, *The Black Body in Ecstasy*, 2.

52 Joseph R. Roach, *Cities of the Dead: Circum-Atlantic Performance* (New York: Columbia University Press, 1996), 3. Writing on Narcissister's work in the context of post-Black performance art, Cesar Garcia argues that the artist presents "bodies that urge, desire, pleasure, expose, consume, and indulge, and excrete, bodies that through the act of performance reclaim their agency while simultaneously liberating themselves from confining visual paradigms." See Cesar Garcia, "Eroticized Corporealities," *Fore*, exhibition catalog, ed. Thomas Lax et al. (New York: Studio Museum in Harlem, 2012), 70.

53 Robin Bernstein, *Racial Innocence: Performing American Childhood from Slavery to Civil Rights* (New York: New York University Press, 2011), 23.

54 Sigmund Freud, *On Metapsychology: the Theory of Psychoanalysis: Beyond the Pleasure Principle, The Ego and the Id, and Other Works*, trans. James Strachey (London: Penguin, 1985).

55 Narcissister first performance of *The Dollhouse* aired on *America's Got Talent* on June 28, 2011. The artist performed *The Dollhouse* at The Box in January 2017.

56 Diana Ross, "Upside Down," recorded 1980, track 1 on *Diana*, Motown Record Corporation, LP.

57 Grover Washington Jr. and Bill Withers, "Just the Two of Us," on *Winelight* (Elektra Records, 1980).

58 Kimberly Wallace-Sanders, *Mammy: A Century of Race, Gender, and Southern Memory* (Ann Arbor: University of Michigan Press, 2007), 35. She writes, "African American slave women may have given dolls like these to their daughters as a preparation for a possibility of a life devoted to nurturing two babies: one black and one white. Topsy-turvy dolls are designed for children to play with one baby at a time, and this accurately reflects the division of caregiving that African American women encountered, having to care for white children during the day and their own children at night. These handmade dolls are important, creative expressions of those otherwise silent women we know only as 'mammy.'"

59 A topsy-turvy doll is a soft, two-headed object in which a young white girl is fused with either a Topsy, after the character in Harriet Beecher Stowe's sentimental anti-slavery novel *Uncle Tom's Cabin* of 1852, or a Black mammy. Historically, topsy-turvy dolls existed before Stowe's character Topsy. But after the novel's publication, the doll was often called Topsy-Eva, further establishing in the US public imaginary the pickaninny, a stereotypical representation of Black children as blacker than black, unkempt, and primitive. Pickaninny imagery—bulging eyes, big red lips, broken dialect—is rooted in blackface minstrelsy, and pictures of Topsy in American visual and material culture illustrate these tropes.

Her Blackness (she is "one of the blackest of her race—odd and goblin-like"), her ugliness, her filthiness, her insensate nature, and her inability to know her age and parentage are contrary to Eva, who represents childhood innocence. Devoid of sociable instincts until Eva's touch transforms her into a being capable of feeling, Topsy is essentially antisocial, an attribute of undesirability brought to bear in Narcissister's solo performance. "One of the blackest of her race—odd and goblin-like" is the caption for James Daugherty's full-page illustration of Topsy in Stowe's novel. See Harriet Beecher Stowe, *Uncle Tom's Cabin* (New York: Coward-McCann, 1929), 229. Special thanks to Tammy Owens for this language and reference. Narcissister performs the mammy figure in *The Basket*, a video work of 2012. She also performs as an Eastern European peasant and scantily clad video vixen among other stereotypes in this video, again demonstrating her interests in image scavenging, multicultural archives, and the Black female body.

60 Bernstein, *Racial Innocence*, 174.

61 Bernstein, *Racial Innocence*, 87.

62 For a thorough study of this phenomenon within a performance studies context, see Tavia Nyong'o, *The Amalgamation Waltz: Race, Performance, and the Ruses of Memory* (Minneapolis: University of Minnesota Press, 2009).

63 Katie Cercone, "Lorraine O'Grady & Narcissister Do Future Feminism at the Hole," *Posture Magazine*, September 30, 2014. Lorraine O'Grady's performance art and writings are a point of departure for Narcissister. O'Grady's influential text, "Olympia's Maid: Reclaiming Black Female Subjectivity," critiqued sexual and racial hierarchy in the West to institute a shift toward winning back the position of the black female as a questioning subject with agency, in the art world and society at large. O'Grady's text can be found here: http://lorraineogrady.com/wp-content/uploads/2015/11/Lorraine-OGrady_Olympias-Maid-Reclaiming-Black-Female-Subjectivity1.pdf. The first part of the text was published in *Afterimage* 20, no 1 (Summer 1992). The revised version, including "Postscript," originally appeared in *New Feminist Criticism: Art, Identity, Action*, ed. Joanna Frueh, Cassandra L. Langer, and Arlene Raven (New York: Icon, 1994). The essay has subsequently been reprinted in Grant Kester, ed., *Art, Activism, and Oppositionality: Essays from Afterimage* (Durham, NC: Duke University Press, 1998); and Amelia Jones, ed., *The Feminism and Visual Cultural Reader* (London: Routledge, 2003).

64 Sigmund Freud, "The Uncanny," in *Literary Theory: An Anthology*, 2nd ed., ed. Julie Rivkin and Michael Ryan (Oxford: Blackwell, 1998/2004), 418–30. See also Sigmund Freud, "The 'Uncanny,'" trans. Alix Strachey (First published in *Imago*, Bd. V., 1919; reprinted in *Sammlung*, vol. 5).

65 Freud's theory, though central to critical race studies scholarship like that of Robin Bernstein and Amber Musser, neglects race and racial difference, which is why I rely on Bernstein in my explication of Narcissister's racialized doll personae.

66 For an expanded discussion on this history, see Chris Hassold, "The Double and Doubling in Modern and Postmodern Art," *Journal of the Fantastic in the Arts* 6, no. 2/3 (1994): 253–74.

67 Here, I follow Sianne Ngai's account of animatedness. For more on animatedness and the racial epistemology of liveliness, see Sianne Ngai, *Ugly Feelings* (Cambridge, MA: Harvard University Press, 2005).
68 Cruz, *The Color of Kink*, 4.
69 Alphaville, "Forever Young," recorded 1984, track 6 on *Forever Young*, Warner Elektra Atlantic Records.
70 Def Leppard, "Photograph," recorded 1983, track 2 on *Pyromania*, Mercury Records.
71 Nat King Cole, "Unforgettable," recorded 1952, track 1 on *Unforgettable*, Capitol Records.
72 Rihanna, "Birthday Cake," recorded 2011, track 6 on *Talk That Talk*, Def Jam Recordings.
73 Jared Sexton, *Amalgamation Schemes: Antiblackness and the Critique of Multiracialism* (Minneapolis: University of Minnesota Press, 2008), 7.
74 Nyong'o, *The Amalgamation Waltz*, 165.
75 Nyong'o, *The Amalgamation Waltz*, 165.
76 For a consideration of race, sex, and performance along these lines, see *Radical Presence: Black Performance in Contemporary Art*, exhibition catalog, ed. Valerie Cassel Oliver et. al., (Houston, TX: Contemporary Art Museum Houston, 2013); and *Women & Performance* 27, no. 1, special issue, "Reading and Feeling after *Scenes of Subjection*," ed. Sampada Aranke and Nikolas Oscar Sparks (2017).
77 Nyong'o, *The Amalgamation Waltz*, 175.
78 To realize the utopian vision at the core of critical legal studies and intersectionality, Mari J. Matsuda suggests that scholars and lawyers look to the bottom, a facet of minoritarian life, as a new epistemological source for knowledge and repair. For Matsuda, the bottom is more than the tiers of society occupied by "the least advantaged," namely Black and poor people. It is also grassroots organizing and "the actual experience, history, culture, and intellectual tradition of people of color in America." "Looking to the bottom for ideas about law," she acknowledges, that "victims of racial oppression have distinctive normative insights" that can lead "to concepts of law radically different from those generated at the top." See Mari J. Matsuda, "Looking to the Bottom: Critical Legal Studies and Reparations," *Harvard Civil Rights-Civil Liberties Law Review* 22, no. 2 (Spring 1987): 325–26.
79 Jennifer C. Nash, "Re-Thinking Intersectionality," *Feminist Review* 89 (2008): 8.
80 Narcissister, "Narcissister Organ Player," *Narcissister* (n.d.), www.narcissister.com/film.
81 Osterweis, "Public Pubic," 115.
82 "Chopped and screwed" music is a genre of hip-hop developed by DJ Screw in early 1990s Houston, Texas. It refers to a technique where remixes of hip-hop music are achieved by slowing the tempo of a song down to between sixty and seventy quarter-note beats per minute and incorporating skipped beats, record scratching, and stop-time that results in a "chopped-up" version of the original.
83 The costumes in *Ass/Vag* and in *Hand Dance* that follows completely cover Narcissister. In *Hand Dance*, the upstage prop is now a puppet whose breasts are on

display; its legs are bent and splayed at impossible angles. The puppet's legs move up and down as Narcissister uses her own legs to move the fingers of the hand costume to "pleasure herself" to an electronic sound score composed of more moans and screams that oscillate between sexual excitation and the soundtrack of a horror film.

84 Leo Bersani, "Is the Rectum a Grave?," *October* 43, special issue, "AIDS: Cultural Analysis/Cultural Activism," ed. Douglas Crimp (Winter 1987): 222.

85 Darieck Scott, *Extravagant Abjection: Blackness, Power, and Sexuality in the African American Literary Imagination* (New York: New York University Press, 2010), 259.

86 Scott, *Extravagant Abjection*, 257.

87 Susan Fraiman, *Cool Men and the Second Sex* (New York: Columbia University Press, 2003), 135, quoted in Maggie Nelson, *The Argonauts* (Minneapolis: Graywolf, 2015), 69.

88 Anna Martine Whitehead, "Expressing Life through Loss: On Queens That Fall with a Freak Technique," in *Queer Dance: Meanings and Makings*, ed. Clare Croft (Oxford: Oxford University Press, 2017), 282.

89 Whitehead, "Expressing Life through Loss," 282.

90 In the past twenty years, feminist scholars have questioned how the psychoanalytic theory of narcissism fails to account for Echo's radical difference. See Tania Modleski, "Feminism and the Power of Interpretation: Some Critical Readings," in *Feminist Studies/Critical Studies*, ed. Teresa de Lauretis (Houndmills: Macmillan, 1986), 121–38. The figure of Echo poses ethical questions crucial for deconstructing canonical texts and disciplinary scripts, a project central to Narcissister's practice. Indeed, Echo is traditionally marginalized in analyses of the myth of Narcissus. Given the namesake of the artist discussed in this essay, I too neglect Echo in order to tease out the disorderly, racialized, and anti-relational aspects of her performance.

91 Lee Edelman, *No Future: Queer Theory and the Death Drive* (Durham, NC: Duke University Press, 2004), 4.

92 See Amber Jamilla Musser, *Sensual Excess: Queer Femininity and Brown Jouissance* (New York: New York University Press, 2018); Roderick A. Ferguson, *Aberrations in Black: Toward a Queer of Color Critique* (Minneapolis: University of Minnesota Press, 2003); Tavia Nyong'o, *Afro-Fabulations: The Queer Drama of Black Life* (New York: New York University Press, 2018); and José Esteban Muñoz, *Cruising Utopia: The Then and There of Queer Futurity* (New York: New York University Press, 2009).

93 Muñoz, *Cruising Utopia*, 23.

CONCLUSION

Epigraph: The Combahee River Collective, "A Black Feminist Statement," in *All the Women are White, All the Blacks are Men, But Some of Us are Brave: Black Women's Studies* (New York: Feminist Press, 1982), 18.

1 Kaiama L. Glover, A Regarded Self: Caribbean Womanhood and the Ethics of Disorderly Being (Durham, NC: Duke University Press, 2021), 220.
2 Anne Anlin Cheng, "Psychoanalysis without Symptoms," *differences* 20, no. 1 (2009): 98. Emphasis in original.
3 Kara Walker quoted in *Art21 Exclusive*, 204; "Kara Walker: 'A Subtlety, or the Marvelous Sugar Baby,'" dir. Ian Forster, aired May 23, 2014, https://art21.org /watch/extended-play/kara-walker-a-subtlety-or-the-marvelous-sugar-baby-short/.
4 Here I follow Darby English's call for both a language that adeptly captures the desire of Black historical subjects—namely Emmett Till—beyond that of iconic victimhood, as well as Michel Foucault's concept of work. Work Foucault writes, is "that which is susceptible of introducing a significant difference in the field of knowledge, at the cost of a certain difficulty for the author and the reader, with, however, the eventual recompense of a certain pleasure, that is to say, of access to another figure of truth." See Darby English, "Emmett Till Ever After," in *Black Is, Black Ain't*, exhibition catalog, ed. Hamza Walker and Karen Reimer (Chicago: The Renaissance Society at the University of Chicago, 2013), 92–93. See also Michel Foucault, "Des Travaux," in *Dits et Écrits*, vol. 4 (Paris, FR: Editions Gallimard, 1994), 367, quoted in English, "Emmett Till Ever After," 99.
5 Sandra Ruiz, "Crossing the Line: The Here and Now of Race and Gender and the Entanglements of Love in Performance Art and Pedagogy," in *Autumn Knight: In Rehearsal* (Urbana, IL: Krannert Art Museum and Kinkead Pavilion with Project Row Houses, 2018), 52.
6 Caitlin Cherry quoted in Tyler Akers, "Caitlin Cherry," *Gayletter* 16 (Fall 2022): 110.
7 Cherry quoted in Akers, "Caitlin Cherry," 110.
8 Caitlin Cherry quoted in Tina Rivers Ryan, "Caitlin Cherry: Caitlin Cherry on Digital Abstraction and Black Femininity," *Artforum*, July 20, 2020.
9 Cherry quoted in Ryan, "Caitlin Cherry." Emphasis mine.

INDEX

Page numbers in *italics* indicate Photos

ABOUT THE AUTHOR

Dr. Tiffany E. Barber is an internationally recognized scholar, curator, and critic whose writing and expert commentary appears in top-tier academic journals, popular media outlets, and award-winning documentaries. Recipient of the Smithsonian's 2022 National Portrait Gallery Director's Essay Prize, Barber is currently Assistant Professor of African American Art at UCLA, where her research and teaching focuses on artists of the Black diaspora working in the United States and the broader Atlantic world.

www.ingramcontent.com/pod-product-compliance
Lightning Source LLC
LaVergne TN
LVHW020506100826
845148LV00003B/702

* 9 7 8 1 4 7 9 8 2 9 2 8 6 *